Crime Fiction as World Literature

Literatures as World Literature

Literatures as World Literature takes a novel approach to world literature by analyzing specific constellations—according to language, nation, form, or theme—of literary texts and authors in their world-literary dimensions. World literature has been mapped and theorized in the abstract, but the majority of critical work, the filling in of what has been traced, lies ahead of us. *Literatures as World Literature* begins the task of filling in the devilish details by allowing scholars to move outward from their own area of specialization. The hope is to foster scholarly writing that approaches more closely the polyphonic, multiperspectival nature of the world literature we wish to explore.

Series Editor:
Thomas O. Beebee

Editorial Board:
Eduardo Coutinho, Federal University of Rio de Janeiro, Brazil
Hsinya Huang, National Sun-yat Sen University, Taiwan
Meg Samuelson, University of Cape Town, South Africa
Ken Seigneurie, Simon Fraser University, Canada
Mads Rosendahl Thomsen, Aarhus University, Denmark

Volumes in the Series
German Literature as World Literature
Edited by Thomas O. Beebee
Roberto Bolaño as World Literature
Edited by Nicholas Birns and Juan E. De Castro
Crime Fiction as World Literature
Edited by Louise Nilsson, David Damrosch, and Theo O. D'haen
Danish Literature as World Literature
Edited by Dan Ringgaard and Mads Rosendahl Thomsen
Romanian Literature as World Literature (forthcoming)
Edited by Mircea Martin, Christian Moraru, and Andrei Terian
Brazilian Literature as World Literature (forthcoming)
By Eduardo F. Coutinho

Crime Fiction as World Literature

Edited by
Louise Nilsson, David Damrosch, and Theo D'haen

Bloomsbuy Academic
An imprint of Bloomsbury Publishing Inc

B L O O M S B U R Y
NEW YORK · LONDON · OXFORD · NEW DELHI · SYDNEY

Bloomsbury Academic
An imprint of Bloomsbury Publishing Inc

1385 Broadway	50 Bedford Square
New York	London
NY 10018	WC1B 3DP
USA	UK

www.bloomsbury.com

BLOOMSBURY and the Diana logo are trademarks of Bloomsbury Publishing Plc

First published 2017

© Louise Nilsson, David Damrosch, Theo D'haen, and Contributors 2017

Whilst every effort has been made to locate copyright holders, the publishers would be grateful to hear from any person(s) not here acknowledged.

All rights reserved. No part of this publication may be reproduced or transmitted in any form or by any means, electronic or mechanical, including photocopying, recording, or any information storage or retrieval system, without prior permission in writing from the publishers.

No responsibility for loss caused to any individual or organization acting on or refraining from action as a result of the material in this publication can be accepted by Bloomsbury or the editors.

Library of Congress Cataloging-in-Publication Data
A catalog record for this book is available from the Library of Congress.

ISBN: HB: 978-1-5013-1932-7
PB: 978-1-5013-1933-4
ePub: 978-1-5013-1934-1
ePDF: 978-1-5013-1935-8

Series: Literatures as World Literature

Cover design: Simon Levy

Typeset by Newgen Knowledge Works (P) Ltd., Chennai, India

Contents

List of Illustrations   vii

Introduction: Crime Fiction as World Literature   *Louise Nilsson, David Damrosch, and Theo D'haen*   1

Part 1   Global and Local

1. The Knife in the Lemon: Nordic Noir and the Glocalization of Crime Fiction   *Andreas Hedberg*   13

2. After Such Knowledge: The Politics of Detection in the Narconovelas of Elmer Mendoza   *Michael Wood*   23

3. Red Herrings and Read Alerts: Crime and its Excesses in *Almost Blue* and *Nairobi Heat*   *Tilottama Tharoor*   33

4. The Detective is Suspended: Nordic Noir and the Welfare State   *Bruce Robbins*   47

5. Four Generations, One Crime   *Michaela Bronstein*   59

Part 2   Market Mechanisms

6. With a Global Market in Mind: Agents, Authors, and the Dissemination of Contemporary Swedish Crime Fiction   *Karl Berglund*   77

7. So You Think You Can Write ... Handbooks for Mystery Fiction   *Anneleen Masschelein and Dirk de Geest*   91

8. Covering Crime Fiction: Merging the Local into Cosmopolitan Mediascapes   *Louise Nilsson*   109

9. Surrealist Noir: Aragon's *Le Cahier noir* and Pamuk's *The Black Book*   *Delia Ungureanu*   131

Part 3 Translating Crime

10 Detective Fiction in Translation: Shifting Patterns of Reception *Susan Bassnett* — 143

11 Making it Ours: Translation and the Circulation of Crime Fiction in Catalan *Stewart King* — 157

12 "In Agatha Christie's Footsteps": *The Cursed Goblet* and Contemporary Bulgarian Crime Fiction *Mihaela P. Harper* — 171

13 A Missing Literature: Dror Mishani and the Case of Israeli Crime Fiction *Maayan Eitan* — 187

14 World Detective Form and Thai Crime Fiction *Suradech Chotiudompant* — 197

Part 4 Holmes Away from Home

15 Holmes Away from Home: The Great Detective in the Transnational Literary Network *Michael B. Harris-Peyton* — 215

16 Sherlock's Queen Bee *Theo D'haen* — 233

17 Sherlock Holmes Came to China: Detective Fiction, Cultural Meditations, and Chinese Modernity *Wei Yan* — 245

18 A Sinister Chuckle: Sherlock in Tibet *David Damrosch* — 257

19 Detecting Conspiracy: Boris Akunin's Dandiacal Detective, or a Century in Queer Profiles from London to Moscow *Elizabeth Richmond-Garza* — 271

Notes on Contributors — 291
Index — 297

List of Illustrations

5.1	"Four generations" comparison chart	62
8.1	Covers for Maj Sjöwall and Per Wahlöö, *The Laughing Policeman*, and for Arne Dahl, *Misterioso*	115
8.2	Cover Arne Dahl, *Misterioso*	117
8.3	Covers for Håkan Nesser, *Am Abend des Mordes*, and for Arne Dahl, *Ungeschoren*	122
8.4	Cover for Kristina Ohlsson, *Engelbewaarders*	126
18.1	Cover for Jamyang Norbu, *The Mandala of Sherlock Holmes*	269

Introduction: Crime Fiction as World Literature

Louise Nilsson, David Damrosch, and Theo D'haen

In place of the old local and national seclusion and self-sufficiency, we have intercourse in every direction, universal interdependence of nations. And as in material, so also in intellectual production. The intellectual creations of individual nations become common property ... and from the numerous national and local literatures, there arises a world literature.
— Marx and Engels, *Communist Manifesto* (1848)

Well, we haven't had a good, juicy series of sex murders since Christie. And they're so good for the tourist trade. Foreigners somehow expect the squares of London to be fog-wreathed, full of hansom cabs and littered with ripped whores, don't you think?
— Alfred Hitchcock, *Frenzy* (1972)

In Alfred Hitchcock's movie *Frenzy* a serial killer hunts down women in London and strangles them. The quote above is from a scene showing two men in a bar talking about the killer. They dwell upon the desire behind the need to kill, reflecting on the fascination people feel for serial killers. As Marx and Engels would have expected, this fascination has come to have a worldwide literary market with substantial economic consequences, not only for bestselling writers such as Agatha Christie but even for the tourist trade. There's something that captures human attention, and that sells, when it comes to gruesome murders, and crime fiction has a long history of entertaining readers as well as moviegoers. Today the genre is a multimillion-dollar industry and its stories circulate in a multimedia landscape, through books and television and movie adaptations that spread the world over. In cities all over the world "crime tourists" follow the trails of their favorite fictional characters, while on crime-novel-ridden campuses scholars try to figure things out when it comes to the phenomenon of crime fiction and its popularity.

This collection treats crime fiction as a significant participant in the international sphere of world literature. Our point of departure is the question of world literature in relation to society, for which crime fiction offers a particularly rich area of inquiry. Often discussed largely in terms of elite productions, world literature has been studied too little in terms of more popular writings, even though bestselling genre fiction fully illustrates what Marx and Engels enticingly describe as world literature's "intercourse in every direction." By bringing crime fiction into the sphere of world literature, this collection aims to open up further knowledge about the transnational flow of literature in the globalized mediascape of contemporary popular culture, and to offer new insights into the crime fiction genre itself, as our contributors follow the creative transformations of transnational plots and motifs in very different local settings around the world.

Crime fiction is certainly one of the most widespread of all literary genres. It is both part of our literary heritage and intimately intertwined with the rise of today's consumer society. Crime novels are read worldwide, and crime writers around the world inspire each other. The genre's history and development are connected to modernization and industrialization, and exemplify today's globalization and the changes in the book market. The switch from national publishing houses to international multimedia conglomerates, digitalization and the rise of the e-book, and the rapid circulation of popular authors in translation are all topics to be discussed in this collection.

Crime fiction circulates in ways that go quite beyond common understandings of the diffusion of the novel from European centers to non-Western peripheries, as traced by Franco Moretti, or the competition for recognition in Paris or New York emphasized by Pascale Casanova in *The World Republic of Letters*. It is notable that the first modern detective stories were written not in Europe or the United States but in China, where several seventeenth- and eighteenth-century writers elaborated old tales of a Tang Dynasty magistrate named Di Renjie, famous in the eighth century for his acumen in solving crimes and punishing the criminals. In 1949 the Dutch diplomat, linguist, and writer Robert van Gulik published *The Celebrated Cases of Judge Dee* in Tokyo, where he was then stationed. The book is a translation of the eighteenth-century Chinese detective novel *Dee Goong An*. Van Gulik went on to write a further series of detective novels based on the figure of Di Renjie, published originally in Chinese and Japanese, later in English in which Van Gulik had originally composed them.

Today, American crime writers are as likely to be inspired by Swedish authors as the reverse, while writers in Bangkok closely follow the work of their Japanese and Italian peers. In his "Conjectures on World Literature" (2000), Franco Moretti emphasized the importance of not approaching world literature as an object but as a problem that has to be analyzed from new angles and with new methods. A significant factor here is the globalization of the novel. Through worldwide literary systems of distribution, both digitally and in print, widely read works of national literature become a shared world literature. Rather than reflecting a single, "flat" economic landscape, international publication and distribution involve complex, overlapping, disjunctive networks and sub-networks. In this context, crime fiction becomes a highly relevant area for investigation. To date, however, studies of crime fiction have largely been confined to individual national or at most regional traditions, generally within the realm of studies of popular fiction. Typical of such studies are Barbara Pezzotti's *The Importance of Place in Contemporary Italian Crime Fiction* (2012), or the numerous studies dealing primarily with British and/or American crime fiction, including *The Cambridge Companion to Crime Fiction* (2003), Andrew Pepper's *The Contemporary American Crime Novel: Race, Ethnicity, Gender, Class* (2000), Hans Bertens and Theo D'haen's *Contemporary American Crime Fiction* (2001), Peter Messent's *The Crime Fiction Handbook* (2013), and most recently Richard Bradford's *Crime Fiction: A Very Short Introduction* (2015) or Peter Swirski's *American Crime Fiction: A Cultural History of Nobrow Literature as Art* (2016).[1]

Various collections such as *The Oxford Companion to Crime and Mystery Writing* (1999) have included Continental as well as Anglo-American writers, and studies have begun to appear that take a directly transnational approach, such as Marieke Krajenbrink and Kate M. Quinn's collection *Investigating Identities: Questions of Identity in Contemporary International Crime Fiction* (2009) and Vivien Miller and Helen Oakley's *Cross-Cultural Connections in Crime Fictions* (2012), which discusses relations between Swedish and English-language novels and films. Yet with the partial exception of Anderson, Miranda, and Pezzotti's primarily European collection *The Foreign in International Crime Fiction* (2012), no study of truly global scope has yet been attempted.

Scholars of world literature have neglected crime fiction, focusing instead on elite writers in preference to mass-market or "airport" novels. Yet while crime fiction is among the most popular of genres, it has a long history of interrelation with more elite productions as well. Sophocles' *Oedipus Rex* provides an early example of a work centered on the investigation of a crime, in a drama already showing a sophisticated play on expectations as the royal detective discovers that he himself is the object of his search. Dostoevsky's *Crime and Punishment* (1866) gives a signal case of the use of popular fictional form by a major world writer, a pattern that can be seen today in novels such as Orhan Pamuk's *My Name Is Red*, whose vivid opening chapter is narrated by a recently murdered Ottoman miniaturist, eager to enlist the reader's aid in determining his killer's identity.

Conversely, fine art and literary classics often play a role in crime fiction, serving not only as plot devices but also as a means by which cultural knowledge is spread. In one way, if you read about Henning Mankell's detective Kurt Wallander you learn about opera, and Michael Connelly's detective Harry Bosch (named after Hieronymus Bosch) listens to jazz artists such as John Coltrane and Art Pepper. If you read Thomas Harris you find a serial killer obsessed with William Blake, and if you watch David Fincher's movie *Seven* you learn about Milton and about Dante—whose *Commedia* was memorably translated for Penguin by the prominent detective story writer Dorothy Sayers. T. S. Eliot was a great fan of Dashiell Hammett and Raymond Chandler.

Traditionally the focus of studies in comparative and world literature studies has been on a Western classical canon, but over the past fifteen years the field of world literature has rapidly expanded to include much more of the world's literatures. By exploring the genre of crime fiction, we want to show the value of not dividing literature into watertight categories of high and low art and culture. The most ambitious crime novels occupy a space in between both categories or even participate in both, varying according to time, place, and readership. Even the most purely popular crime fiction shares important features with elite works of world literature, especially the characteristic of combining universal themes with local settings. At once highly stylized and intensely localized, crime fiction is a preeminently "glocal" mode of literary creation and circulation.

The globalized and hybridized genre of crime fiction, dealing with universal questions about life and death, crime and punishment, conflicting values and moral systems, is known for portraying the darker sides of society and formulating a social critique upon its own native context. At the same time, it is a genre that entertains readers worldwide, and its authors write within a tradition, continuously reshaping the genre's way of telling stories about crime. Within the genre, cities like Bangkok, Beijing, Cairo, London, Los Angeles, Milan, or

Stockholm become settings for exciting plots while at the same time highlighting vernacular and national discourses that, with the novels' translation, spread to a cosmopolitan audience for whom the works become ambassadors for their country of origin.

This collection works with an open definition of crime fiction, but with a primary focus on detective and police novels that are produced for the mass market and that have spread globally. An open definition of the genre is necessary, but we have chosen to let the presence of the detective be the starting point for our definition of crime fiction, given the character's central function in the genre. The detective can be found within institutional settings (the police/forensic science) or represent an individual (the private eye). The crime itself becomes a crime in relation to its society's legal apparatus and juridical system, which defines what to punish or what not to punish in the society in question. Through the detective's investigations, power structures, institutions, police procedures, and civil codes are portrayed, as are human behavior and psychology. As a genre, crime fiction is complex and comprises a spectrum of stories that can be grouped in numerous subgenres or categories, such as hard-boiled, suspense or noir fiction, the spy novel, lesbian crime fiction, the clue puzzle or whodunit, and historical crime fiction; these categories often merge and create subgenres.

A significant aspect our collection explores is the literary system that surrounds the books and makes them accessible to the reader—a sociological approach that is becoming increasingly important in world literature scholarship today. The spread of literature in a transnational context is fueled by commercial interests and by the international book markets. These activities in turn intersect with the globalized media market, and marketing is a crucial part of the process of distributing a book and selling it in the global market. Today world literature comes into play through international multimedia conglomerates and publishing houses, driven by commercial interests. The eminently worldly genre of crime fiction offers a particularly interesting lens through which to view these developments today.

This collection is divided into four parts. The first part, "Global and Local," features essays on the global spread of crime fiction and how these stories become ambassadors for a specific nation and culture, with special emphasis on political issues. The essays in this section examine how the novels give local expression to such global phenomena as human trafficking, human rights, upheavals in gender, class, or political relations, and globalization itself. Andreas Hedberg argues that, when adapted to a new cultural mileu, the frame of the crime story can be filled with almost any narrative material, incorporating the latest fashion trends and current affairs. In this respect, crime fiction is world literature par excellence. Michael Wood shows how the Mexican crime novelist Elmer Mendoza portrays a world saturated by crime, from which the old theological certainties of classic detective fiction have vanished: crimes can be solved, as the genre requires, but then our detective has to solve the solution. None of his hard-boiled heroes are as hard-boiled as they think they are, and their cryptic, ironic tone that seeks to escape from emotion, often hides (or fails to hide) a distress that is thoroughly political.

Turning to readings across borders, Tilottama Tharoor discusses how two recent novels—Carlo Lucarelli's *Almost Blue* and Mũkoma wa Ngũgĩ's *Nairobi Heat*—follow the narrative formula of prevalent crime genres: one is about serial killings set in Bologna; the other a trans-Atlantic murder mystery involving an African American detective. In both, though, the formulas and codes are displaced through red herrings and misdirections, necessitating relocations and reconfigurations—much as the assembling and interpretation of world literature requires. Bruce Robbins probes the complex relations between Swedish detective fiction and the welfare state that the noir detective seems to oppose but that the genre ultimately supports, a political valence that is largely lost on American readers, who tend to see the novels in terms of their own anti-statism. Michaela Bronstein examines the allure of what she calls "utopian crime" in a chain of novels by Dostoevsky, Conrad, Ngũgĩ wa Thiong'o, and Mũkoma wa Ngũgĩ, ranging from nineteenth-century Russia to twentieth-century Africa and America. Utopian crime exposes the secret kinship between the ideology of aesthetic endurance and that of revolution: both appeal to the judgment of the future against the present.

Part 2, "Market Mechanisms," focuses on the literary systems and marketing strategies that surround the genre. It sheds light on changes in the publishing industry, and on the use of different media to spread crime fiction globally, including film adaptations and remakes. Karl Berglund discusses the new global conditions for Swedish crime fiction as an illustration of changes in the contemporary book trade. Today, Swedish agents think big when they take on new crime writers, and Swedish writers are following suit. Ironically, then, Swedish crime fiction is increasingly being produced with translations, adaptations, and global popularity in mind, at the same time as the impact of the genre owes much to its regional characteristics (or its purveying of images of Nordic exoticism). Thus the example of Swedish crime fiction shows how center and periphery work in new ways in the global literary economy of the twenty-first century. Anneleen Masschelein and Dirk de Geest show that there has been a remarkable boom of crime writing handbooks in recent decades, demonstrating the popularity of the genre not only for readers but also for aspiring writers. Insofar as these handbooks try to present a set of good examples, they establish a world literature canon of their own. Louise Nilsson looks at book covers, examining the negotiation going on between a book's content and its representations in different cultural contexts, showing how marketing strategies enable Nordic Noir to become a globally shared literature. Delia Ungureanu examines how Aragon's *Le cahier noir*, whose peculiar publication history she sees as a mystery in itself, functions as one of the main intertextual sources for Orhan Pamuk's *The Black Book*. She thereby traces one of the unrecognized legacies that Pamuk is engaging with in a book that played a key role in his literary and social trajectory toward the Nobel Prize, as he exploited the resources of surrealist noir fiction to reach a global audience.

Part 3, "Translating Crime," investigates the relation between the global genre, local voice, and the metropolitan writer. If the local becomes the global, how does it change as it travels abroad? Susan Bassnett sees the recent global boom in crime fiction as having been facilitated by translation. Focusing on European crime fiction, Basnett suggests that the boom is fueled by major shifts in European consciousness, connected to questions of cultural memory and identity. Stewart King uses Catalan crime fiction as a case study to draw attention to the ways in translation can contribute to the creation of a homegrown crime fiction tradition, as the crime genre moves between and within different polysystems. Mihaela P. Harper inquires into the reasons for the availability and popularity of Agatha Christie's crime novels in communist Bulgaria prior to 1989, and shows how Lora Lazar's *The Cursed Goblet* participates in the global genre while invoking local history as well as distinct social problems and dynamics. Maayan Eitan argues that Hebrew literature has had no serious crime fiction tradition, because unlike the soldier or heroic Mossad agent, an ordinary policeman has rarely seemed worth depicting. However, Dror Mishani's *The Missing File* (2011) shows a genre reinventing itself, negotiating the distances between the Middle East and the West, origin and translation, and local and global. Suradech Chotiudompant traces the development of Thai crime fiction from the dawn of the twentieth century up to two contemporary Thai authors, Prapt and Jatawaluck. Though their award-winning works follow the pattern of international crime fiction, on a closer analysis their works reveal the fears and anxieties prevalent in present-day Thai society.

Finally Part 4, "Holmes Away from Home," looks at ways in which crime fiction today increasingly plays on its own generic history, building on the established canon of the genre's classics in new ways and giving new life to a metropolitan genre in peripheral locations. Michael Harris-Peyton argues for the "great detective" stock character as a site of complex interactions between apparently national (or nationalist) literary marketplaces and the transnational origin of the stock character as a literary device. The figure of the typically British "great detective" is, in fact, transnational from the beginning, and its colonial (and particularly postcolonial) embodiments subvert center and periphery, the geography of literary hierarchy and colonialism. Theo D'haen shows how Laurie King's Mary Russell and Kate Martinelli series build on the popularity of a world author, a world character, and a world genre to make a number of points on gender and society. Wei Yan focuses on the interaction between world crime fiction and Chinese detective writings during the Republican period. She studies how Western detective fiction was introduced and adapted to the Chinese context, but also the mixed feelings of native writers toward the pressure of Western modernity as embodied in Western detective literature, and their strategies of cultural resistance drawn from traditional Chinese literature and values. David Damrosch demonstrates how the Tibetan activist Jamyang Norbu tells the tale of the "missing years" between Sherlock's supposed death at the Reichenbach Falls and his reemergence. Exploring the complex cultural politics of Norbu's hilarious pastiche of Kipling and Conan Doyle, Damrosch shows how the archetypal British detective and his loquacious Indian sidekick Hurree Chunder Mukherjee are enlisted in the struggle for Tibet's political independence and cultural survival. Finally, Elizabeth Richmond-Garza illustrates how Russia's Boris Akunin has created a kind of "pulp fiction for the intelligentsia" in period stories that embed thoughtful and witty commentary on Putin's Russia, via the chronotope of late imperial Russia.

We hope that the essays collected here will appeal both to students and to devotees of crime fiction, and more generally will show people working in comparative and world literature that detective fiction opens up exciting new ways to think about globalized literary production today.

Note

1. Other examples include Stephen Knight's *Crime Fiction, 1800–2000: Detection, Death, Diversity* (2003 and 2010), John Scagg's *Crime Fiction* (2005), Lee Horsley's *Twentieth-Century Crime Fiction* (2005), Leonard Cassuto's *Hard-Boiled Sentimentality: The Secret History of American Crime Fiction* (2008), and Charles Rzepka and Lee Horsley's *Companion to Crime Fiction* (2010).

Part One

Global and Local

1

The Knife in the Lemon: Nordic Noir and the Glocalization of Crime Fiction

Andreas Hedberg

It has often been argued that crime fiction, more than any other genre, mirrors its contemporary reality. In his book *The Pursuit of Crime: Art and Ideology in Detective Fiction* (1981), Dennis Porter discusses the verisimilitudinous character of crime fiction, its relationship to the realist tradition, and its fidelity to contemporary social reality:

> [M]ainstream detective fiction respects the conventions of the realist tradition. That is to say, it situates its actions in contemporary social reality, limits the type of crime and the methods of detection to what passes for rationally plausible, and chooses as its characters easily identifiable human or social types. Further, detective stories present themselves to their readers as substitute worlds or mirrors that reflect directly the reality beyond. (Porter 1981: 115)

Porter makes his point using notions from the Marxist tradition, citing Antonio Gramsci's writings about cultural hegemony, describing the domination of a culturally diverse society by a ruling class which manipulates that society's culture, beliefs, explanations, perceptions, and values so that its worldview is imposed and accepted as the cultural norm (Porter, 117–18). Porter claims that "the most popular detective fiction everywhere represents an ideal form of policing insofar as it is in conformity with the most cherished behavioral norms of a given society" (129). Porter also differentiates between the British and American traditions of crime fiction, arguing that they mirror different cultural ideologies (128–9).

In this article, I set out to make a point similar to Porter's, but focusing more strongly on the parallel developments of crime fiction and consumer society, of markets and forms. While crime fiction is a product of the mass market, what interests me is the stereotypical form of crime fiction itself and its importance for the genre's status as world literature.

Wherever crime fiction is produced, the form is usually recognizable. Here lies, in part, its great success. The reader of crime fiction looks for a certain experience and finds it. If s/he didn't, s/he would be disappointed and rightly so. However, this is not to say that all crime fiction is the same. The elements common to all crime fiction—or at least to the great majority of the genre—are the form and the focus on producing a certain reader response, particularly, a feeling of suspense and/or curiosity. Perhaps paradoxically, this strictly standardized frame offers unparalleled possibilities for variation. When adopted into a new cultural milieu, the given mold of the crime story can be filled with almost any narrative material. Crime fiction is therefore able to attract the consumer by incorporating the latest fashions, trends, and current affairs. The standardized form is what makes this operation possible. Thus, since crime fiction is recognizable everywhere it surfaces, it is an excellent pedagogical example of how literature and especially literary genres (rather than single works) change when crossing from one linguocultural sphere to another. It is also a genre that can be called "glocal," in that it easily permits the writer to combine global patterns with local themes (Damrosch 2009: 109). In order to further discuss these phenomena, I would like to examine two cases from the Swedish crime fiction genre, or Nordic Noir: Sofie Sarenbrant and Kåre Halldén.

Sofie Sarenbrant's *Visning pågår* and the Swedish housing bubble

On the back cover of Swedish writer Sofie Sarenbrant's fifth crime novel, *Visning pågår* (a title that can be translated as Open House or House Viewing), there is a striking image of a glass bowl containing a lemon pierced deeply by an expensive kitchen knife. Above this picture the following back cover text meets the reader's eye: "The morning after a house viewing in Bromma, Stockholm suburb, a father is found dead by his six-year old daughter Astrid. There are no signs of a break-in, and the murder weapon is one of the family's own kitchen knives" (English translation provided by the publishing house for promotional use). The front cover is even more graphic. On the sidewalk of a suburban street, tinted in blue, sits an open house sign, its upper right corner stained crimson with blood. The street is completely empty, producing an eerie sense of abandonment.

This quite novel theme for a crime novel—the housing market—came not unexpectedly for Swedish critics or the Swedish general reading public. Although a rather uncommon subject for popular fiction, real estate is currently a constant topic of conversation in Sweden, and especially in the nation's capital, Stockholm. The choice of theme can be interpreted as a marketing strategy to rise above the competition within crime fiction, a world in many ways as profit-driven as real estate. In the genre fiction industry, where the bestseller list is often the standard of a writer's success, this is then "a genius move"—as one internet reviewer put it—to write about what readers are discussing, thinking, and concerned with at the moment:

> Most of us have some experience selling houses or flats. I've been to a ton of open houses, once as the seller. Every time I start thinking about selling, I also start worrying about everything that needs to be done before the open house—it feels like I have an insurmountable hill to climb. This feeling is combined with the fear that not enough people might come. Maybe our house won't get sold! Maybe the price will be too low! What will happen then? (Evhammar 2016, my translation)

Since the mid-1990s, house prices in Sweden have more than doubled and are now at a historical high. For Stockholm, this means that prices, as of 2015, have surpassed USD 1,000 per square foot. This raises concerns that the market for owner-occupied housing may be overvalued and that Sweden may be headed for a significant drop in house prices. Thus, the Swedish National Bank (Riksbanken) and the Swedish Fiscal Policy Council (Finanspolitiska rådet) have recently published extensive reports analyzing trends in the Swedish housing market and discussing the resulting risks to economic and financial stability.

Another consequence of the housing bubble is the increasing use of creative home staging; since prices are at a record high, there is a strong incentive to be the most attractive to buyers. This is also reflected in the paratext of Sarenbrant's novel *Visning pågår* by the lemon and the knife on the back cover. For some reason (perhaps because they are typically associated with freshness and purity), fruit—especially citrus—has been a recurring prop in real estate ads in Stockholm papers. Therefore, the knife in the lemon can be interpreted in several ways: as simply something familiar to the reader, as a light parody of the real estate market, or as a poignant threat aimed at the Stockholm bourgeoisie and its superficial ways.

For *Visning pågår*, her breakthrough novel and her third featuring, as protagonist, police inspector Emma Sköld, Sarenbrant adapts this topical theme to the already enormously popular Nordic Noir genre. And she does so with hyperbolic frenzy, as is clear in the following synopsis of the novel's plot:

While rain starts to fall in the early hours of April 1, police inspector Emma Sköld, in her 30s and a few weeks pregnant with her first child, is summoned to a fashionable address in the Stockholm suburb of Bromma, where Hans Göransson—husband to the much younger Cornelia and father to six-year-old Astrid—a man who has invested a lot of money in real estate, has been found dead, brutally stabbed with a kitchen knife. The first suspect is Cornelia, who claims she has been repeatedly beaten and abused by her alcoholic and unfaithful husband, to whose millions she is the sole heir. But Emma Sköld's investigation quickly grows more complicated as the "Open House killer" strikes again. This time, the victim is Hans Göransson's one-time business partner, the cruel and unscrupulous real estate agent Benjamin Weber, who is killed together with his employee and mistress, the ambitious and, again, much younger Helena Sjöblom, just minutes before another open house in another fashionable Stockholm suburb.

As the book continues, Emma Sköld must also handle problems in her personal life. Until recently, she has been living with Hugo, a photographer who works for the apartment listings section of Stockholm newspapers. The couple broke up when they were unable to have children. Emma's current boyfriend, Kristoffer, the father of her unborn child, is a successful but workaholic real estate agent whom she met during apartment-hunting after the break up. Hugo is morbidly jealous and stakes out Emma's apartment. He also visits Kristoffer's open houses to berate the homes, loudly pointing out that the walls smell of mold or that neighboring houses are too close, not letting in enough sunlight.

As this description shows, the Stockholm of Sarenbrant's novel is steeped in real estate terms and thinking. There is also a certain amount of criticism, though admittedly somewhat vague and unoriginal, of the strictly profit-driven real estate industry. Sometimes it is not entirely clear if passages concerning the buying and selling of flats should be read as ironic. For instance, when Josefin, Emma's older sister, learns that her husband and the father of her three children has fallen in love with another woman, her first thought is: "What about the house? What real estate agent should we go for? Will the neighbors run around during the open house, judging our interior design?" (Sarenbrant, 39, my translation). When Cornelia Göransson has discovered her husband murdered and is forced to leave her house—now a crime scene surrounded by police officers—she immediately asks herself: "How are we supposed to sell the house now ... Who will want to live here after this?" (Sarenbrant, 81, my translation).

Not surprisingly, the murderer also has a connection to the real estate industry. Throughout the book, the reader follows him through short chapters of first-person narrative. The novel's very first chapter is one of these. As a result, the reader gets to know the killer and is—at least on a narratological level—closer to him than to anybody else, since the killer is the only character who speaks in first person, intriguing the reader even more as to his identity. At first, it seems to be someone unknown, not otherwise mentioned. But gradually, perhaps with a chill, the reader understands that this voice is actually that of another character central to the plot, Emma's boyfriend Kristoffer, as is wholly revealed in the very last of the book's 105 chapters.

As a reader, it is hard not to sympathize somewhat with Kristoffer, even if he is the murderer sought by Emma Sköld. In the third of his short chapters, he speaks about his "project" to "bring justice" (Sarenbrant, 79, my translation). He sees himself as a righteous killer, punishing those who take advantage of society's weak and poor as he feels his greedy and materialistic victims do. (The somewhat ironic fact that Kristoffer himself, as a real estate agent, is part of this greedy industry is never addressed in the novel). In this regard, he joins the ranks of sympathetic killers motivated by a just cause, a role lately revitalized in popular culture by the American TV show *Dexter* (2006–2013).

The killer's voice also serves the tepidly anti-materialistic undercurrent of Sarenbrant's novel, for Kristoffer shares the narrative voice's critical view of the real estate industry as profit-driven and amoral. As a result, these two voices—one homodiegetic, the other heterodiegetic (Genette 1980: 245)—come together to formulate a moral vision. When describing Benjamin Weber, the second victim of "the open house killer," the narrator shows disgust, emphasizing Weber's least flattering traits. In the first-person narrative, the killer claims that his victims, Hans and Benjamin, only have themselves to blame; it is their consistent and blatant disregard for anything but their own personal economic gain that makes them deserve death. But what seems an entirely altruistic motive is later revealed to be much more personal: revenge for the fact that Hugo and Benjamin indirectly caused the death of Kristoffer's adopted daughter Felicia (from a previous relationship) at a construction site for a modern housing project against which Kristoffer was protesting at the time. In this way, *Visning pågår* follows the pattern of another mode of successful Scandinavian crime fiction: the widely popular Danish–Swedish TV drama *Bron* (2011–), which has spurred several international versions (e.g., *The Bridge* in the United States [2013–2014]; *The Tunnel* in the United Kingdom/France [2013–]).

Sarenbrant's strategy—the fusion of the Nordic Noir format with the topic of real estate—has proven successful. *Visning pågår* was published in March 2014. The novel was aggressively marketed and quickly became a commercial success. Including the pocketbook edition—released in April 2015—it has sold over 100,000 copies in Sweden, quite an accomplishment in a country of 9.8 million inhabitants (although paling in comparison to the first installment of Stieg Larsson's Millennium Trilogy, *Män som hatar kvinnor*, 2005 [*The Girl with the Dragon Tattoo*], which sold more than 1,000,000 copies in Sweden). Nevertheless, in May and June 2015, *Visning pågår* was the most widely sold pocketbook crime novel according to statistics from *Svensk bokhandel*, the Swedish book industry's official news magazine. The novel's translation rights have been sold to publishers from Denmark (*Åbent hus*, 2014), Germany, Portugal, and the Czech Republic (*Dům na prodej*, 2015). Also, *Visning pågår* was the first novel by Sarenbrant to be translated into English. Under the title *Killer Deal*, it was published in the United States in May 2016 by the Swedish publisher Stockholm Text, which specializes in marketing Scandinavian bestsellers worldwide. On the front cover of the American edition, Sarenbrant is confidently dubbed "the new Queen of Scandinavian Crime."

Kåre Halldén and the Wine Crime series

Sarenbrant's *Visning pågår* is one of several novels in which the format of Nordic Noir is infused with contemporary concerns/topical matters. The Swedish book market has seen numerous examples of this kind of marketing mentality of late. Competition for crime fiction readers has become so fierce that writers must be extremely creative when searching for something to set them apart. An author in this vein is Kåre Halldén (b. 1969), the creator of the Wine Crime series published by Damm förlag, which also published Sarenbrant's first six novels. On his personal web site, Halldén describes the Wine Crime series as

> a suspense genre in a modern puzzle detective format that takes place in various known wine districts. Intrigues and power games. Glamour and family battles. War and heroes. With this series I hope that a lot of people will discover the

fascination and unique history of the wine world. Imagine Falcon Crest meets Agatha Christie. (Halldén, "Wine Crime")

For the second book of the series, *Cavakungen* (The Cava King, 2012), Halldén came up with the tagline "Will you ever dare to drink wine again?" (my translation). The back cover text combines a picturesque milieu—the sort often praised in Swedish travel magazines—with the threat of death and murder:

> In a small village just outside of Barcelona a hidden war has been fought. Since time immemorial, two of the world's biggest producers of cava have been competing with each other. They haven't stopped at threats, nor at corruption nor murder. Of this, Harald and Isabelle know nothing when they move to the village, having decided to produce their own cava. But when Isabelle's friend is found dead in their garden, they soon realize what a dangerous world they have entered. (my translation)

Halldén's wine crime novels, *Cavakungen* (2012) and *Champagneführern* (The Champagne Führer, 2011), seem an attempt similar to Sarenbrant's to attract a contemporary audience through current topics of conversation. In Sweden, interest in fine wines has been growing for several years. Already by the end of the 1970s, wine, for the first time, surpassed liquor as the most popular alcoholic beverage in Sweden. Since 1996, wine consumption has increased 65 percent. The average Swede drinks more than twice as much wine as the average American per year. Halldén, one of Sweden's leading experts on sparkling wines and the author of two books on the subject, including *Champagne: Din guide till bubblornas värld*, (Champagne: Your Guide to a World of Bubbles, 2007), sprinkles his thriller with facts about wine-making. In *Cavakungen*, we are given an explanation of how irrigation affects the grapes as a vineyard is mistakenly sprayed with radioactive water.

However, even though his strategy is similar to Sarenbrant's, Halldén's crime novels have not had the same success. *Cavakungen* remains the latest of the Wine Crime series, which has stopped short after this second installment. Nevertheless, in 2013, *Champagneführern* was translated into Dutch (*Het champagnehuis*), followed by a Finnish edition of *Cavakungen* (*Cavakuningas*) in 2014.

Crime fiction as glocal literature

Using Sarenbrant and Halldén as my main examples, I argue that crime fiction as a format is especially suitable for the incorporation of everyday topics or local cultural phenomena, like the Swedish housing bubble or the fashionable interest in fine wines. Crime fiction, as a mold, can be set anywhere and everywhere and can be filled with whatever readers' interests are. The strategy of Sarenbrant and Halldén can be further understood in the context of what David Damrosch—in his book *How to Read World Literature*—calls "glocalism," an authorial strategy that, according to Damrosch, takes two forms: the exportation of local situations abroad and the importation of global situations at home (Damrosch 2009: 109). It is mainly the first form that applies here. Per Damrosch, this means treating "local matters for a global audience." As an example, he discusses the work of Rudyard Kipling, where local (Indian) customs are introduced and explained for a British, and, later on, a global, audience (110–12). As indicated by the terms "strategy" and "audience," the glocal approach is the author's attempt to reach more readers. What I posit is that crime fiction is glocal, for it easily permits the writer to combine a global pattern with local themes. The larger goal, as in Damrosch's discussion, is to reach a greater audience. Yet, for glocal writers like Sarenbrant and Halldén, the first goal is not to reach an international/global audience, rather a local one.

By virtue of their glocal character, the examples of Swedish crime fiction discussed here can be considered world literature. However, there is a need to further clarify this point, especially since the concept of world literature is still very much debated. Johann Wolfang von Goethe's original understanding of the term is cosmopolitan and antinationalistic. In a much quoted passage, he says that "National literature means little now … the age of Weltliteratur has begun … everyone should further its cause" (Goethe [1827], 2013: 11). Goethe's stance is idealistic, and in a way emancipating, even though he keeps a normative emphasis on the quality of literature. In a globalized world, we are quite bound to study literature as an international, border-crossing phenomenon. "In hindsight," as Mads Rosendahl Thomsen puts it in *Mapping World Literature: International Canonization and Transnational Literatures*, "Goethe's hope for a future wherein the national literatures would not be dominant, and works would be received around the globe, was too optimistic" (Rosendahl 2008: 11). In his discussion of "the concept of world literature between idealism and realism," Rosendahl Thomsen classifies Goethe as an idealist.

The concept of world literature later developed into an instrument used to update old literary canons, as posited by Harold Bloom in *The Western Canon: The Book and the Schools of the Ages*, 1994. Damrosch, Rosendahl Thomsen points out, "argues that canons do not present themselves with the same validity as they did decades ago ... the dominance of old colonial powers is regarded with some skepticism" (2008: 18). Damrosch, for his part, envisions a canonical system with three prongs: "a *hypercanon*, a *counter-canon* and a *shadow canon*" (cited in Thomsen 2008: 18).

In the context of canonized literature, the main object of study in Rosendahl Thomsen's book, crime fiction hardly qualifies as world literature save for a few unique exceptions such as Edgar Allan Poe ("The Murders in the Rue Morgue," 1841) or Umberto Eco (*The Name of the Rose*, 1980). When I discuss crime fiction as world literature here, I have a different understanding of this concept, one very much influenced by Franco Moretti. For him, world literature is not a set of works as it is for Bloom or Damrosch—it is not even "an object, it's a *problem*, and a problem that asks for a new critical method" (Moretti 2013: 161–2). World literature, his argument continues, should be a new way to study literature as a border-crossing phenomenon and on a much larger scale than before. Ergo, Moretti is much more interested in genres and the spread and development of genres throughout the world (Thomsen 2008: 16). Using his trademark method of distant reading, he identifies configurations common to literary development in several different cultures. He uses these pieces of evidence "to reflect on the relation between market and [literary] forms" in order to uncover what he terms "*laws of literary evolution*." The first such law discussed in Moretti's seminal theoretical article "Conjectures on World Literature" (2000) is this: "When a culture starts moving towards the modern novel, it's always a compromise between foreign form and local materials" (Moretti 2013: 163).

This brings us back to David Damrosch and his term glocalism, the combination of global patterns and local themes. It also brings us back to the core of my argument in this article: that popular fiction, especially crime fiction, is, in a certain sense, *more* world literature than canonized literature. The more standardized the literary form or genre, the easier it travels. If a literature no longer aims to be wholly loyal to a particular situation, no longer aims to restrict its form to a unique human experience shaped by a specific culture or milieu, if it then casts off the auratic character of canonized modernist art (to use Walter Benjamin's term; Benjamin 2008), doesn't that also mean that when it comes to literary form, it becomes more cosmopolitan, more a form of world literature?

Crime fiction—as the Swedish examples discussed here show—makes it possible to combine cosmopolitan patterns with vernacular themes. Crime fiction is a travelling structure, applicable everywhere and thereby a world literature par excellence. For, as Moretti's theory indicates, when a new genre adapts in a new literary environment, it is always a compromise between foreign and local, between cosmopolitan and vernacular. This is something that happens spontaneously. But for the Nordic Noir writers discussed here, it is something else. It is a marketing strategy, poignantly symbolized by the back cover of Sarenbrant's *Visning pågår*: the kitchen knife plunged into the lemon.

Works Cited

Benjamin, Walter (2008). *The Work of Art in the Age of Mechanical Reproduction*. London: Penguin.

Bloom, Harold (1994). *The Western Canon: The Book and the Schools of the Ages*. New York: Harcourt Brace.

Damrosch, David (2003). *What is World Literature?* Princeton and Oxford: Princeton University Press.

Damrosch, David (2009). *How to Read World Literature*. Malden and Oxford: Wiley-Blackwell.

Evhammar, Joachim. "Visning pågår av Sofie Sarenbrant—Recension." http://www.deckarhuset.se/visning-pagar-av-sofie-sarenbrant-recension/ (Accessed January 7, 2016)

Genette, Gérard (1980). *Narrative Discourse: An Essay in Method*, trans. Jane E. Lewin. Ithaca and New York: Cornell University Press.

Goethe, Johann Wolfang (von) ([1827], 2013). "On World Literature." In *World Literature: A Reader*, ed. Theo D'haen, César Dominguez, and Mads Rosendahl Thomsen. London and New York: Routledge, 9–15.

Halldén, Kåre (2012). *Cavakungen*. Stockholm: Damm förlag.

Halldén, Kåre "Wine Crime—A Journey through Time & Space." http://www.winecrime.org/eng/wine_crime_genre.cfm (Accessed January 7, 2016)

Moretti, Franco ([2000/2003], 2013). "Conjectures on World Literature and More Conjectures." In *World Literature: A Reader*, ed. Theo D'haen, César Dominguez, and Mads Rosendahl Thomsen. London and New York: Routledge, 160–75.

Porter, Dennis (1981). *The Pursuit of Crime: Art and Ideology in Detective Fiction*. New Haven and London: Yale University Press.

Sarenbrant, Sofie (2014). *Visning pågår*. Stockholm: Damm förlag.

Thomsen, Mads Rosendahl (2008). *Mapping World Literature: International Canonization and Transnational Literatures*. London and New York: Continuum.

2

After Such Knowledge: The Politics of Detection in the Narconovelas of Elmer Mendoza

Michael Wood

Elmer Mendoza began his literary career as a short-story writer, turning to the longer form of the novel through a particular provocation. In 1994, the Mexican presidential candidate Luis Donaldo Colosio was assassinated. The origins and full context of this event are still far from clear, but its implications were visible immediately to anyone who lived in or thought about Mexico. The Institutional Revolutionary Party, its name alone a sort of political parable, had been in power since 1946—or longer if we include its earlier incarnations, dating from 1929. The party was broad-based in its ideology and practice, including old socialists and new capitalists, but it was also exclusive. If you were not in it, politically you were nowhere. The outgoing president traditionally nominated his successor—the naming itself was called "el dedazo," the pointing of a finger—and Carlos Salinas de Gortari had nominated Colosio in November 1993. Between this date and that of Colosio's death five months later, the two men had a falling out, and the old guard of the party was disturbed by some remarks Colosio had made about democratizing the one-party system. The official view was (and still is) that the murder was the work of a lone killer, Mario Aburto Martinez, who is still in jail. Almost no one believed this. What everyone did believe, and what seemed even truer because of this assassination, was that the old system was bankrupt, and within six years, the party lost an election for the first time, and the opposition took power.

Listening to talk about Colosio's assassination, Mendoza said, made him realize that "a myth was forming ... and I thought of writing a novel."[1] The myth engaged with a brutal fact and a series of shifting political and economical realities, and a sense that stories were being spun around them. The truth was not nonexistent or entirely relative, as some modernist modes of skepticism have suggested in other situations, but was hidden, and perhaps too dangerous to be talked about directly. Still, it was talked about in fantasy and gossip, and some of the talk may even have been true. When the talk became material for a fully developed literary fiction, the fiction represented the missing truth—in the senses both of standing in for it and of keeping a place for it—and invited readers to imagine alternatives.

There are elements of this vision, or this relation of fiction to history, in the work of Gabriel García Márquez and other Latin American writers of the later twentieth century, but the full theory and practice emerge with the claim of Ricardo Piglia, in relation to the "disappearances" in Argentina in the 1980s, that a novelist's material is "the already narrated," *lo ya narrado* (Piglia 2005: 230). In his example, no one had ever seen a train carrying corpses to the sea, but everyone knew someone who had seen the train. This is exactly the kind of experience on which Mendoza bases his shift to the novel. His first work in this form, *Un asesino solitario* (1999) arose "from what I heard. I learned everything related to the death of Colosio afterwards. It was the journalists who told me [Fueron los periodistas que me lo contaron]" (Rey Pereira 338).

I'm not going to linger over this very good novel here, and shall note only that it sets the terms for Mendoza's later work in an exemplary way. The book knows what the reader does not know, cannot know in advance since it concerns fictional people and events, but that knowledge, once transmitted, can be related to other forms of knowledge in many ways. The novel can be seen as copying reality, inverting it, running alongside it, filling in its gaps, making travesties of it. Of course all fiction may be read in this fashion, but when the chief event is a crime that closely parallels its historical source, the game in the reader's mind can become especially intense. And all of Mendoza's novels, even without a nameable individual historical event in the background, reflect and compete with a violent contemporary scene, in particular with the fictions of the Mexican nation state and of what is happening in the place that has come to be called Narcoland.[2] A trivial but not uninteresting fact is that Mexican bookstores now stock Mendoza's books among "national literature" rather than crime fiction. He has published eight novels since *Un asesino*, four of them involving the brooding detective Edgar Mendieta, and I want to concentrate on the first and the most recent of that series, *Balas de plata* (2008), translated as *Silver Bullets* (2015) and *Besar al detective* (2015; North American edition 2016).

Mendoza's hero has many elements of the classic literary detective in his style. He believes murders are messages, reads appearances and odors, like Arsène Dupin and Sherlock Holmes.³ He goes in for irony and worldly epigrams, like Sam Spade and Philip Marlowe.⁴ But I want to associate him most closely with a larger, more recent and less easily codifiable development in crime fiction. This is what Piglia calls looking at society from the point of view of crime rather than the other way round. We might say this is already happening in Hammett and Chandler, as it is not in the English mystery from Dorothy Sayers to P. D. James; but then the degree and kind of looking keep changing. American society is under keener critical scrutiny in the novels of Ross Thomas, say, than in those of his predecessors.⁵ Crime is so ordinary in the Sicilian world of Leonardo Sciascia that in the novel *To Each His Own* (1966) only the amateur detective does *not* know who committed the murder he is investigating. In Ian Rankin's recent work *Even Dogs in the Wild* (2106), the old gangster worlds of Glasgow and Edinburgh are falling apart, there are opportunities for a new generation of crooks, and if not all policemen are corrupt, there is no surveillance team that does not have at least one member who has sold out to the enemy. And in Rankin as in Mendoza, the legally identified public enemy, the serial killer or the gang boss, is not always the worst of the bad guys. There is a passage in *Even Dogs* where John Rebus, a retired police detective, all but decides that crimes have to be solved not because the criminals are in the wrong but because the detective's life has to be perceived as having made some sort of sense. A young man, Brian Holroyd, has been killing off the people involved in the sexual abuse of his father as a child, and a witness to part of the story says they should wish the boy luck.

> Rebus ... stayed where he was ... He couldn't help feeling that the man had a point, and Rebus was no longer a cop. What did it matter if Brian Holroyd was out there, picking off his abusers and their abettors? Yet somehow it did—it did matter. Always had, always would. Not because of any of the victims or perpetrators, but for Rebus himself. Because if none of it mattered, then neither did he. (Rankin, 285)

A similar question arises in *Silver Bullets* when Mendieta chooses to hand over a criminal to a drug chief rather than to his colleagues, the representatives of the law. Or when, in *Besar al detective*, he discovers that he is willing to save the life of an individual human crook at the expense of his loyalty to a theoretically abstract, pragmatically corrupt system.

I should say at once that these reflections and actions offer no solution to the moral and professional questions they raise—the questions are almost unmanageably complex, however crisply Rankin and Mendoza present the instances. But they do clearly belong to the perspective of society viewed from the point of view of crime, and we can perhaps be a little more precise about this. Eva Erdmann makes two helpful claims in this respect. First, she says that "[t]he crime novel of the last decades is distinguished by the fact that the main focus is not on the crime itself but on the setting ... crime fiction's distinguishing characteristic has become the *locus criminalis*" (Erdmann 2009: 12); and second that "[d]eep within our crime fiction world ... there is a paradox that is hardly noticed any more. The unusual occurrence of murder has become the norm" (17). We should not insist too much on the idea of a setting as distinct from the crime itself—and probably we should not to be too sure we know what the crime itself is—but the drift of this claim is suggestive. In a great deal of older crime fiction the "setting," let's say the whole imaginary moral and material world in which the story is situated, is pictured as a realm of order invaded by the disorder of crime. In Poe's "The Murders in the Rue Morgue," for example, the disorder doesn't even have a human source, so it is sheer disorder, not even a crime. And in all such cases, even with human agents, order returns when the mess is cleared up, that is, when the mystery created by the crime is explained. Needless to say, such a picture of order is usually as much of a fantasy as its disruption. In more recent fiction, the notion of order is still present, and murder has not quite become the norm, as Erdmann says it has, since it is still exceptional enough, most of the time, to start an investigation. But there is more than one order, and the solution of the crime is often just the beginning of another story, the gateway to more crimes perhaps, or a path that leads only to an impasse, since there is no one to whom the "truth" can be told, and no authority who can or will act on it.

Much of the wit and intellectual energy of the characters in Mendoza's novels comes from their attempts to cope with this situation. In *Silver Bullets* the witnesses of an act of violence say nothing because they think "With the Mexican police, the farther away the better, same story with the killers" (Mendoza 2015: 9).[6] Forensic technicians are never surprised, because "in their departments anything could happen and everything did" (14).[7] When a crime scene is so full of clues that could lead investigators almost anywhere, Mendieta's colleagues attribute the deed to Jack the Ripper for starters: "in other words all the prints in the world and good luck finding the culprits" (95).[8] A woman says, "in this country justice is in the hands of the criminals" (136),[9] and the criminals themselves are apt to boast of their social achievements or their old-fashioned ethics. A drug lord speaks of the neighborhoods he has developed in the city, of all the jobs he has created—far more than the government has ever managed—and we learn elsewhere of his many charitable works. A professional assassin complains to Mendieta about the sensationalist habits of the newer generation of customers, and in what is perhaps the fiercest of Mendoza's Swiftian jokes, says, "We get more and more requests for services where they want the target cut to pieces, drawn and quartered, castrated, what is that all about, ours is an ethical firm, we would never accept those contracts, it's a human being we're going to kill not a wild animal" (131).[10] There are after all ways of respecting life even when you take it away. In one of Mendieta's own finest literary moments, he thinks "power corrupts, dissolute power corrupts dissolutely" (74).[11]

The second of Mexico's non-PRI presidents, Felipe Calderón (in office from 2006 to 2012), declared an open war on drugs, which informs the world of *Balas de plata*. The government is widely thought to have lost this war—indeed to have been in no position to win it in the first place, because it didn't have enough weapons or soldiers and because too many of its own representatives were playing for both teams. Calderón's successor, Enrique Peña Nieto, whose election signalled the return of the PRI to power—or to a diluted form of power, since the old order was never going to revive—has governed largely by silence, neither waging the war nor declaring it over. This means, in Mendoza's more recent novel, *Besar al detective*, that many of the narcos think the war belongs to the past and easier days lie ahead for them—as if the war had not been easy enough. Some anonymous others are also said to have thought the war "had reached its end, but the dead people kept on appearing."[12] A gay restaurant owner reminds Mendieta that "because the dead people don't show up in the newspapers doesn't mean they don't exist" (Mendoza 2016: 6).[13]

In this novel Mendieta mocks the idea of the narco with the heart of gold, but only to replace it with a modest twin. "The narco world is full of decent people. Yes, of course, and I am Little Red Riding Hood, a very happy little girl" (127).[14] It's not immediately clear whether Mendieta is speaking of himself in mockery or ventriloquizing a line for Samantha Valdes, who has inherited her father's drug empire. She's not a decent person, and she's not Red Riding Hood, but she has her principles and her loyalties and she pays her moral debts.

But then if the obvious bad guys are not the worst offenders, who are? There are almost too many contenders for the honor, including newer generations of narcos, corrupt policemen and politicians, top-flight international assassins, and hundreds of members of the conspiracies of silence that haunt the country. In *Besar al detective*, the FBI is a candidate at least for a place among the finalists. But Mendoza seems to want to award the prize to the faceless central authorizers of violence against criminals (and against the innocent where necessary), to those whose mission is to make sure that crime continues to serve state power rather than interfere with it. Dissolute power not only corrupts dissolutely, it secretly and securely sustains absolutism. There are horrible echoes here of an ongoing case in Mexico where the inquiry into the murders of forty-three students in Ayotzinapa appears to be permanently stalled, the bodies not yet found, for fear of who might turn out to be involved, what person or what arm of government could have known about the event before it happened, or would have more to lose if the pieces of the puzzle were coherently put together. The case is quietly evoked in *Besar al detective* when the mention of "so much senseless dying" in Mexico, *tanto muerto sin sentido*, is followed by the thought that we need to add forty-three to that sum (202). And the methods of these silent senior powers are in the air from the beginning of the novel. Who wants to kill the gang boss Samantha Valdes and why? A rival gang, obviously, and for obvious reasons. But what if the rival gang was put up to it? Who would be behind that, and why is there an assassin in the wings in case the gang doesn't do the job? As in fact it doesn't. Samantha is in hospital, wounded but not fatally, and from the point of view of those whose existence we can scarcely guess at, the chief risk appears to be not that she will die or escape but that she will be arrested—will fall, that is, into the arms of a too public form of government. That she manages to see off two assassins doesn't make her a heroine of political freedom, any more than she was Red Riding Hood to start with, but it does make us wonder, with Mendieta, how to fight the good fight, and whether it can be fought at all.

This is all very local, Mexican, and apparently not global; but we are, in these novels, looking at instances of world literature all the same, and I must try to spell out the reasons. There are many, but two will do for now. First, the global is not necessarily opposed to the local; each may be a dimension of the other. Even the global has to start somewhere, and to continue to live somewhere, and quite often manages the extraordinary feat of staying at home and traveling abroad. And the local may already be intensely globalized, as is certainly the case with Mendoza's fiction.

Some critics are inclined to deplore this fact. Fernando Fabio Sanchez, for example, having evoked some of the intertexts of Mendoza's first novel *Un asesino solitario*—Charles Bronson, Pedro Infante, Valentin Trujillo, *Star Wars*,

Natural Born Killers, Trading Places, Back to the Future, Flashdance, Saturday Night Fever—invites us to see these allusions as signs of "the penetration of global culture into local culture," where the global is "a deathly presence that invades that which was already dying: the post-revolutionary symbolic world" (Fabio Sanchez 2010: 156). This is a very astute comment on the current or recent condition of the Mexican national myth that identified the PRI with order, and it is true that the drug wars brought death to what was already dying. It's hard to believe that *Flashdance* and *Saturday Night Fever* were part of the problem, though, and although their presence in Mexican imaginations—inside and outside of fiction—must be symptoms of something, we don't have to think of international culture as death.

If we take a moment to add to the mix a few more names, chosen more or less at random, we shall find, in *Balas de plata*, James Bond, *Brokeback Mountain*, Robbie Williams, Christina Aguilera, *The Good, the Bad, and the Ugly*, Joe Cocker, Joe Lennon, Edvard Munch, as also Mexican figures like Frida Kahlo, Carlos Fuentes, Juan Rulfo, Fernando del Paso, and other Latin Americans like Gabriel García Márquez and Ricardo Piglia. A similar trawl through *Besar al detective* yields the Beatles, *Playboy*, Ferguson Missouri, Steve Jobs, *Fast and Furious*, Superman, Spider-Man, and John Denver, as also the Latin American writers Juan Carlos Onetti and Mario Vargas Llosa. We might discount the names from pop and rock music, since such instances are everywhere in Mendoza's novels, part of his signature as much as of Mendieta's. But then we are left with an image, a collage of cultures that could belong in principle to anyone who lives in a world that contains television sets and cinemas and the internet. One could avoid such a world, or edit it out of one's writing or life, but the act would be drastic and willful. It is only an apparent contrast to such a claim to insist on the intensely Mexican, idiomatic language of Mendoza's writing and of Mendieta's style of thought. The texts are littered with jokes, aphorisms, turns of phrase that native speakers—not just of Spanish but of Mexican Spanish—will recognize from the slangiest moments of their lives or occasionally may not recognize at all because they don't move in the right circles. We can, and most of us do, live locally and globally, hardly pausing to distinguish between what is village folklore and what is general knowledge; and detectives with catholic minds will not separate highbrow from lowbrow allusions.

David Damrosch reminds us that "world literature is not an infinite, ungraspable canon of works but rather a mode of circulation and reading" (Damrosch 2003: 5), and I wish only to add that the mode will often have a sort of precondition, a situation in which worldliness of a certain kind is itself part of local culture. This is important in Mendoza's case, since he is scarcely setting out on his way toward world literature if our criterion is translation and a movement "out into a broader world" (6). As of this writing, only two of his books, *Balas de plata* and *La prueba del acido* (2010), have been translated into English (2015, 2016). The same two have been translated into German (2010, 2012) and Italian (2010, 2012) and the second has been translated into French (2014). We might say that the Spanish language spoken all over a sub-continent constitutes a world; but it seems more interesting to linger over the idea of world literature in the making rather than fully made.

There is another sense, however, in which Mendoza belongs to world literature already, and this is the second of the reasons I evoked earlier. It is a matter of genre. If crime fiction is always world literature *in potentia*, as I believe it now is—it was not always so—then any rich example of it, even if insufficiently known in the world at large, becomes part of an ongoing dialogue with other examples. I have mentioned Sciascia and Rankin in connection with Mendoza, and there is an elegant Mexican play on the idea of worldliness in *Besar al detective*. Héctor Belascoarán Shayne, the sleuth hero of the best-selling novels of Paco Ignacio Taibo II, appears in Mendoza's novel, hoping to help in some way. After an amicable lunch with Mendieta, he returns to Mexico, realizing that as a mere metropolitan he has no sort of purchase on the provincial subtleties of Northwest Mexico. This is a way of saying that neither Mendoza nor Mendieta have to pass through the capital to reach the world, any more than Rankin and Rebus need to go to London.

Latin American commentary on detective fiction, usually called *literatura policial*, whether any sort of police is involved or not, has not always regarded the larger world, and still shows a markedly Anglo-American tilt. Whether we read Jorge Luis Borges (1980) or Ricardo Piglia (2005), Rodolfo Walsh (1987) or Carlos Monsiváis (1973), the lineage looks much the same: Poe-Conan Doyle-Chesterton-Christie/Sayers-Hammett-Chandler. There is often a suggestion that such mysteries and solutions cannot apply to Latin American realities, or can apply only in parodic ways. And yet Monsiváis, in 1973, was not only being provocatively anachronistic when he claimed that no thrillers of any note were being written in Mexico; he was actually defining the genre itself as many have now come to think of it. "Among us," he wrote, "there is no crime fiction because there is no confidence in justice and everyone is afraid to identify with the suspect, is afraid to defend him or her"[15] (Monsiváis 1973, n.p.). I'm not sure confidence in justice or identification with the suspect were ever essential requirements for readers of Anglo-American thrillers and detective fiction, and Monsiváis's phrasing brilliantly gives another game away. This is precisely what society looks like from the point of view of crime, an angle I have already drawn from Piglia and associated with Eva Erdmann, but need now to complicate with a more desperate, troubled coloring. Chandler's mean streets are a long way off here, because the meanness is everywhere—not in reality, we trust, but in every plausible imagining of our fragile city. The balance is beautifully held by two remarks made by Paco Ignacio Taibo in an interview: "Criminality forms part of the system" (Taibo 1997: 147); and "I suppose Mexican readers find in my novels a broken mirror, a proposition that invites them not to surrender to an immoral reality" (145).

The mirror of fiction at its best always belongs to a particular place, reflects a quite specific history. But the breakages bear striking resemblances from one history to another, and the cracks and consequent distortions of our faces allow for all kinds of parallels and analogies, for the tracking of patterns of harm in many parts of the world. No crime and no mirror, we might say, is ever entirely alone.

Notes

1 Interview with Ricardo Rey Pereira, my translation. The Spanish reads "Me di cuenta que se estaba formando un mito ... y pensé en hacer una novela" (337).
2 *Narcoland* is the English title of Anabel Hernández's *Los señores del narco*.
3 See *Silver* Bullets, 78, 88–9, 136; *Besar al detective*, 18, 89.
4 *Balas*, 115.
5 See especially *Briarpatch* (1985) and *The Porkchoppers* (1972).
6 *Balas*, 20: "Con la policía mexicana cuanto más lejos mejor y de los matones también." Further references to the English translation in the text
7 *Balas*, 26: "En sus departamentos podía pasar y pasaba cualquier cosa."
8 *Balas*, 116: 'o sea, todas las que es posible dejar en el mundo y ubiquen las del culpable si pueden."
9 *Balas*, 160: "la justicia está en manos de los delincuentes."
10 *Balas*, 155: "cada vez más seguido nos llegan solicitudes de servicios donde quieren al objetivo despedazado, arrastrado, castrado, qué es eso, nosotros somos una empresa con ética y jamás hemos aceptado esas comisiones, es un ser humano el que vamos a matar, no un animal salvaje."

11 *Balas*, 91–2: "El poder corrumpe, el poder disoluto corrempe disolutamente."
12 *Besar al detective*, 41. My translation; "había llegado a su fin, pero los muertos seguían apareciendo." Further page references in text.
13 "que los muertos no salgan en los periódicos no quiere decir que no existan."
14 "el narco esta lleno de gente decente: si, cómo no, soy Caperucita Roja, una niña muy feliz."
15 "Entre nosotros no hay literatura policial porque no hay confianza en la justicia y todo el mundo teme identificarse con el sospechoso, teme defenderlo."

Works Cited

Borges, Jorge Luis (1980). "El cuento policial." In *Borges Oral*. Barcelona: Bruguera.
Damrosch, David (2003). *What is World Literature?* Princeton: Princeton University Press.
Erdmann, Eva (2009). "Nationality International." In *Investigating Identities*, ed. Marieke Krajenbrink and Kate M. Quinn. Amsterdam: Rodopi, 11–26.
Fabio Sanchez, Fernando (2010). *Artful Assassins*, trans. Stephen J. Clark. Nashville: Vanderbilt University Press.
Hernández, Anabel (2013). *Narcoland*, trans. Iain Bruce. London: Verso.
Mendoza, Elmer (2015). *Balas de plata*. Mexico: Tusquets Editores, 2008. *Silver Bullets*, trans. Mark Fried. London: MacLehose Press.
Mendoza, Elmer (2016). *Besar al detective*. New York: Literatura Random House.
Monsiváis, Carlos (1973). "Ustedes que jamás han sido asesinados." *Revista de la Universidad de México* 7, March, n.p.
Piglia, Ricardo (2005). "Lectores imaginarios," in *El Ultimo Lector*. Barcelona: Editorial Anagrama.
Piglia, Ricardo (2013). "Afterword" to Rodolfo Walsh, *Operation Massacre*, trans. Daniella Gittlin. New York: Seven Stories Press.
Rankin, Ian (2016). *Even Dogs in the Wild*. London: Orion.
Rey Pereira, Rodrigo (2008). "La condición social de México en los escritos del autor: entrevista con Elmer Mendoza." *Anales de la Literatura Hispanoamericana*, vol 37, 331–42.
Taibo, Paco Ignacio (1997). Interview with Ilan Stavans. In Stavans, *Antiheroes: Mexico and its Detective Novel*, trans. Jesse H. Lyttle and Jennifer A. Mattson. Madison: Fairleigh Dickinson University Press.
Walsh, Rodolfo (1987). *Cuentos para tahúres y otros relatos policiales*. Buenos Aires: Puntosur.

3

Red Herrings and Read Alerts: Crime and its Excesses in *Almost Blue* and *Nairobi Heat*

Tilottama Tharoor

Carlo Lucarelli's 1997 detective novel, *Almost Blue*, set in the Italian city of Bologna, opens with a principal character, the young man Simone, informing us:

> I'm blind. I've been blind since I was born. I've never seen colors or light or movement of any kind. I listen. I scan the silence around me the way as an electronic scanner sweeps the airwaves for sounds and voices, tuning automatically into any and all frequencies. I know how to use both my scanners perfectly, the internal one that I've had in my head for the past twenty-five years, ever since I was born, and the electric one in my room next to my stereo. If I had any friends, I know they'd call me Scanner. I'd like that. (Lucarelli, 5–6)

This blind Simone receives the outside world through headphones and electronic scanners, and listens to an assortment of radio and telephone conversations—snatches of exchanges between truck drivers, Bologna residents, students, and the police. The snippets that float and crackle in his ears are random, disjointed, and truncated; Simone deciphers and responds to them mainly by the sensory suggestions they convey.

As "Scanner" he stumbles into a serial killer drama in Bologna when he overhears frantic police chatter about a vicious killing, followed by the disturbing, though desultory, words of the killer himself, and is subsequently enlisted to help the police investigation.

The quote that introduces Simone as an acute listener and intuitive interpreter, and prepares the reader for his investigative role, seems highly pertinent for both the mystery-solving procedures of crime fiction and the negotiation of texts in their constitution as world literature. There is silence—at times baffling or intractable—but with the promise of decipherability, even coherence. The detective or the reader may enter the material "blind," but senses that there's light: of explanation, possibly revelation, from diverse interpretive strategies. And each scans, diligently and methodically: the detective, conducting the investigation, tunes into "any and all frequencies," collecting snatches and glimmers, seeking the "internal scanner" (M. Poirot's famed "grey cells"; Sherlock Holmes's notion of the "elementary") to infer and deduce toward a solution. World literature's transmission is inevitably from great distances; it comes tangled and is unraveled in wires of translation, and is received through frequencies of wavering lengths. The "scanners" of demand and circulation, of comparison and thematic alignments, of enabling compatibilities and easing disjunctures—such scanners are employed in construing and pursuing world literature. Through external scanners—the translation industry, the circulation centers—we listen. But then internal scanners, developed by world literature's textual imperatives, decode and recode, mediate local textual contingencies and reclaim into contingent signifying systems of world literary regimes. World literature sometimes assumes a "blindness" to the obscurities of textual locations in order to illuminate with other, more assimilable, contexts and categories.

The insights that *Almost Blue* enables into both crime fiction and world literature will be addressed in this chapter by comparing it with another, later work, *Nairobi Heat* (2010), by Mũkoma wa Ngũgĩ. While the two novels are instructive versions of crime fiction writing from recent times, they are also usefully different. *Almost Blue* follows the serial killer format, with police (led by the female Inspector Negro and helped by Simone's electronic and sensory skills) tracking a deranged killer as he destroys young student victims. It is set entirely in the city of Bologna, involving all Bologna natives, except Inspector Negro specially assigned from her forensics post in Rome. *Nairobi Heat* begins in Madison, Wisconsin, where a white young girl's dead body is found sprawled outside the house of a Rwandan immigrant, Joshua Hakizimana, a famous savior of Rwandan genocide victims. The chief detective—intriguingly named Ishmael—is African American, and makes his first trip to Africa, to Kenya, to discover the identity of the victim and the reasons for her death. In Nairobi, American detective thriller format contends with local police methods and local histories and politics—of white settler colonialism, refugees from the Rwandan tragedy, and corruption in international aid agencies—which acquire global ramifications. New worlds and codes are accessed and delivered in a genre that relies on American cop culture while accommodating the turbulent energies of Nairobi streets and bars and economic plight.

Nairobi Heat would appear to exemplify transnational, multicultural tensions and urgencies, while *Almost Blue* captures local particulars in the Bologna student milieu and police practices, except that the title *Almost Blue* is a direct reference to Chet Baker's famous jazz piece, the composition that Simone listens to before switching on his scanners. *Almost Blue* conjures both the American jazz that is Simone's favorite, and structures of American crime fiction playing over the Bologna scene. Both books qualify for the field of world literature, as permitting "windows into worlds" in diverse ways—mixtures of local and global form and content—though neither has achieved the status of classic nor has acquired the kind of global circulation and prestige associated with much of world literature's canon. Rather they comprise what Ronald Walker and June Frazer observe in their introduction to *The Cunning Craft*: "the increasing output of Crime Fiction around the world ... which significantly broaden the possibilities of the form as a mirror of cultural dynamics" (Walker and Frazer 1990: i).

The allusion to the broadening of "the possibilities of the form" is a reminder that early theorists had circumscribed crime fiction in a distinctive, often constricted, formal structure, which, at its most basic level of plot, involves a commission of a crime that intrigues, baffles, potentially endangers, engenders other crimes, and is eventually solved. Formalist theorists, such as Tzvetan Todorov in "The Typology of Detective Fiction" and Franco Moretti in "Clues" from *Signs Taken for Wonders*, have famously reified the form by eliciting and prescribing narrow preordained norms of narrative austerity that, they claimed, determine the satisfaction provided by crime fiction. Peter Brooks's insistence that "to a greater degree than other popular fiction, the detective story is governed by rigid canons and must comply with certain formulas" (Brooks 1984: 25) further conferred a conservative intransigence on the form.

Such conservatism regarding form is also perceived to apply to ideological intent when Franco Moretti asserts crime fiction's role in inscribing and legitimizing the operations of formidable state power. In "Controlling Discourse in Detective Fiction," Carl Lovitt similarly claims that crime fiction delivers a strict and simple lesson: the criminal is caught and justice is always done. "Bourgeois legality, bourgeois values, bourgeois society always triumph in the end." It is thus "soothing, socially integrating literature, despite its concerns with crime, violence and murder" (Walker and Frazer 1990: 63). Dennis Porter too alludes to it as "the literature of reassurance and conformism, principally intended for the enjoyment of a privileged class and describes detective fiction as "a hymn to culture's coercive abilities" (Walker and Frazer 1990: 143).

However, later critics have challenged this unequivocal compliancy of crime fiction with rigid narrative rules or conservative social purposes. It is widely acknowledged that the best of crime fiction does not simply fulfill formulaic criteria without disruption or departure. The innovations in Borges's "Death and the Compass" and Orhan Pamuk's *My Name is Red* coexist with, and indeed deploy, the techniques, format, and "norms" of a crime plot while expanding and transforming their literary genres. *Almost Blue* and *Nairobi Heat*, I plan to demonstrate, amplify the possibilities of crime fiction, disturb cultural pieties, as they participate in world literary modalities and concerns.

World literature also engages a tension between conformity and dispersal: it encompasses works of sumptuous diversity, even dazzling invention, yet they negotiate and also manifest, a self-explanatory correspondence with rules. World literature texts are often expected to contain and transmit their own rules for reading, and to provide clarity of their codes in order to be accommodated within preassigned categories in world literature anthologies. In *How to Read World Literature*, David Damrosch avers, "usually ... a work fits well enough within a form whose rules we know" (Damrosch 2009: 8)—though he earlier suggests that "writers sometimes push the envelope with genre-bending experiments" (8).

Postcolonial critics detect a conservative, controlling propensity in world literature. The postcolonialists' complaint about world literature is that it renders literary production, circulation and its study too benign and reductive, suffused in a false consciousness of equivalence and universality, impervious to the inequities and iniquities of power structures, and indifferent to postcoloniality, its struggles, valuable interventions, and theoretical contributions.

However, the incipient conservatism of both world literature and crime fiction is not absolute, and is available (indeed hospitable) to challenges and alterities. It can be argued that world literature has displaced a hegemonic Western canon, engaged alternative literary histories, even privileged non-Western cultural connections and exchanges. Often choices are not determined exclusively in Paris or New York: erstwhile margins can exert cultural pressures from recovered pasts or substantial presents. They can expose injustices in literary selections, negotiate and redress cultural asymmetries, and deploy postcolonial methodologies.

Almost Blue and *Nairobi Heat* offer useful material to examine features of crime fiction and world literature, since they adhere to narrative norms of crime plot while extending their provenance. *Almost Blue* opens with Inspector Negro's realization of the existence and continuing menace of a serial killer through her forensic work of assembling and detecting a pattern in several scattered but similar deaths. The launching of the serial crime investigation coincides with Simone inadvertently overhearing the killer's assignation on a phone line, thus becoming the only person who knows the killer's voice. The story of the investigation is filled by discoveries of the unknown killer's identity and psychologically troubled history, and his capture is assured only after Simone becomes the object of his murderous desire.

On the surface, *Nairobi Heat* observes all crime fiction proprieties, especially of the action thriller and noire variety. The crime already committed—the dead white girl on the Madison doorstep—is such a total mystery that even the victim's identity is completely unknown. So not only is it a whodunit, but a who-got-done. The confounding murder contains all the prior histories, political intrigues, enmities, and venalities that are incrementally aligned and interpreted, accompanied with more violence and surprises for the truth to emerge. The detective Ishmael follows clues to Kenya, collaborates with a local police officer, Detective O, and the two conduct an investigation, replete with car chases, shootouts in bars, and attempts on their lives in the mean streets of Nairobi. The plot engages current politics—the treacheries that attended the Rwandan massacres, the miseries of a Nairobi slum, and the perfidy of aid agencies—that could both enrich the story line and provide a viable world literary context.

Both novels challenge Moretti's contention that "there is little interest in what may cause criminality," when crime fiction seeks mainly to protect and sustain the dominant social order. In their different ways, *Almost Blue* and *Nairobi Heat* evince a narratively invigorating interest in the causes of the respective crimes they uncover. Sections of *Almost Blue* are presented from the perspective of the killer, and his agonizings, obsessions, as well as police findings tracing the history of childhood neglect and grievances that precipitated his sociopathy and his need to ravage himself and his victims with mutilating frenzy. *Nairobi Heat* probes the betrayals and institutional chicanery attendant on and following the Rwanden atrocities, in order to establish the greed and venality that cause a young woman's murder. The cause conceals several secrets and their unfolding comprises the political and social abominations that exercise the novel—ethnic hatred that causes a revered school headmaster to secretly facilitate gruesome killings; the secret conversion of a refugee-assistance charity into a money-making enterprise for its founders.

The causes of criminality are intricately linked to the plot, but they are not simply subsumed to supplying plot; they are developed as relevant subjects for delineating and deepening the social worlds in which the fictions operate. In this respect, they correspond to Catherine Nickerson's assertion in "Murder as Social Criticism" that crime fiction often "releases explosive cultural material" that cannot be suppressed or erased even when the crime is punished and social order is validated.

The explosive cultural material, and the effectiveness with which it is combined with the narrative structures of crime and detection, are indicative of the texts' viability as world literature as well as their success in the crime fiction genre. *Almost Blue* and *Nairobi Heat* suggest the "radical possibilities" that Peter Messent claims are offered in the "social ruptures and tremors" that attend the criminality and its enactments (Messent 2013: 13). The investigation leads to the interception and indictment of the criminal/s, but in the process it also indicts elements of the social order it seeks to reinstate. And the reconstituted closure does not necessarily entail erasure of such disclosures: ideological tensions, social corruptions, and perfidies, or compromised systems of authority and values. Messent quotes David Stewart to suggest how the popularity of crime fiction may be connected to its examination of serious contemporary issues in urban life and a rapidly expanding capitalist economy. It confronts "an ambivalence about criminality and its relation to the dominant social order," and provides a "necessary and thrilling release from the disciplinary procedures of capitalism, the laws and behavioral practices" sustaining "an increasingly regimented social order" (Stewart 1997: 689).

Messent posits the "hard boiled crime novel" as progressive rather than conservative, as it "traces an ongoing chain of violent criminal action, the way it proliferates and its relationship to a contaminated larger social body rather than foregrounding the exceptional and relatively discrete nature of the single criminal act as in the classic case." Messent follows Stewart's conclusion that this genre represents "in a generally realistic style the most anxiety-producing issues and narratives of a culture" (Messent, 744–5).

Furthermore, Messent's contention about the modern police novel that "at its best has mutated into an ongoing enquiry into the state of the nation, its power structures, and social concerns" (2013: 44), connect with the most compelling aspects of *Almost Blue* and *Nairobi Heat*, signaling their plenitude and their intervention in social criticism. These novels contain the "three-way focus" that Messent writes about: "on individual law enforcers and the policing communities to which they belong; the exercise of state power and bureaucracy; on general health (or lack) of social system they represent" (44). As *Almost Blue* and

Nairobi Heat portray, these factors are characteristically embodied in the figure of the detective who is "often non-conformist, resistant to official procedures or interests" (45).

In *Almost Blue*, Grazia Negro, as lead detective, possesses institutional authority but is constrained both by gender and city politics. As a senior official in the Forensic Department of the Unit for Analysis of Serial Crimes at Rome headquarters (which "investigates homicides with no apparent motive and serial carnal violence"), she has meticulously assembled and analyzed records of "cold cases"—unsolved and seemingly unrelated violent deaths in Bologna—and has come to the conclusion that Bologna has a vicious, elusive serial killer targeting vulnerable students. But her findings are received by the Bologna police chief, the Questore, with fury and dismay at the adverse impact on Bologna's reputation. While she worries about the safety of Bologna's population of 200,000 students, the Questore prioritizes the assuaging of urban fears. He is consistently more concerned about containing publicity than in supporting Grazia's hunt for the killer (Lucarelli 1997: 23–8). Following a bungled mistaken identification of the killer, the news does erupt in sensationalized headlines, and incurs further fury from officialdom. Grazia Negro reacts with contrition and declares her willingness to resign, suggesting her imbrication in a system that values its own preservation and prestige above the ingenuity and dedication of an officer like her. The system presents limitations and obstructions; she is familiar with both the submission and the struggle within it.

Grazia's unrelenting struggle is most strikingly rendered in gendered terms that expand the novel's codes from a local crime plot to more generalized constructions of female authority struggling in a male-dominated social order. At times, her female subjectivity is glaringly overdetermined: even as she marshals her considerable forensic and technological expertise to present a convincing case about the existence of the serial killer (*assassini seriali*), she is convulsed by menstrual cramps. Her professional composure and proficiency are juxtaposed with the information that "her stomach ached ... pressure in her kidneys along her back," and "under her padded jacket and sweatshirt, under her thin cotton camisole, her breasts felt heavy and sore" (22). This conflating of her femininity and police role is consummately encapsulated by the image of "tampons in her jacket pocket next to the spare Beretta cartridge clip" (23).

The composite subjectivity is often tenuous and fractured; "in wool dress and black stockings ... she looked more like a woman than usual," and "despite the bomber jacket and Police ID," other policemen assume she's a student or a journalist. The local sergeant repeatedly addresses her as "signorina" till she reminds him with asperity that she is Ispettore (41, 42). The assisting officers, Sarrina and Matera, blatantly direct "brazen and ironic" gazes at her, and smile "lewdly" (56, 57). Her brusque, peremptory rejoinders have no shaming effect, and she endures a torrent of insolent remarks—that she tries "to show you're better than a man," that she doesn't have a boyfriend, and won't "spread your legs" till her elevation to *"commissario capo"* (57). The egregious comments uttered without fear of retribution shockingly demonstrate the prevalence of an unreconstructed, unabashed sexism in the police force and perhaps the larger society, and define the debilitating environment in which Grazia is obliged to function. The casual normativeness of this sexist discrimination and abuse is emphasized by Grazia's seeming submission to it—she fumes inwardly, she refutes and reasons, but does not express outrage nor seek redress. There is a further essentializing of her femininity by the frequent reference to her desire to cry when frustrated or agitated. However, she is also fierce and fearless in action, plunging at the end into physical combat with the killer to save the blind Simone.

The novel thus affords complex and troubling insights into gender politics. Grazia is endowed with professional agency and prowess; yet her femininity is figured as disabling rather than empowered. The evocation of a conventional femininity can be attributed to the narrative's need to make her a suitable love interest for Simone, as *Almost Blue* also incorporates their growing closeness and eventual union. Here, the conventions of the crime plot are further distended to accommodate the requirements of an unusual romantic attraction—between an authoritative police detective and an isolated, sightless man who alone has the sensory power to apprehend the killer. Grazia acknowledges his power, but more significantly, finds comfort in his inability to see her, since "Simone can't ogle" or inspect the physicality that is often enfeebling (126).

Nairobi Heat also presents the predicaments of policing in a politically contested, socially inequitable environment. The complications are intriguingly signaled by the opening sentence, articulated by Ishmael, the African American detective: "A beautiful young blonde was dead, and the suspect, my suspect, was an African male. I was travelling to Africa in search of his past. What I found there would either condemn or save him. As you can imagine, my business was urgent" (Ngũgĩ 2010: 1). The "business" of solving the crime is enmeshed in the circumstances, especially the potent racial politics, suggested by this sentence. Ishmael is particularly aware of the inflamed public interest in the crime. The dead body's femaleness and whiteness, and the Africanness of the chief suspect who lives in an upscale, mainly white, neighborhood, ignite Madison's codes of race and class. Additionally, the chief of the city's predominantly white police force is black, which compounds the pressure he exerts on Ishmael to find a swift solution. Not only would Ishmael's success "be advantageous for black people in the force" (15), but it would also diffuse simmering racial disquietude. This prompts Ishmael's wry "advice to black criminals—do not commit crimes against white people because the state will not rest till you are caught. Black-on-white crime does not grow cold" (6), reflecting his sardonic acknowledgment of an asymmetrical justice system.

Especially at the opening, the novel addresses several issues arising from Ishmael's blackness in America. Ishmael avers that his marriage collapsed because his wife's resented his role as a black cop serving a system of white privilege. He also observes that journalists crowding the police precinct don't recognize him as an officer since they're accustomed to "two kinds of blacks in the police station—those in handcuffs and the Chief" (19). Later he hears in the speech patterns of his Kenyan counterpart, Detective O, that "Americanisms had filtered into Kenyan culture through movies and music video," but as an ambitious African American in white America "I was trained to disdain colloquialisms by middle-class parents" (47). He confesses to Detective O that contesting claims of race and class have shaped his identity and life choices, making him a "rebel." After college he abandoned further academic advancement because it represented "aspirations to whiteness" and concomitant race betrayal. Joining the police force seemed a form of service to the black community. Yet ironically his blackness blurs in Kenya and his Americanness superimposes its privilege; to his chagrin, Ishmael is frequently addressed in Nairobi as "Mzungu," a white man.

The issues of class and race are thus located and problematized in *Nairobi Heat*'s dual worlds of America and Kenya, allowing local experiences and identities to be experienced and examined in a global frame. In contrast to Ishmael, Detective O had aspired to higher status, but he was denied access to the only university, and had chosen police work since "it was either this, join the army or become a criminal" (51). When Ishmael confides about his wife's contempt for his policing, Detective O indignantly remonstrates that she works for Shell Oil, which plunders Africa, "and she thinks you are a bad guy 'cos you're a black cop" (50).

The attitudes and actions of the American and Kenyan policemen correspond with what Messant calls "Transgressor Fiction, a minority strand of crime fiction which asks questions more openly about the nature and justice of the dominant social order" (Messant 2011: 59). For Ishmael, this questioning translates into an insistent sympathy for the unnamed, unclaimed, brutalized white girl and a commitment to secure justice for her. Her abject victimhood obscures the white privilege earlier accorded her; privilege becomes attached to her killers, important individuals (mainly Africans) who earned social glory and absolution through (and despite) cynical exploitation of the Rwandan tragedy. To expose the crime and pursue the desired justice, Ishmael enacts the role of "transgressor" cop on multiple occasions. He obtains copies of documents about the corrupt practices of refugee aid agencies that implicate socially prominent individuals—venerated humanitarians and heads of governments and international organizations—who facilitated and profited from the fabrications and embezzlements. Toward the end, the mystery of the girl's identity is solved, but the initial suspect, Joshua, a confessed perpetrator of atrocities, is exonerated of her killing. Ishmael is dissatisfied with the official legal outcome as a travesty of justice. Acting outside approved legal processes, he turns lone avenger, and his scheme seeks to avenge multiple social injustices—he manipulates the racial prejudices of a local KKK leader to eliminate the white girl's killer and also terminate the KKK bigot himself. Justice is convoluted, it is extrajudicial, but it triumphs against many social obstacles and iniquities.

The sequences in Kenya often show Detective O circumventing the finer processes of law as he punishes wrongdoers. Armed and even unarmed men are ruthlessly shot when legal scruples might dictate their arrest. Detective O explains the "fury and logic of his actions" by claiming that in Kenya "we live in anarchy: life is cheap and the rich and criminal can buy a whole lot of it" (Ngũgĩ, 67). Ishmael, initially discomfited by Detective O's recourse to arbitrary violence, eventually accepts it, especially when repeated encounters confirm the immunity and impunity with which the "rich and criminal" suborn and command the system, not just in Kenya but globally.

Such narrative complexities, elaborations of issues of race, gender, causes of criminality and social discontents in diverse geographical contexts, enrich the format of crime fiction and provide avenues for world literature. The stringency of form, privileged by critics such as Todorov and Moretti, would deny their relevance, even demand their suppression. The imperative of simplicity—in form, narration, and language—makes crime fiction for Morretti (as for Todorov) "an anti-literary form because its object is to obliterate an excess of clues and signifiers" (Moretti 1997: 137). While Moretti acknowledges the sociocultural dimensions of crime fiction, he focuses on a univocality that dissipates the genre's insurgent energies.

From this perspective it might seem that crime fiction—in its composition and reading—is congenial to the procedures of a depoliticized understanding of world literature. For works to circulate beyond their time and place and transcend national cultural affiliations, world literature might discipline excess, might chastise the estrangement of irreducible untranslatabilities into approximations, and wither an abundance of signifiers into malleable motifs. But it is apparent that world literature has need of the excess. The poetics in any language cannot be shrunk into silence: it is the tumult of tropes, the abundance of signifiers that construct the world to which the literature "provides a window." If these are red herrings, they still demand a reading. When our scanners tune in and encounter the "excess," we are compelled to listen.

I would argue that excess gives *Almost Blue* a literary presence and success as crime fiction, even though it functions within an intensely localized context; while, in spite of its impressive attempts at "global" worldly bustle, *Nairobi Heat* occasionally falters when important subjects are treated more perfunctorily than they deserve.

Almost Blue envelops and expands its crime plot with the explorations of Grazia's gendered role and the killer's tormented, disfigured history. But most of all, the blind scanner, Simone—whose technology and tactile perceptions command luxuriant, copious detail—captures our interest, and the solving of the crime never either seeks or achieves the diminution of this excess. The novel also slips away from a clear formula in pursuit of the crime to revel in vivid descriptions of Bologna, rendered quite poetically in several paragraphs that start with the refrain, "This city isn't like any other" (Lucarelli, 108)—particularly noticed by Inspector Negro who is from Rome, lingering in its shadowed arcades and student hangouts. Music pulsates through the novel, sometimes strategic, sometimes character-defining (Grazia Negro is evocatively identified with the mood and lyrics of "In the Summertime"), sometimes ambiently amplifying, and often utterly incidental to the crime and detection imperatives.

Signifiers float and forage, aesthetics are languorously, at times luridly, assembled and nurtured. Even the love story—which many theorists deplore as extraneous or injurious to detective fiction—charmingly develops. Yet, despite all the excess, the novel remains a taut, compelling, meticulously planned, astutely directed work of crime fiction. The rules of sequence, suspense, and closure, expected by the reader, are fulfilled. In a climactic meeting between Simone and the killer, Simone's sensory recognition of him is intensified by the killer seeing that Simone "is not staring at me, but towards me. Through me. Inside me ... he knows who I am ... he can even see the bells ... ringing in my head" (140). Predictably, suiting the best norms of detective fiction, the killer is caught in his own trap.

Nairobi Heat gains literary power when the tropes and themes that hover around the plot are probed and developed: for instance, the sections that explore Ishmael's African American identity in Madison and Nairobi, or that evoke the horrors of the Rwandan past through several harrowing narrations. But elsewhere, the story lurches through rushed encounters, gunfights, dropping bodies, and attempted rape, and the surrounding context becomes attenuated. This leanness means that detective leads are few: in fact the identity of the victim is discovered not by any diligent or brilliant deduction, but by stumbling on a fading newspaper clipping in a chanced-upon country church. Literary leads are introduced in the form of quotes from Derek Walcott and Langston Hughes, but are not sufficiently attached to the story. A postcolonial literary expansion into a "Heart of Darkness" is attempted through a Kurtz-like figure, an English Lord Thompson gone flamboyantly native, who inhabits a palace with South African mercenary guards, and is "a sickly balding Gandhi-like figure wrapped in a sheet" (Ngũgĩ, 56), in a room which "reeked of decay: unwashed feet, rotting teeth and death" (55). Rumors of "rapes and disappearances" whisper around him, but he is betrayed by servants and killed by Detective O. Lord Thompson symbolizes fading, discredited colonialism, performing a perverse postcolonial parody. But his representation is a flutter of "excess" that dissolves. So too, the African American detective's decision to leave America at the end and move to Kenya is intriguing, but deeper literary subtexts of trans-Atlantic migrations and returns are unexplored, even unintimated.

Perhaps excess is often at the mercy of the disciplinary protocols of crime fiction and world literature. But the literary is vivified by excess; the literary can resist the policing. Indeed, Moretti too appears to recommend the role of excess in world literature: "because it showed that world literature was indeed a system—but a system *of variations*. The system was one, not uniform. The pressure from the Anglo-French core *tried* to make it uniform, but it could never fully erase the reality of difference" (Moretti 2000: 64). As *Almost Blue* and *Nairobi Heat* illustrate, crime fiction relies on particularities of location and avocation, on variations to shape its plots of harm and healing, of the violent ruptures in societies and the yearning for justice.

Works Cited

Brooks, Peter (1984). *Reading for the Plot: Design and Intention in Narrative*. Cambridge, MA: Harvard University Press.
Damrosch, David (2009). *How to Read World Literature*. Oxford: Wiley-Blackwell.
Lucarelli, Carlo (1997). *Almost Blue*, trans. Oonagh Stransky. San Francisco: City Lights Books.
Messent, Peter (2013). *The Crime Fiction Handbook*. Oxford: Wiley-Blackwell.
Moretti, Franco (1997). *Signs Taken for Wonders*. London: Verso.
Moretti, Franco (2000). "Conjectures on World Literature." *New Left Review* (January–February), 54–68.
Mŭkoma wa Ngũgĩ (2010). *Nairobi Heat*. New York: Melville House Publishing.
Nickerson, Catherine (1997). "Murder as Social Criticism." *American Literary History* 9:4, 744–57.
Stewart, David M. (1997). "Cultural Work, City Crime, Reading Pleasure." *American Literary History* 9:4, 676–701.
Todorov, Tzetvan (1977). *The Poetics of Prose*, trans. Richard Howard. Ithaca: Cornell University Press.
Walker, Ronald G., and June M. Frazer, eds. (1990). *The Cunning Craft: Original Essays on Detective Fiction and Contemporary Literary Theory*. Macomb: Yeast Printing.

4

The Detective is Suspended: Nordic Noir and the Welfare State

Bruce Robbins

There is a moment in the TV serial *The Killing* (the original Danish version, henceforth *Forbrydelsen*) when it looks like Detective Sarah Lund is going to lose her job on the police force for ignoring orders or in some other way overstepping her authority. It makes sense that she should be at risk of losing her job. Conflict between her and the state authority she works for has been simmering for some time. The police bureaucracy has resisted her efforts to do that job, efforts we know to be well-meaning and well-directed, even inspired, and that come at great sacrifice to her personal life. There are hints that some corrupt figure in city government may be covering up for the killer, or maybe even *is* the killer. The parallel plot dealing with the campaign of a reform candidate to be elected mayor of Copenhagen and the suspicion hovering over various political operatives and opponents makes the same point. Her superiors in the bureaucracy are suspects. Government is part of the problem to which it is supposed to be the solution.

In offering us a detective who is under threat of suspension by state authorities who are themselves under suspicion, *Forbrydelsen* is consistent with the astonishingly engaging and influential tradition of Nordic noir that readers around the world began discovering in police detectives Martin Beck (Maj Sjöwall and Per Wahlöö) and Kurt Wallander (Henning Mankell). "Martin Beck shrugged his shoulders. He was very tired, but the conversation interested him. 'I might possibly have been suspended'" (Sjöwall and Wahlöö 2010: 9). "They can suspend me,' said Wallander. 'They can fire me. But they can't ever make me apologize" (Mankell 2010: 103–4). The title of this chapter is meant to refer, then, to what seems like the inevitable first hypothesis about the relationship between Nordic noir and the welfare state: namely, that Nordic noir is centrally and enthusiastically engaged in a critique of the state, specifically the welfare state.

This proposition seems uncontroversial. One early discussion of the Stieg Larsson trilogy in *n+1* is called "The Man Who Blew Up the Welfare State." "To read the 1,082 pages" of Stieg Larsson's trilogy, it begins, "is to be told that, for all their perceived virtue, the institutions of social democracy are a farce." "Larsson brings the ostensibly protective welfare state to the fore," the article goes on, "making it not just a backdrop but a central force and, in a way, a villain" (MacDougall). Slavoj Žižek says similar things about Henning Mankell, in whose novels he sees "the long and painful decay of the Swedish welfare state." This is also the thesis of Andrew Nestingen and Paula Arvas' highly respected *Scandinavian Crime Fiction* (2011).[1] No doubt there is considerable truth in this account, especially as seen from within Scandinavia. And no country can be denied the right to the self-critique of its own choosing. But the idea of Nordic noir as national or regional self-critique does not seem to me the whole truth, and the part of the truth it leaves out seems considerably more interesting, especially as seen from the other side of the Atlantic.

In the United States, critique of the welfare state is largely a right-wing or, to be more precise, a pro-capitalist phenomenon. The ideological energy behind it comes in the main from what we have come to call neoliberalism: the belief that the state must be reduced in size as far as possible in favor of the so-called free market. The state is fine, the neoliberals say, as long as it serves the market, but it should be deprived of all power to regulate or otherwise interfere with the market. The state is the last remaining antagonist the market faces, and it must be brought down or, even better, made to serve the market. That's the neoliberal line. Nordic noir replies that the state is serving the market all too well; look at its collusion with rich industrialists, real estate developers, rapists, neo-Nazis. This sounds like critique of neoliberalism from the left. But a very similar sounding case can be made from the right, especially when it is an individual who is confronted with or even victimized by the state bureaucracy. Some of the genre's success outside Scandinavia, in countries like the UK, the United States, and Germany (and perhaps some of its success inside the Scandinavian countries as well) clearly comes from the audience's broader and deeper anti-statism, which is to say its susceptibility to neoliberal ideology.

In America, critique of the state is a cliché of the noir genre, as of other popular genres (e.g., the Western). It begins long before the ascendancy of neoliberalism. And it too is politically ambiguous. There is almost always a moment when the detective is suspended from his duties (once upon a time, it would have necessarily been a he) because he has been doing those duties too well. There are close parallels in *The Wire*, *True Detective*, and *Justified*, as well as the American remake of *Forbrydelsen*, *The Killing*. In *True Detective*, not only is the detective suspended and his badge and gun taken away, but the premise throughout Season 1 is that the detective is himself being investigated by his fellow police officers. The same is true of the more conventional series *Justified*. The threat of suspension that hangs over the detective is in fact entirely conventional, and this makes perfect sense in the United States because America's cultural traditions are so deeply anti-statist. American audiences are always already prepared to suspect the public authorities of being corrupt or merely fronting for private interests. And most often, this is in direct alignment with the refusal of the Americans to be suspicious of capitalism as such, a system seen as essential to the nurturing of individual freedom. In the period of the old liberalism, most of the critique of the state that has been hardwired into the mystery genre since Sherlock Holmes (think what stupid bunglers Holmes is always revealing the police to be) and in the United States since the classic Western (think of Gary Cooper throwing away his badge in disgust at the end of *High Noon*)—most of this is not inconsistent with right-wing or at least pro-capitalist politics.

If it were true, then, that Nordic noir is constitutively critical of the welfare state, at this point in history that would not be self-evidently a desirable thing. But again, this seems to me at best a very partial truth. My argument here will be that the success of Nordic noir both domestically and for export contains some affirmation of the welfare state. The genre's characteristic Nordic progressivism is not uncritical of the welfare state, certainly, but neither is it unwilling to abandon all the commitments and institutions that global capitalism has taken such pains to dismantle and dissolve. In order to see that productive ambivalence, however, you have to look at the texts themselves, not as bodies of sociological evidence or symptoms of the Zeitgeist but (if you will forgive the expression) as works of art—that is, artifacts that function to expose social contradictions and are organized so as to stimulate serious reflection rather than a simple yea or nay.

I will have more to say about how such reflection structures the characterization of the detective and the plot, but it can be observed at the micro level as well as the macro. Consider one brief instance (not one in which he is threatened with suspension) in which Wallander expresses the shakiness of his faith in the system he serves, a system in which the state collaborates with and trusts private capital. "He had spent his life," Wallander tells us, "in the loyal and unhesitating belief that Swedish business practices were as above reproach as the emperor's wife. The Swedish export industry was at the heart of the country's prosperity, and as such was simply above suspicion. Especially now, now that the whole edifice of the welfare state was showing signs of crumbling, its floorboards teeming with termites" (Mankell 2010: 169). The first thing to notice about this passage is how it hesitates. It neither asserts nor denies that the termites eating away at the welfare state are a figure for Swedish industry. It does not say whether the welfare state has only itself to blame for its dilapidated condition or whether the fault lies elsewhere. The implication is no doubt that Swedish business is corrupt—perhaps more so than the state. But Wallander also implies that once upon a time, before the "especially now," before it became infested with termites, the welfare state was perhaps sound enough in its construction and foundations. If this is disillusionment, as so many have suggested, it's not clear that it's disillusionment with the *principle* of the welfare state. The passage does not tell the reader what to think; it puts a question mark in our minds and demands that we reflect. It certainly leaves open the possibility that a residual commitment to the welfare state's progressive principles is as close to the moral and political core of these narratives as their slow pace, melancholy landscapes, and morose and maladjusted characters.

At least in *Forbrydelsen* and *Bron/Broen* (in English, *The Bridge*), the key evidence of ambivalence about the welfare state is the female protagonist: a distinctively "difficult" or unsocialized or even autistic woman, lacking the social skills usually demanded of and thus associated with women. Lisbeth Salander, the best known of the Nordic noir heroines, is very literally a victim of the state, raped and abused by those delegated by officialdom to deal with her case. But the most obvious thing to say about detectives Sarah Lund and Saga Norén is very nearly the opposite: they are the face of the state. Why did these shows elect to give the state a new and female face? Perhaps, women being expected to be *more* socialized than men, choosing an un- or undersocialized woman to embody law enforcement, the state's most basic and uncontroversial function, has the effect of making the state itself seem unsocialized, awkward, and unnatural. In other words, here too the intention could well be antistatist critique. But this interpretation seems unpersuasive. In spite of all the awkwardness, or perhaps because of it, audiences both male and female clearly identify with the unsocialized woman. Indeed, they identify quite strongly and surprisingly, for example, by buying Sarah Lund's unsexy Faroe Island sweaters in enormous quantities. What is it they are identifying with *if not* the state in this new guise?

Identification is probably not the most accurate term for the typical viewer relation to Saga Norén, who is a more extreme and challenging example. Ostentatiously lacking in empathy, she forces her questions on potential witnesses who are lying in their hospital beds, severely damaged, after having been poisoned or shot. Her strict obedience to official protocols is inscribed in the opening credits, where we see her signature Porsche in the right lane, being passed by other cars. Yet to see this powerful sports car that is holding itself back, choosing not to exceed the speed limit, is to see more than an individual's eccentricity; it's a mini-drama in motion. Like Norén's failures of empathy, it suggests that the value of the state and its rules is not to be taken for granted, but is in play—indeed, that it needs to be put under surveillance.

What does it say about the state that these wildly successful examples of Nordic noir choose to represent it by means of women who manifest some failure of socialization?[2] This failure can be read as a mark of a loss or lack. But it makes more sense if seen as a voluntary sacrifice—a sacrifice of personal life, even of personality or personhood. But also (there is no way to avoid the somewhat insipid vocabulary) a sacrifice in the interest of the public welfare. Here the distinctiveness of Scandinavia shows clearly in contrast to the United States, which has its share of undersocialized heroines who are similarly made to pay a price for their competence and efficiency. In the United States, the god on whose altar the woman's sacrifice is made is more often presented as *work*, which is to say the world of money and career. In America, in other words, the dimension of publicness is missing or muted. Thus the woman's choice can look like the very reverse of sacrifice: that is, like empty careerism, self-interest, greed. In Scandinavia, on the other hand, it seems important that whatever doubts may be suggested about the high cost of this sacrifice—and they are many—the higher good itself is never thrown into question. In that sense what audiences are identifying with is in fact the legitimacy of the state as the guardian of the general wellbeing and thus also as the proper recipient of personal sacrifice, the site of a dramatic and perhaps even tragic trade-off between private good and public good.

The insistence on the higher good manifests itself in another innovation that *Forbrydelsen* brings to the police procedural: the extended screen time that the narrative chooses to devote to the Larsens, the family whose daughter has been murdered. At one end of the murder mystery's emotional spectrum, the victim can serve as merely a puzzle to be solved, a stick figure or functional necessity with no personal presence or emotional hold over the reader. In such cases, knowledge of the victim is nothing more than evidence relevant to exposing the murderer. Season 1 of *Forbrydelsen* occupies the other end of this spectrum. There the grieving family is treated with the close attention usually reserved for suspects. The more time we spend with them, the more their loss becomes our loss. This adds the audience's emotional pressure to the pressure Sarah Lund already feels to keep working on the case, even if working on the case means the sacrifice of her relations with her fiancé and her son. We forfeit the privilege of taking the detective's motivation for granted. (This is also true, if to a lesser degree, of the first novel in Mankell's Martin Beck series, *Roseanna*.) The narrative urges the audience to embrace the protagonist's sacrifice, and thus puts us on the side of the state.

This is not a comfortable place to be in. After all, as spectators in front of our televisions we are enjoying our leisure. We are enjoying our leisure, that is, as we watch the heroine work. And yet we are obliged to root for her to work harder, to surrender more and more of her own leisure. This structural contradiction does not kill the viewer's enjoyment—on the contrary, one might say—but it suggests what such narratives in the deepest sense are *about*.

Intensifying the pressure on the female protagonist to sacrifice her life to her mission is one thing that's accomplished by keeping the focus on the family and its loss. But there is another. We scrutinize Nanna Birk Larsen's family as much as if they were suspects, and the reason is that in a sense they *are* suspects. Not suspects in their daughter's murder (though her mother's sister almost makes it into that category). They are suspects in a crime that has not yet happened, but toward which much of the series points: the crime of revenge for their daughter's murder. The mother and father blame the government. And because they blame the government, they are tempted to take matters into their own hands. This temptation to express their grief and anger against their daughter's assumed killer by acting on their own, thus preempting due processes of law and rescinding the state's monopoly of the legitimate use of violence, is one of the series's explicit motifs. The grieving family is the main onscreen bearer of lack of trust in the state, which they accuse of failing them in their hour of need. The family is antistatist. This antistatism turns out to be a terrible mistake, almost a fatal mistake. The killer is not, as they suspect, the foreigner, wrongly protected by the state (and himself a teacher, a state employee). The actual killer (Vagn—note how different a choice the American remake made: in America, the killer is a representative of politics!) comes from their own household: he is as close to being a member of the family as anyone can be without benefit of blood or marriage. This is an allegory. The family blames the state, as it blames foreigners. It turns out that the daughter's embrace of a foreigner was unacceptable to Vagn, the almost-family member. After directing suspicion both to a foreigner and to the state, the story places final responsibility at the family's outside edge, if not quite within it.[3] Left to itself, the family would strike out viciously and blindly. The murder can only be properly dealt with, the moral goes, from *outside* the family: by the cold, unexpressive, unlikely representative of the state.

And that is why this representative of the state must be cold, unexpressive, unlikely. Consider the following coincidence: ideologically speaking, the final scene of Season 1 of *Forbrydelsen* is echoed with uncanny precision in the final scene of Season 1 of *The Bridge*, where Saga comes between Martin and Jens on the bridge, wounding Martin in order to stop him from killing the man who has murdered his son. In both cases, an individual who has been grievously wronged seeks private revenge against a murderer, and the murderer *wants* the revenge to happen. If it does happen, in the eyes of the law (and, it appears, in the eyes of Scandinavian society) the vengeance-seeking individual will also be in the wrong, no matter how natural his act seems.[4] One might even say that the murderer will have managed to make the detective *as wrong as the murderer himself.* (In which case the murderer will have disabled moral judgment as such, at least in its habitual forms. The show's willingness to flirt with this position, even if they end up rejecting it, is another sign of the high philosophical ambitions animating this agreeable entertainment.) In order to prevent a moral leveling, the plot requires the intervention of someone lacking in "natural" or "normal" feelings. For the principle behind this intervention is the same on which the state is founded: the necessary transfer of the right of punishment away from the individual to an impartial, impersonal, rule-bound authority. In other words, if from one perspective the unsocialized women may represent a problem, from another perspective she represents the *solution* to a problem. Justice needs her.

In the case of *The Bridge*, Season 1, Saga's effort is explicitly an effort to stop her fellow detective from being suspended. If Martin had killed his son's murderer, she explains afterward, then whether or not he went to jail, he would certainly have lost his position in the police force forever—he would have been banished from the work that gives his life meaning. That goal is seen as important enough for it to have been Jens's own motive: he doesn't want to kill Martin, but to *get* him suspended. And Martin's psychological victory in Season 2 involves getting the imprisoned Jens to act and feel like a policeman again.

You can see how the unsocialized woman is also a response to critiques of the state in another sense. Her excessive concern for following the rules, which seems to come out of her absolute refusal of all merely personal feeling and motive, is also a refusal of that kind of "normal" social relationship that would ordinarily permit and even encourage state corruption: favoritism, cronyism, collusion with private economic interests, and so on. These are exactly the charges that Nordic noir is usually taken to be leveling at the welfare state. The protagonist's inability to function normally in her social interactions is a high price to pay for a state that would be above suspicion. But that seems to be the one clear logic behind it. In that sense too, she is both a problem and the solution to a problem.

On American television, as Merve Emre has pointed out, the figure of the "female sociopath" has become "central to workplace dramas like *Damages, Revenge, Bones, The Fall, Rizzoli and Isles, Person of Interest, Luther*, and *24*" (Emre, online). It is of course tempting to see women who hate empathy as a fitting response to men who hate women (the Swedish title of *The Girl with the Dragon Tattoo*). But nothing could be farther from *Forbrydelsen* or *Bron/Broen*. The fashion in the United States is to treat gender inequality as if it were an adequate excuse for women to embrace corporate ethics—that is, for you to climb the corporate ladder or otherwise pursue your advantage without any of the customary shame or inhibition while, if necessary, stomping on the fingers and other body parts of those below you. This is feminism-as-neoliberal-propaganda. Men can enjoy it too. The Scandinavian female protagonists are different. Yes, they work too hard and suffer for it in their private lives. But what they do is not just work. It's work for the common good.

Here it may help to consider, for purposes of contrast, the infamous section of Roberto Bolaño's novel *2666* that deals with a series of murders of women in a thinly disguised Ciudad Juarez on the US–Mexican border. A woman's body is discovered. The details of the crime scene are supplied, including the terrible things that have been done to that body. But the murder does not generate a mystery. The machinery of investigation does not rumble into action. Nothing happens. Then another body is discovered. Again, a list of grisly details is provided. Again, the details are unbearable. And they are more unbearable because there is again no investigation, no promise of knowledge, no move toward punishment, resolution, exorcism from society of the source of violence. Those who were most vulnerable remain just as vulnerable, and there is no help in sight. The pattern continues: more bodies, and still more bodies, one by one by one, but no mystery, no narrative. In context, the point seems clear: in this area of the world, there is no functioning state, and in the absence of a functioning state, there can be no murder mystery genre. In other words, the existence of the genre depends on the partial but real confidence that, despite some degree of corruption and much complicity with the interests of private money, the designated authorities are, more often than not, making a good faith effort to do their job. In northern Mexico, no such confidence exists. In Scandinavia, on the other hand, it does. Indeed, confidence is more justified than in most other countries. That is one reason for the exportability of Nordic noir.

Like the state, the noir genre has its rules. If one were to take these narratives as attempts to reflect Scandinavian society as it exists today, one would be struck not only by the statistically implausible accumulation of murders but also by the extraordinary degree of sexual perversity among the murderers—for example, the incestuous passion for a sister that "explains" the dénouement of Season 2 of *The Bridge*. But this would of course be a misunderstanding of how this or any artistic genre works. The murderer's motivation must be obscure; if it were a matter of transparent self-interest, it would be too easy to guess and the narrative machine would cease to function. Perversity is better seen, then, not as a psychosocial phenomenon that ought to elicit the concern of sociologists and therapists, but as a formal and structural requirement of the genre. These semi-autonomous artistic rules make one pause before putting too much weight on any item of "social content." Still, this does not make either the murderer's motive or the welfare state irrelevant.

Indeed, the linkage of the two is worth mentioning as a final piece of evidence. Both in Season 1 and Season 2 of *The Bridge*, the killers make themselves known to the public by means of an extraordinarily creative, symbol-laden PR campaign, which presents them as paying attention to the general good—more attention than the state that is trying to track them down. In Season 1, the killer highlights the plight of addicts, the homeless, and the elderly. In Season 2, the crimes are supposedly committed in the name of animals and the environment. In both cases, one might say the point is to insist on the state's unfulfilled responsibilities. It's as if the killers were goading the state to extend its reach by entering into a competition over who can best represent the most vulnerable elements of the human and nonhuman population, those who do not yet fully or adequately benefit from the state's protective care. In both cases, the killers are very brutal. In spite of their brutality, however, the measures they take subtly echo the unpalatable harshness of Saga Norén. She too acts as if she cannot protect society unless she can also bully and perhaps even change it.

In both cases, of course, the killers' politicking turns out to be a smokescreen meant only to conceal the true motives, which (as usual) are merely private. And as usual, the revelation of the truth as the private can be read as neoliberal in the Margaret Thatcher sense: there is no such thing as society, only individuals with individual interests. Here, however, as so often, the narrative is more seriously interested in the motive that turns out not to be true. And rightly so.

Notes

1 The strongest version of this case is attributed to Maj Sjöwall and Per Wahlöö: "Because social democracy concealed its reactionary subservience to capitalism in the notion of the solidary nation, Marxist-Leninist critique sought to expose the welfare state's fascist nature" (Nestingen and Arvas, 3).

2 As it happens, the lack of social skills is more salient in the woman detective's dealings with her coworkers than in her dealings with the public. But this aspect of the police procedural may be less of a problem for my interpretation than it seems. In a sense, the state is an exemplary workplace, a workplace on which the citizen audience eavesdrops. In other words, the competition of egos and the negotiation of personalities that the audience observes as coworkers try to get along with each other while getting the job done is a social and political microcosm. The same principle applies to the detective/buddy pairing, or for that matter the detective's relations with her lazy and troublesome secretary in Yrsa Sigurdarsdottir's Icelandic thriller *The Silence of the Sea*. Like *Bron/Broen*, the American version of *Forbrydelsen*, *The Killing*, acknowledges the woman detective's lack of social skills as a problem by giving her a male colleague or sidekick who, though her subordinate, possesses the skills she lacks and uses them very ostentatiously and successfully to push their investigation forward. The sidekick, however damaged in other ways, or perhaps because he is damaged enough to pick up on and address a diversely injured population, has some version of the common touch. The exploring of the relationship between the two is another way to do the noir genre as social microcosm.

3 One of the motives behind antistatism in the United States, though this is perhaps less true of Scandinavia, has been the perception that the state enforces a high standard of fairness in the hiring of women and (especially) minorities, a standard higher than what is currently acceptable to portions of the majority.

4   As Wallander says in *The Fifth Woman* (1996), "it never solves anything for people to take the law into their own hands" (160–1). Note the frequency with which the murderer who must be caught or killed is carrying out a revenge that the reader will be inclined to see as justified.

Works Cited

Emre, Merve (2014). "The Female Sociopath." *Digg*, May 14. http://digg.com/2014/the-female-sociopath.

Macdougall, Ian (2010). "The Man Who Blew Up the Welfare State." *N+1BR*, issue 6 February 27.

Mankell, Henning (2003). *Sidetracked*, trans. Steven T. Murray. New York: Vintage.

Mankell, Henning (2010). *An Event in Autumn*, trans. Laurie Thompson, New York: Vintage.

Nestingen, Andrew, and Paula Arvas, eds. (2011). *Scandinavian Crime Fiction*. Cardiff: University of Wales Press.

Sjöwall, Maj, and Per Wahlöö (2010). *The Terrorists*, trans. Joan Tate. New York: Vintage.

Žižek, Slavoj (2003). "Parallax," *London Review of Books* 25:22 (November 20), 24. http://www.lrb.co.uk/v25/n22/slavoj-zizek/parallax

5

Four Generations, One Crime

Michaela Bronstein

Here's an old story: a man who appears to be a hero turns out to be concealing a terrible moral failing. When the failing is discovered, the world turns against him; he is killed in vengeance or kills himself to escape.

Specifically, this is the plot of four novels, written in Russia, England, Kenya, and the United States across about a century and a half. Each novel directly inspired the next: Dostoevsky's *Demons* (1871–72) lurks behind Joseph Conrad's *Under Western Eyes* (1911); Conrad's novel is the conscious model for Ngũgĩ wa Thiong'o's *A Grain of Wheat* (1967/1986); Ngũgĩ's son Mũkoma wa Ngũgĩ has reworked his father's plot both in a series of hard-boiled detective novels and in a more literary work. Ranging across genres as well as across continents, each novelist aims at both a very immediate audience and a transhistorical one.

These novels are part of a tradition of what I'll call *utopian crime*—violence, particularly on the left, on behalf of a better future. These are not stories of civil disobedience: characters in these works commit assassinations and set explosions; occasionally, they commit suicide to make a philosophical point. They commit what are, in Camus's terms, "crimes de logique" (Camus, 15). Crime is always a political problem, but in these works, it is also a form of political action—a strategy and a philosophical commitment. All these writers examine the ways in which the idea of "crime fiction" opens up questions about the gaps between law and morality. Novels of unsettled or outrageous legal regimes, they focus on the rising anxiety that precedes revolution: the moment when crossing an ethical boundary—violently breaking the law—still seems fateful and potentially monstrous. Crime is the nexus where the utopian dreams of radical ideology meet brutal realist fact.

The most familiar story we have about the politics of crime fiction comes from the American hard-boiled tradition, which, like the novels of utopian crime, shifts uneasily back and forth between self-consciously literary writing and pulpy genre fiction. There, crime fiction's politics reflects the American naturalist emphasis on crime as a social problem—as the symptom of a diseased social order.[1] Exemplified by novels like Dreiser's *An American Tragedy* (1925) and Wright's *Native Son* (1941), naturalism shows crime as often unplanned and almost unintentional. The worlds of the novels put their protagonists into situations where their crimes are scarcely even conscious choices. This same social outlook, Garry Scharnhorst suggests, has a genre fiction incarnation: the "hard-boiled crime fiction of the 1920s and 1930s … was a spin-off of the naturalistic crime novel" (Scharnhorst, 350). Naturalism's inquiry into corrupt social systems, Scharnhorst argues, finds an expression in the hard-boiled detective's pessimism and moral ambiguity.[2] The pulp tradition, like its naturalist cousins, sees the border between a law-abiding member of society and a violent criminal as porous and haphazard, constituted only by luck and privilege.

By contrast, the authors of the novels of utopian crime instead foreground precisely the border naturalism found so permeable, and examine conscious choices to violate legal and moral codes. These authors treat a diseased social order as an occasion for concentrating the agency of individuals rather than diffusing it across social structures.[3] Under what conditions, they ask, is crime—especially violent crime—the right form of political activism? How can it be ethical to sacrifice a life today for the uncertainties of the future? Many of these authors are skeptical of revolutionary action. They focus on the violence of radicals in order to question the possibility of change. The radical novelist Chernyshevsky tells stories of revolutionary ideology leading to socialist cooperatives and equality of the sexes; the Slavophile Dostoevsky anatomizes the ways it can lead to violence.

Yet as the four generations of authors here transform the plot I sketched at the outset, they slowly turn away from seeing criminality—even utopian crime—as an ethical dilemma particular to the left. Despite Conrad's hostility to the idea of revolution, the changes he makes to Dostoevskyan plots mark a sudden ambiguity in what constitutes a crime. Counterrevolutionaries are as guilty as assassins; as in the hard-boiled tradition, the world is full of violence and brutality on every side. But this is not naturalism: the crimes remain calculated, philosophical. Ngũgĩ takes this transition even further in an anticolonial context where by its nature the "law" is criminal, a colonial imposition.[4] Mũkoma wa Ngũgĩ takes this to an extreme in *Black Star Nairobi*, where an act of utopian crime is plotted by American political powerbrokers. Revolutionary utopian crime has disappeared: it is now only the work of the global elite.

This specific line of connection—Dostoevsky to Conrad to Ngũgĩ to Mũkoma—also reflects two intersecting pressures for these authors and for literary scholarship more broadly: to conceive of writing on the one hand as embedded in and intervening in its own moment; and on the other, to see it as crossing historical boundaries and appealing to the future as well as the present. Utopian crime has a particular power over the literary imagination as a potential vision of the relation between the present and the future. Looking at these texts as part of a network of transhistorical, as well as transnational, affiliation suggests one way of thinking about the transhistorical dimensions of art without resorting to notions of timelessness and universality: these are all very *timely* texts, embedded in complex sets of discourses in their own times and places even as they appeal to others.[5]

In literary studies, the strongest theories of futurity come from the world of queer theory. Most famously, Lee Edelman analyzes what he calls "reproductive futurism," arguing that most conceptions of futurity are inherently heteronormative and conservative, sacrificing today's diverse individuals for a future that will only ever reflect the past: this accords well with literary studies' current suspicion of the idea of transhistorical artwork as a denial of the political claims of the present. By contrast, José Muñoz declares in *Cruising Utopia*, "The future is queerness's domain ... Queerness is essentially about the rejection of a here and now and an insistence on potentiality or concrete possibility for another world" (Muñoz, 1). In analyzing other forms of utopian thinking—literary and political—we might take our cues from Muñoz's queer futurities.[6] The future might be a way of disregarding the present. But it is also the specter—the hope—of radical, rather than incremental, otherness and change.

The futures in which these novels were rewritten and repurposed across time form a literary version of the problem of utopian crime: how can one act (or write) for a time beyond one's own? I'll suggest an unlikely kinship between the authors and the revolutionaries: unlike Muñoz's consciously radical artists, these novelists find themselves confronting a radical vision of futurity (sometimes against their own wishes) in the very act of trying to write for an unknowable audience beyond the present. Crime is the path their characters take to reach the future; writing is their own. And, as utopian crime gradually escapes the association with the left with which it began, it risks losing its status as a potential pathway to literary futurity.

The shifting political valences of the central crimes in the novels are registered in their plots. I've provided a chart setting out some of the plot parallels (Figure 5.1). This is a mixture of extremely well-known parallels and others

	Dostoevsky, *Demons*	Conrad, *Under Western Eyes*	Ngũgĩ wa Thiong'o, *A Grain of Wheat*	Mũkoma wa Ngũgĩ, *Nairobi Heat*
False Hero/ Tragic Traitor	Stavrogin	Razumov	Mugo	Joshua Hakizimana
False Hero/ Comic Traitor	Peter Stepanovich Verkhovensky	Peter Ivanovitch		Samuel Alexander
Betrayed by Hero	Shatov	Victor Victorovich Haldin	Kihika	Macy Jane Admanzah
Victim's Sister; Confidante of Tragic Traitor	Darya Shatov	Natalia Victorovna	Mumbi	
Narrator and Onlooker	Anton Lavrentievich G___v	English teacher	"We" (unnamed members of community)	Ishmael
Sinister Agents of Mob Will	Fomka and Fedka	Nikita Necator	General R; Lt. Koina	Jim (KKK member)
Holy Fool	Marya Timofeevna	Tekla		
Patroness of Liberalism	Varvara Stavrogina	Madame de S___		
Confessor/ Interrogator	Tikhon	Mikulin		
Assassination Victim		Mr. de P___	District Officer Robson	
Female Voice of Revolution	Unnamed student	Sophia Antonovna	Wambui	Muddy
Audience of Betrayal		General T___	John Thompson	
Love Triangle Members		English Teacher, Razumov, Natalia	Karanja, Gikonyo, Mumbi	

Figure 5.1 *"Four generations" comparison chart.*

that are less obvious. Particularly in the comparisons between Dostoevsky and Conrad and between Conrad and Ngũgĩ, the specificity with which the later authors reworked even minor roles is notable. All three of the rewritings I'm discussing here are historically founded: this is influence, not just comparison; these parallels arise from specific knowledge of one author's text by the next, and are not just more general workings of an archetypical plot or stock narrative.[7]

As each novelist reworked the plot of his predecessor, they slowly shifted the moral emphasis of the crime away from the ways the acts of left-wing revolutionaries violate the law. A full plot summary of the two central novels, which have the closest relation to each other, shows the transformation. The plot is this: a young man with no parents or family lives in a time of great political strife—Razumov, in late nineteenth-century Russia, or Mugo, during the State of Emergency surrounding the Mau Mau uprising. This young man is asked for aid by a revolutionary figure who has just committed an assassination: Haldin and Kihika. Razumov and Mugo both choose to turn in the revolutionaries to the authorities: General T__ and John Thompson. Afterward, no one is aware of the betrayal, and the protagonists are treated as heroes of the revolution. Yet guilt rises; and each confesses, first to the sister of the dead man—Natalia, Mumbi— and finally to the broader group of revolutionaries, after which Razumov is brutally beaten into premature frailty, while Mugo is executed in secret offstage.

Juxtaposing Conrad's or Ngũgĩ's iteration of the utopian crime problem with Dostoevsky's makes visible a reversal of the ethical problem of utopian crime in later writers. Narratively, Mugo and Razumov align with Stavrogin: guilt-ridden figures in novels that play out the consequences of their actions. But the political orientation is inverted for Ngũgĩ and Conrad. In *Demons*, Shatov, the betrayed victim of the protagonists, is a suspected informant against the revolutionaries; in Conrad and Ngũgĩ, the protagonists *are* the informants who betray revolutionaries to the police. The later novels are less concerned by the deaths of Mr. de P___ or D. O. Robson than by the ethical transgressions of Razumov and Mugo, who turned in their assassins.

In other words, when we view these novels in the larger context of the network of texts in which they reside, it becomes more significant that the central crime in the Conrad and Ngũgĩ novels lies not in violators of the law, but in those who violate moral obligations by upholding the law. Both novels are designed to bring their readers to a place where the word "crime" suggests anything but illegality. Crime, as an English word, has a legal dimension first but carries strong moral connotations. Most other English words with similar meanings tend to be primarily moral in our mind—sin, evil, wrong, iniquity. It is, however, not a neutral word like "transgression," which carries few if any implications about the nature of the rule being broken. This tendency of the English word to start in a legal register but shift quickly to a moral one is literally enacted in the plot of Mũkoma's *Nairobi Heat*: the protagonist starts out an American police officer, an agent of the law, but becomes a private detective working in the realm of individual morality in Nairobi by the end.

This shiftiness between legal and moral contexts is especially useful in the novels of utopian crime, where the ambiguity of the word *crime* often signifies the failure of existing legal standards. The novels exploit the uncertainties of replacing a legal violation with a moral one. Razumov and Mugo follow the "law," such as it is; and the point of both novels—even Conrad's, with all his hostility toward radical types—is that doing so is no guarantee of acting justly.

In *Under Western Eyes*, the word "crime" is applied again and again to the activities of the revolutionaries, but it also rings increasingly hollow. At the beginning it's forceful: Razumov hears of the assassination from Haldin and thinks himself confronted with "the appalling presence of a great crime and the stunning force of a great fanaticism" (Conrad, 26). The judgment is cloaked in all the authority of typical Conradian syntactical parallelisms. But only a few pages later, he resorts to tautology in trying to convince himself to turn Haldin in: "For it is a crime … A murder is a murder" (28). Even he can't quite see the assassination as ordinary crime. By the time he goes through with the betrayal, he shifts his ground entirely, deciding that murder is irrelevant to Haldin's real crime: "He was a wretch from my point of view, because to keep alive a false idea is a greater crime than to kill a man … I did not hate him because he had committed the crime of murder … I hated him simply because I am sane" (79). Legal crime is now irrelevant next to questions of psychology. Razumov has to define crime in precisely the most invidious possible way—as thoughtcrime—in order to explain his actions to himself.

At the same time, the word "crime" starts to show up in an oppositional sense: the two female revolutionaries we see, Sophia Antonovna and Tekla, ascribe their families' misfortunes to "the crime of a society" (202) and "the crime of the upper classes" (119). And by the time of his confession to Natalia, Razumov applies the term *crime* to himself. It was as if, he says, describing his decision to spy on the revolutionaries for the government after Haldin's death, circumstances conspired "to help me on to further crime" (273). The sentence implies, though does not quite say, that Razumov's earlier action was also a crime. If the crime is the absent center of a detective novel, as Todorov suggests (46), the fact that Razumov's betrayal *is* a crime is the absent center of Conrad's novel, and one of the driving problems of utopian crime in general.

This inversion of the legal associations of crime goes a step further in Ngũgĩ's work. The word scarcely appears in *A Grain of Wheat*, but it's there at the climax as Mugo thinks that "He would stand there and publicly own the crime" (Ngũgĩ, 235). The crime was entirely moral when he committed it, but at that moment it has become a legal crime as well: the day of his confession is the day of independence, and the leaders of the town plan to punish those who failed to support the uprising previously. Mugo's moral failing was also a failure to follow the laws of a future that had not yet come to pass. The anticolonial context of *Grain of Wheat* makes utopian crime more utopian and less criminal: the laws that make a particular act a crime are the laws of an occupying force. The removal of the British flag and the raising of the Kenyan one under cover of darkness mark a moment of hope that law and morality might finally coincide.[8]

Utopian crime, in other words, raises a temporal problem about the nature of crime. One act becomes a crime only in retrospect after a change in a legal regime; another switches from crime to heroism with the same change. Utopian crime spurs characters to think about the law as unfixed, and to think about their actions in relation to legal systems that are beyond the horizon of the immediate future. Characters find themselves constantly theorizing and weighing political and personal futures. Razumov's fatal choice to turn Haldin in for the assassination in *Under Western Eyes* comes out of a very unabstract concern for his most immediate future: "am I to have my future, perhaps my usefulness ruined by this sanguinary fanatic?" (Conrad, 34) Note the contrast between the familiar language of "future" and "usefulness" against the absurdly elevated "sanguinary fanatic." Razumov feels that he can sacrifice Haldin because Haldin's future is less real than his own. Haldin, meanwhile, describes his own future is terms that are abstract but much more familiar than Razumov's elevations: "Men like me leave no posterity but their souls are not lost ... The Russian soul that lives in all of us. It has a future" (24–25). The future is the arbiter and ultimate priority for all of them.

These novels too, have in some cases been better received by the future than in their own times. Conrad in *Under Western Eyes*, in particular, is fascinated by literary as well as political futurity. While the novel does not imagine a utopian future for Russia or for its characters, it is obsessively concerned with its own textual future. The material of the story is intricately mediated through its multiple narrators (in theory, the novel is narrated by an unnamed English teacher who has access to Razumov's diary). This mediation extends to the form of the book itself, where a character's statement in the novel is adapted into an epigraph. The novel came out in 1911; Conrad's 1920 Author's Note confesses to the failure of the novel in England when it first appeared, but sketches a picture of its becoming ever more relevant and influential as events in Russia took their course: recent news stories, he declares, testify "to the clearness of my vision and the correctness of my judgment" (5). In a strange way, he implies, the Russian Revolution rescued his novel's own future as literature, just as it would have rescued the moral meaning of an act like Haldin's.

Conrad's self-congratulation testifies to a strange problem in the novels of utopian crime: here, the ideology of transhistorical aesthetics finds an uncanny doppelganger in the ideology of revolutionary activity, not because either seeks autonomy apart from history, but because both turn to the future as a justification for the choices of the present. Just as the perpetrators of utopian crimes strive to create with their acts a new legal regime that will judge them innocent, the authors of these novels strive to balance the urgency of their immediate audience with the perspective of an unknown future readership. The revolutionary, like so many modernist novelists, imagines being an outcast in his own time and feted by the judgment of the future. Writing for the future here is not a conservative rejection of the possibility of political engagement; it is an enmeshment in the difficult politics of radical violence and utopian yearning. In *Under Western Eyes* and *A Grain of Wheat*, Conrad and Ngũgĩ use complex frame narratives to measure the past against the future it brings about; in both cases, that future is not exactly a utopia, but framing forces readers and characters alike to look towards the ends to measure the value of the means. In other words, even Conrad's condemnation of revolution implicitly adopts in form revolution's evaluation of the choices of the present by the standards of the future they create.

Contemplating utopian crime, then, forces a relatively conservative novelist like Conrad to recognize, by historical irony, a kinship between the ethical calculations of novel-writing and those of violent political action. And it allows a novelist like Ngũgĩ, writing simultaneously for Kenyan, pan-African, and global audiences, to stake a claim on the political attention of a Western audience who still had a fairly dismissive approach to Mau Mau in the late 1960s.[9] By juxtaposing the atrocities of the British past with the never-quite-pure moment when a Kenyan future begins, his novel uses the literary and political past to call into being the future audience he hopes a postcolonial world will allow.

The fear that there might be an inverse relationship between writing for an urgent political problem of the present and writing for the future haunts these writers both within and outside of their novels. Famously, Dostoevsky worried in a letter that *Demons* would be only a "pamphlet" (Dostoevsky 1986, 112), but thought his political purposes were more important than the artistry. In the novel, a character asks, "which is more beautiful, Shakespeare or boots, Raphael or petroleum?" (485). Both within and outside of the novels, these authors set the appeal of lasting art against the urgency of the needs of the present. At the same time, however, Conrad's transport and reimagining of *Demons* suggests that writing novels-as-pamphlets could make them even more capable of speaking to the future, rather than less so.

What happens, then, when the aesthetically and politically fraught tradition of utopian crime collides with the different political and media world of the hard-boiled crime series? Mũkoma wa Ngũgĩ has rewritten his father's plot twice: first in the serial Ishmael detective novels; then in a more traditionally literary mode in *Mrs. Shaw* (2015). The Ishmael novels, consisting of *Nairobi Heat* (2010) and *Black Star Nairobi* (2013), confront the problems of the border between law and morality characteristic of the utopian tradition; they also render a noir world where violence and corruption are everywhere, rather than the subject of rare ethical dilemmas. These works self-consciously turn to crime as a separate and specific genre: in its American edition, *Nairobi Heat* bears the imprint "Melville International Crime" on the cover, and the cover design disaffiliates from any association with "literary fiction": on a green background, the shape of Africa in black merges with the silhouette of a revolver. It is, in other words, packaged to look like disposable entertainment, not identifying itself as art with ambitions upon future readers—even though, of course, its very existence testifies to the influence and reach of the genre.

In *Nairobi Heat*, the story of the false hero comes closest of all to moral clarity—and crime no longer has any association with left-wing radicalism. But it also ultimately erases the secret kinship between the artist and the assassin. Mũkoma turns further away from crime as the actions of radical idealists: the false hero turns out to be the perpetrator of the murder with which the novel begins, and his motive is entirely selfish. The novel might have made an ethical dilemma out of this: the murderer, Joshua Hakizimana, is thought to be a hero of the Rwandan genocide who sheltered fleeing victims. In fact, he sold them out to a militia. As the novel opens, he's serving as a figurehead for a charity, and the murder victim is the daughter of one of his former victims. Mũkoma never balances any good done by a charity against his monstrosity: there is no claim here of an ethically justified moral compromise, no lie Joshua tells himself about the sacrifice being for a greater good. "Only what you do when you meet the Joshuas of this earth matters," says Ishmael (Mūkoma 2010, 199). Ishmael's attempt to bring Joshua to justice is portrayed as a contest against pure evil. This is, on some level, a return to the moral world of *Demons*: although Dostoevsky's characters are more morally ambiguous, the Western ideas that possess them are unambiguously destructive. Like Stavrogin, whose experiments with various ideas catastrophically infect everyone around him, Joshua is a charismatic figure to whom everyone turns at their peril: for safety amidst atrocity, for a hopeful image of heroism to the survivors of the genocide, and for the expiation of American consciences via charity. And like Stavrogin, he is a fraud. Dostoevsky's critique of the promises of nineteenth-century radicals echoes in Mūkoma's critique of the dreams of twenty-first-century international aid.

In the sequel, *Black Star Nairobi*, there is, however, a central ethical dilemma that *does* take the form of utopian crime. The protagonists have been trying to track down the leader of the shadowy organization that has planted a bomb with an eye to wiping out all the leading politicians in Kenya and starting afresh; Mūkoma suggests in the novel that they're modelling their revolution on Bush-era pre-emption doctrine (Mūkoma 2013: 247). Just as they are successful in stopping the plot, Ishmael and his companions find themselves unexpectedly tempted to set the bomb off themselves. One of them is a Rwanda survivor and sees the need for drastic measures to prevent a descent into another genocide in the aftermath of the contested 2007 elections in Kenya. Suddenly the old Conradian language of the madness of idealism reappears: "We had gone insane," Ishmael thinks as they contemplate the bomb, "and entered a universe of calculation and logic" (258). The schemes of idealistic radicals have become those of the global elite, equally mad in their intellectual clarity and scorn for reality.

Yet they don't set off the bomb. And not because stepping over the edge into violence is too dangerous—these are very bloody books; more people have died than our protagonists have bothered to count. Instead they decide that somewhere the violence has to end. These novels take place in a world where violence is always lurking, a product, as in the naturalist tradition, of the systemic injustices of global power; our heroes resolutely stick to their human-scale narrative. "I didn't want to impact forty-two million lives for better or worse all at once—I just wanted see justice for Amos and Mary" (259). The border between criminal and innocent has become porous again. And it's happened by ending contemplation of the future: Ishmael wants justice for the past, not to be an architect of utopia. The future holds no ethical claim on him.

Mũkoma's crime novels are a challenge to the insoluble ethical agonies of the novelists of utopian crime, in their insistence that we must weigh the present according to the terms of the future. The genre novelist, however, foregrounds neither a literary nor a political future. In *Black Star Nairobi*, it is the villainous representatives of powerful countries who say that "the future is worth a little bloodletting in the present" (244–5). Mũkoma's genre novels, in other words, are both signs of the persistence of the literary past and a rebuke to its self-consciously transhistorical aspirations; they're also a rejection of the political futurities of utopian crime.[10]

Mũkoma's more "literary" novel, *Mrs. Shaw*, even more directly revisits the plot of *A Grain of Wheat* and its predecessors: this time, the protagonist Kalumba from the fictional nation of Kwatee returns home after the end of the rule of a repressive dictator. His presence—and his desire to speak openly about the massacres that precipitated his exile—disrupts the fragile status of the new democratic government. Though he doesn't remember it, he had given up the names of his fellow dissidents under extreme torture before his flight; the revelation of this fact leads his oldest friend (Ogum) to kill him to save the new regime. Kalumba's story evokes *A Grain of Wheat*'s Mugo's, but his missing memories make his crime without guilt and without volition. In this, the novel also echoes those naturalist crime novels of murder without intention.

The novel has all the moral inquiry that the Ishmael novels deliberately refuse. It is full of stories about history that turn out to be false—knowledge of the massacre is suppressed; the murder of a British colonial officer by freedom fighters (which supposedly kicked off the struggle for independence) turns out to have been committed by his abused wife; Kalumba is the exiled hero who actually, through no fault of his own, was also responsible for the violence he escaped. These false stories have changed the course of Kwatee's history. And determining the meaning of Ogum's final choice to kill Kalumba requires measuring the value of all those truths about the past against present and future outcomes. Ogum, like Razumov and like Dostoevsky's revolutionaries, justifies his act in terms of the future—but he also finds the future inextricable from the past and the present: "He had done it: he had avenged his father; no, he had saved Sukena from Kalumba; no, he had saved the nation from a counterrevolution led by Kalumba. Yes, this was his sacrifice" (Mũkoma 2015: 234). Running through potential justifications for an act he can scarcely bear, he moves from the past (vengeance for his father, dead in the massacre) to the present (saving his fiancée from connection with Kalumba) to the future (the nation he wishes to create). The political future, his thoughts suggest, is merely a cover for a more personal present and past.

Futurity creeps into this novel in precisely the spaces of ambiguity and outrage that the Ishamel novels refuse. The violence committed against and by Ishmael and his friends is genre violence: they acclimate to it as the norm of the world they inhabit. The violence in *Mrs. Shaw* is traumatic, haunting: it demands moral judgment from the future and refuses to stay in the past. *Mrs. Shaw* returns to the thematics of utopian crime I outlined before. But, like the Ishmael novels, it is also an exposure of their political limitations. If the novels of utopian crime confront the past in order to reach the future, *Mrs. Shaw* anatomizes the devastating consequences of failing to see the past: the constant erasure and rewriting of history ensures that the future will never be radically different.

Simon Gikandi's account of the temporal twistiness of *A Grain of Wheat* can help illuminate the difference: in the novel, he says, "the restoration that was expected to justify the whole history of Kenya ... has not come about. And it is in this context that a debate emerges in the novel on whether the past can be more usable in its commemoration or forgetfulness" (Gikandi, 120): the characters measure the past's failings to live up to the myths they've told about it against the disappointed expectations of the present and future. Just as the horrors of the past seemed justified at the time by appealing to the hope of independence, the limitations of the present prompt them to look back to the hopes of the past. The problem here is not that the future resembles the past—at least not yet; this is a novel before the rise of the neocolonial state depicted in Ngũgĩ's next novel, *Petals of Blood*. The problem is that independence brings its own new shadows.

But in Mũkoma's novel, there is scarcely a distinction between future and past. The novel concludes with the survivors "stagger[ing] out of the airport and into the new and old Kwatee Republic" (Ngũgĩ 2015: 235). *New and old*, not *old and new*: this is not the same country tinged with change, but a country pretending to be new haunted by the fear that it is the same old place. In other words, radical change no longer seems possible.[11] In *Black Star Nairobi*, a sharp break from the past was the plot of villains; here, it is the perpetual, deluded dream of the heroes: they keep on thinking they'll create something new, and only the elderly characters are there to remind them that these stadium spectacles, decade after decade, all resemble each other as each new form of liberation is announced (159). The tragedy of *Mrs. Shaw* is not that acting for the future requires sacrificing the present; it is that the future will scarcely be anything beyond the present. The transportable quality of novels by Dostoevsky, Conrad and Ngũgĩ lies in part in the way they confront—with fear and suspicion—the genuine possibility of radical change, both on a literary and a political level. Mũkoma, writing in pulp and cloth alike, suggests that neither literature nor politics can count on the future to do anything more than reproduce the present. Either way, literary authors, whether in embracing or in rejecting futurity, face both the hopes and the failures of revolution.

Notes

1. For a discussion of Dostoevsky's critique of similar thinking in nineteenth-century Russia, see Ruttenburg (126–39).
2. Alongside the hard-boiled tradition in America, of course, there rose the true-crime novel, which Lana A. Whited discusses as another genre developing out of naturalism.
3. In this sense, it is possible to position novels of utopian crime halfway between the noir novel of a corrupt world and the British golden age detective novel of social order broken and restored: in utopian crime, the advent of violence is a fateful step in a way that isn't necessarily true in Hammett's world but is in Christie's; but unlike Christie, novelists of utopian crime see little possibility of restored order by the revelation of the crime. On the difference between the figure of the detective in American and British contexts, see Porter (129).
4. *A Grain of Wheat* is famously influenced by Frantz Fanon, whose *The Wretched of the Earth* had appeared in 1963. Fanon's depiction of radical violence has something of the naturalist emphasis on crime as a response to a social problem about it: "the almighty body of violence" on the part of the colonized arises "in reaction to the primary violence of the colonizer" (Fanon, 50). But he also emphasizes the cathartic force of an active choice to commit to violence: "Claiming responsibility for the violence also allows those members of the group who have strayed or have been outlawed to come back, to retake their place and be reintegrated" (44). Violence is both an organic, collective movement and a crisis point in individual commitment.

5 For a recent analysis of the competing claims of the historical and the transhistorical – and a defense of the latter—see Felski (150–85).

6 Muñoz's work is based in performance studies, and shares with others in that field the idea that live performance might be a strategy for instantiating utopian possibility for an audience today (see, e.g., Dolan). Utopian crime, of course, take the opposite tactic – obsessed with the problem of ends justifying means and deferring utopia to that distant and desirable future; enacting violence so that violence might cease to be necessary.

7 The best-studied connection is that between Dostoevsky and Conrad; see, for example, Carabine, Kaye. Although Conrad always disclaimed interest in Dostoevsky's work, critics have found this claim impossible to believe. Ngũgĩ explicitly declared his fascination with Conrad; recent work includes Bronstein, West-Pavlov.

8 The ironies of this hope became complex as Ngũgĩ's career extended into postindependence Kenya. His next novel *Petals of Blood*, for instance, is even more explicitly a detective story. The novel is framed as a mystery: an arson attack has burned down a brothel and killed three wealthy and rapacious men; the police interview the novel's four protagonists as suspects. The novel specifically raises the possibility that the act might be political activism in order to deny it: "They came for him that Sunday" (Ngũgĩ 2000: 3) is the first line, raising the image of nefarious government repression. The local socialist organizer is one of the suspects; but the actual culprit is another character who has spent most of the novel attempting to fit in with rather than to change society. With the shift to the neocolonial context, in other words, calculated violence becomes less utopian for Ngũgĩ—although other forms of crime retain their political powers.

9 Ngũgĩ's well-known shift to focusing on the local audience represented by his choice to write in Gikuyu in works after *Petals of Blood* (1977) connects to his decreasing interest in utopian violence: when both the audience and the political stakes are immediate rather than distant, the present is no longer merely a sacrifice.

10 Mũkoma's novels share this critique with another contemporary descendent of the Russian classical tradition—Tom Stoppard, whose disillusioned idealists in the *Coast of Utopia* trilogy come to realize that their failure was in their privileging of the future over the present. Vissarion Belinsky cries, "I'm sick of utopias!" (Stoppard, 180); Alexander Herzen declares, "later is too late ... It's only we humans who want to own the future too" (223). Theater, like genre fiction, often seeks action in the present rather than sacrificing the present for the future.

11 In this sense, the depiction of utopian crime in *Mrs. Shaw* matches the depiction of reproductive futurism in Lee Edelman's account: sacrificing the present in the name of a future that is actually a reproduction of the past.

Works Cited

Bronstein, Michaela (2014). "Ngũgĩ's Use of Conrad: A Case for Literary Transhistory." *MLQ* 75:3, 411–37.
Camus, Albert (1951). *L'Homme révolté*. Paris: Gallimard.
Carabine, Keith (1996). *The Life and the Art: A Study of Conrad's "Under Western Eyes."* Amsterdam: Rodopi.
Conrad, Joseph ([1911], 2013). *Under Western Eyes*, ed. Roger Osborne and Paul Eggert. Cambridge: Cambridge University Press.
Dolan, Jill (2005). *Utopia in Performance: Finding Hope at the Theater*. Ann Arbor: University of Michigan Press.
Dostoevsky, F. M. (1986). *Polnoe Sobranie Sochinenii*. Vol. 29, Bk. 1. Leningrad: Akademiia Nauk.
Dostoevsky, F. M. ([1871–72], 2000). *Demons*, trans. Richard Pevear and Larissa Volokhonsky. New York: Everyman's Library.
Edelman, Lee (2004). *No Future: Queer Theory and the Death Drive*. Durham: Duke University Press.
Fanon, Frantz (2004). *The Wretched of the Earth*, trans. Richard Philcox. New York: Grove Press.
Felski, Rita (2015). *The Limits of Critique*. Chicago: University of Chicago Press.
Gikandi, Simon (2000). *Ngũgĩ wa Thiong'o*. Cambridge: Cambridge University Press.
Kaye, Peter (2006). *Dostoevsky and English Modernism 1900–1930*. Cambridge: Cambridge University Press.
Mũkoma wa Ngũgĩ (2010). *Nairobi Heat*. New York: Melville House Publishing.
Mũkoma wa Ngũgĩ (2013). *Black Star Nairobi*. New York: Melville House.
Mũkoma wa Ngũgĩ (2015). *Mrs. Shaw*. Athens, OH: Ohio University Press.
Muñoz, José (2009). *Cruising Utopia: The Then and There of Queer Futurity*. New York: NYU Press.
Ngũgĩ wa Thiong'o (1986). *A Grain of Wheat*. Rev. ed. Oxford: Heinemann.
Ngũgĩ wa Thiong'o (2000). *Petals of Blood*. New York: Penguin.
Porter, Dennis (1981). *The Pursuit of Crime: Art and Ideology in Detective Fiction*. New Haven: Yale University Press.
Ruttenburg, Nancy (2010). *Dostoevsky's Democracy*. Princeton: Princeton University Press.
Scharnhorst, Gary (2011). "Naturalism and Crime." In the *Oxford Handbook of American Literary Naturalism*, ed. Keith Newlin. New York: Oxford University Press, 339–53.
Stoppard, Tom (2007). *The Coast of Utopia: Voyage, Shipwreck, Salvage*. New York: Grove Press.

Todorov, Tzvetan (1977). *The Poetics of Prose*, trans. Richard Howard. Ithaca: Cornell University Press.

West-Pavlov, Russell (2015). "The Politics of Spaces and Voice: Ngũgĩ's *A Grain of Wheat* and Conrad's *Heart of Darkness*." *Research in African Literatures* 44:3, 160–75.

Whited, Lana (2003). "Naturalism's Middle Ages: The Evolution of the American True-Crime Novel, 1930–1960." In *Twisted from the Ordinary: Essays on American Literary Naturalism*, ed. Mary E. Papke. Knoxville: University of Tennessee Press, 323–43.

Part Two

Market Mechanisms

6

With a Global Market in Mind: Agents, Authors, and the Dissemination of Contemporary Swedish Crime Fiction

Karl Berglund

On 27 August, 2015, David Lagercrantz's *Det som inte dödar oss* (*The Girl in the Spider's Web*) was published simultaneously in twenty-five countries, and an additional fifteen countries or so followed soon after. The book was launched and marketed as the "official sequel" to Stieg Larsson's enormously successful Millennium Trilogy, and everyone in the business expected it would be a big hit. The first sales figures indicate that this is indeed the case. According to *Svensk Bokhandel*, the Swedish book trade journal, *The Girl in the Spider's Web* reached the number one spot in September 2015 in nearly all the national bestseller charts covered by their study, including the United Kingdom, the United States, France, Germany, and the Netherlands, and, of course, Sweden (Utländska topplistor).

Much can be said about the rather dubious marketing strategies used for this particular book—the publisher, the agent, and the copyright holders are obviously exploiting a dead author's name and reputation to generate yet more money. But that is not my interest here. In what follows, I will use the example of the global success of Swedish crime fiction in the 2000s to discuss the book trade mechanisms that enable and even foster phenomena such as the Lagercrantz story. In my opinion, if we are to understand global trends in popular fiction, we have to try to identify the circumstances in which such fiction is produced and disseminated—circumstances have changed beyond all recognition for writers of Swedish crime fiction over the last twenty years.

Of particular interest in this case is the fact that Lagercrantz and the other crime writers discussed here are Swedish (or, more broadly, Scandinavian or Nordic)—that is, authors writing from a periphery. What I aim to highlight is that the traditional relationship between centers and peripheries in the global book trade—between the global and the local—has been altered in recent decades.

A discussion of the term world literature has much to gain from paying close attention to these structural changes. After all, in David Damrosch's words, "world literature is not an infinite, ungraspable canon of works but rather a mode of circulation and of reading" (Damrosch, 5), and it includes all sorts of works "circulating out into a broader world beyond its linguistic and cultural point of origin" (6). With such a definition, the successful Swedish crime fiction of the 2000s is emphatically world literature. Stewart King says as much in his article "Crime Fiction as World Literature," though he follows it with the sour observation that this has seldom been the case in studies of world literature (King, 11–12). He sets out to look beyond national contexts when discussing crime fiction, and instead analyzes the genre in a global context from the start. In order to do so, King notes, we need to shift our focus:

> Moretti observes that "world literature is not an object, it's a *problem*, and a problem that asks for a new critical method." Likewise, Damrosch proposes that world literature is not so much an object of study, a canon of great works that must be read, but a reading practice, a way of analyzing literary texts outside of the cultural and intellectual tradition from which they come. The practice of reading world crime fiction requires a shift from studying the production of crime fiction to its consumption. That is, a shift from writers to readers. (King, 13)

I agree with King, but would take his argument a step further, for I hold that the practice of reading crime fiction as world literature also requires a shift from studying its writers and readers to looking at its material conditions and the book trade that produces and disseminates it. In general, this follows Ann Steiner's point that "world literature is conditioned by sale systems, publishing traditions, translations, government support, taxes, and everything else related to the economy of literature" (Steiner 2012, 316).

I use the example of Swedish crime fiction in the 2000s, then, to (1) point out how peripheral and local attributes of popular fiction are used as global selling arguments, and (2) how such trends, in turn, always depend on book market structure. One of my main points is that the book trade and the fiction it distributes are always closely intertwined. First, I sketch the Swedish background to the rise of crime fiction and literary agents. Then, I connect this development to the bigger changes in the global book trade. Finally, I consider the terms world literature and the global–local distinction, and argue for what I understand as a market-driven literature produced with the intention of becoming world literature.

Swedish crime fiction and Swedish literary agents

Following the success of Henning Mankell in the late 1990s and early 2000s, many authors have added to the reputation of Swedish and Scandinavian crime fiction abroad. With Stieg Larsson, this interest rose to heights never seen before. According to his Swedish publisher, Larsson's books have been translated into fifty languages and sold over 80 million copies worldwide ("Millennium"). In 2010, *Publisher's Weekly* said of Larsson's popularity in the United States that "If we had to name the author of the year, Larsson would lead the parade. With a combined weekly total of 202 weeks on the 2010 bestseller charts and an impressive 59 of those in the #1 spot, his Millennium trilogy ... outpaced all other bestsellers" (Maryles, 18).

When the Millennium Trilogy became part of what is perhaps best called the hypercanon of contemporary popular fiction, along with other blockbuster megasellers such as Harry Potter, the Twilight saga, and the Fifty Shades of Grey trilogy (see Steiner 2014, 42–46), it brought along a seemingly inexhaustible demand for more stories in the same vein. This sudden global interest in a specific national tradition of crime fiction in turn meant Swedish publishers and bestselling crime writers began to rake it in—as did their literary agents. The latter are especially interesting in the present case. Compared to the Anglo-American book trade, the history of literary agents in Sweden is much shorter and the position they hold different. Traditionally, agents have had little or no importance in Swedish publishing for the domestic market; however, since 2000 things have changed, as a great many literary agencies have been founded, and new ones are constantly being added. Of the currently active Swedish literary agencies, around two-thirds were founded in the 2000s, and around 40 percent in 2010 and later (Berglund 2014, 73).[1]

The simultaneous rise of the Swedish literary agent and the successful dissemination of Swedish crime fiction is of course no coincidence. All the new agents relied heavily on the translation rights to Swedish and other Scandinavian crime fiction (as well as adaptation rights and a variety of immaterial rights;

see Murray, 37). The Salomonsson Agency, founded in 2000 and the biggest literary agency in Sweden at the moment, exemplifies this, for a majority of the authors it represents globally are crime writers, and when it comes to number of rights sold, the dominance of crime fiction is even more palpable (Salomonsson Agency; see Berglund 2014, 76).

What has happened, then, is that the demand for Swedish crime fiction simultaneously created a new market for Swedish agents: it created business opportunities that simply did not exist before. The rapid growth of Sweden's literary agencies is thus to a great extent due to the crime fiction boom. Yet the opposite has also been true: the popularity of Swedish and Scandinavian crime fiction abroad has of course been helped by all the new Swedish agencies.

This, in turn, has had a drastic effect on Swedish publishing. Traditionally, the Swedish book trade has been keen to embrace foreign literature—it has been a culture of literary imports. The export of Swedish literature mainly focused on the other Nordic countries and Germany, while the UK and US book markets were typically out of reach for most Swedish authors (of course, though, with individual exceptions) (Svedjedal, 50–52). Due to the symbiotic rise of Swedish crime fiction and Swedish literary agents, this has now started to change. *Svensk Bokhandel* even speaks of a rights trade turned upside down (Pettersson, 11).

The literary agent Magdalena Hedlund underlines the fact that Stieg Larsson's books changed the rules for selling Swedish literature abroad:

> Even if many Swedish authors had succeeded abroad before, it was never successes of that magnitude. Suddenly the world understood that "Wow, Swedish fiction can become a world hit!" … After Stieg Larsson it was apparent that everyone was looking for the next Stieg Larsson. And when more publishers got interested in Swedish literature they acquired the tools needed: they sought contact with professional readers and translators that knew the language.[2] (Laxgård, 19–20)

Moreover, the speed with which rights are sold has accelerated considerably. In the book trade it is now not unusual to have rights sales of *options*—that is, before the novel in question is completed. Agents spread digital proposals to publishers and their scouts around the world, with the intention of selling as many rights as possible before the original text has even been published (Høier, 15).

There have been quite a few such examples of Swedish crime fiction in recent years. Two that stand out, at least in Sweden, are *Strindbergs stjärna* (2010, *Strindberg's Star*) by Jan Wallentin and *Den andalusiske vännen* (2012, *The*

Andalucian Friend) by Alexander Söderberg. The former was the main title presented by Bonniers, Sweden's largest publishing house, at the London Book Fair of 2010, even though at the time it had not only not yet been published in Sweden, it was not even finished. During the fair, over twenty countries bought the rights to the novel in its unedited condition, which gave its author the largest advance in Swedish publishing history. Söderberg's book made headway at the Frankfurt Book Fair of 2012 on even less substance. The agency arrived armed with a rough translation of the first 100 pages. With the help of a two-page synopsis, the novel was sold to over twenty countries (Laxgård, 22).

It is important to stress here that these novels were both debuts. Wallentin and Söderberg had not published anything before, and they were not otherwise well known. Why their rights sold so well, then, was solely a matter of hype. And of course this hype was mostly due to the earlier successes of Swedish crime fiction. The translation rights to these novels were sold on the assumption that they might be the next Millennium Trilogy. As it turned out, though, neither of them was.[3]

Since the contemporary book trade is largely dominated by front-list bestsellers, publishers try hard to spot the forthcoming ones. This leads to a business culture in which publishers outbid one another in the scramble for what everyone thinks will be the next big hit, or the next *big book* to use John B. Thompson's term (192–4). Agents are only too happy for this to continue, since their income is a share of the rights sales (typically around 15 percent) (Clark and Phillips, 92). This does much to explain why a debut novel can be sold to twenty countries well in advance of publication. It also makes it easier to understand why suddenly the whole world wanted to read crime fiction from Scandinavia. Literary agents are key players in the creation of such book trade buzz.

The case of David Lagercrantz is thus an example of this business culture, but one taken to the extreme. Regarding *The Girl in the Spider's Web*, it was not the hope that it might turn out to be the next Stieg Larsson that drove market speculation to heights never seen before but the fact that it *was* the next Stieg Larsson (or, to be more precise, the closest one could get to a new Larsson novel, being an official sequel, written by another author but with a marketing spiel that made it appear that Larsson himself had been brought back to life). From a strictly commercial perspective, it was in many ways the perfect book launch: an unknown book by an almost unknown author, which everyone who had read the Millennium Trilogy would want to read.

It should also be noted that the person who came up with the original idea of writing a sequel to the Millennium Trilogy was Magdalena Hedlund, the agent who holds the rights to Stieg Larsson's work (Strömberg). It is literary agents, and not publishers, who are the main winners in a literary economy where hype and speculation push up the prices of rights.

Book fairs as places of dissemination

If agents are the influential individuals in the dissemination of literature today, the most influential places are the major book fairs, which have become an increasingly important arena for the transaction of translation rights. The most important one of all is the Frankfurt Book Fair. According to the fair's website ("Literary Agents & Scouts Centre"), "More than 300 agencies with more than 600 registered agents from over 30 countries" were represented there in 2015. The plan for the rights center shows over 400 small tables, each one a physical space where, for five days every October, a stream of translation rights are traded and where deals between agents and publishers are constantly being struck.

The Frankfurt Book Fair has restyled itself over the years. Where it was once primarily a marketplace for books, it is now a marketplace for various sorts of intellectual property rights. Simone Murray takes this evolution to represent the "twenty-first-century view of the book: that of a content platform interlinked with more recently emerged media through networks of IP [intellectual property] rights dealing" (Murray, 84).

Murray's interest lies in adaptations, but her argument also works for translations. She understands these fairs as a "sociological window into the *making* of the literary," and, with a suitably tart metaphor, she describes the action staged at such rights centers as speed-dating in immaterial rights (85–86). Today, it is at these book fairs that the dissemination of literature begins. In a very tangible way, this is where world literature is created in the contemporary, globalized book trade (see Murray, 102).

A very influential essay on the structural and sociological aspects of literary translation in a global perspective is Johan Heilbron's "Towards a Sociology of Translation" from 1999. He conceives of published translations as an international system with a hierarchical structure that basically consists of three levels of languages: central, semi-peripheral, and peripheral (Heilbron, 433). English, of course, is the most central of the languages in his model. Swedish is identified as semi-peripheral (around 1–3 percent of the total number of translations involve Swedish as the source or target language) (434).

Crucially, Heilbron identifies central languages as intermediary languages:

> Distinguishing languages by their degree of centrality not only implies that translations flow more from the core to the periphery than the other way around, but also that the communication between peripheral groups often passes through a centre. What is translated from one peripheral language into the other depends on what is translated from these peripheral languages into the central languages. In other words, the more central a language is in the translation system, the more it has the capacity to function as an intermediary or vehicular language, that is as a means of communication between language groups which are themselves peripheral or semi-peripheral. (Heilbron, 435)

He emphasizes the importance of being translated into these central languages, which in fact seems to mean being published in the UK or the United States:

> Much of the international communication about books works in this manner and is dependent on the role of the leading centers of the international system. Once a book is translated into a central language by an authoritative publisher, it immediately catches the attention of publishers in other parts of the globe. The simple fact that an American or English publisher will publish an author from a semi-peripheral language is used extensively by the original publisher, because it is the best recommendation for publishers elsewhere to acquire the translation rights. (Heilbron, 436)

Interest from British and American publishers is still of crucial importance to all authors of popular fiction who want to make it abroad, of course. Yet in one respect, Heilbron's model has been superseded. Nowadays, it is not translations that generate further translations, but the sale of translation rights. As shown above, rights sales precede translations, and it is at the overheated rights auctions at book fairs such as Frankfurt and London that the global interest in further translations is established.

If the rights to a Swedish crime novel are sold to a major UK and US publisher at a major book fair, that is all the argument the publishers need to persuade semi-peripheral and peripheral countries to also buy the rights. Meanwhile, if the translation rights to the same novel at the same book fair are instead sold first to about fifteen peripheral and semi-peripheral book markets, this will most likely generate interest from British and American publishers.

Thus, what drives the dissemination of popular fiction today is first and foremost hype. Success breeds success; interest, further interest. This holds true for both single titles and bigger literary trends in the trade (such as the Swedish crime fiction fad in the early 2000s). And in such a trade culture, the importance of book fairs and their rights auctions can hardly be overrated.

The global and the local—producing world literature

In the production of a world literature of popular fiction, then, literary agents are key players and the major book fairs are key places. If we keep the analysis on a structural level—that is, if we do not dwell on single examples of crime novels that might have made the big time across the globe for this or that reason—the two obvious factors in the boom in Swedish crime fiction are genre (crime fiction) and nationality and/or language (Swedish).

Regarding Stieg Larsson's impact, Ann Steiner states that "international success is more often linked to genre than to language" (Steiner 2012, 322). I cannot agree with this entirely. Her main point, and it is a fair one, is to show that global bestsellers can be of any national origin, even if many of them are written in English. However, I would not go so far as to claim that Larsson's Swedish origins were less important than his chosen genre. Of course, the Millennium Trilogy's status as crime fiction is fundamental to its success, but I would say that the same also holds true of its Swedishness. The key to its success lies in the combination: it is, after all, a Swedish crime novel. This is exactly what the Scandicrime phenomenon is built upon.

That places and settings are important in contemporary crime fiction is not something unique to the Swedish or Nordic traditions. On the contrary, it is fundamental to the genre as a whole, as noted by, among others, Eva Erdmann:

> Surprisingly, the crime novel of the last decades is distinguished by the fact that the main focus is not on the crime itself, but on the setting, the place where the detective and the victims live and to which they are bound by ties of attachment. The surroundings where the investigations take place are portrayed with increasing inventiveness, to the extent that the crime itself appears to be at best merely a successful stunt. It almost seems as if the inventories of criminal motives and case histories have been exhausted, so that crime fiction's primary distinguishing characteristic has become the *locus criminalis*. (Erdmann, 12)

Jean Anderson, Carolina Miranda, and Barbara Pezzotti take the argument one step further when they connect the popularity of "foreign" environments in crime novels to a more general desire among the reading public to read about something that to themselves appears as "exotic" (either in a positive or a more negative way):

> As for the exotic environment, the proliferation of detective novels with foreign settings brings the genre into close proximity to travel writing and may have both entertainment and didactic value for readers. Whether they are able to judge the accuracy of these representations remains, however, a moot point: their choices—along with the authors'—may reflect genuine interest in other cultures or instead constitute a desire for a kind of cultural Disneyland in which plot, setting and characters are subsidiary to overt or covert stereotypes. (Anderson, Miranda, and Pezzotti, 3)

The importance of the exotic elements in Swedish and Scandinavian crime fiction is well known, and is evident in the titles to popular surveys of the tradition, for example, the German anthology *Fjorde, Elche, Mörder* (2006, Fjords, Elks, Murder) or the British *Death in a Cold Climate* by Barry Forshaw (2012). Foreign curiosity about the Swedish climate and distinctive cultural features has also resulted in a perhaps more unexpected side effect for the Swedish book trade. When it comes to popular fiction—and especially, of course, when it comes to crime fiction—players in the Swedish book trade nowadays think big when they take on new authors. They do not focus solely on a Swedish audience; they have a global market in mind. Put simply, the major audiences are foreign, as is the real money. And due to the fact that it is the "exotic" features of the genre that the global reading public looks for, this has led to an increased emphasis on the supposed Swedishness and Nordic characteristics of the literature in question.

This is at its most evident in the snowy covers given to Swedish crime fiction published outside Sweden (see Broomé 2014; Louise Nilsson elsewhere in this volume),[4] but it has affected literary production right down the line, from writing to rights selling to marketing. A number of Swedish authors in the 2000s started to write crime fiction at least partly for strategic reasons, with an eye on the market. And, to use the present essay's principal example, the frequent descriptions of snow and snowfalls in Lagercrantz's *The Girl in the Spider's Web* are no coincidence. Ironically, then, Swedish crime fiction seems to be increasingly written and produced with translation, adaptation, and global popularity in mind, at the same time as the impact of the genre is due to its regional characteristics (or to put it more cynically, due to the exoticism of the Nordic countries and their climate).

According to David Damrosch, literary works "become world literature by being received *into* the space of a foreign culture" (Damrosch, 283). And world literature, as he says, is "always as much about the host culture's values and needs as it is about a work's source culture." Today, Swedish authors and agents are trying to *produce* world literature by deliberately addressing the demands and needs of the host cultures. By emphasizing the national characteristics of Swedish crime fiction they are in effect trying to hijack—or at least speed up—the processes that create world literature.

This is probably not something unique to the Swedish tradition of crime fiction, even though the example is a telling one. It is likely that the need for rapidity and the altered conditions for the translation of popular fiction in the global book trade, in combination with the preoccupation with location and place in contemporary crime fiction—the genre's *topophilia*, to use Anne Marit Waade's term (Waade, 43)—have fostered an industry that gives prominence to new and global takes on the genre, but where the meaning of "new and global" is in constant flux. In the early 2000s, the global fad of non-Anglophone crime fiction has no doubt been crime fiction from Sweden and Scandinavia. What regional or national tradition that might follow is yet to be seen.

In this respect, then, the globalized book trade of the twenty-first century seems to have opened up new doors to the center of the publishing world for popular fiction from peripheral and semi-peripheral nations and languages such as Swedish. The United States and the UK are still the natural starting points for most global bestsellers, but are no longer the only ones. In today's globalized book trade, crime fiction that is local in the extreme is potentially also global, and the periphery can end up being the center. Thus, the production of world literature has in this sense been helped by the new conditions of the book market. We should not forget, however, that this holds true for commercially strong popular literature, but not for literature in general.

Conclusion

To conclude, the boom in Swedish and Scandinavian crime fiction, together with the current structural changes to the book trade, has changed Swedish publishing, with a slew of new literary agents and a far greater focus on literary exports as the result. This, in turn, has made it possible for Swedish authors to figure large in what could be called the "world literature of contemporary popular fiction"—translated and published in twenty countries or more, and read and discussed by a far larger audience than exists in Sweden or Scandinavia alone. This opportunity simply did not exist twenty years ago, perhaps not even ten, for Swedish authors of popular fiction.

The process of translating also has been sped up. Today, a previously unknown author from Sweden can almost instantly be an author of world literature, at least in a technical sense. In its essentials, the current publishing climate means that what you need as an author of contemporary popular fiction intent on making it into world literature are a skillful agent, a big book fair, and an ongoing hype.

When it comes to Swedish crime fiction, the bonanza may now have passed, but the business infrastructure remains in place and will perhaps continue to generate global interest in Swedish literature. At least, this is what Swedish literary agents are hoping for. As one of them put it, "Now it's a hard fact that Swedish literature is out in the world to stay."[5] In order to be able to compete in the global arena of popular fiction, however, Swedish authors and agents hoping for global success must still remember their country's marginal position. Write on the periphery, and you have to be branded (or to brand yourself) as exotic in some way or another, as something that differs from the Anglophone tradition. In this respect, "otherness" or "exoticness" are at the same time a requirement and an opportunity.

Notes

1 For an extensive review of the history of Swedish literary agents and the ways they differ from their Anglo-American counterparts, see Berglund 2014, 69–77.

2 Agent Magdalena Hedlund interviewed in Laxgård: "Även om många svenska författare hade lyckats utomlands var det aldrig av den magnituden. Plötsligt förstod världen att shit, svensk litteratur kan bli en världssuccé! ... Efter Stieg Larsson var det klart att alla började leta efter nästa Stieg Larsson. Eftersom fler utländska förlag blev intresserade av svensk litteratur skaffade fler också rätt verktyg: man sökte kontakt med lektörer och översättare som kunde språket." (All translations are my own unless otherwise indicated.)

3 *Strindbergs stjärna* sold reasonably well in Sweden, but failed abroad. *Den andalusiske vännen* did not sell as well as expected at home or abroad.

4 The covers of Swedish crime fiction published in Sweden are a different story, though (see Berglund 2016).
5 Agent Elisabet Brännström interviewed in Laxgård: "Nu är det reella fakta att svensk litteratur är ute i världen för att stanna."

Works Cited

Anderson, Jean, Carolina Miranda, and Barbara Pezzotti (2012). "Introduction." In *The Foreign in International Crime Fiction: Transcultural Representations*, ed. Jean Anderson, Carolina Miranda, and Barbara Pezzotti. London: Continuum International, 1–8.

Berglund, Karl (2014). "A Turn to the Rights: The Advent and Impact of Swedish Literary Agents." In *Hype: Bestsellers and Literary Culture*, ed. Jon Helgason, Sara Kärrholm, and Ann Steiner. Lund: Nordic Academic Press, 67–87.

Berglund, Karl (2016). *Mordförpackningar: Omslag, titlar och kringmaterial till svenska pocketdeckare 1998–2011*. Uppsala: Uppsala University.

Broomé, Agnes (2014). "The Exotic North, or How Marketing Created the Genre of Scandinavian Crime." In *True North: Literary Translation in the Nordic Countries*, ed. B. J. Epstein. Newcastle upon Tyne: Cambridge Scholars Publishing, 269–82.

Clark, Giles, and Angus Phillips (2008). *Inside Book Publishing*. 4th ed. London: Routledge.

Damrosch, David (2003). *What Is World Literature?* Princeton: Princeton University Press.

Erdmann, Eva (2009). "Nationality International: Detective Fiction in the Late Twentieth Century." In *Investigating Identities: Questions of Identity in Contemporary International Crime Fiction*, ed. Marieke Krajenbrink and Kate M. Quinn. Amsterdam: Rodopi, 11–26.

Fjorde, Elche, Mörder: Der skandinavische Kriminalroman (2006), ed. Jost Hindersmann. Wuppertal: NordPark.

Forshaw, Barry (2012). *Death in a Cold Climate: A Guide to Scandinavian Crime Fiction*. Basingstoke: Palgrave Macmillan.

Heilbron, Johan (1999). "Towards a Sociology of Translation: Book Translations as a Cultural World-System." *European Journal of Social Theory* 2:4, 429–44.

Høier, Anneli (2012). *Den litterära agenten då och nu*. Stockholm: Svenska Förläggareföreningen; Stockholms universitetsbibliotek.

King, Stewart (2014). "Crime Fiction as World Literature." *Clues* 32:2, 8–19.

Laxgård, Kalle (2013). "Det som går upp som en sol." *Svensk Bokhandel* 62:20, 11–28.

"Literary Agents & Scouts Centre." *Buchmesse.de/en*. Frankfurt Book Fair, 2015. Web. November 3, 2015. http://buchmesse.de/en/fbf/registration/table_registration/literary_agents_and_scouts_centre/.

Maryles, Daisy (2011). "Bestsellers '10." *Publishers Weekly* 139: January 10, 18–21.

"Millennium." *Norstedts.se*. Norstedts, 2015. Web. November 3, 2015. http://www.norstedts.se/millennium.

Murray, Simone (2012). *The Adaptation Industry: The Cultural Economy of Contemporary Literary Adaptation*. New York: Routledge.

Pettersson, Jan-Erik (2010). "Agentroll i förändring." *Svensk Bokhandel* 59:16, 10–22.

Salomonsson Agency. *Salomonssonagency.se*, 2015. Web. November 3, 2015.

Steiner, Ann (2012). "World Literature and the Book Market." In *The Routledge Companion to World Literature*, ed. Theo D'haen, David Damrosch, and Djelal Kadir. London: Routledge, 316–24.

Steiner, Ann (2014). "Serendipity, Promotion and Literature: The Contemporary Book Trade and International Megasellers." In *Hype: Bestsellers and Literary Culture*, ed. Jon Helgason, Sara Kärrholm, and Ann Steiner. Lund: Nordic Academic Press, 41–65.

Strömberg, Niklas. "Agent bakom den nya Millennium-titeln." *Svensk Bokhandel*, 2013. Web. November 3, 2015.

Svedjedal, Johan (2012). "Svensk skönlitteratur i världen: Litteratursociologiska problem och perspektiv." In *Svensk litteratur som världslitteratur: En antologi*, ed. Johan Svedjedal. Uppsala: Uppsala University, 9–81.

Thompson, John B. (2010). *Merchants of Culture: The Publishing Business in the Twenty-First Century*. Cambridge: Polity

"Utländska topplistor: De titlarna sålde bäst i september" (2015). *Svensk Bokhandel* 64:16, 30–31.

Waade, Anne Marit (2013). *Wallanderland: Medieturisme og skandinavisk tv-krimi*. Aalborg: Aalborg universitetsforlag.

7

So You Think You Can Write ... Handbooks for Mystery Fiction

Anneleen Masschelein and Dirk de Geest

Detective fiction has evolved into one of the most intriguing and most symptomatic phenomena of our contemporary culture. Since its very emergence, the genre has contributed to the partial destruction and reorganization of cultural hierarchies (Monroe, 253–4). Far beyond an assortment of banal popular texts, it has become one of the major literary genres, praised and practiced by numerous famous writers all over the world. Intellectuals and scholars no longer feel ashamed about reading detective fiction, as in the days of W. H. Auden. Moreover, elements from detective fiction have proven of crucial importance in the establishment as well as the canonization of diverse prestigious cultural phenomena such as postmodernism (with Umberto Eco and Paul Auster, to name only these), postcolonialism (Alexander McCall Smith with his No. 1 Ladies' Detective Agency series), gender fiction (Janet Evanovich), graphic novels (Frank Miller's *Sin City*), and most recently, quality television series (from *Hill Street Blues* to *True Detective*).

Yet at least one important aspect of the genre has been largely overlooked so far. Apart from the immense literary production and the ever-growing body of literary criticism, there is an impressive industry of handbooks that aim to instruct and guide the aspiring writer of detective fiction. This corpus illustrates both the textual construction of detective fiction and its complex institutional embedding in an exemplary way, since it attempts to stimulate the production of successful detective novels. These handbooks and other instances of the so-called literary advice industry (including guidelines for literary awards but also memoirs and essays of advice by established writers of the genre) may be considered as examples of normative narratology, focusing on how detective stories *should be* written, instead of how they are actually written (De Geest and Goris). They also negotiate between two, mostly opposing, dreams: commercial and popular success versus literary prestige and becoming a "writer." Finally, handbooks provide their readers with an overall picture of the writing process, from its inception until publication and even the organization of book tours.

By concentrating on seminal moments in the history of advice for aspiring writers of mysteries (as the genre is usually called in such works), we want to indicate several aspects in which mystery fiction is an exemplary genre for literary advice. First, advice for mystery fiction has been around since roughly the beginning of the twentieth century—when the genre was still young and gaining importance. Today it continues to occupy a significant part of the market and is spread over various media. Second, mystery advice embodies the essence of literary advice for genre fiction because it is strongly rule-based. Due to the constitutive internal logic of the mystery genre, moreover, its rules don't just outline stylistic constraints for beginning authors but also serve to guarantee the relation between author and reader. Third, handbooks for writing detective fiction demonstrate the crucial tensions inherent in all literary advice. On the one hand, handbooks and other types of advice are instruments to quickly detect and communicate the genre's evolutions and changes. On the other hand, due to their conservative nature, they also safeguard the genre's basic "universal" features across time, media, and national traditions.

In what follows we demonstrate how contemporary advice is in many ways still dependent on its early forms, in spite of a stronger emphasis on specialization, efficacy, and self-referentiality across media. At the same time, the awareness of the genre's historicity and its link to national literatures has all but disappeared, despite the strong emergence of regional subgenres, like the Nordic Noir in the 1960s. Yet national diversity is considered subsidiary to the genre's universal pretensions; regional and historical factors—as well as elements related to the genre's "modernity," such as race, nation, and gender—are present, but they are relegated to the realm of particular examples (and the silent omission of others) or found in interviews with authors. The overall ideology of universality ultimately demonstrates how our handbooks still prefer a rather conservative and safe stance over innovation and extension of the genre. If detective writing is "world literature," according to the handbooks, this is primarily because it addresses a global market, governed by a very different logic than simply a high/low division, in the most universal and neutral way.

A brief history of literary advice

Mystery advice is part of a larger body of metaliterature—writings about literature addressed to writers—that has been around since the end of the nineteenth century (Wandor, 108). In the first decades of the twentieth century, published literary advice differentiated into various types that can still be found today. A first type of advice, still the most widespread today, is that provided by the "literary advice industry" in magazines, books, and websites (Hilliard, Levy). This type of advice caters to the demands of the commercial market and formulates strict rules related to specific genres and subgenres, based on relatively stable forms. Next to this rather static approach, the circuit of Creative Writing was founded in the 1930s as an academic institution (Myers, McGurl, Wandor). Creative Writing pedagogy is mostly associated with the workshop form (in MFA programs or summer courses), but some of its teachers, for example, Janet Burroway, John Gardner, and Robert Olen Butler, have also published important manuals and anthologies. A third type of advice that emerged in the 1930s and 1940s brings literary advice close to the self-help industry (Wandor, Peary). Popular handbooks such as Dorothea Brande's *Becoming a Writer* (1934) or Brenda Ueland's *If You Want to Write: A Book about Art, Independence and Spirit* (1938) no longer concentrate on technical advice, but promote creative processes in general and a writerly life. They appeal to folk psychology (Brande) or to mysticism (Ueland) in their advice to stimulate the unconscious and the creative spirit/muse and to overcome all kinds of mental blocks.

Although Andrew Levy observes a waning of literary advice in the 1950s and 1960s—though with some classics like Brande and Ueland remaining in print—publishers like The Writer and Writer's Digest have managed to retain their position up to the present day. Instead of disappearing with the advent of the internet, a huge revival of handbooks and other types of advice occurred toward the end of the twentieth century. This "new wave" coincides with a massive diversification of the market and the appearance of some "newer" forms and formats in various media. First of all, manuals come closer in design to school textbooks, incorporating exercises and worksheets. Software writing programs such as Scribnr incorporate these worksheets and plans in their design. Second, "writer's memoirs" by many well-known authors—Stephen King, Patricia Highsmith, John Gardner, Nathalie Goldberg, and Anne Lamott—take their authors' successful careers as the vantage point for advice and inspiration (Wandor, 115).

Advice is also increasingly found in interviews, following the famous *Paris Review* interview series that focuses on "*The Art of* ...." *(Fiction, Screenwriting* and *Poetry)* (Masschelein, 26). Finally, the genre looks for original, often parodic formats to sell its wares in a highly saturated market, for example, by offering negative formats like *How Not to Write a Novel* (Mittelmark and Newman) and *How NOT to Get Published* (Gilman), or *The Writer's Rehab* (Gilles), a twelve-step program for writers.

The rules of the game

Although Edgar Allan Poe is generally considered the father of both the detective genre and of literary advice in general, he never provided direct advice about the detective or mystery writing. Still, according to Carolyn Wells, Poe is a "Necromancer," a master of the mystery tale, and therefore "we do no better than to study both his own stories, and his essays in criticism of them" (Wells, 291).[1] Wells's *The Technique of the Mystery* was commissioned in 1913 by Joseph Berg Esenwein, founder of the Home Correspondence School and the classic series "The Writer's Library" (Levy, 97). A blend of criticism and advice for aspiring writers, often in the form of warnings or prohibitions, the book is full of examples. Wells not only discusses a large repertoire of detective fiction, she also refers to a lot of writings about the detective story, although it is not clear where this information comes from, due to the lack of an index and bibliography.

Wells's title highlights that the mystery story is about technique rather than art. In fact, this constitutes the most important feature of early advice on the detective genre, that is, its definition not in terms of literature but in terms of an intellectual game or puzzle. Throughout the first decades of the twentieth century this analogy colors the rhetoric used to describe the genre:

> There will be less "beautiful" passages, fewer lofty flights, and the flow of English will not be so charming; but, these qualities aside, all the remaining points go to the mystery as a genre. For ingenious plot, logical movement, relentless subordination of means to ends, suppression of the irrelevant and unimportant character contrasts, sustained and climactic interested, and all the qualities that go to make up absorbing narration, the mystery yarn is unsurpassed. It is like a fictive game of chess, a story-telling foxchase, a promising literary bass strike—combined. (Esenwein in Wells, xii)

As a riddle, the mystery fits in a very long tradition of world literature, going back to the Sphinx in Greek and Egyptian mythology, to Buddhist and Arabic literature (Wells, 41). In terms of a game, it is likened to particularly British pastimes: chess, bridge, foxhunts, or cricket.

The definition of the mystery story as an intellectual game leads to a number of characteristics that are hardly literary as such. First, the genre appeals to the intellect, the driving motor for the reader being curiosity, the desire to find the solution to the mystery or puzzle. Second, the reader is conceived as a mirror image of the detective. What brings the two together is the notion of deduction, as the reader too strives to read the clues and piece them together. As readers become more familiar with the genre, the competition with the detective provides an additional pleasure for readers, but also a challenge for writers. Third, in order to guarantee the fairness of the game, it is governed by strict rules that writer and reader must observe. One of the main functions of advice, therefore, is to clarify the nature of the game and to outline the specific rules of the genre.

The most classic examples of sets of rules that are regularly reprinted and still circulate on the internet are those issued in the late 1920s by famous detective authors S. S. Van Dine, author of the Philo Vance series, and Father Ronald Knox, a British priest. S. S. Van Dine's "Twenty Rules for Writing Detective Fiction" first appeared in 1928 in *American Magazine* and served as "a sort Credo, based partly on the practice of all great writers of detective stories and partly on the promptings of the honest author's inner conscience." Quite a number of Van Dine's rules have to do with the fair play between reader and writer. Thus rule number 1 that states that "The reader must have equal opportunity with the detective for solving the mystery. All clues must be plainly stated and described" (Van Dine). Other rules are quite specific: there can only be one detective and one culprit, who cannot be a professional criminal or mafia member. The crime must be murder, because "three hundred pages is far too much pother for a crime other than murder."

One year later, Ronald A. Knox issued even sterner advice in his "Ten Commandments for Detective Fiction" (1929/1935), which first appeared in a magazine and was later used as an introduction to a collection of *Best Detective Stories*. Knox formulates his rules in terms of fervent interdictions, things that "must/must not" be done, "are ruled out," or that "no accident must ever help." However, in the accompanying article, he tones down the absoluteness of the commandments, emphasizing that they are not set in stone and providing counter-examples to his sometimes surprisingly specific rules, for example, no Chinamen (rule V) and no twin brothers and doubles (rule X). Contrary to Van Dine and Wells, Knox does not deduce his rules from his own practice and from other detective stories; instead, they follow directly from his definition of the mystery story in terms borrowed from classical poetics. The mystery is a "*hysteron—proteron*," in other words, "the true essence of the detective story... is that in it the action takes place before the story begins." The "highly specialized rules" required for this type of story emphasize the importance of both plot and plotting.

Wells also suggested that the mystery must be written "backward, if need be; but see to it that every incident and every episode, every speech of the characters and every hint of the author have their direct bearing on the statement of the problem or the quest to its solution" (Wells 291–2). She attributes this idea to Poe, but she also underpins it by listing extensively the exact work methods used by lesser-known authors such as Dr. Nevil Monroe Hopkins, Henry Kitchell Webster, including a diagram of Mr. Gelett Burgess.

Some common characteristics are striking in this early stage of advice. First, these authors have a penchant for lists. Second, they implicitly or explicitly refer to a body of literary advice that circulates in this period. Early advice authors possess a good knowledge of their own genre, so they can illustrate their arguments with examples. Third, in connection with the awareness of the genre, there is the dominance of negative rules, that is, things that a writer must *not* do, especially in order to avoid certain stereotypes of the genre. Wells repeatedly warns her readers against clichés, sometimes in almost dramatic terms: "And oh, young writer, avoid, as you would the plague, the introduction of shreds or threads of wearing apparel as incriminating evidence!" (Wells, 175). Similarly, Van Dine's twentieth rule rounds up plot devices that "have been employed too often, and are familiar to all true lovers of literary crime."

From Poe to Aristotle: Mystery as literary genre

Throughout the 1930s and 1940s, quite a lot of advice continued to appear in small writers' magazines such as *The Writer* and *The Spicy Detective*, alongside the first "criticism" of the genre, usually not only by famous detective authors, but also by fans of the genre. In this body of meta-literature, we gradually perceive the outlines of a new phase in the writing on the detective story that can be related to an evolution within the genre itself. In the definition of the mystery story, the emphasis shifts from the notion of puzzle towards that of literary genre, albeit of a specific kind. An interesting testimony in this respect is a lecture delivered by one of the British star authors of the 1930s. In "Aristotle on Detective Fiction" Dorothy Sayers proposes an Aristotelian model for the detective story: "Now, to anyone who reads the *Poetics* with an unbiased mind, it is evident that Aristotle was not so much a student of his own literature as a prophet of the future ... what, in his heart of hearts, he desired was a Good Detective Story" (Sayers,24).

In Sayers's account, the detective story completely conforms to Aristotle's prescriptions for the tragedy: it evokes fear and pity and leads through intellect and emotion to catharsis. Moreover, the detective plot is also based on a three-act structure consisting of Peripety, Discovery (the process of detection), and Suffering. Finally, Sayers borrows a term from Aristotle, "paralogism—the art of the false syllogism," to reformulate the core of the mystery story in ethical, rather than in ludic terms: the detective story is the "art of *framing lies in the right way* ... the right method is to tell the *truth* in such a way that the *intelligent* reader is seduced into telling the lie for himself" (30–31). By ironically treating the mystery as the rightful heir of the tragedy, the highest literary genre, Sayers achieves a double goal: she heightens its literary and moral status and at the same time she fixes its form as an established, universal formula—a basic fixture in a lot of literary advice—that is, Aristotle's three-act structure.

In his 1948 *Harper's Magazine* essay "The Guilty Vicarage. Notes on the Detective, by an Addict," W. H. Auden highlights milieu rather than plot and character (usually the focus of early advice) in order to come to a new definition of the figure of the detective. No longer conceiving the genre as a mere intellectual game, he arrives at an ethical point of view: "The interest in the detective is the dialectic between innocence and guilt" (Auden, 406). This idea not only guides Auden's discussion of the most perfect representatives of the genre—Sherlock Holmes, Inspector French, and Father Brown—but it also allows him to pinpoint the difference between the detective story and genuine literature, for, like his predecessors, he is adamant that the detective is "escape literature, not works of art" (Auden, 412).[2] If literature has the uncanny ability to make the reader identify with a murderer, the detective story raises suspicions but ultimately appeases all forms of guilt (whether Freudian or Christian). This is the reason why Auden compares the pleasure of the genre not to a game between writer and reader but to an "addiction." Like tobacco or alcohol, the reader keeps craving for the fake Edenic restoration of a fallen universe by the *deus ex machina* of the detective, even when he knows that there is no innocence in the world.

Hence, the detective novel is a guilty pleasure that cannot be considered art due to its formulaic nature. However, as an "anti-literary" genre it stands in dialectical relation to art, in that it shows negatively what literature is. Paradoxically, Auden values the detective story precisely because it is everything that (high modernist) literature is not. This view is shared by Father Knox, who is adamant that "You cannot write a Gertrude Stein detective story." Likewise, the most commercial handbook from the period in our selection, Marie F. Rodell's *Mystery Fiction. Theory and Technique* (first issued in 1943, and republished for the British market in 1954) is very specific about the type of literature to which the detective story belongs: "modern escape fiction" (Rodell, 85).

Paradoxically, then, while there is a tendency to highlight classical characteristics of the mystery, seemingly in order to elevate its literary status, there is also an acute awareness of the exact position of the genre. As one of the higher genres within a "literature of escape," it is a suitable, intellectual pastime for readers of serious literature. Moreover, the detective genre is valued—also by modernist authors such as T. S. Eliot, Auden, and Walter Benjamin—precisely because of its modernity.

The detective story as a modern genre

A fascinating plea for the genre's modernity is found in Howard Haycraft's *Murder for Pleasure* (1941), a curious mix of literary history, criticism, and literary advice that constitutes an essential moment in the consolidation of the mystery genre. Haycraft sketches the evolution of the detective genre from strict formulaic writing toward a more literary style and subtler characterization. In addition to his emphasis on the literary qualities of the detective novel, he also advances a new argument for its value that is directly related to the time of his writing, the beginning of World War II. In his view, detective fiction is increasingly popular and topical in times of war, because it combines distraction with a moral stand as it defends democratic values and the modern institution of juridical procedures. In chapter XV, "Detectives, Democrats and Dictators," Haycraft argues that the detective novel is a quintessential modern genre, one that requires the emergence of a police system as well as democracy. For this reason the genre has been strongest in the democratic countries of England, France,

America, and to a lesser extent Scandinavia, as opposed to Germany and Central Europe (Haycraft, 315).

In his book Haycraft brings together the existing norms of advice, including some German and French sources and a number of early manuals, most of them from the 1930s. He boils down the essence of the detective story to two basic principles: fair play and readability (225). He also emphasizes how emotion and drama must be balanced against the puzzle element. Although Haycraft's advice is in many respects close to Wells's from 1913, he links it to different periods, types, and fashions of the genre, most notably the difference between the British and the American style. Indeed, his book is consistently structured around the juxtaposition of Britain and America in various eras. From the perspective of literary advice, the rise of the American or hard-boiled detective story is a direct response to the emphasis on rules and rigid formulas.

As discussed earlier, the superiority of the English detective stories is often assumed in writings of the 1930s. At the same time, it is not a coincidence that Raymond Chandler explicitly attacks Sayers in "The Simple Art of Murder" (1945). In his view, English detective fiction is dull and predictable; it lacks interesting psychology and is badly written. Instead, he advocates first and foremost a new, realistic style, exemplified by Dashiell Hammett. Moreover, by suggesting that Hammett may have been influenced by Hemingway, he reclaims it as an American genre while at the same time boosting its literary status. When we take a closer look at the list of rules attributed to Chandler, we see how besides unity of plot, necessity of solution, and fair play, new elements such as realism, credibility, simplicity, and style gain in importance (Parsons, 129).

The difference between the English and American mystery story is not just a literary or stylistic matter; it is also related to the literary life in which the detective writer is embedded. Haycraft addresses this side of writing when he discusses issues such as manuscript length, copyright, and possible revenues from books, magazines and detective writers' clubs and associations both in England and America. As a historical genre, detective fiction faces both an internal and an external threat. Internally, the genre could either be on the verge of exhausting itself by lack of quality (as Van Doren Stern suggests), or (and this is Haycraft's position) it may have reached maturity, able to be maintained by regular internal renewal. This renewal—the rise of several subgenres (e.g., the character detective in England and the hard-boiled style in the United States)—must be regarded as "essentially sub-developments, sidelines, of the main issue" (Haycraft, 325). The external threat is related to the conception of the detective story as a democratic genre. Although the genre receives a boost during the war, it may be threatened by the same forces that threaten the world at large. Ultimately, Haycraft concludes that the political victory of America will also determine the genre's future:

> by sheer compulsion of world events the future of the detective story may well lie in America. If this should prove to be the case, the present book can conclude its major argument on no more useful note than a plea to American publishers: to study the form seriously; to insist on at least the same standards which they *require* of their general fiction (and adherence to the special rules as well); to eschew cheap and shoddy craftsmanship, even at the sacrifice of immediate profit. (Haycraft, 326, emphasis in original)

One of the authors who may have heeded Haycraft's plea is Marie F. Rodell, a prominent editor of crime fiction and a mystery author herself (Weiman). Her *Mystery Fiction: Theory and Technique* first appeared in 1943 and was republished for the British market in 1954. Rodell is an interesting figure, because she moves away from the mix of criticism and advice, and hence a mixed audience of fans and aspiring writers. Throughout, she addresses beginning authors, who are interested in making a living from their pen. Rodell's practical and commercial stance entails a new perspective on the reader. No longer a participant in an intellectual game, the reader is a client whose expectations must be satisfied. Whereas Haycraft saw genres as primarily stylistic variations to ensure the internal dynamism of the genre, Rodell takes genre expectations very seriously and adapts her advice to the different mystery subgenres (the detective story, the horror story, the mystery-adventure story, and the literary mystery). In an odd mixture of Freudian terminology and commercial reasoning, she also issues a number of taboos, rather than rules, especially related to sexuality and politics. These topics may offend (female) readers and hence affect sales. "As escape literature, the mystery is not designed to preach a message, correct an evil, or advocate Utopia. Controversies on questions such as these are among the things the reader is trying to escape from" (Rodell, 68–71).

Rodell's book marks a clear shift in mystery advice for various reasons. Her advice is "businesslike" (xii), "wise and sensible" (xv), and above all practical. She proposes a clear work plan—first the plotting of the crime, then the plotting of the detection process, and finally the actual writing—and illustrates it with a story that she makes up from scratch, not with reference to existing examples. She also diversifies the genre and the market, not only by foregrounding different subgenres and their audiences and by differentiating between the American and the English market, but also by including different media. Rodell's advice is encompassing but it is also highly specialized and precise, both in the guidelines she issues and in the audience she addresses. This new feature marks a break with the earlier tradition in which advice and criticism are intertwined and announces the direction that mystery advice will take in the last half of the twentieth century and into the twenty-first.

The contemporary mystery market

Like the genre they deal with, contemporary handbooks have become more varied and seemingly also more complex. And yet, it is quite striking that mystery advice still projects a more or less constant image, manifesting unity in diversity rather than a multitude of approaches and methods.[3] A first observation is the large number of advice books in the market since the 1990s.[4] Clearly the idea of one single method has become subsidiary to the commercial value of this branch of publications, with now dozens of titles on writing detective fiction. Written by "star" teachers or by mystery authors, they are primarily distributed and produced by specialized publishing houses, often within series of advice for different genres. Since the advent and popularity of quality detective series on television, contemporary handbooks no longer define the genre as an intellectual game but as a transmedial genre, based on realism and plausibility. Although most advice authors do recognize that fiction is different from reality, they invariably emphasize the importance of getting all the details and procedures right and of doing a lot of research. This has led to highly specialized reference series such as Writer's Digest's "Howdunit," which includes volumes dealing with police procedures (Wingate and Stevens) or poisons (Stevens with Klarner).

Unlike earlier advice books, contemporary handbook titles do not refer to art, technique or craft, but they all foreground the act of writing: *Writing the Modern Mystery* (Barbara Neville), *Writing and Selling the Mystery Novel: How to Knock 'em Dead with Style* (Hallie Ephron), *How to Write Killer Fiction* (Carolyn Wheat), *How to Write a Mystery* (Larry Beinhart), *Writing the Mystery* (G. Miki Hayden), *The Weekend Novelist Writes a Mystery* (Robert J. Ray and Jack Remick), *How to Write a Damn Good Mystery* (James Frey), *Now Write! Mysteries* (edited by Sherry Ellis and Laurie Lamson), and *Masterclass: Writing Crime Fiction* (Rowe). The writing process is described in phases that are reminiscent of the "five Canons" of classical Aristotelian rhetoric. The first phase is that of "invention" (finding the ideal material for the story, usually a news event or a real life case). This is followed by "arrangement" (plotting crime, process of detection, characters, and setting) and the choice of "style," that is, determining the exact "subgenre" of the mystery. The phase of "delivering" is the actual writing of the story. This phase usually receives more attention than in earlier handbooks and includes discussions of narrative components—for example, beginning and ending, conflict and tension, building authentic characters—alongside style, grammar, and dialogue. The final classical rhetorical phase is "memory" (the actual pronunciation of the speech). In handbooks, this is transposed to entering the market (sending the manuscript in the right format and approaching publishers and agents) and becoming a writer. Because of the commercial goal of handbooks, this part has become quite specific, sometimes including sample letters and indicating which letter font is preferable. Moreover, advice authors also talk about the many challenges of literary life—from writer's block and dealing with rejection to the impact of a literary agent, copyright, and the organization of book tours—and they give advice on further reading, both literary reading and other manuals and reference books.

In general, the expansion and evolution of mystery advice in the past few decades can be summarized under the heading of professionalization. While handbooks stress that writing is (hard) work, at the same time they convey the illusion that if you follow all the instructions and do the exercises, you may have a manuscript ready to be published by the time you've finished reading the handbook. While dos and don'ts remain very important in handbooks, the normativity is toned down by the use of examples and exercises in writing and rewriting. Thus, contemporary advice presents an ambiguous picture. On the one hand, the tone is informal, often colloquial, and the approach offered is hands-on, by using examples or a step-by-step approach. In this way, manuals adopt the professionalism of the workshop. They present themselves as private coaches and address the reader in a motivational manner. At the same time, they also position themselves as part of the mystery field itself, primarily through style and layout that mimic detective novels (often using colors like black, red, and yellow and visual motifs associated with crime and detection, like guns or magnifying glasses). Moreover, the handbook author's prestige within this particular genre is stressed. Not only the writers of handbooks, but also the many interviewees who testify about their career or talk about specific aspects, are invariably presented as award-winners and experts. Finally, because these books often address screenwriters as well as people writing for publication, the mystery market appears as a relatively independent field that covers several media. This explains the huge influence of screenwriting terminology—for example, dialogue, story beats, conflict and tension, and three-act structures—and the emphasis on seriality in contemporary handbooks, used interchangeably with the older models and formulas that have remained virtually the same as in early advice.

Conclusion

The first aim of our overview of mystery advice is to demonstrate the scholarly importance of this neglected corpus in various respects, both from a synchronic and a diachronic point of view. First of all, handbooks for creative writing offer an exemplary perspective on readers' and writers' expectations. They formulate, so to say, a kind of "normative poetics," indicating what a good detective novel should (or should not) be. Moreover, they play an important role in outlining the genre and its different subgenres. Whereas early handbooks primarily stressed the genre's intrinsic characteristics and addressed a broad audience of aspiring authors, fans, and literary critics, contemporary handbooks are specialized and focus on all aspects of the writing process, from its very inception up to the publication of a successful title.

The literary dimension of detective fiction is dealt with in a rather ambiguous way. Initially, detective stories were evaluated in terms of the intellectual challenges they offered to their readers, as compensation for their low literary status. Moreover, their modernity also increased their popularity with elitist modernist writers, not as literary artefacts but as fascinating, even addictive signs of contemporary life. In spite of the attempts in the 1930s and 1940s to increase the literary status of the genre and its later adoption by postmodern authors, contemporary handbooks are conspicuously ambiguous about the genre's literary status. On the one hand, they discuss all kinds of literary concepts and literary questions: point of view, characters, plausible narration, and stylistic refinement. Some chapters clearly bear influences from modern(ist) poetics. Yet the literary ambition of the aspiring writer remains secondary to the intrinsic mechanisms of detective fiction as such, regardless of its literary prestige. Instead, prestige is sought within the subfield of the mystery genre. Moreover, the market for detective and mystery fiction is now profoundly transmedial.

Finally, with regard to the detective novel as world literature, we have come to the remarkable conclusion that the national pedigree of the detective story all but disappeared from the manuals written at the end of the twentieth century. Our predominantly Anglo-Saxon corpus is canonical in the sense that it is a standard body of advice referenced by mystery writing sites and other handbooks. Within this corpus we see a clear evolution. Whereas earlier handbook writers were concerned with national traditions, contemporary handbooks generally perpetuate a conservative and universalist poetics. At the same time, advice writers today are well aware of the diversity of the genre and its multiple subgenres (e.g., cozies, police procedurals, private investigators or private eyes), but this aspect of writing is treated as a relatively minor question and is seldom related to regional factors. In our view, this is because Anglo-Saxon handbooks are more concerned with the potential of different media than with different international markets.

While literary advice books also exist in other languages including French, German, and Dutch, when it comes to more commercial genres, they are largely constituted of translations of English manuals. When we were looking for literary advice specific for the "polar" or "thriller" on the French market (where there is a proper tradition of literary advice and ateliers d'écriture), we have found no original manuals for the mystery novel and very few book-length translations (Jute). A notable exception, though, is *Comment écrire un polar suédois sans se fatiguer* (Lange), a translation of a Swedish graphic novel from 2015. This advice book is a newer, more playful format that incorporates all the different dimensions of advice outlined earlier, and offers writing advice starting from successful Swedish classics by writers such as Stieg Larsson and Henning Mankell.

Scandinavian crime fiction has been a successful fixture in the international mystery scene since the 1960s and has recently been very successful on television. This evolution was already predicted by Haycraft in 1941, and there are a number of recent critical studies of the phenomena on the market (Forshaw, Peacock, and Bergman). And yet, this important regional variant's international success is not reflected in contemporary handbooks. In our corpus, we have not encountered references to Scandinavian crime fiction.

To conclude, then, while mystery advice is and always has been attuned to changes in the market, today, unlike at the beginning of the twentieth century, it no longer includes regional and national variations in its instructions. Heeding the lessons of the most commercial of early advice authors, Marie F. Rodell,

Anglophone mystery advice nowadays prefers neutrality over diversity and technical accuracy over cultural specificity. Highly professional in its pedagogy and accessible to all, the advice industry primarily wants to keep the customer satisfied, by fostering the idea that everyone can write a mystery and that all mysteries are created equal.

Notes

This research on Handbooks for Creative writing is part of the "Literature and Media Innovation" project, funded by Belspo. The authors thank Arne Vanraes and Gert-Jan Meyntjens for their useful comments.

1. According to its editor, Wells's textbook is "the first exhaustive study of the genre that has ever been brought out" (Wells, xiii) and also the earliest one we have found. This is a common claim made by handbook authors; see also Roddell. A comprehensive list of early critical and advisory writings on the detective genre is given in the chapter "Friends and Foes of the Detective" in Howard Haycraft's *Murder for Pleasure* (1946). From Haycraft's accompanying bibliography, it seems that Carolyn Wells's *The Technique of the Mystery* (1913) is the first advice book, and that it long occupied "top-position among the 'how-to-do-it' manuals in America, despite its age and its somewhat desultory and repetitive treatment of the subject" (Haycraft, 274).
2. The term "escape literature" or "literature of escape" in this period is opposed to "literature of expression" and coincides with the distinction between popular and serious or high (modernist) literature.
3. Levy notes a similar trend for short story handbooks and points out that despite differences in style and tone, the continuities are in fact more evident (Levy, 105).
4. Our selection is based on a number of bibliographies, found on websites like Goodreads and The Thrilling Detective as well as on Amazon searches.

Works Cited

"Listopia. Best Books on Detective Fiction." http://www.goodreads.com/list/show/92010.Best_Books_on_Writing_and_Editing_Mystery_Suspense_Thriller_and_Crime_Fiction

"Murder in the Library: Bibliography." http://www.thrillingdetective.com/trivia/biblio.html

Auden, W. H. (1948). "The Guilty Vicarage. Notes on the Detective, by an Addict" *Harper's Magazine*, May, 406–12.

Beinhart, Larry (1996). *How to Write a Mystery.* New York: Ballantine Books.
Bergman, Kerstin (2014). *Swedish Crime Fiction: The Making of Nordic Noir.* Stockholm: Mimesis International.
Brande, Dorothea ([1934] 1981). *Becoming a Writer.* New York: Jeremy P. Tarcher.
Burroway, Janet (2014). *Writing Fiction. A Guide to Narrative Craft.* 9th ed. New York: Longman.
Butler, Robert Olen (2006). *From Where You Dream. The Process of Writing Fiction.* New York: Grove Press/Atlantic Monthly Press.
Chandler, Raymond (1934). *The Simple Art of Murder.* New York: Curtis Publishing.
Chandler, Raymond (1985). "Ten Commandments for Detective Novels." Parsons.
De Geest, Dirk, and An Goris (2010). "Constrained Writing, Creative Writing: The Case of Handbooks for Writing Romances." *Poetics Today* 31:1, 81–106.
Ellis, Sherry, and Laurie Lamson, eds. (2011). *Now Write! Mysteries.* New York: Jeremy P. Tarcher/Penguin.
Ephron, Hallie (2005). *Writing and Selling Your Mystery Novel: How to Knock 'em Dead with Style.* Cincinnati, Ohio: Writer's Digest Books.
Forshaw, Barry (2013a). *Death in a Cold Climate: A Guide to Scandinavian Crime Fiction (Crime Files).* Basingstoke: Palgrave MacMillan.
Forshaw, Barry (2013b). *Nordic Noir.* Harpenden: Pocket Essentials.
Frey, James N. (2004). *How to Write a Damn Good Mystery: A Practical Step-by-Step Guide from Inspiration to Finished Manuscript.* New York: Saint Martin's Press.
Gardner, John ([1983] 1991). *The Art of Fiction. Notes on Craft for Young Writers.* New York: Vintage Books.
Gilles, D. B. (2013). *The Writer's Rehab. A 12 Step Guide for Writer's Who Can't Get Their Act Together.* Los Angeles: Michael Wiese Production.
Gilman, Claire (2013). *How NOT to Get Published.* Abingdon: Teach Yourself.
Goldberg, Natalie ([1986] 2005). *Writing Down the Bone:. Freeing the Writer Within.* Boston: Shambhala Publications.
Grimstad, Paul (2016). "What Makes Great Detective Fiction According to T. S. Elliot?" *The New Yorker* (February 2). http://www.newyorker.com/books/page-turner/what-makes-great-detective-fiction-according-to-t-s-eliot?
Haycraft, Howard (1941). *Murder for Pleasure: The Life and Times of the Detective Story.* New York: Appleton-Century.
Hayden, Miki G. (2001). *Writing the Mystery: A Start-to-Finish Guide for Both Novice and Professional.* Philadelphia: Intrigue Press.
Highsmith, Patricia (1983). *Plotting and Writing Suspense Fiction.* New York: Saint Martin's Griffin.
Hilliard, Christopher (2006). *To Exercise our Talent: The Democratization of Writing in Britain.* Cambridge, MA: Harvard University Press.
James, P. D. (2009). *Talking About Detective Fiction.* New York: Knopf.

Jute, André (2003). *Comment écrire un thriller: L'art et la manière de composer et de réussir à la publier*, trans. Martine Falguières. Paris: Gremese.

Kaplan, Alice (2007). "Writer Brenda Ueland and the Story She Never Shared." *The American Scholar* (September 1). https://theamericanscholar.org/lady-of-the-lake/#.V02e17597ox

King, Stephen ([2000] 2012). *On Writing: A Memoir of the Craft*. London: Hodder Press.

Knox, Ronald A. (1929). "Ten Commandments for Detective Fiction." http://gadetection.pbworks.com/w/page/7931441/Ronald%20Knox%27s%20Ten%20Commandments%20for%20Detective%20Fiction

Lamott, Anne (1980). *Bird by Bird: Some Instructions on Writing and Life*. New York: Anchor Books.

Lange, Hendrik (2015). *Comment écrire un polar Suédois sans se fatiguer*. Paris: Editions ça et là.

Levy, Andrew (1993). *The Culture and Commerce of the American Short Story*. Cambridge: Cambridge University Press.

Masschelein, Anneleen, Christophe Meurée, David Martens, and Stéphanie Vanasten (2014). "The Literary Interview: For a Poetics of a Hybrid Genre." *Poetics Today* 34:1–2, 1–49.

McGurl, Mark (2009). *The Program Era: Postwar Fiction and the Rise of Creative Writing*. Cambridge, MA: Harvard University Press.

Mittelmark, Howard, and Sandra Newman (2008). *How Not to Write a Novel: 200 Classic Mistakes and How To Avoid Them—A Misstep-by-Misstep Guide*. London: William Morrow Paperbacks.

Monroe, Jonathan (2015). "Genre." In *Literature Now: Key Terms and Methods for Literary History*, ed. Sascha Bru, Ben de Bruyn, and Michel Delville. Edinburgh: Edinburgh University Press, 252–64.

Myers, David Gershom (2006). *The Elephants Teach: Creative Writing Since 1880*. Chicago: University of Chicago Press.

Nestingen, Andrew, and Paula Arvas, eds. (2011). *Scandinavian Crime Fiction*. Cardiff: University of Wales Press.

Norville, Barbara (1986). *Writing the Modern Mystery*. Cincinnati: Writer's Digest Books.

Parsons, Nicholas, ed. (1985). *The Book of Literary Lists: A Collection of Annotated Lists, Statistics and Anecdotes Concerning Books*. London: Sidgwick and Jackson.

Peacock, Stephen (2014). *Swedish Crime Fiction: Novel, Film, Television*. Manchester: Manchester University Press.

Peary, Alexandria (2014). "Taking Self-Help Books Seriously: The Informal Aesthetic Education of Writers." *The Journal of Aesthetic Education* 42, 86–104.

Ray, Robert J., and Jack Remick (1998). *The Weekend Novelist Writes a Mystery*. New York: Dell Trade Publishing.

Rodell, Marie F. ([1943] 1954). *Mystery Fiction: Theory and Technique*. London: Hammond, Hammond and Company.

Rowe, Rosemary (2014). *Masterclass. Writing Crime Fiction*. London: John Murray Learning.

Sayers, Dorothy L. (1936). "Aristotle on Detective Fiction." *English* 1:1, 23–35.

Stern, Philip Van Doren (1941). "The Case of the Corpse in the Blind Alley." *Virginia Quarterly Review* 17: 227–36.

Stevens, Serita Debora, with Anne Klarner (1990). *Deadly Dose: A Writer's Guide to Poisons*. Cincinnati: Writer's Digest Books.

Ueland, Brenda ([1938] 2007). *If You Want to Write. A Book about Independence, Art and Spirit*. New York: Graywolf Press.

Van Dine, S. S. (1928). "Twenty Rules for Writing Detective Stories," *The American Magazine*, (September). http://gaslight.mtroyal.ca/vandine.htm

Wandor, Micheline (2008). *The Author is Not Dead, Merely Somewhere Else: Creative Writing Reconceived*. Basingstoke: Palgrave MacMillan.

Wells, Carolyn (1913). *The Technique of the Mystery Story*. Boston: The Writer's Library.

Wheat, Carolyn (2003). *How to Write Killer Fiction*. Santa Barbara: Perseverance Press.

Wingate, Anne (1992). *Scene of the Crime: A Writer's Guide to Crime-Scene Investigations*. Cincinnati: Writer's Digest Books.

8

Covering Crime Fiction: Merging the Local into Cosmopolitan Mediascapes

Louise Nilsson

When browsing online or in a bookstore, we often find ourselves—despite the adage—judging books by their covers, for the cover locates the work generically and in many other ways. Crime fiction in particular gives itself away with ominous, iconic images of guns, silhouettes, bodies, and settings, as well as a predictable color palette. These jackets, emblazoned with the typically aphoristic title, eye-catching font, and gruesome images, deploy the aesthetic not only to establish the novel as crime fiction, but also to create a mood of suspense (perhaps even providing clues and leads about the plot and suspect), evoking the corresponding allure in the target reader. This approach illuminates the power of representation and how easily the book cover frames the narrative on a commercial book market and within a specific genre.

A crime novel's cover visually carries the narrative it encloses. To serve as a marketing strategy, it must use a noir aesthetic resonant with both contemporary society and a cultural heritage to create a certain perception of the story while intersecting with a profit-driven transnational book market. Though these significant functions are seldom considered by scholars, book covers are exquisite sources to help us better understand how a domestic literature circulates in a transnational context. The narrative's framing involves a negotiation—deeply rooted in marketing strategies—between a book's content and its context in a commercial market. Through marketing and the use of symbols, book covers shed light on how literature becomes meaningfully represented outside its domestic context.

When analyzing covers, many aspects warrant consideration: genre, aesthetics, domestic publishing patterns and traditions, target groups, existing values, and specific cultural and national contexts. This essay examines the negotiation between a book's content and its representation in different cultural contexts by showing how marketing strategies have enabled Swedish crime fiction to become a globally shared or world literature. The subgenre Nordic Noir is known narratively for its uniqueness or exoticism and aesthetically for its wintery book covers. This seemingly logical, straightforward encapsulation belies the complexity of marketing foreign literatures in new transnational, cosmopolitan mediascapes, oversimplifying the metamorphosis of domestic crime fiction into the international phenomenon Nordic Noir, a literary transformation of once uncertain success.

When a domestic literature is integrated—and often assimilated—into another national and cultural context, the appearances of the books become especially crucial, either in reinforcing the branding of a known author or series, or else in setting the tone for a new entry into the market. A foreign publication joining the ranks of a publisher's series is couched by preconceptions. In France and Italy the domestic crime series *Actes Sud* and *Il Giallo* integrate Swedish crime fiction into the established context of well-known series for crime fiction. Book series and publishers build on their reputations, and thus novels serve to brand the author or connect to other successful authors within the genre. Bestselling Henning Mankell, followed by the overwhelming success of Stieg Larsson, paved the way for Nordic Noir as it emerged as a subgenre within the globally spread crime fiction genre. The bestseller is also an opportunity for a film company to try and generate a blockbuster. The movie adaptation, in turn, opens up a host of new opportunities to associate the book with a new set of activities and images. By boosting sales of the novel it may pave the way for a writer's international success. In such a scenario, the book cover becomes the face of the book as well as the further iteration connecting it to the movie.[1]

The cover designs for foreign editions must adjust to the sociocultural context of potential buyers outside the book's own national context. An interesting ripple effect emerges as a book becomes an international bestseller: suddenly, a specific cover or aesthetic gains recognition worldwide and the book begins to travel the globe, often in the company of similar cover images. An example of such images are the now iconic covers for Stieg Larsson's Millennium Trilogy with their abstract covers in yellow, orange, and silver, with drawings of dragons, fire, and hornets that blend into the colors. Another example is Jamyang Norbu's *The Mandala of Sherlock Holmes*, which travels the globe with different covers and titles that tone down the book's complexity and political agenda, and instead emphasize its place in the crime fiction genre.

Such universality lies at the heart of this essay, which aims to show how crime fiction, as a domestic literature, is integrated through its covers into a media landscape and reaches popular culture internationally to become, through marketing, a visually propelled glocal literature.

While covers position all sorts of books for their expected markets, crime fiction covers are particularly notable in two respects: first, in the ways they do or do not attempt to represent the story's local setting (already highly stylized in most crime fiction); and second, in the reciprocity stemming from the genre's popularity, whereby successful crime novels regularly become motion pictures, and images from those in turn adorn the original novels' covers; the film remarkets the book. I argue that the marketing strategies behind crime fiction covers circulating in different media contexts not only hearken to narrative and genre conventions, but they also follow an aesthetic invoking specific associations, often loosely connected to the narrative yet situating the work in a broader cinematic and literary-historical context. Here the puzzle pieces of the death aesthetic fall into place, revealing a cosmopolitan collage deeply rooted in macabre visual expressions presented for leisure and entertainment, a trend dating back through centuries of cultural history and folklore.

Breaking down covers

A common approach to studying covers is quantitative, and finds its inspiration in the work of Gérard Genette, statistically surveying paratexts (blurbs on the back cover, titles, additional text appearances on the cover).[2] Another common approach in book-market studies stems from Pierre Bourdieu's work on distinction and the separation of products into high- and low-brow literatures, drawing upon sociological studies about the book market's changes and flows.

My own approach is qualitative and employs discourse analysis as a theoretical and methodological point of departure. I understand crime fiction as a discursive field—a network consisting of elements and nodal points that connect and build on each other. The nodal points forming this discursive field can include subgenres, iconic works, authors, and domestic literature. This discursive field is not static but flexible, yielding an openness where new nodal points can emerge. An established genre, crime fiction holds a hegemonic position on the book market, intersecting with a number of discourses: entertainment culture, social critique, self-positioning as a literature that is political and that challenges cultural norms and views on gender, ethnicity, morals, ethics, and so on. This approach follows Ernesto Laclau's and Chantal Mouffe's development of discourse as a system of social relations consisting of both linguistic and nonlinguistic phenomena, including forms of behavior or visual representations (Howarth 2000: 101; Laclau and Mouffe 1985).

My analysis of book covers connects specifically to this nonlinguistic dimension. Within this discursive field, elements appear continuously, striving to establish identities and subject positions. Elements then compete to strengthen their position and become nodal points, which are constructed through linguistic as well as nonlinguistic practices. Consider a foreign literature or unknown writer, both elements within this discursive field. Through articulatory practices including the many elements that go into the construction of a compelling paratext, these can merge successfully into the field, connecting to other nodal points, then establishing independent identities to become fixed nodal points connected to others. As discourses are open, identities continuously change and evolve. Meaning, therefore, is only partially fixed within the field (Howarth 2000: 101–7).

Swedish crime fiction as a whole, I claim, has gone from being a foreign element to a well-established nodal point in many markets, by successfully articulating its own identity and by connecting to other nodal points of the discursive field via genre, nationality, author-branding, bestseller status, or place-representation and its specific geography. As Laclau and Mouffe discuss, a subject position can possess a number of social relations, all providing different identities. Thus, a domestic literature may represent the vernacular or national, and can circulate within the transnational field as a cosmopolitan literature. A crime fiction novel may spur entertainment-oriented movie or television adaptations, yet at the same time spotlight a specific social problem (thereby connecting to another discourse).

This essay will discuss how the articulatory practices surrounding Swedish crime fiction connect to the international discursive field of crime fiction and how it, as a domestic literature, visually merges with a cosmopolitan mediascape. Using Arne Dahl's *Misterioso* as my point of departure, I'll then expound on how a domestic literature visually merges with crime fiction's global discursive field and its cosmopolitan mediascape.

Cover stories

Misterioso (1999) is the inaugural novel in Dahl's series about a Stockholm-based crime-fighting squad called the *A-gruppen* (A-unit, the Intercrime Group in English translation). Its plot centers on a set of business leaders' murders, each shot twice in the head while a recording of Theolonius Monk's album *Misterioso* plays. While hunting the killer, the squad engages with several exciting red herrings such as the Russian Mafia, though the real villain turns out to be a Swedish everyman. A recording of Monk's classic piece at the Five Spot Café in New York in 1958 plays an important part in providing a lead to the killer: a bank clerk from southern Sweden who has gone violent after having been beaten up by a former customer whose loan application he had rejected. The villain suffered this abuse in a bar (where he'd gone to play a game of darts) with *Misterioso* playing from a tape deck. The trauma catapulted the bank clerk into seeking vengeance on wealthy businessmen, the symbols and guardians of an abusive economic system.[3]

In Sweden, Dahl's crime series has been adapted for the screen and in this format has been exported to Argentina, Chile, Finland, Germany, Japan, and the UK, among other countries. The book itself has been translated into thirty languages and launched in Europe, North America, Asia, and beyond. In translation, the majority of the book's publishers have kept its domestic title: *Misterioso*. Exceptions include the UK English translation, entitled *The Blinded Man* (the American edition was released as *Misterioso*).[4]

Most *Misterioso* covers of translated editions echo the plot and display conventional crime fiction images. Monk's *Misterioso* itself is a common theme: jackets for American, French, and Greek editions feature a cassette or close-ups of piano keys. The US Pantheon hardcover shows two crossed darts, while the Vintage Crime/Black Lizards paperback has a cassette, as does the Greek Metaichmio edition. The French *Point Policiers* jacket shows a cassette broken in half.[5] The German Kindle edition has a dartboard. An additional French edition from Seuil, published in the *Policiers* series, combines a dart with two hands playing a piano.[6] Although covers adjust to local commercial contexts, these similarities are evidence that symbols and images often replicate—without duplicating— each other, demonstrating how a book's themes tend to recur as they spread across national borders and into different cultural contexts. Intriguingly, the cover for the Italian edition, published in the *Il Giallo* series for domestic and foreign crime fiction, has a silhouette of a man holding a gun against a blue background patterned with faded black music notes. Baltos Lankos, publisher of the Lithuanian edition, designed a similar front cover: an aerial photograph of a seated person holding a gun (like the novel's killer-in-waiting). The UK cover for *The Blinded Man* depicts a male figure standing on a road. The Polish edition from Muza Publisher has a crucified hand (from a detective's encounter with the Russian Mafia). Despite diverging from the *Misterioso* theme, all these covers follow well-established crime genre conventions: guns, threatening silhouettes, violence, and another common genre trait—colors like red and blue.[7]

Il Giallo's *Misterioso* cover reflects a decision to bind its edition to the publishing house's aesthetic, integrating the foreign work into a new domestic context. By publishing the book in a well-established domestic series, the publisher outfits the foreign with its own brand and look, designed to let a potential reader identify the foreign as familiar crime fiction. The fragmented iconography of fear functions as a marketing trope, as seen repeatedly in the jacket designs for Swedish crime fiction in translation. Måns Kallentoft's *Midwinter Blood* and Åsa Larsson's *Until Thy Wrath Be Past* have covers with close-ups on a victim's hand. Dahl's *Ungeschoren* displays a dark shadow behind a blurred surface, a theme that echoes on the Slovakian cover for Arne Dahl's *Misterioso* that depicts a pale hand, pressing against a surface, reaching out from an unknown shadowy body. In the rerelease of the *The Laughing Policeman* by Swedish crime writers Maj Sjöwall and Per Wahlöö, the front cover shows a close-up on a bloody hand against foggy glass, so does the Slovakian edition of Dahl's *Misterioso* (see Figure 8.1). Thus, the foreign becomes accessible.[8]

The different covers for Dahl's *Misterioso* also intersect with another local, vernacular context. The cover art honors an established noir aesthetic—the cassette (exotic by now in its technological antiquity), the darts game (ludic but dangerous), the man with a gun/ silhouette/ crucified hand (implicit or explicit violence), all branding the book as crime fiction. Yet none of these covers aspires to depict the novel's highly ideological, left-wing plot with its inferred criticism of capitalism. Then comes the deviation.

As can be seen in Figure 8.2, the jacket design for the 2010 Spanish Ediciones Destino translation of Dahl's novel (and also used for the 2013 Spanish Kindle release),[9] bucks the trends of translated editions on the transnational book market. This front cover has a drawing of a face against a white circle, reminiscent of a full moon. The only other body parts are two arms, emerging from an unseen body, hands raised toward the face. The head lacks hair. There is no clothing. The

Figure 8.1 *Covers for Maj Sjöwall and Per Wahlöö,* The Laughing Policeman (New York: Vintage, 2009), *and for Arne Dahl,* Misterioso (Bratislava: Příroda, 2014).

Figure 8.1 *Continued*

Figure 8.2 *Cover Arne Dahl,* Misterioso (Barcelona: Destino, 2010). *Cover for the hardcover, paperback and Kindle editions.*

face, with its lips, looks female. Towards the upper left corner, an arrow stretches out from a pine tree, emphasizing the full moon behind. Below, the novel's title is written in white and the author's name is typed in red. The rest of the cover is black. The face's eyes are covered by black birds, giving the impression that the birds are the eyes. From the birds run trails of black, as if dark blood is pouring from these unseen eyes, down and over the arms. The back cover offers a blurb in white letters, then a short biographical note about Dahl. Beneath are two translated quotes from book reviews. Selected from France's *Le Devoir* and Sweden's *Aftonbladet*, these are typed in red.

This visual deviation is indicative of a larger pattern traversing crime fiction's genre aesthetics. Though the Spanish *Misterioso* cover appears at first as an aberration, it actually conforms to the well-established framing of crime fiction outside its national context, exemplifying how a domestic crime fiction literature meets a cosmopolitan media landscape and merges with the glocal crime fiction genre. Destino's jacket design, with its bleeding bird-eyes, exhibits an element connecting to a set of nodal points in its discursive field, transforming itself into a new nodal point in the field.

Misterioso was launched in 2010, in Destino's prestigious series *Colección Áncora y Delfín* consisting of both domestic and translated works. The series publishes both well-established writers, such as Nobel Prize winner Camilo José Cela, and newcomers. Thus this surrealist cover image, diverging from crime fiction genre conventions, reflects an adaptation to the series *Colección Áncora y Delfín*, a way of locating it by binding it to the corresponding nodes. As such, it shows a foreign and so-called lowbrow genre-fiction novel getting embedded in a new commercial context via aesthetics which, following Bourdieu, endow it with cultural capital.

Still, this distinctive cover is also deeply enmeshed in crime fiction's discursive field. Black and red are present, and the eerie image of the bleeding bird-eyes foretells pain, violence, and suffering. But the narrative has nothing to do with birds, nor with eyes getting pecked out. There are no female victims. Still, this empirically deviant cover makes perfect sense, illustrating a complex way a foreign literature joins a visually cosmopolitan aesthetic. Looking at the Spanish *Misterioso* cover, beyond the fact that *Misterioso* translates as "mysterious" in Spanish, we nevertheless understand that this is a crime fiction novel. This cover frames the content as a story about violence, and about metaphorical blindness, themes likewise picked up by the UK edition titled *The Blinded Man*, and alluding to the traumatized killer suffering from a blind rage (in this case, against society's economic structures, which he attacks by killing its businessmen). The metaphor of blindness is common in crime fiction; contemporary examples include the cover of Swedish author Lars Kepler's *Fire Witness*, showing a girl, lying naked on a bed, pressing her fingers against her eyes, the white sheets spattered with blood. Blindness is also an age-old cultural trope, as in Sophocles' *Oedipus Rex*. Thus it serves as a ready-made marketing strategy. This technique was similarly applied to the German release of the opening novel of Stieg Larsson's Millennium Trilogy. The German translation changed the title from the domestic *Män som hatar kvinnor* (Men Who Hate Women) to *Verblendung*, a term that can be interpreted as being blinded as well as unable to see despite being physically able to do so.[10]

Employing certain images, symbols, or metaphors assists the integration of a vernacular and foreign literature into a cosmopolitan book market, and so the cover shown in Figure 1a makes perfect sense for catching the potential buyer's eye. Destino's surreal cover-image echoes a history of seeing and visual culture, despite appearing more modern than the other covers. But *seeing* also has an intimate relation to crime fiction; it is the detective or "private eye" who so often solves the murder by seeing what the untrained eye cannot.

Edgar Allan Poe's short story "The Man of the Crowd" (1840) points to the changing practice of spectatorship, specifically in a modern urban setting. The story's central theme is how the unidentified narrator sees and visually reads the city's flow of bodies and spectacles as he strolls through London, dissecting the crowd with his gaze. This story, as analyzed by Dana Brand and Tom Gunning building on the work of Walter Benjamin, typifies the rise of different modes of spectatorship, marked by the experience of urban modernity: bright, colorful advertising signs, electric lights, shop windows with gleaming glass and captivating displays. Here, Poe forged the link between visual pleasure and the culture of consumption, and three modes of seeing come into shape: the flâneur, the gawker, and the detective.[11]

The modern marketing of literature arose within this context of flowing visuals, seeking to get noticed by utilizing everything showy as well as cultural, including mythologies, media spectacles, belief systems, folklore, literature, and then film. With new printing technologies came the mass production of literature, rendering the jacket design of great importance to identifying genres on the world market. It is in this milieu that arose what we can call the *death aesthetic*. The death aesthetic evolved out of crime fiction's discursive field, inseparable from its historical, cultural, and contemporary contexts, and became associated with the commercialized framing of a novel's content, intersecting with these cultural dimensions to form a flow of images that represent crime fiction. From a marketing perspective, the Destino cover transcends the death aesthetic that evolves from the discursive field for crime fiction. Yet the cover enables Dahl's *Misterioso* to appear meaningful and enticing to a potential buyer outside its domestic context by connecting to established genre symbols like eyes, blood, birds, and seeing, letting the jacket design intersect with a cluster of different nodal points centered on canonized films and novels.

These associations spread out to encompass the array of symbols, images, iconic scenes, characters, film directors, and authors behind these other narratives. Consider the birds covering the eyes that appear to be bleeding, or perhaps pecked out by the birds. These feathered creatures recur in folklore, religious texts, paintings, mythology, and cinema, conferring an aesthetic that connects to that array of existing nodal points. A selection of classic examples might be Jacob and Wilhelm Grimm's tales such as "Seven Birds," "The Golden Bird," "The Raven," or "Fitcher's Bird," though the most obvious literary allusion is to Edgar Allan Poe's "The Raven," adapted to the screen as early as 1915 as a silent film, with its latest incarnation in 2012. Poe, often dubbed the father of crime fiction, constitutes a nodal point in crime fiction discourse, epitomizing dark and lurid tales, influencing writers worldwide. Birds too, especially crows or ravens, are iconic. Placed on a book or DVD cover, these immediately trigger myriad cultural, mythological, religious, and folkloristic references, inducing the spectator to associate the item with a specific discourse.

Macabre tropes, so often resting on the shoulders of world literature, are important nodes within the discourses of crime fiction and its neighbor, horror. Both genres possess an overlapping aesthetic, as seen in *The Omen* movies (1976–1981) about the birth of Satan's son on earth, which use a raven on the film poster for the second movie, and in which birds peck out the eyes of an investigative photojournalist; blinded, she runs in front of a car. For this particular scene the producers hired the bird-trainer Ray Berwick (1914–1990), who worked with Hitchcock on *The Birds* (Spoto 1992: 332).

Birds occur often in Alfred Hitchcock movies, most notably *The Birds* (based in turn on a literary work, Daphne du Maurier's story). *The Birds* features multiple shots of people with eyes pecked out by birds, notably Mitch's mother's friend Dan, whom she finds leaning dead against his bedroom wall, eyeless. When adapting Robert Bloch's *Psycho* for film, Hitchcock let the killer Norman Bates nurture an intimate and highly personal relationship to birds, both as a concept and in the physical form of a stuffed bird—an echo back to Poe's raven (Spoto, 329–36). Given Hitchcock's iconic status, he is another nodal point that other elements connect to when positioning themselves in the genre's discourse and that marketing seeks to link up to as well. The birds and pecked-out eyes, then, besides relating the work to other books and genre tropes, link to the cinema nodes within crime fiction's discursive field. The intimate relation between literature and film plays a key role in marketing, and not just when the screen adaptation provides the novel's cover with new images—for future releases, remakes, and editions—taken from its visual retelling of the plot.

Hitchcock himself was also strongly influenced by Poe. He states in his essay "Why I Am Afraid of the Dark" (1961) that "Poe has a very particular place in the world of literature," as a romantic and a precursor of modern literature, and says that as a director, he tried to carry out in his films what Poe did in his writing. Poe's influence echoes in *Psycho* and *The Birds*, as well as in *Rear Window*, when the photographer L. B. Jefferies, housebound with a broken leg, discovers a murder while watching his neighbors. In this movie the main set, apart from Jefferies's apartment, is his courtyard. The viewer can glimpse the city's crowd passing by from dawn to dusk in the background, offering a dioramic quality of urban spectatorship that leads us to Poe as well as the city's gazes.[12] In *Rear Window* Hitchcock also tellingly lets Jefferies's nurse from the insurance company remark about his newborn neighborhood-watching hobby that Americans are becoming "a race of Peeping Toms," and she also refers to Jefferies's camera as a portable keyhole.

It is thus not surprising that black birds appear so often on crime fiction covers. Ravens are depicted on all three mass-market paperback covers of American crime writer Michael Connelly's trilogy about a killer named *The Poet*, in which Poe's works are an important clue for solving the case. On the first novel's cover, the bird circles over a red-colored Los Angeles, embedded in black.[13] So too, it is no surprise that birds frequently appear on the covers of Swedish crime novels. *Mensch ohne Hund* and *Die Einsamen*, the German translations of two of Håkan Nesser's works, have sepia windows through which birds can be seen. The American edition of Liza Marklund's *Lifetime* carries the silhouette of a bird with its wings spread against murky yellowish tones. The German translation of Arne Dahl's *Ungeschoren* depicts a snow-covered pine tree with two black ravens, leading the mind into a winter-mystery (see Figure 8.3, left). The original title *En midsommarnattsdröm* (A Midsummer Night's Dream) shows that the plot actually takes place in June. Black birds also figure in winterish covers

Figure 8.3 *Covers for Håkan Nesser,* Am Abend des Mordes, *and for Arne Dahl,* Ungeschoren (Munich: Piper Verlag, 2009).

Figure 8.3 *Continued*

depicting such features as snow-covered fields or forests, blending the two aesthetics. Another example can be seen in Figure 8.3 (right side), with the cover for Håkan Nesser's *Am Abend Des Mordes*, featuring a red house in the forest flanked by a black bird. Another example is the Dutch edition of Kristina Ohlsson's *Engelbewaarders*, showing a black, blood-dipped feather against white snow. These nodal points serve as models for other points or elements to apply in new, emerging narratives, or to be challenged as established points of reference by new entries on the market, for the discursive field is not fixed but flexible, permitting changes and new formations of points and clusters. In this way, Swedish crime fiction has built a cluster of nodes, of which its aesthetics are a seminal part, but not the only one.

However enticing these Nordic Noir covers are in the outside market, snowy images don't furnish an exotic and unique framing in Sweden, where the literature originates, or for the Nordic countries in general; the domestic covers rarely feature these snowy "Nordic" landscapes, focusing instead on the more "universal" tropes of guns, cityscapes, threatening silhouettes, images of victims, and other iconic markers of the genre. Another common trait for the Swedish domestic book market is the design of crime fiction covers that connect directly to the plot.[14]

As I've previously argued (Nilsson 2016), the representation and perception of Nordic Noir intersects with a set of different expressions that goes far beyond the narrative itself. Media discourses (such as articles about authors or reviews) contribute to its representation, as well as the film adaptations that tie in with the marketing of the narratives. These media expressions embedment of the narratives in a winterish frame connect to a greater set of universally spread ideas about *north* as a mysterious place.

A part of Nordic Noir's foreign allure rests upon a culturally forged idea of *the north*, found worldwide in various cultural expressions such as myths, folklore, fairy tales, literature, and contemporary cinema and trails centuries back in history worldwide. Renaissance historian Peter Davidson writes in *The Idea of the North* (2005) that everyone carries a notion within of the north; the specific territory and topography are only part of this concept. No matter where one is, "north" is always farther, a compass pointing towards an *elsewhere*. Danger often awaits in the north, from the climate to evil beings. The portrayal of the north as an imaginary location has a long, rich tradition in art and literature, intimately entwined with ghost stories and the fantastic: the Snow Queen or Ice Witch, as in Hans Christian Andersen's tale *Snow Queen*

(1844) about a heroine who journeys to save her friend, kidnapped by the Snow Queen.[15]

This multifaceted idea of the north (gravitating between its physical appearance as a place and geography and a state of fantasy and imagination) is a common theme and aesthetic in film and literature worldwide. Two contemporary examples include the Twilight movie series, where a vampire battle takes place on a snow-covered field, and Quentin Tarantino's bedazzling Japanese winter garden for the sword-fight in *Kill Bill*, where the heroine Beatrix Kiddo fights her enemy O-ren Ishii.

The fascination that infuses the idea of the north resonates in how Nordic Noir is perceived abroad and this provides a *local* color to the narratives, even though crime fiction covers for Nordic Noir can connect to other aesthetic expressions, as we've seen in the deviating Spanish *Misterioso* cover. When employed as a strategic marketing tool, the northern imagery gives Swedish literature a dramatic setting and labels domestic crime fiction through its home geography and topography.

Following Borges in his essay "The Argentine Writer and Tradition" (1951), we can understand this local color as something that only matters to foreign readers, the point that Borges makes with his famous remark that there are no camels in the Qur'ran, as they were part of everyday reality and taken for granted, just as there are no snowy forests on the covers of the domestic editions of Nordic Noir. This exemplifies how the perception of a novel is indeed a negotiation between context and content. Just as Larsson's Millennium Trilogy is perceived as stories about a classic detective and a *final girl* (as Carol Clover would say) who survives in the end, the political red thread in *Misterioso* is toned down in favor of other elements and nodal points in the discursive field for crime fiction.

The aesthetic that embraces the Nordic Noir narratives shows how the vernacular and cosmopolitan becomes a mélange through marketing strategies. A blood-dipped feather against white snow (Figure 8.4) not only gives the novel a local flavor for the foreign eye, but also positions the narrative on the map of an international genre and its transnational book market. A close-up on a hand pressed against a window or a shadowy figure behind a curtain becomes here more than a cover trope; it connects domestic crime fiction to a wider culture for literature and film. This is exemplified, for example, by the rerelease of *The Laughing Policeman* by Sjöwall/Wahlöö with a cover that aesthetically connects to Hitchcock's iconic shower scene in *Psycho*. Swedish crime fiction has thus

Figure 8.4 *Cover for Kristina Ohlsson,* Engelbewaarders (Amsterdam: The House of Books, 2012).

become its own cluster of nodal points, positioning itself in the discursive field as a vernacular literature through marketing, worldwide sales, and film adaptations. Here, the vernacular meets the cosmopolitan aesthetic, as in the case of a snowy cover enhanced by birds and bleeding eyes. At other times—as in the deviating Spanish *Misterioso* cover—the narratives of Nordic Noir become embedded in a fabric of nodal points, disperse over time and media, tracing back in history to Poe and at the same time intersecting with the movie industry's iconic scenes and films. It is also notable that the now well-known cover design for Stieg Larsson's novels, with its color palette in yellow, red, and silver and accompanying abstract drawings of dragons, hair, and wasps, is aesthetically far removed from the common description of Nordic Noir's wintery covers (Nilsson 2016).

To conclude, the representation of Swedish crime fiction comes together as a fabric woven of transnational media discourses, marketing strategies, literary echoes of folklore, fairy tales, and literatures. Media expressions, like movie adaptations, go further, giving a visual narrative and embedding stories in the cinematic. This, in turn, refocuses the limelight on the literature, allowing the book to be rebranded for new sales. This mediascape embeds the domestic literature—here Swedish crime fiction—and lets it rise as a world literature, as its images and discourses circulate on a transnational book market as a cosmopolitan death aesthetic.

Notes

1. For further reading on the evolution of the book market, see: Claire Squires (2009), Angus Phillips, "How Books are Positioned in the Market," in Matthews and Moody (2007), Steiner (2012), and also John B. Thompson (2010) and Schiffrin (2000).
2. Gérard Genette (1997). See also Berglund (2016) and Matthews and Moody (2007). For a solid and introducing study to literature and its commercial context see Claire Squires (2009). Book covers are still an unexplored area, and most common are compilation of covers, offering an historical overview and surveys over a specific company or series, for example: Phil Baines (2005) and Thomas L. Bonn (1982).
3. Arne Dahl is a pen name for Jan Arnald, who started out as a literary writer and then in the 1990s began writing crime fiction under the Dahl pen name.

4 For information about translations and film adaptations of Dahl's novels, see: http://www.arnedahl.net (visited January 28, 2016).
5 Dahl (2013, 2010b, 2009a, 2009b).
6 Dahl (2008, 2011a).
7 Dahl (2009c, 2012, 2011b), Arne Dahl, *Misterioso*, Muza, 2010, see also: "Marsilio," Italian Publishing House, accessed October 28, 2010, http://www.marsilioeditori.it/
8 Kallentoft (2011), Larsson (2011), Dahl (2014), and Sjöwall and Wahlöö (2009).
9 Image applies to both hardcover and paperback editions, Dahl (2010a).
10 Louise Nilsson (2016, forthcoming), Stieg Larsson (2007, 2008, 2009).
11 Gunning (1998: 60–4) focuses upon the difference between early cinema and later narrative film, departing from how a visual culture of spectacles fostered a cinematic spectatorship. Gunning argues that nineteenth-century urban culture nurtured and produced a visual experience that raised a gaze perfectly adapted for the film medium. My interest here is the visual dimension that cuts through crime fiction and the detective's eyes; here Dana Brand (1990, 1991, 1999) forms a central source of inspiration for my discussion. Compare with King (2016).
12 My discussion here follows Dana Brand (1999). For Hitchcock's essay, see Gottlieb (1995:142–5, quote 144).
13 The specific mass-market paperbacks used here were printed in 2006, 2009, and 2010. These cover images have also been used for hardcover editions. The very first editions of Michael Connelly's trilogy were published in the following order: *The Poet* (1996), *The Scarecrow* (2009), and *The Narrows* (2004). On Poe in popular culture, see, for example, the TV series *The Following* (2013–15) created by Kevin Williamson: http://www.imdb.com/title/tt2071645/?ref_=nv_sr_1
14 I connect here to Karl Berglund (2016), who discusses the design of Swedish crime fiction mass-market paperbacks for its domestic book market.
15 For further reading about the idea of north in cultural history, see: Peter Davidson (2005), especially 6–9, 19, 7–20, 67–8.

Works Cited

Baines, Phil (2005). *Penguin by Design: A Cover Story 1935–2005*. New York: Penguin Books.

Berglund, Karl (2016). *Mordförpackningar. Omslag, titlar och kringmaterial till svenska pocketdeckare 1998–2011*. Uppsala: Avd. för litteratursociologi, Uppsala universitet.

Bonn, Thomas L. (1982). *Under Cover: An Illustrated History of American Mass Market Paperbacks*. New York: Penguin Books.
Brand, Dana (1990). "From the Flâneur to the Detective: Interpreting the City of Poe." In *Popular Fiction: Technology, Ideology, Production, Reading*, ed. Tony Bennett. London, New York: Routledge.
Brand, Dana (1991). *The Spectator and the City in Nineteenth-Century American Literature*. Cambridge: Cambridge University Press.
Brand, Dana (1999). "Rear-View Mirror: Hitchcock, Poe, and the Flaneur in America." In *Hitchcock's America*, ed. Jonathan Freedman and Richard Millington. New York, Oxford: Oxford University Press.
Clover, Carol (1992). *Men, Women and Chainsaws: Gender in the Modern Horror Film*. Princeton: Princeton University Press.
Connelly, Michael (2006). *The Narrows*, New York: Grand Central Publishing.
Connelly, Michael (2009). *The Poet*, New York: Grand Central Publishing.
Connelly, Michael (2010). *The Scarecrow*, New York: Grand Central Publishing.
Dahl, Arne (1999). *Misterioso*, Höganäs: Bra böcker.
Dahl, Arne (2008). *Misterioso*, Paris: Seuil.
Dahl, Arne (2009a). *Misterioso*, Athens: Metaichmio.
Dahl, Arne (2009b). *Misterioso*, Paris: Points.
Dahl, Arne (2009c). *Misterioso*, Venezia: Marsilio.
Dahl, Arne (2009d). *Ungeschoren*, Munich: Piper Verlag: Piper Taschenbuch.
Dahl, Arne (2010a). *Misterioso*. Barcelona: Destino.
Dahl, Arne (2010b). *Misterioso*, New York: Pantheon.
Dahl, Arne (2011a). *Misterioso*, Piper EBooks Kindle.
Dahl, Arne (2011b). *Misterioso*, Vilnius: Baltos Lankos.
Dahl, Arne (2012). *The Blinded Man*, New York: Vintage.
Dahl, Arne (2013). *Misterioso*, New York: Vintage Crime/Black Lizard.
Dahl, Arne (2014). *Misterioso*, Bratislava, Slovakia: Príroda.
Davidson, Peter (2005). *The Idea of North*. London: Reaktion Books.
Genette, Gérard (1997). *Paratexts: Thresholds of Interpretation*. Cambridge and New York; Cambridge University Press.
Gottlieb, Sidney (1995). *Hitchcock on Hitchcock*, Berkeley: University of California Press.
Gunning, Tom (1997). "From Kaleidoscope to the X-Ray: Urban Spectatorship, Poe, Benjamin, and Traffic in Souls (1913)," *Wide Angle* 19:4, 25–63.
Howarth, David R. (2000). *Discourse*. Buckinghamshire and Philadelphia: Open University Press.
Kallentoft, Måns (2011). *Midwinter Blood*. London: Hodder & Stoughton.
Kepler, Lars (2014). *The Fire Witness*. London: Blue Door.
King, Stewart (2016). "Chief Inspector Javier Falcón." In *Crime Uncovered: Detective*, ed. Barry Forshaw. Bristol: Intellect.

Laclau, Ernesto, and Chantal Mouffe, Chantal (1985). *Hegemony and Socialist Strategy: Towards a Radical Democratic Politics*. London; New York: Verso.
Larsson, Åsa (2011). *Until Thy Wrath Be Past*, New York, London: Maclehose Press.
Larsson, Stieg (2007). *Verblendung*, Munich: Heyne Verlag.
Larsson, Stieg (2008). *Verdammnis*, Munich: Heyne Verlag.
Larsson, Stieg (2009). *Vergebung*, Munich: Heyne Verlag.
Marklund, Liza (2013). *Lifetime*. New York: Atria/Emily Bestler Books.
Matthews, Nicole, and Nickianne Moody (2007). *Judging a Book by Its Cover: Fans, Publishers, Designers, and the Marketing of Fiction*. Aldershot: Ashgate.
Nesser, Håkan (2007). *Mensch ohne Hund* München: Btb Verlag.
Nesser, Håkan (2011). *Die Einsamen* München: Btb Verlag, 2011.
Nesser, Håkan (2012). *Am Abend Des Mordes*. München: Btb Verlag.
Nilsson, Louise (2016). "Uncovering a Cover: Marketing Swedish Crime Fiction in a Transnational Context." *Journal of Transnational American Studies 7:1, 1–16*.
Ohlsson, Kristina (2012). *Engelbewaarders*. Amsterdam: The House of Books.
Schiffrin, André (2000). *The Business of Books: How International Conglomerates Took Over Publishing and Changed the Way We Read*. London and New York: Verso.
Sjöwall, Maj, and Per Wahlöö (2009). *The Laughing Policeman*. New York: Vintage Crime/Black Lizard.
Spoto, Donald (1992). *The Art of Alfred Hitchcock: Fifty Years of His Motion Pictures*. 2nd ed. New York: Doubleday.
Squires, Claire (2009). *Marketing Literature: The Making of Contemporary Writing in Britain*. Basingstoke: Palgrave Macmillan.
Steiner, Ann (2012). "World Literature and the Book Market." In *The Routledge Companion to World Literature*, ed. Theo D'haen et al. London and New York: Routledge, 316–24.
Thompson, John B. (2010). *Merchants of Culture: The Publishing Business in the Twenty-First Century*. Cambridge; Malden: Polity.
Online sources:
http://www.arnedahl.net/?rID=1056&page=internationellt
http://www.marsilioeditori.it/
http://www.imdb.com/title/tt2071645/?ref_=nv_sr_1

9

Surrealist Noir: Aragon's *Le Cahier noir* and Pamuk's *The Black Book*

Delia Ungureanu

The global popularity of crime fiction has made it a pathway to a world market for many authors from peripheral countries, including highly ambitious writers much more interested in winning the Nobel Prize than an Edgar Award from the Mystery Writers of America. A leading example is the 2006 Nobel Prize winner Orhan Pamuk, who has enjoyed both popular and critical success with a series of novels that play sophisticated variations on themes and techniques of crime and detective fiction, including his best-known novels *Snow* and *My Name Is Red*, each built around investigations of mysterious murders. Pamuk didn't start out as a popular writer, either in his intentions or his audience; he began his writing career with two brilliant novels that were very much indebted to the high modernist tradition: *Cevdet Bey and His Sons*, modeled on Mann's *Buddenbrooks*, and *The House of Silence*, modeled on Faulkner's *As I Lay Dying*. His approach changed when he lived in New York for three years in the mid-1980s, while his wife was a graduate student at Columbia. During this time, Pamuk began to develop a new literary and market formula that would bring together his interest in recovering the Middle East cultural legacy and his engaging with the great writers of the European modernist tradition, now leavened with a new focus on mystery and detective fiction. *The Black Book* was the novel that resulted from this trip and that launched Pamuk as a real world writer.

Genre framing proved key in *The Black Book*'s success: the noir, mystery, and detective fiction were among the first things that the book reviewers of the first English translation remarked in 1994. On the cover of the 2006 second English translation of Pamuk's *Black Book*, by Maureen Freely, the editors at Faber and Faber framed the work as a "detective novel" (*Independent on Sunday*), a "dark, fantastic invention" (Patrick McGrath), and a "mystery" (the editors themselves). An investigation into its sources sheds an interesting light on crime fiction as world literature, for the prime model for the novel that Pamuk wrote in New York wasn't American at all, but French.

Pamuk had always believed that the road to literary success led to the old cultural center—Paris—ideally by being published by the prestigious Gallimard, whose books had been central acquisitions in his father's library, which he grew up reading. Introduced there by the translator Münevver Andaç, he had a contract signed as early as 1984, and Gallimard's Sebastien-Bottin Street was for Pamuk "a magic place": "Together with Rousseau, Paris, the encyclopedists and Truffaut, Gallimard is to me a part impossible to dissociate from my image of France" (Pamuk 2011). Within this context, crime fiction might never have attracted more than popular or commercial interest, if not for a surprisingly avant-garde legacy: that of surrealism. It was the Parisian surrealists who first began to take crime fiction seriously within the field of French letters, and it is a surrealist text that most directly underlies Pamuk's *Black Book*.

During the 1930s the surrealists contributed not only to the recuperation of gothic and noir fiction, but also to the development and legitimation of the mystery and detective fiction and, in general, to the development of art and literature bordering on dream, reality, and the fantastic. As early as 1929, *Le surréalisme au service de la révolution* showed an interest in the mysteries of life at night in a magical Paris, sometimes mapped like an erotic female body (Eluard 1931), but also explored through the creative dimension of detective fiction. What surrealism had in common with detective fiction was a representation of reality as a texture of objects interrelated through an inner logic, not obvious to everyone, that gave reality a whole new meaning. The surrealists were drawn to solving puzzles and mysteries, as well as interpreting the whole network of coincidences that they saw as coming together in the surrealist objects that translated the subject's materialized subconscious desire. One good example is the column dedicated in *Le surréalisme au service de la révolution* to news published in other newspapers, where we can read about a series of leftist writers who became spies for the French secret police. One thing that qualified them for the job was the poet's logic that could see a pattern of connections among the objects of reality different from the obvious one. Even if Paul Eluard and Benjamin Péret, who wrote the column, cited with irony another journalist who praised these intellectuals who became spies—Jean Richard Bloch, Pierre Kisling, Léon-Paul Fargue—the example remains illustrative for the kind of subjects that preoccupied the surrealists: "'to disentangle the skein of a complicated matter it helps to have this experience of things and people that literature offers and also to use the poet's intuition,' writes in *Mercure de France* on February 15, Mr. Ernest Raynaud, poet and police commissary" (Eluard and Péret 1933: 26).

As an example, another column focuses on another piece of news about a bloody murder: the sisters Léa and Christine Papin, brought up by nuns at the monastery in Mans, kill their bourgeois employer's wife and daughter. The news itself is read by Eluard and Péret as a consequence of the religious education that brings out vice, a situation in which they saw a continuation of Sade's moral critique and the symbolic rebellious crimes of Lautréamont's antihero Maldoror: "[The Papin sisters] emerging from a canto of Maldoror armed to the teeth" (Eluard and Péret 1933: 28). The article is paired with a drawing showing a virtuous nun who lifts up the seam of her dress to show sexy garters underneath. Ultimately, the interest in detective fiction is shown through an ironic photo of a man reading the recently founded *Détective* magazine, under which we read: "A singular evolution: Mr. [Brice] Parain, former manager of *Détective*, is currently writing the book review column in *L'Humanité*" ("Une évolution singulière" 1930). What is interesting to note is that *Détective* published all sorts of news, not necessarily detective fiction, in the same note as the news commented on by Eluard and Péret, so in a way, the surrealists were interested in events that would later become the specialty of detective fiction.

The surrealist magazine *Minotaure* continued and refined all these genres—noir, Gothic, mystery, detective fiction—as well as specific mechanisms associated with these—the surrealist object, the mannequin, the automaton. Crimes that come out of bourgeois morality and religious education like the Papin sisters' crime had a precedent in the Marquis de Sade, and the surrealists found in his writings not only elements that overlapped with the noir novel, but also elements that anticipated the current development of mystery fiction. Young Jacques Lacan dedicated an entire article to the mysterious crime of the Papin sisters: "Motifs du Crime Paranoïaque" in *Minotaure* (Lacan 1933).

But the real opening of the noir novel to the contemporary world, benefiting from the surrealists' practice, comes from Maurice Heine's "Promenade à travers le roman noir" (Heine 1934). Heine defines the noir novel as a genre open to the circulation of ideas between cultural spaces: "all fiction that is dominated by the joint effects of terror and the surnatural can be termed noir novel ... such exchanges between the literatures of neighboring countries [England, France, Germany] surprises us less than this general taste of the European audience for the terrifying novel that has lasted for half a century" (1). With its variants—the gothic noir, the fantastic noir, noir realism, the burlesque noir (irony, satire, caricature)—noir fiction was already developing under surrealism's influence toward a transnational genre that would also integrate poetry. Maurice Heine believed that the genre could still develop in new directions: "today even the storyteller delves ... into a region of terror and grandeur where it meets poetry; shouldn't we explore this climate of mystery and violence from which so many new season can be born?" (4). Orhan Pamuk's *Black Book* would certainly not have disappointed him.

Louis Aragon and *La Défense de l'infini*, a novel for posterity

What is perhaps most striking is that Pamuk's novel wasn't the first to bear this title. In 1926, Louis Aragon, one of the leading surrealist poets, the most well-read of the group and the first translator of *The Hunting of the Snark* into French, published in *La Revue européene* a story called "Le cahier noir," a first-person narrative about a love triangle between a narrator who changes identities (Firmin, Ledoux), the woman he loves, called Blanche, and her lover Gérard. Aragon expanded the story into a long, never-completed novel, *La Défense de l'infini*, in which the love triangle appears in two different variants: either Firmin is married to Blanche who leaves him for Gérard or she's married to Gérard and Firmin is gnawed by jealousy. A quest for identity through writing a black book, two mysterious lovers who seem to be the projections of an insomniac's mind, and love as a journey to death: this is all strikingly similar to Pamuk's own *Black Book*, which tells the story of Galip, who sets out to find his wife Rüya, who has disappeared mysteriously with her step-brother, the journalist Celal. Galip finds himself in a detective fiction world where Celal is himself and Rüya becomes the world of dreams/fiction that he enters. Galip's search for his loved wife ends with death: both Rüya and Celal are found dead.

But could Pamuk have read Aragon's story? We know for a fact that he was reading the NRF collection brought out by Gallimard that his father purchased from Paris in the 1950s and that became one of Pamuk's greatest sources of modern literature: "It is thus that I discovered Gallimard at the age of five. My father explained to us the importance of this publishing house, with its white books softly yellowed which fifty years later I was to show to Antoine Gallimard during his visit to Istanbul" (Pamuk 2011). It was in the same NRF collection that

Aragon's "Le cahier noir" was republished in 1986 by Edouard Ruiz, as part of Aragon's unfinished novel, *La Défense de l'infini*. A writer with Pamuk's interest in what appeared in the NRF collection would have certainly been interested in the discovery, sixty years later, of a text that was to have been the most ambitious modernist novel had Aragon never abandoned it. The timing was good too: in 1986, Pamuk was just starting to work on *The Black Book*, which came out in 1990.

The story of how Aragon's "Le cahier noir" was produced and circulated is a mystery novel in itself, and is connected with stories of doubles, changed identities, spying, and fiction that mixes with reality. Having abandoned his medical studies and enrolled with Breton on the barricades of surrealism, Aragon lost his family's support and was in bad financial need. Poetry didn't pay, but it was a contradiction in terms to write novels while being a surrealist: André Breton had deemed the genre the epitome of submitting to the commercial bourgeois enterprise. Though Gallimard announced in 1926 that they would be publishing Aragon's 1500-page novel in six volumes, it remained just a dream. Devoted to Breton and the surrealist cause, Aragon in 1927 burned almost 1300 pages of his projected novel; thereafter he published pornographic novels such as *Le con d'Irene* under the pseudonym Albert de Routisie and sold off parts of his unfinished novel that his lover had saved from being destroyed. In 1929, he sold a manuscript called *Le Mauvais plaisant* to the American publisher Edward Titus, who owned a bookshop in Montparnasse, At the Sign of the Black Manikin (4, rue Delambre)—all too apt signs for Pamuk's episode with the underground mannequins who appear in his *Black Book*.

The manuscript was the original and Aragon didn't make a copy. *Le Mauvais plaisant* was a story in three parts. The first was a first-person narrative of an insomniac and a dreamer who rambles through the underground of the Parisian metro at night to discover a whole secret world of crimes and unleashed sexual fantasies. The second part was a Gogol-like story modeled on "The Nose" that told the adventures of a huge, elegantly dressed penis strolling through the streets of Paris. The third part was "Le cahier noir," framed as a story within a story about a black book from which several pages are torn, found in a brothel after someone had left it behind or forgotten it.

The first part of *Le Mauvais plaisant* was the result of a pact Aragon had made in 1923 with his patron, the clothing designer Jacques Doucet: for 600 francs a month, Aragon would act as Doucet's double in the nightlife of Paris and would provide his patron with pages that told Aragon's nighttime adventures that spanned the gamut from cafés, the metro, and the brothels to the literary séances at Breton's place. In a similar way, Pamuk's Galip would act as Celal's spy on the streets of Istanbul, moving between ghostly streets, secret newspaper archives, and mysterious stories of predestined lovers. Doucet was too old and too respectable for this kind of life, so he wanted at least to enjoy it like a voyeur and Aragon and his adventurous life were just the thing to put in a Black Book about the ghostly night places in Paris. Aragon's wondrous and wandering destiny proved to be the manuscript's too.

Edward Titus disappeared mysteriously from the Parisian stage together with Aragon's manuscript, moving to the United States and losing himself in some peripheral Midwestern town. Years later, in the 1960s, when Aragon was a well-known poet, he wanted to find the Titus manuscript and recuperate his identity as a surrealist novelist, but reality seemed against him: Helena Rubinstein, who had been married to Titus back in the 1920s, had gotten a divorce years before and the last thing she knew about him was that he had married a much younger woman, moved to the Midwest, and was already dead by the time Aragon was seeking to track him down. Even more mysterious was the fact that the young and not very cultivated widow had sold all her husband's archives before disappearing herself. The manuscript seemed forever lost, until Edouard Ruiz found it in a private collection and brought it to light in 1986 at Gallimard.

The two black books

When it was recuperated by Ruiz in a fragmented form in the 1980s, the novel *La Défense de l'infini* that included the Titus manuscript could represent a great potential for contemporary writers. What Breton thought wouldn't work in the 1920s proved paradoxically to push the surrealist legacy forward when a future world writer like Orhan Pamuk could consider *Le cahier noir* and *Le Mauvais plaisant* worthy to engage with.

"Le cahier noir" and *The Black Book* are constructed symmetrically: both explore the ghostly side of a city—Paris or Istanbul—and its secret nightlife, and both are centered on the problem of the double. Both use epigraphs in an ironic relationship with the text itself, and both draw on their own local legacy: whereas Aragon's epigraphs are taken mainly from French writers as well as other figures associated with surrealism as proto-surrealists, Pamuk cites not only Islamic and Sufi thinkers next to his own character's creations but also his own European masters. There are some authors cited by both Aragon and Pamuk, like Lewis

Carroll, and put to similar use: Pamuk cites "Must a name mean something?" (Pamuk 2006: 66) and turns the main character's name Rüya—*dream*—into the very atmosphere of the book, equating *fiction* to *dream*; Aragon plays too on the name *Blanche* and turns it into the illuminating light of the cornea of the authorial eye that writes the black book, the light in the night:

> A whiteness [*blancheur*] makes me reticent. The radiance of this woman is comparable to a cornea ... The real and the fictional marry like the foliage on the tree where a strange flower blooms. If I see Blanche today, it's because she's the girl I saw yesterday in my mind's eye; and Gérard didn't speak to me as an accomplice, as if he knew I might have witnessed what passed between the two of them. He doesn't understand that I'm the one who's directing him for everything that I imagine diminishes him in the eyes of the Blanche in my mind's eye. (Aragon 1997: 218, 225–6)

Other writers are cited only obliquely, also by Pamuk: Part I of the Titus manuscript cited Baudelaire calling Poe a *farceur*, whereas Pamuk's final metatextual chapter, "But I who write," is prefaced by Poe's "Shadow—A parable." Poe the farceur is also Poe the creator of the diabolic double William Wilson, whereas Rimbaud's *Je est un autre* structures both *Black Books*: "to be someone else" is the problem of both Firmin/Ledoux and Galip, but it's only "Le cahier noir" that gives an epigraph from Rimbaud.

Gérard, like Celal, doesn't have a material presence himself; he disappears when he approaches Blanche and reappears like her shadow whenever he takes some distance: "This kind of shadow of hers, Gérard, returns the moment I leave ... This distances me and makes me return to her, only to see Gérard stepping back, who was smelling her" (Aragon 1997: 218–9). This leads to the only plausible conclusion: Gérard is Ledoux's double, just as Celal is Galip's double: "I allow myself to love another man's woman with all the force of this other, multiplied in my crossed arms" (219). It is in this love for the nocturnal, in the desire to penetrate others' dreams that Ledoux will be a good model for Galip: "The nights are not as short as one thinks. The pulse of curiosity is painful. I am soothing it with the cruel milk of imagination ... Nights, nights, nights. We're playing cards [Manille]. I penetrate in the intimacy of each of them. Blanche/White ..." (223).

The black final pages of Pamuk's novel are the memories of a sleepwalker, and in this he comes closer to Aragon's framing of *Le cahier noir*. As in Aragon's case, the blackness of the notebook stands for silence—the silence of memory—and this is perhaps the most important point where we can analyze *Le cahier noir* as one of the structuring, unnamed sources of *The Black Book*. The black pages of a found manuscript are framed by Aragon with a distanced voice, a third-person narrator distanced presumably both in time and in space from the first-person narrator of "Le cahier noir." Thus the frame opens with the silence that these black pages invite us into:

> The man who was speaking, the man who crossed this world, fell silent. A sort of mist enveloped the time. What time is it? But above all, what year? It seemed as if great upheavals had taken place everywhere: but maybe they are insignificant. It's always the one who wasted his life following the city's movements who had to abandon these streets, these crossroads where he dedicated himself to a task impossible to understand today. He hated this bastard universe, this monster that lives only to devour itself. (Aragon 1997: 193)

With Pamuk, the third-person framing takes the shape of a second I, someone who is one head above our Galip, and who takes the same distance from his hero who, like Aragon's hero, is fed up with rambling on the endless Istanbul streets, in a city that devours itself:

> Reader, dear reader, throughout the writing of this book I have tried ... to keep its narrator separate from his hero ... That, dear reader, is why I would prefer to leave you alone on this page—alone, that is, with your memories ... This would do justice to the black dream that descends upon us at this point in the story—to the silence in my mind, as I wander like a sleepwalker through the hidden world. For the pages that follow—the black pages that follow—are the memoirs of a sleepwalker, nothing more and nothing less. (Pamuk 2006: 442–3)

Galip's greatest dilemma, which runs throughout the 460 pages of the novel, is whether he can become someone else. Chance encounter or not, the narrator of Aragon's *Cahier noir* started off with the same dilemma: "Could it be that all of a sudden he accepted to define himself as being this one and not the other one? Very unlikely. However, it is what he wanted us to think of him in this small black book which has no title and in which everything is told as if his name were Ledoux. Absurd will of fiction" (Aragon 1997: 193).

As it will happen in Pamuk's *Black Book*, the narrator of this *cahier noir* leaves these black pages behind him, and they are connected to the problem of memory and oblivion that is at the heart of Galip's/Pamuk's writing. For Aragon's narrator, the black pages we read are what the narrator chose or wanted to forget, to leave behind him in a brothel: "The dreadful country prostitutes, whom we see in the brothel of a big market town. They are three, two are snoring, and the third one is the oldest. That's enough. The man left. The only thing he forgot is [the story that] follows" (Aragon 1997: 194).

Ruiz's 1986 version of *La Défense*—the "phantom-novel" as Aragon called it—closes with a final paragraph that *Le cahier noir* gives between parentheses, in which the final image is one of flying sheets of paper, sheets that have been torn from the black book. This leaves open the question about *where* is the real text of the Black Book—in the text we've just read, or in the invisible text that was removed by the man who disappeared when our fiction started:

> (The manuscript stops here. It should have contained a few more pages, as the torn ten pages testify. The one who forgot it, did he want to destroy these ten pages or did he want to save only those and destroy what was before? Very likely he himself has no idea, being as we could see one of those men who believe that nothing can ever be destroyed, even if envy isn't missing, but who know that at least we can always *break it into pieces*). (Aragon 1997: 232)

Celal's unfinished text, broken into his daily columns, is just as fragmented and open as "le cahier noir," and we'll never know where the real Celal was, whether in these columns or in the ones written by Galip.

Celal's and Galip's—and the surrealists'—favorite activities include graphological analysis, palm reading, dream interpretation, and most important, reading riddles in faces. The title of Pamuk's 24th chapter, "Riddles in Faces" had a precedent in the surrealists' practice of anamorphosis, in which they could identify in an image a second, secret message, and even a third hidden image. Coincidentally or not, in 1938 Georges Hugnet published in the surrealist magazine *Minotaure*, under the title "Devinettes," a series of anamorphotic images, one of them entitled "The Sultan and His Favorite." If it is turned upside down, what seemed to be a sultan's portrait turns out to be the portrait of a beautiful veiled beauty who is the sultan's favorite (Hugnet 1938: 35). Even better, the sultan's coiffure camouflages two lovers kissing. Just as Pamuk superimposed the image of the two mysterious lovers Rüya and Celal on Galip's face, if we were to turn Pamuk's own covert self-portrait in *The Black Book* upside down, we'd perhaps find his favorite: Louis Aragon's portrait in "Le cahier noir."

Works Cited

Aragon, Louis (1997). *La Défense de l'infini*. Édition renouvelée et augmentée par Lionel Follet. Paris: NRF, Gallimard.
Eluard, Paul (1931). "Nuits partagées." *Le surréalisme au service de la révolution* 3, 14–6.
Eluard, Paul, and Benjamin Péret (1933). "Revue de la presse." *Le surréalisme au service de la révolution* 5, 19–28.
Heine, Maurice (1934). "Promenade à travers le roman noir." *Minotaure* 5, 1–4.
Hugnet, Georges (1938). "Devinettes." *Minotaure* 11, 34–5.
Lacan, Jacques (1933). "Motifs du Crime Paranoïaque." *Minotaure* 3–4, 25–8.
Pamuk, Orhan (2006). *The Black Book*, trans. Maureen Freely. London: Faber and Faber.
Pamuk, Orhan (2011). "J'ai découvert Gallimard à 5 ans." *Le nouvel Observateur*, February 3. http://bibliobs.nouvelobs.com/actualites/20110203.OBS7438/j-ai-decouvert-gallimard-a-5-ans-par-orhan-pamuk.html (Accessed February 27, 2016).
"Une évolution singulière" (1930). *Le surréalisme au service de la révolution* 2, np.

Part Three

Translating Crime

10

Detective Fiction in Translation: Shifting Patterns of Reception

Susan Bassnett

The archetypal global detective figure is Sherlock Holmes, the creation of a young doctor, who went on to become Sir Arthur Conan Doyle, and who acknowledged a debt to Wilkie Collins, Edgar Allan Poe, and Emile Gaboriau as his precursors to writing detective fiction. Holmes made his debut appearance in *A Study in Scarlet*, published in *Beeton's Christmas Annual* in 1887, and although that first short novel was not an immediate success, the series of Holmes stories that began to appear in the *Strand* magazine were immensely popular and established Conan Doyle's reputation. He, however, did not see himself as a detective story writer, and came to resent the popularity of his protagonist to such an extent that in 1893 he killed Holmes off, in "The Final Problem," the story that saw Holmes fall to his death along with his archenemy, Professor Moriarty, from the Reichenbach Falls.

The story of how subscriptions to the *Strand* Magazine plummeted, and how Conan Doyle then bowed to public opinion and brought Holmes back from the dead in "The Adventure of the Empty House" is too well-known to relate here. Once Holmes had been returned to Baker Street and to his large body of fans, Conan Doyle continued to write stories featuring Holmes and Dr. Watson until shortly before his death in 1930. His preface to a collection of his last twelve stories, *The Case-Book of Sherlock Holmes*, which came out in 1927, opens with a statement that today appears prophetic:

> I fear that Mr Sherlock Holmes may become like one of those popular tenors who, having outlived their time, are still tempted to make repeated farewell bows to their indulgent audiences. This must cease and he must go the way of all flesh, material or imaginary. One likes to think that there is some fantastic limbo for the children of the imagination, some strange, impossible place where the beaux

of Fielding may still make love to the belles of Richardson, where Scott's heroes may still strut, Dickens' delightful Cockneys still raise a laugh, and Thackeray's worldlings continue to carry on their reprehensible careers. Perhaps in some humble corner of such a Valhalla, Sherlock and his Watson may for a time find a place, while some more astute sleuth with some even less astute comrade may fill the stage which they have vacated. (Doyle 1951: 7).

The heavy irony of this preface serves to reinforce the mixed feelings that Conan Doyle had for his creation, who had seemed to acquire a life beyond the page. Holmes's afterlife has continued apace, with other writers continuing to produce stories of his adventures, and with the international success of Holmes and Watson as characters in film and television adaptations, the most recent being the hugely successful BBC television series, *Sherlock*, written by Mark Gatiss, Steven Moffat, and Stephen Thompson, and featuring Benedict Cumberbatch and Martin Freeman, in which the sleuth and his sidekick are transposed into twenty-first-century London. Conan Doyle's detective stories have been so frequently translated into other languages that his name is listed as fourteenth in the list of most translated authors in the world, according to the *Index Translatorum*. Holmes and Watson are recognizable characters all over the world.

Yet Conan Doyle's success pales when compared to that of the woman named as the world's most translated author, Agatha Christie. The *Index Translatorum* ranks her as number one, while sales figures are over two billion copies. The website for Agatha Christie lists her as the world's best-selling author of all time, after the Bible and the works of Shakespeare. Her books have sold some two billion copies and have been translated into one hundred and three languages at the last count. Her fictional detectives, the Belgian Hercule Poirot and the English spinster, Miss Jane Marple, have been recreated many times for the cinema and for television, and repeats, particularly of the successful Poirot episodes, as played by David Suchet, continue to be broadcast around the world. As with Conan Doyle, Christie had initial problems in finding a publisher, but once John Lane at the Bodley Head had signed her for that first detective novel, he contracted her immediately to write another five. Hercule Poirot first appeared in 1920, and her other well-known detective, Miss Marple, appeared in 1927, and there have been dozens of film, stage, and television versions of Christie's novels and short stories. Compared to other best-selling twentieth-century English detective fiction writers, such as Dorothy Sayers, Ellis Peters, or, more recently, P. D. James and Ruth Rendell, Christie's international reputation is enormous.

In 2012 the British journalist Mark Lawson made a fifteen-part series for BBC Radio 4, *Foreign Bodies*, which explored aspects of European history through a range of well-known detectives. Lawson started his exploration with Sherlock Holmes, ending it with Harry Hole, the detective created by one of today's best-selling crime writers, the Norwegian Jo Nesbø, whose sales figures globally are estimated at over fifty million copies. In an essay published in *The Guardian*, Lawson points out that crime novels routinely provide a mass of minute social detail, which means that they can be viewed as case-files of their times:

> Crime fiction is a magnifying glass that frequently reveals the fingerprints of history before they become visible to politicians or journalists. And—as in a forensic investigation—separate pieces of evidence begin to reveal patterns (Lawson 2012).

To illustrate this, Lawson notes that Ian Rankin's DCI Rebus novels systematically depict the ways in which Scotland began to re-examine its identity over the quarter of a century leading up to the Scottish independence referendum in 2014. Discussing the rise of what has come to be termed Nordic Noir, Lawson notes that future historians when considering why Sweden holds the improbable distinction of being the only Western democracy to have both its prime minister and foreign minister assassinated in modern times—or why a racist gunman killed seventy-seven people in Norway in 2011—will find clues to the forces behind those events in crime novels written at least a decade earlier (Lawson 2012).

Lawson's interest is in tracing patterns in postwar European crime fiction, and he is particularly interested in the visible connections between writers and their characters. He points out that Andrea Camilleri's Inspector Montalbano is named after Manuel Vasquez Montalban, creator of the Barcelona private eye, Pepe Carvalho, while Henning Mankell has admitted that his detective, Kurt Wallander, derives from Martin Beck, protagonist of the detective novels by the Swedish writers Maj Sjöwall and Per Wahlöö. Lawson finds this kind of genealogical thread intriguing. He sees Holmes as the prototype for highly intelligent, yet deeply flawed detectives such as Harry Hole or Josef Skvorcky's Inspector Boruvka, but claims that the most influential of all European crime writers in terms of what he calls prose tone and structure is Georges Simenon, the most translated French-speaking author of the twentieth century whose books have sold over 800 million copies. Simenon's Commissaire Maigret, unlike the amateur genius Sherlock Holmes, is a professional policeman, and Simenon does not avoid describing the darker aspects of police work. In contrast, by using the character of Dr. Watson as narrator, it is Dr. Watson's opinions and perspectives that prevail, which according to Lawson render Conan Doyle invisible. To support the idea of the seminal importance of Simenon's work, Lawson reports that Andrea Camilleri and Jakob Arjouni have both acknowledged the fundamental importance on their writing of Simenon's novels, as has P. D. James. This strong sense of succession, Lawson claims, is underlined by "the almost universal tendency of leading crime novelists to acknowledge predecessors as inspiration" (Lawson, 212).

Interestingly, Lawson pays little attention to Agatha Christie, apart from noting that she would often locate her novels in exotic places such as cruises down the Nile, depicting "trips that the majority of her audience was unlikely ever to experience" (Lawson 2012). He implies that Christie wrote more escapist literature than many other European writers, whereas "it is scar tissue from the great global conflicts of the twentieth century that runs through European crime fiction," and he notes that in the Commisaris Van der Valk novels, written by the British writer, Nicholas Freeling and set in Amsterdam, many of the plots revolve around bringing to light a hidden history of war-time collaboration during the Nazi occupation of Holland.

Lawson's radio series stressed both the interconnectedness of European postwar detective fiction and the implicit political dimension of many novels in which plots hinge on experiences of occupation, life under dictatorship, stories of collaboration with the enemy, organized crime, government corruption, and, most recently, migration and people trafficking, all of which is a long way away from Baker Street or an English village. If it is indeed the case that crime fiction captures the history of a period, then the English tradition established by Conan Doyle and Agatha Christie, if we can call it that, reflects a very different history from the rest of Europe, which is evident today in the ambiguous English relationship with the European Union. It is worth noting, however, that Christie did make Poirot a refugee from war-torn Belgium, while there are hints that Jane Marple's unmarried state was due to the death of so many young men of her generation in the trenches.

In his famous essay of 1948, which appeared in *Harper's Magazine*, W. H. Auden declared himself to be an addict of detective stories. Explaining his addiction, he listed two essential criteria: the novel must conform to specific formulae and must convey a sense of immediacy that will compel the reader to read on with urgency. Auden's essay is entitled "The Guilty Vicarage," and he admits that he finds it difficult to read a detective story that is not set in rural England. He declares that there are only three "completely satisfactory" detectives, one of whom is Sherlock Holmes, another G. K. Chesterton's Father Brown, and the third, Inspector Joseph French, created by Freeman Wills Crofts, an Anglo-Irish writer whose work has been largely forgotten but may be due for a revival. The task of the detective, according to Auden, is "to restore the state of grace in which the aesthetic and the ethical are as one" (Auden 1948: 409). For Auden, detective fiction is very definitely escapist writing, in which the "magical satisfaction is the illusion of being dissociated from the murderer" (412). This emphasis on escapism leads him to challenge Raymond Chandler, who "has written that he intends to take the body out of the vicarage garden and give murder back to those who are good at it," arguing that Chandler is not a writer of detective fiction, which is inevitably escapist literature in Auden's view, but rather a writer who produces serious studies of a criminal milieu, hence his "extremely depressing" books should be "judged as works of art" (408). What Auden could not have foreseen was how his binary distinction between types of detective fiction would continue to widen, as the detective story developed in the hands of very different writers, in very different social contexts.

Not only was Auden writing from the safety of the United States, at a distance from the trauma of postwar Europe, but he was writing in an age when challenges to the high literary canon from feminism, deconstruction, postcolonialism, and so on had not yet happened, hence literature was still divided into Great Works and what the Germans term *trivialiteratur*, which included detective fiction, romantic fiction, children's literature, memoirs, and a whole range of other popular writing. Yet, as Andre Lefevere points out in his book on the many agencies behind the movement of texts within and across cultures, *Translation, Rewriting and the Manipulation of Literary Fame*, the vast majority of readers are what he calls "non-professional readers":

> It is my contention that the process resulting in the acceptance or rejection, canonisation or non-canonization of literary works is dominated not by vague, but by very concrete factors that are easy to discern as soon as one decides to look for them, that is as soon as one eschews interpretation as the core of literary studies and begins to address such issues as power, ideology, institution, and manipulation. (Lefevere 1992: 2)

He goes on to note that "high" literature is increasingly read only in educational settings, that is, in schools and universities, and does not constitute the preferred reading matter of the nonprofessional reader. For it is the nonprofessional reader who buys the books that make the best-selling lists and who drives up the sales figures to millions.

Lefevere was trying to make a case for broadening literary studies (hence addressing what he called professional readers within the academy) to include the study of forms of rewriting—translations, anthologies, literary histories, reviews, editions, film and television adaptations, abridgments, plot summaries in reference works or magazines, and so forth. Most readers, even those who can be termed professional readers, in Lefevere's view have some kind of construct of a literary work in their minds, say of *War and Peace*, for example, based not on a reading of the novel itself, but on a combination of plot summary, opinion, maybe film adaptations, that they have acquired over time. And, of course, even those who have read the novel in its entirety have read it in a translation unless they are fortunate enough to know Russian and French. Nonprofessional readers of detective fiction appear to enjoy both the escapist variety, if we follow Auden's binary distinction, and the more overtly politicized variety of contemporary detective fiction, judging by the sales figures for both, as exemplified by the continuing popularity of Agatha Christie and the high sales figures for very different writers such as Jo Nesbø or Patricia Highsmith.

Since the 1990s when Lefevere's book came out, there have been great changes in publishing and in the global distribution of books, with greater recognition of the value of translation in both the book market and the academy. There have also been great changes in taste, and one notable shift of focus has been the rising popularity of detective fiction across the world, accompanied by television series, some of which are based on novels and some of which are not. Once seen as marginal, detective fiction has not only proliferated but has also acquired greater status with its greater prominence. Anecdotally, when I served as a judge for the Independent Foreign Fiction Prize in 2003, and then as judge for the IMPAC Dublin Prize in 2012, which involved reading a total of nearly 300 novels, with some 180 being translations, what was striking on both occasions was the number of detective novels entered for each competition, by publishers in the first case, and by librarians in the second. Reading through the entries confirmed Mark Lawson's point about the significance for many European writers of life in the aftermath of the Second World War and other later conflicts, including the dictatorships in Spain and Portugal. Many of the novels were beautifully written and the plot line with the solving of a crime frequently involved uncovering dark secrets withheld from a later generation. From those two prizes, in those two years, it is safe to say that the dominant genre of books the judges were sent to read was the detective novel.

In her essay on world literature and the book market, Ann Steiner notes that in 2009 the most widespread books in the world were Stieg Larsson's three novels and four novels in the *Twilight* vampire series by Stephanie Meyer. She draws attention to the vast commercial enterprises that make up international publishing, the threat caused by overpublishing, the power wielded by large media conglomerates, but she also warns against generalizing about the effect of global marketing on what readers choose to read. As she points out, following the large number of websites that enable readers to discuss and exchange ideas, the traditional hierarchies of the book trade have been overturned. BookCrossing, GoogleBooks, book blogs, pirated copies of e-books, cooperative writing communities, and fan fiction are a few of the novel phenomena that have changed what can be defined as world literature, as most of these are on global sites (Steiner 2012: 320).

Steiner also points out that, to her surprise, the best-seller lists showed that English is not the dominant world language. She cites crime fiction, written in Swedish, as highly significant in the international market, and to this we should add crime fiction in other Nordic languages, particularly Norwegian, with Jo Nesbø as the prime example. She concludes that translation, along with the publishing industry and the global book trade help to shape what readers choose to read, and the fact that many of the titles that reach the best-seller lists internationally may have been written in minority languages shows that the national and the international are inextricably linked.

One of the major lines of enquiry that has opened up within Translation Studies since its inception in the 1970s is the question of the unpredictability of text reception. As noted already, neither Conan Doyle nor Agatha Christie found an enthusiastic publisher for their work straight away, yet within a few years both had become not just best-selling authors but phenomenally successful global authors, and in a pre-electronic age. The rise to global prominence of Nordic detective fiction over the last twenty years, with writers like Peter Høeg, Stieg Larsson, Henning Mankell, Matti Joensuu, Yrsa Sigurdsdottir, Arnaldur Indridason, Anne Holt, and Jo Nesbø, all of whom write in minority languages in countries with small populations and advanced welfare systems is another good example of the unpredictability of success. All these writers have acquired global access through translation.

In what has come be seen as a seminal essay, "The Position of Translated Literature within the Literary Polysystem," Itamar Even-Zohar, one of the founders of Translation Studies, proposed a basic model for tracing and understanding the movement of texts across cultural and linguistic frontiers. The terminology of that essay sounds dated today (he was writing in the early 1970s) and his idea of "weak" and "strong" literatures has long since been challenged, but what is still valid is the case he makes for textual production and reception varying at different historical moments. Under certain conditions literary systems import ideas or literary forms that result in the creation of new literary models, and he sketches out three principle conditions when this kind of transformation happens: when a literature is "young" and in the process of establishing itself, when a literature perceives itself as "weak" or "peripheral," or when there are "turning points, crises, or literary vacuums in a literature" (Even-Zohar 2000:194).

In short, when there is a lacuna, a gap in a literary system, new forms arise to fill it. Moreover, the dynamics within a literary system mean that there are points when established models are no longer tenable for a new generation. At such moments, importing texts through translations can be of enormous significance, and to look back at literary history from such a translationist perspective can show clearly how different literatures were either boosted or renovated by the importation of new literary models. The shift from epic to romance in the twelfth century, the Renaissance and Reformation, the Enlightenment, the nationalist movements of the nineteenth century such as the Czech Revival, or the beginnings of Finnish literature are all examples of great cultural change where translations played a central role. It could be argued that the present translation boom in China is another example of a similar process.

Even-Zohar's work has given rise to a great deal of research on the role of translation in national literary histories, though attention has all too often been focused on well-known or canonical texts. However, the idea of the vacuum that can be unpredictably filled can equally apply to noncanonical literature. In recent years there have been good examples of unpredictable success stories that are both interlingual and intralingual: we might think of the *Twilight* vampire books, The Hunger Games, *Game of Thrones* and, most remarkable of all, J. K. Rowling's Harry Potter books. The Harry Potter success story is all the more intriguing since not only was Rowling turned down by several publishers, but the received wisdom at the time was that children had moved on from stories about magical powers, also that the boarding school story was a product of a bygone more elitist age, and that children's writers should aim to write more realistic stories for a much less naive generation. Rowling's books defied all pedagogical presuppositions and led on to dozens of imitative versions, fan fiction, films, comics, and so on just as the unexpected success of *Game of Thrones* has led to reinvigorated versions of the sword and sorcery genre that was popular in the 1970s.

Returning to Agatha Christie, what is apparent is that she wrote in a way that appealed to her contemporary readers and has somehow continued to do so. Christie's writing is not outstanding, her plots are formulaic, as are her characters. There is always a denouement, when the truth is revealed to all parties concerned and the guilty person is finally exposed. Before the final exposure, readers are led down blind alleys, so that the narrative builds up to the moment of revelation. This theatricality has meant that Christie's work can be comfortably adapted for other media, notably the one- or two-hour television episode format. In Christie's work, no matter how many people die, no matter how brutal the murders (which are never described in the kind of detail that we find in many contemporary writers), there is a final resolution when, as Auden puts it, the detective story addict is restored to a state of innocence in the Garden of Eden, the reader's ultimate fantasy of escape. But Christie also locates her narratives within a particular milieu, that of upper-class England. Her characters move in high social circles, with titled aristocracy and lavish country houses. This too is escapist, a fantasy of a world as foreign to her readers as the pyramids of Egypt, which also feature in some of her narratives, since after her marriage to an archaeologist she developed an interest in travel and in Egyptology.

It is possible that one of the attractions of Christie's fiction is her idealized Englishness, which is packaged in such a way as to be accessible to both English and non-English readers. This accessibility contrasts with the novels of Christie's contemporary, Dorothy Sayers, whose sleuth, Lord Peter Wimsey, is so much a caricature of the English class system as to make him objectionable to many readers, including Auden who described him as a priggish superman and whose adventures rely on understanding the nuances of the English class system. That same idealized fantastical England can be seen today in the television series *Midsummer Murders*, one of ITV's most successful programs. Based on the Inspector Barnaby books by Caroline Graham, the writer Anthony Horowitz adapted them for television. Horowitz, it should be noted, has also written two Sherlock Holmes novels and, most recently, a James Bond novel, having been commissioned by the Conan Doyle and Ian Fleming estates. *Midsummer Murders* has run through eighteen series, and has been sold to 225 territories. It is reputedly Angela Merkel's favorite program and is so successful in Denmark that in 2015 there was a joint Anglo-Danish episode, "The Killings of Copenhagen," which featured the stars of the British show and two Danish actresses who had become well-known in Britain through Danish television series, Anne Eleonora Jorgensen from *The Killing* and Birgitte Hjort Sørensen from *Borgen*.

This marriage of stars from two completely different traditions, from the tough realist Danish programs and the tongue-in-cheek pastoral idyll of the English program, appealed to fans in both cultures. *Midsummer Murders*, like Agatha Christie's writings, offers a safe space where murders happen, but where order is always restored, and that order is reinforced by the idealized rural English setting. Indeed, it is the fantasy of Englishness that seems to appeal, as much as, if not more so than the ridiculous plots and pasteboard characters, a fantasy that has kept Agatha Christie at the top of the list of most-translated authors in the world for over half a century.

Besides the lavish country house settings of Christie's stories, some are set in luxurious hotels, and here we can see another tendency of a certain kind of contemporary detective fiction, which is the location in which the stories take place. As Lawson puts it, detective fiction can operate as a sort of imaginative travel agency, taking readers across borders and introducing them to other cultures. Location is important in the Inspector Chen books by Qiu Xiaolong, or Keigo Higashino's detective, Kyochiro Kaga, with details of contemporary Chinese and Japanese society serving as compensation for the stilted English and weak plot lines. Interestingly, the cover blurbs use the device of associating the Chinese and Japanese writers with well-known European figures, so Inspector Chen is described as "Morse of the Far East," while Keigo Higashino becomes "the Japanese Stieg Larsson." Michael Dibdin's detective novels featuring Aurelio Zen are set in Italy, as are Donna Leon's, while the success of the televised versions of Andrea Camilleri's Montalbano novels has actually led to organized Montalbano tours round Sicily, which are apparently popular with fans from Britain and Northern Europe.

Camilleri began writing detective fiction in his late sixties, his first Montalbano novel appearing in 1994. In an interview with Mark Lawson, as part of the latter's BBC series, Camilleri explains how he chose to write novels that would engage with some of the major social problems of his native Sicily—government corruption, the power of the Mafia, drug and people trafficking, a climate of violence and terror not experienced since the 1940s, and he tells the interviewer, "I deliberately decided to smuggle into a detective story a critical commentary on my times" (Camilleri 2012). Part of his strategy is to write the novels in a mixture of standard Italian, Sicilian dialect, and a Sicilian variant of Italian. Montalbano is able to move between these three linguistic registers, well aware of the shifting power relations as he does so. Camilleri explains why he chose to use these linguistic variations: "the dialect is always confidential, a non-institutional relationship, intimate, a friendly atmosphere. The use of Italian language creates an immediate officialness, a distance. It is used to make law, to suggest intimidation, power, distance, emphasis" (Camilleri 2012).

The Sicilian location is essential to the novels, not as a colorful backdrop but as a real place where the struggle against state and local corruption is played out every day. Camilleri's deliberate use of different linguistic registers is fundamental to his strategy to "smuggle in" a critical commentary on his own time. But the English translator, Stephen Santorelli, faced with the impossibility of finding equivalents, opts for standard English throughout, except for the character of the stupid Catarella, who is given an invented English part-Cockney, part-Bronx, a literary invented language devoid of any political significance. Indeed, Camilleri's novels in English lose their political dimension, and fit cozily into the escapist category. The contrast between the brightly colored covers of the English versions and the plainer covers of the Italian versions highlights the difference in marketing strategies. Camilleri, the political novelist, has been repackaged as a writer of escapist fiction in a holiday setting.

The success of Nordic detective fiction has led to the republication of the godparents of Nordic Noir, Maj Sjöwall and Per Wahlöö. A husband and wife team, both communists, writing in the 1960s, their novels revealed a darker side to the idealized picture of the Swedish welfare state. The detective, Martin Beck, is an unheroic figure, whose private life is far from perfect, is bored with his job, depressed by the misery and violence he encounters, suffering from dyspepsia, but is widely acknowledged as the prototype for the Nordic detectives who have become so well-known in recent years. In a preface to the 2006 edition of *Rosanna*, first published in 1965, Henning Mankell pays tribute to the work of Sjöwall and Wahlöö: "I think that anyone who writes about crime as a reflection of society has been inspired to some extent by what they wrote. They broke with the previous trends in crime fiction ... broke with the hopelessly stereotyped character descriptions that were so prevalent" (Mankell 2006: vii).

In their 2007 preface to *The Laughing Policeman*, first published in 1970, novelists Sean and Nicci French make a similar point, noting how the Martin Beck books succeed as detective stories and yet at the same time work as social commentary, "because, despite it all, despite politics that are as far removed from the reactionary Christie as it is possible to get, Sjöwall and Wahlöö never lost their pleasure in the machinery of the whodunit" (French 2007: viii).

The global success of detective fiction is a complex phenomenon, but the binary distinction made somewhat patronizingly by W. H. Auden appears to have some credibility. The continued success of formulaic, reactionary writers like Agatha Christie and her many successors has to be offset against the success of writers who are more politically engaged and who use the format of the detective novel on more than the level of simple plot resolution. This division is particularly apparent when we consider the unexpected popularity of Nordic Noir in translation, which demonstrates a need for a different kind of detective fiction than the safe whodunit. That Camilleri should have been translated for English readers in such a way (and the television programs are also dubbed into standard English) as to remove the multilayered and ideologically charged linguistic dimension, suggests that there is still a wide readership for escapist detective fiction also.

Europeans are living in a time of immense social and political changes, and the detective story format provides a useful frame for exploring what is going on at the grass roots level. The idealized Nordic states have been shown to have darker undercurrents, political and judicial corruption reached its nadir in Italy during the Berlusconi years, the unresolved pain of the end of the Franco era without a process of truth and reconciliation continues to haunt Spanish writers, just as the break-up of Yugoslavia and the atrocities of the Balkan wars continue to haunt Serbian, Croatian, and Slovene writers. Stories of war-time collaboration with the Nazis continue to come to light, as do stories of pedophilia in the Catholic Church. In Britain, the rise of Scottish independence has raised the possibility of the end of the Union. The euro lurches from crisis to crisis, and today images of the suffering of the millions of refugees displaced by wars outside Europe created by Europeans in the Middle East and North Africa appear daily on television screens. The term "people trafficking" has entered daily parlance. And since major sociopolitical changes always have epistemological consequences, it may well be that the rise of detective fiction, both in terms of sales figures and in status is indicative of something that nonprofessional readers are reaching out to. Some favor the dark, gruesome variants, others opt for escapism, but both are opting for the detective story format and of this those of us who are professional readers would be well-advised to take note.

Works Cited

Auden, W. H. (1948). "The Guilty Vicarage, Notes on the Detective Story by an Addict." *Harper's Magazine* May, 4406–12.

Camilleri, Andrea in conversation with Mark Lawson (2012). *The Guardian* July 6.

Doyle, Arthur Conan ([1927]1951). *The Case-Book of Sherlock Holmes* London: Penguin.

Even-Zohar, Itamar ([1978] 2000). "The Position of Translated Literature in the Literary Polysystem." In *The Translation Studies Reader, ed.* Lawrence Venuti. London and New York: Routledge, 192–7.

Lawson, Mark (2012). "Crime's Grand Tour: European Detective Fiction," *The Guardian* October 26.

Lefevere, Andre (1992). *Translation, Rewriting and the Manipulation of Literary Fame.* London and New York: Routledge.

Steiner, Ann (2012). "World Literature and the Book Market." In *The Routledge Companion to World Literature, ed.* Theo D'Haen, David Damrosch, and Djelal Kadir. London and New York: Routledge.

11

Making it Ours: Translation and the Circulation of Crime Fiction in Catalan

Stewart King

The first of Georges Simenon's eighty-seven Maigret novels, *Pietr-le-Letton* (1930), opens with an act of translation. The apparent gobbledygook of "C.I.P.C. à Sûreté Paris Xvzust Cracovie vimontra m ghks triv psot uv Pietr-le-Letton Bréme vs tyz btolem" is identified as the secret international police code and is translated by his detective chief inspector protagonist as "Commission internationale de Police criminelle à Sûreté générale, Paris: Police Cracovie signale passage et départ pour Bréme de Pietr-le-Letton" (Simenon 1977: 7) ["International Criminal Police Commission to Police Judiciaire in Paris. Krakow police report sighting Pietr the Latvian en route to Bremen" (2013: 1)].[1] While Simenon perhaps points to the beginnings of transnational policing, we can also interpret the translation into French of a code "utilisé dans les relations entre tous les centres policiers du monde" (Simenon 1977: 8) ["used for communication between all the world's police forces" (2013: 2)] as a self-reflexive acknowledgment of the process by which the crime genre has become a form of world literature.

The role of translation in the development of crime fiction as world literature is perhaps so self-evident that it does not require explication. Edgar Allan Poe, considered by many the founding father of the genre, in fact translated and adapted into English a narrative form that had begun to emerge in German and French with E. T. A. Hoffmann's 1819 detective novella, *Das Fräulein von Scudéri*, and in the work of the real-life detective and memorialist, François-Eugène Vidocq, whose investigative skills he disparages in "The Murders in the Rue Morgue" (1841). Poe was then translated into French by Charles Baudelaire in 1856, and these translations influenced Émile Gaboriau to pen a series of detective novels (1866–76). The translation into English of Gaboriau's *oeuvre* inspired in turn the American writer Anna Katherine Green, author of *The*

Leavenworth Case (1878), and directly influenced the struggling New Zealand playwright Fergus Hume, who studied their methods before producing the world's first international blockbuster, *The Mystery of a Hansom Cab* (1886), set in colonial Melbourne (Sussex 2015: 275–83). Gaboriau's detective, M. Lecoq, was also a major influence on Arthur Conan Doyle's Sherlock Holmes series, despite his protagonist's protestations concerning any similarities between him and the French detective in *A Study in Scarlet* (1887). Doyle, too, has been translated into numerous languages, as have Agatha Christie and Georges Simenon, which has no doubt contributed to their becoming two of the most widely read novelists of the twentieth century. The importance of translation in the global circulation of the genre was further consolidated through celebrated crime collections, many of which contained translated works, such as Gallimard's *Série Noire* in France (1945–), Mondadori's *I Libri Gialli* in Italy (1929–), and Emecé's *El Séptimo Círculo* in Argentina (1945–1983), which was first edited by Jorge Luis Borges and Adolfo Bioy Casares. More recently, the international appeal of so-called Nordic Noir has only been made possible through translation.

Despite its prominent role in the genre's global reach, translation is often overlooked or given short shrift in many crime fiction studies. Much Anglo-American criticism departs from the supposition that translation is unidirectional, moving from the anglophone Atlantic to the rest of the world. US crime writer Walter Mosley, for example, sees the circulation of crime fiction as a form of American cultural expansion. In describing the world as "a kind of global Poisonville" (Mosley 2009: 601), he implies that the international spread of the genre is a consequence of the development of similar levels of corruption, violence, and exploitation in the local context to those investigated by Hammett's Continental Op in *Red Harvest* (1929). Scholars of crime fiction written in languages other than English tend to treat translated fiction in a similar manner, often seeing it as a necessary step toward the creation of the specific national literary tradition that is their object of study and only treating translation as important to the degree to which it contributes toward the development of the national genre (King 2014: 9–10).

My aim in this chapter then is to restore translation practice into the genre's international circulation. "Translation histories are always transnational histories," argues Michael Cronin (2003: 171), and as such a focus on translation draws our attention to the ways in which the crime genre becomes world literature. This chapter has two main aims. First, using Catalan crime fiction as a case study, it shows the ways in which translation can contribute to the creation of an autochthonous crime fiction tradition. Second, it seeks to demonstrate that this cultural exchange is multidimensional and more complex than the mere imposition of a dominant literature over a so-called minor one.[2] David Damrosch reminds us that when travelling beyond the cultural context in which they are produced, literary texts take on new meanings, manifesting themselves differently abroad than at home (Damrosch 2003: 6). Developing this idea further, the translated text also takes on different purposes and functions to those it had in the originating culture. The adoption and adaptation of a foreign genre like crime fiction can, and often does, respond to local concerns (Rolls forthcoming; King and Whitmore 2016). As the example of Simenon's *Pietr-le-Letton* suggests, the implications of this discussion goes beyond the Catalan example and, to this end, the chapter concludes with a brief reflection on the role of translation in the genre's global development.

To understand the place of translation in creating a specific national literary tradition, I draw on an early Catalan term for translation: *anostrar*, meaning to make something ours. In recent Catalan translation scholarship, the process of *anostrament* has come to be associated with domestication. For the Catalan translator and poet Àlvar Valls, the concept of *anostrar* does justice to the process of translation, which he sees as presenting readers with a text that, while faithful to the original, should appear as though it was written originally in the target language (Valls 1998: 53). Domestication, however, is often met with criticism in Translation Studies, implying the assimilation of cultural difference and the reaffirmation of values, beliefs, and representations that already exist in the target culture (Venuti 1995: 17–19). While *anostrar* may have certain affinities with domesticating translations, I interpret it as a "localizing practice," as defined by Lawrence Venuti, for whom "Every step in the translation process, starting from the selection of a source text, including the development of a discursive strategy to translate it, and continuing with its circulation in a different language and culture, is mediated by values, beliefs, and representations in the receiving situation" (Venuti 2011: 180).

As part of the localizing process, the translated text enters into a new literary polysystem where, once accepted, it can potentially modify the native literature. The Israeli scholar Itamar Even-Zohar explains this process by arguing that the translated text occupies one of two positions: the innovatory, or primary, position or the conservatory, or secondary, position (Even-Zohar 1990: 46). In the innovatory position, which is relevant to the development of Catalan crime fiction, translated literature

> participates actively in shaping the center of the polysystem … Through the foreign works, features (both principles and elements) are introduced into the home literature which did not exist there before. These include possibly not only new models of reality … but a whole range of other features as well, such as a new (poetic) language, or compositional patterns and techniques. (Even-Zohar, 46–7)

Even-Zohar identifies three main conditions in which the innovatory position takes place: "(a) when a polysystem has not yet been crystallized, that is to say, when a literature is 'young,' or in the process of being established; (b) when a literature is either 'peripheral' (within a larger group of correlated literatures) or 'weak,' or both; and (c) when there are turning points, crises, or literary vacuums in a literature" (Even-Zohar, 47).

According to Kathryn Crameri, the Catalan literary polysytem arguably fulfils "*all three*" of Even-Zohar's conditions (Crameri 2000: 175; emphasis in original). While its origins in the Middle Ages means that Catalan cannot be considered a "young" literature, from the late nineteenth century it nevertheless has undergone a "process of being *re*-established" and crystallization. As a minority literature in Spain, it also occupies a peripheral position in relation to the larger and more powerful literary polysystem of the Spanish state. Finally, in fulfilment of the third condition, Catalan writers have turned to "American and European literary models when nothing suitable was found in the traditions of either Catalonia or Spain" (Crameri 2000: 175).

Gaps in literary polysystems alone do not fully explain the desire to cultivate specific genres, however. Translations are shaped as much by historical, cultural, and ideological concerns as they are by literary ones (Cavagnoli 2014: 332). This is the case of Catalonia, where the introduction of crime and other popular fictions had a specific nation-building function to resist several centuries of uneven, but persistent Hispanicization from the late fifteenth century to the Franco regime (1939–75). This resulted in high levels of illiteracy among Catalans in their own language,[3] a consequence of which was the adoption of Castilian (Spanish) as the primary vehicle for most literary production and consumption in Catalonia.

To overcome the repeated attempts by successive regimes to undermine the legitimacy of Catalan as a language of culture, many writers sought—with relative success, it must be said—to "maintain the prestige of Catalan as a language of high culture" by producing works of so-called elite literature (Fernàndez 1995: 342–3). As a consequence, Catalan culture was described as a "gran cap sense cos. O, almenys, un gran cap amb un cos miserable i raquític" [a big head without a body. Or, at the very least, a big head with a miserable and rickety body] (Molas 1983: 154). This imbalance toward high cultural forms, however, did little to encourage barely literate readers or ones lacking in confidence to engage with Catalan literature. The need to draw readers to participate in Catalan literary culture was very important because, as Domènec Guansé, an early crime writer, noted, readers who cannot find books that interest them in Catalan "recorrerà[n], sense pensar-s'ho, a un altre idioma" [will fall back on another language without even thinking about it] (quoted in Porta 2007: 239). This other, unnamed, language was, of course, Castilian. In the case of crime fiction, Catalan devotees of the genre either had to read novels in the original language or, more commonly, in Spanish translations, as few Catalan translations existed.[4]

To bridge the gap between readers and Catalan literature, the novelist and critic Rafael Tasis argued that "Ens cal aconseguir un públic, vèncer l'allunyament dels catalans envers el llibre, i si aspirem a emmotllar un dia llurs gustos, no tenim més remei que anar primerament, a oferir-los llurs preferències" [We need to reach an audience, to reduce the distance between Catalans and books, and if we aspire to mould their tastes one day, we have no other option than to make the first step and to cater to their preferences] (Tasis i Marca 1935: 123). This meant there was a need for "fulletonistes, autors de novel·les policíaques, creadors d'ídols sentimentals de porteres i obrers [writers of serial fiction, authors of detective novels, creators who can turn female caretakers and male workers into romantic heroes] (Tasis i Marca 1934: 6). In this context, the production and consumption of crime fiction was not perceived as a threat to Catalan literary culture, as it had been in other national contexts. What we see here instead is the desire to create a popular culture industry consisting of producers, various publishing enterprises, a broad array of products—of which crime fiction was an important part—and consumers, with the aim of strengthening the Catalan literary polysystem against the incursion of Castilian-language culture.

Known originally as "novel·les de lladres i serenos" [cops and nightwatchmen novels] after the figures who patrolled the streets and who carried keys to the front doors of buildings in a particular residential area, the crime novel in Catalan developed rather late in comparison to other national literatures. The genre first entered the Catalan literary polysystem via translations and theatrical and poetic adaptations of Doyle's Sherlock Holmes stories in the first decade of the twentieth century. However, the first known crime story to be written directly in Catalan—the novella *La meva mort* [My Death] by Miquel Poal-Aregall—only appeared in 1924. A handful of novellas and short stories followed shortly afterward and the first full-length crime novel, *El collar de la Núria* [Núria's Necklace], written in the tradition of Wilkie Collins and Doyle, was only published in 1927 by Cèsar August Jordana (King 2015).

This tentative development came to a halt in 1939 with the Franco regime's blanket ban on publishing in Catalan. Following a minor easing of censorship in the 1950s, a few writers, Tasis included, produced the occasional crime story in Catalan, but the genre did not really take off and it was only in the early 1960s that the first sustained attempt to introduce the genre to a broader readership occurred. The main motivator behind this development was Manuel de Pedrolo, a committed Catalan nationalist and author of over one hundred works ranging from avant-garde theater and poetry to science and crime fiction. Pedrolo's major contribution was his editorship of *La Cua de Palla* [The Straw Tail], a now iconic series of yellow-covered crime and detective novels (like the Italian *Gialli*) that were translated in the main from English and French, including works by Sébastien Japrisot, Georges Simenon, Didier Daeninckx, John Le Carré, James M. Cain, Raymond Chandler, Dashiell Hammett, and Ross Macdonald, among others.[5] Pedrolo had two main aims for the series. First, to "facilitar al lector català habitual una mena de literatura que fins aleshores havia hagut de llegir sempre en castellà" [make available for regular Catalan readers the sort of literature that until then they had always had to read in Castilian] and, second, to "proporcionar als nombrosos addictes del gènere poc preocupats per la llengua una oportunitat de practicar la nostra i, eventualment, d'interessar-s'hi, a l'hora de llegir altres llibres" [provide for the numerous addicts of the genre, who were not particularly interested in the language [in which it was written], the opportunity to practise ours and, eventually, by reading other books, to become interested in it], that is, in Catalan literature (Pedrolo 1972: 44).[6] Pedrolo's aims for the series were more extraliterary than purely literary. He saw translated crime fiction as a means of drawing Catalans away from the dominant Spanish literary polysystem and into the orbit of Catalan culture, thereby strengthening the readers' identification with Catalonia.[7] Translated crime fiction, however, also had a literary function, as the translated texts took on an allegorical function of the American nation, which was then mapped onto the Catalan context in order to shed light on the subservient position of Catalonia in Franco's Spain.[8]

These foreign crime novels were transformed into Catalan by dedicated literary translators and also by writers such as Ramon Folch i Camarasa, Maurici Serrahima, Joan Oliver, Josep Vallverdú, Rafael Tasis, Manuel de Pedrolo, and Maria-Aurèlia Capmany, herself an occasional crime writer with two significant titles: *Traduït de l'americà* [Translated from the American] (1959) and *El jaqué de la democràcia* [The Mourning Coat of Democracy] (1972). While the need to translate was a consequence of the impoverished state of the Catalan polysystem, largely thanks to the prohibitions and restrictions placed on publishing and education in Catalan, the fact that some of the best, contemporary Catalan writers were involved contributed to the positive reception of crime fiction in this language. Somewhat hyperbolically, the pioneer popular fiction writer Jaume Fuster claimed the translations were "maravillosas, incluso mejores que las traducciones al francés, etcétera. Yo diría que son tal vez las mejores traducciones" [marvellous, even better than the translations into French, etc. I would say that they are perhaps the best translations] (quoted in Hart 1987: 80).

Other series of translated crime fiction also appeared in an attempt to fill the gaps in the Catalan literary culture of the time: in 1964–65 the publishing house Ayma translated Ian Fleming's James Bond novels and several other thrillers in their *Enjòlit* [In Suspense] series, while Edicions Molino published translations of classic detective fiction, including Christie, in its *L'interrogant* [The Enigma] series (Molas and Gallén 1988: 351). These series, however, were not commercially successful. In the case of *La Cua de Palla*, despite several novels achieving bestseller status, including Pedrolo's *Joc brut* [Playing Dirty] (1965) and *Mossegar-se la cua* [Biting One's Own Tail] (1968), the high cost of the books, the irregular appearance of new translations, and the limited readership for genre fiction hindered sales, and publication ceased in 1970 (Pedrolo 1972: 46).

Although commercially unsuccessful, *La Cua de Palla* and other series made an important contribution to the development of Catalan crime fiction through the translators' creation of a Catalan idiom capable of representing the criminal world common to the genre (Valls 1998: 53–6). For Catalan translators, this meant creating a language in which, in Jaume Fuster's memorable phrase, the cops and the robbers "xamullen com vós i jo" [talk in slang like you and me] (50).[9]

Creating a convincing Catalan idiom for crime fiction was not an easy exercise, as there were few local equivalents for the North American argot contained in many of the novels (Valls 1998: 54). The translators, then, had the unenviable task of creating an idiom that would represent the mean streets of the novels without actually being copied from that environment. For Josep Vallverdú, this meant using "un llenguatge viu i descarat que necessàriament calia que fos un poc artificial" [a lively and cheeky language that by necessity was a little artificial] (quoted in Bonada 1983: 4). Rafael Tasis alludes to this problem of mimesis in the prologue to *Crim al Paralelo* [Crime on Parallel Avenue] (1960), the first of three crime novels he wrote in which he explains that the language of his novel "és volgudament acostat al que és propi en els llocs de l'acció [... però] les meves concessions no arriben al català absolutament depauperat que s'hi sent a cada cantonada" [is close to the language used in the places where the action takes place [... but] my concessions do not go so far as to include the absolutely impoverished Catalan that you hear on every corner there] (Tasis i Marca 1960: 10).

In making foreign crime fiction "theirs," Catalan translators were able to forge a literary language, which at first seemed artificial (Parcerisas 1993: 34), but on which later writers would draw to produce their own fictions. This can be seen in the acknowledgments to Fuster's bestselling *De mica en mica s'omple la pica* [Drop by Drop the Sink Fills] (1972) in which he gives thanks to "tot l'equip de traductors de 'La Cua de Palla', per la seva aportació a un llenguatge típic de les obres policíaques" [the team of translators of *La Cua de Palla*, for developing the typical idiom of detective fiction] (Fuster 1972: np). In this way, the translations became models for new writers, whose original work began to fill this "literary vacuum" in Catalan literature.

The results of the pioneering efforts of Pedrolo and other crime fiction writers were only visible after the death of Spanish dictator, Francisco Franco, in 1975 and during the subsequent transition to democracy. Like elsewhere in Spain during the transition, the popularity of the *novel·la negra*, the Hispanic equivalent of the hard-boiled novel, among readers and writers alike was due to what Pedrolo identified as its "crítica de caràcter social [... i] la càrrega de denúncia d'un sistema i d'una societat [social critique and the aggressive denunciation of a system and a society] that were undergoing profound change (Coca 1973: 30). As a result, numerous authors, such as Jaume Fuster, Andreu Martín, Margarida Aritzeta, Josep-Maria Palau i Camps, the Majorcan writers Maria-Antònia Oliver and Antoni Serra, and Valencian authors, such as Ferran Torrent and Josep Lluís Seguí, experimented with the genre, producing a boom in crime narratives, many of which appeared in new specialist crime series. This was the case of *La Negra*, a *Série Noire*-inspired collection—complete with black covers like its French forebear—published by Edicions de la Magrana and dedicated primarily to publishing original crime novels in Catalan. Publisher Edicions 62 resurrected *La Cua de Palla*, now named *Seleccions de la Cua de Palla* [Selections of the *Cua de Palla*], several novels of which were counted among some of the most widely read texts of the 1980s and 1990s (Pujol 2011: 180).

The impact of translation on crime fiction in Catalan is undeniable, as the genre has grown from a handful of authors and texts in the 1920s and 1930s and again in the 1950s and 1960s to the boom of the 1980s. In the first decade of the twenty-first century—with 176 crime novels published by 125 different authors (Benassar 2011: 328–35)—the crime genre in Catalan is now largely normalized. Indeed, once an importer of crime fiction, Catalan literature now exports the novels of Maria-Antònia Oliver, Teresa Solana, and Marc Pastor, among others, to the—very unequal and competitive—global literary marketplace.

While in some ways, the translation of French, English, and American crime novels into Catalan reinforces the world-literariness of these canonical texts, the brief history of the role played by translation in the development of Catalan crime fiction discussed here demonstrates that translation is not as one-sided as it may first appear. As we have seen, *anostrar*—to make something ours—is here more than just an act of transference from one language to another. It is also the adoption of the foreign text, its adaption to a new context, and its reinvention, later, in Catalan originals.

Shedding light on the literary and extraliterary role of translation in the global circulation of the crime genre has implications beyond the specific Catalan example examined in this chapter. It also draws attention to translation within languages, what Roman Jakobson calls intralingual translation. That is, the "interpretation of verbal signs by means of other signs in the same language" (Jakobson 2000: 114). When we look at intralingual translation, we can see that the process of *anostrament* is not unique to Catalan crime fiction nor is it limited to so-called minor or peripheral national literary polysystems. It is also evident in the creation of a distinctly US crime genre. For isn't "making ours" exactly what Hammett did when, according to Raymond Chandler in his celebrated essay "The Simple Art of Murder" (1944), "he took murder out of the Venetian vase and dropped it into the alley" of the American metropolis (Chandler 1995: 988)? Didn't Hammett make "American" what Chandler described as a quintessentially British genre? Indeed, Hammett localized the genre to the United States and, in so doing, he faced many of the same issues confronting translators of crime fiction, including the need to create a realistic language that was recognizable to native readers, which he achieved by giving his readers "a good meaty drama written in the kind of lingo they *imagined* they spoke for themselves" (Chandler 1995: 989; my emphasis).

In the broader context of the world's crime fiction, the Catalan contribution is undoubtedly small and somewhat peripheral; its marginality perhaps reinforced by the national framework in which it has traditionally been studied. Nevertheless, when examined within the prism of world literature, the Catalan crime genre is no longer bound by the borders of what poet Salvador Espriu calls his "petita pàtria" [little nation] (1989: 2). Instead, as this brief analysis of its development shows, in acknowledging and studying the central role of translation we can better comprehend the complex and multidimensional nature of the circulation, reception, and production of the crime genre between and within different polysystems.

Notes

1 Unless otherwise stated, all translations are my own.
2 Following Damrosch, I use minor literature here to mean the "the literatures of smaller countries" (2009: 194).
3 It is estimated that by the time Franco died in 1975, approximately 50 percent of the population could speak Catalan and even fewer could read it (Woolard 1989: 33). The high level of illiteracy was due to two interrelated factors: the restrictions placed on the teaching of Catalan and the influx of large numbers of monolingual Castilian-speaking immigrants from the 1950s onward.
4 For example, the Catalan poet Gabriel Ferraté translated several of Hammett's short stories into Spanish at the beginning of the 1950s, and Hammett's entire work was available in Spanish by 1958 (Piquer Vidal and Martín Escribà 2006: 48).
5 A complete list of the texts published in the series, including the original titles, can be found in Pujol (2011: 183–7).
6 For a detailed study of *La Cua de Palla*, see Canal i Artigas and Martín Escribà.
7 For an analysis of the way in which writers from Catalonia and Spain's other minority cultures of the Basque Country and Galicia use the genre to promote national identity in these regions and to articulate their difference vis-à-vis the Castilian-dominated center, see King (2011).

8   The ways in which translated crime fiction can act as a bearer of national allegories is analyzed by King and Whitmore (2016).
9   For an overview of the translators and the challenges they faced, see Canal i Artigas and Martín Escribà (2011: 119–32).

Works Cited

Benassar, S. (2011). *Pot semblar un accident. La novel·la negra i la transformació dels països catalans, 1999-2010*, Barcelona: Meteora.

Bonada, L. (1983). "Josep Vallverdú, el 'to' de la novel·la en català," *Avui/Lletres* November 2, 4.

Canal i Artigas, J., and À. Martín Escribà (2011). *La cua de palla: retrat en groc i negre*, Barcelona: Alrevés.

Cavagnoli, F. (2014). "Translation and Creation in Postcolonial Context." In *Language and Translation in Postcolonial Literatures*, ed. S. Bertacco. New York, London: Routledge, 321–48.

Chandler, R. (1995). "The Simple Art of Murder." In R. Chandler, *Later Novels and Other Writings*, New York: Library of America, 977–93.

Coca, J. (1973). *Pedrolo perillós?* Barcelona: Dopesa.

Crameri, K. (2000). "The Role of Translation in Contemporary Catalan Culture." *Hispanic Research Journal* 1:2, 171–83.

Cronin, M. (2003). *Translation and Globalization*, London, New York: Routledge.

Damrosch, D. (2003). *What is World Literature?* Princeton: Princeton University Press.

Damrosch, D. (2009). "Major Cultures and Minor Literatures." In *Teaching World Literature*, ed. D. Damrosch. New York: Modern Language Association of America, 193–204.

Espriu, S. (1989). *Selected Poems of Salvador Espriu*, trans. M. Bogin. New York, London: W. W. Norton.

Even-Zohar, I. (1990). "The Position of Translated Literature within the Literary Polysystem." *Poetics Today* 11:1, 45–51.

Fernàndez, J.-A. (1995). "Becoming Normal: Cultural Production and Cultural Policy in Catalonia." In *Spanish Cultural Studies: An Introduction. The Struggle for Modernity*, ed. H. Graham and J. Labanyi. Oxford: Oxford University Press, 342–6.

Fuster, J. (1972). *De mica en mica s'omple la pica*, Barcelona: Edicions 62.

Fuster, J. (1988). "Lladres i serenos que xamullen com vós i jo." *Serra d'Or* 346, 50–2.

Hart, P. (1987). *The Spanish Sleuth: The Detective in Spanish Fiction*. London: Associated University Presses.

Jakobson, R. (2000). "On Linguistic Aspects of Translation." In *The Translation Studies Reader*, ed. L. Venuti. London, New York: Routledge, 113–18.

King, S. (2011). "Detecting Difference/Constructing Community in Basque, Catalan and Galician Crime Fiction." In *Iberian Crime Fiction*, ed. N. Vosburg. Swansea: University of Wales Press, 51–74.

King, S. (2014). "Crime Fiction as World Literature." *Clues* 32:2, 8–19.

King, S. (2015). "Crime Fiction in Catalan: 1 The Origin." International Crime Fiction Research Group, May 24. http://internationalcrimefiction.org/2015/05/24/crime-fiction-in-catalan-1-the-origins/ (Accessed August 26, 2015).

King, S., and A. Whitmore (2016). "National Allegories Born(e) in Translation: The Catalan Case." *The Translator* 22:2, 144–56.

Molas, J. (1983). "La cultura catalana i la seva estratificació." In *Reflexions crítiques sobre la cultura catalane*, ed. P. Vilar. Barcelona: Generalitat de Catalunya, 131–55.

Molas, J., and E. Gallén (1988). "La literatura popular i de consum." In *Història de la literatura catalana. Part Modern*, Vol. 11, ed. A. Comas and J. Molas. Barcelona: Ariel, 301–53.

Mosley, W. (2009). "1926 Poisonville." In *A New Literary History of America*, ed. G. Marcus and W. Sollors. Cambridge, MA: The Belknap Press of Harvard University Press, 598–602.

Parcerisas, F. (1993). "La traducción en Cataluña." *Antípodas* 5, 27–37.

Pedrolo, M. de (1972). "Que falla, 'La Cua de Palla'?" *Serra d'Or* 419, 44–6.

Piquer Vidal, A., and À. Martín Escribà (2006). *Catalana i crimina: La novel·la detectivesca del segle XX*. Palma: Documenta Balear.

Porta, R. (2007). *Mercè Rodoreda i l'humor (1931–1936): Les primeres novel·les, el periodisme i Polèmica*. Barcelona: Fundació Mercè Rodoreda.

Pujol, D. (2011). "A Catalan Series of Crime Fiction: 'La Cua de Palla' and its Sequels (1963–2009)." *Journal of Catalan Studies* 14, 173–200.

Rolls, A. (forthcoming). "Whose National Allegory Is It Anyway? Or what Happens when Crime Fiction Is Translated." *Forum for Modern Language Studies*.

Simenon, G. (1977). *Pietre-le-Letton*. Paris: Presses Pocket.

Simenon, G. (2013). *Pietr the Latvian*, trans. D. Bellos. London: Penguin.

Sussex, L. (2015). *Blockbuster! Fergus Hume and the Mystery of a Hansom Cab*. Melbourne: Text.

Tasis i Marca, R. (1934). "Falles d'una literatura. Variacions sobre la novel·la." *Mirador* September 27, 6.

Tasis i Marca, R. (1935). *Una visió de conjunt de la novel·la catalana*. Barcelona: Publicacions de la Revista.

Tasis i Marca, R. (1960). "Defensa i il·lustració d'aquest llibre (i d'un gènere literari)." In R. Tasis i Marca, *Crim al Paralelo*. Barcelona: Editorial Selecta, 5–10.

Valls, À. (1998). "Quan els lladres i serenos han de parlar català: l'esclavatge i les angúnies de l'equivalència: una por infundada que cal superar." *Quaderns: revista de traducción* 1, 53–6.

Venuti, L. (1995). *The Translator's Invisibility: A History of Translation*. London, New York: Routledge.

Venuti, L. (2011). "World Literature and Translation Studies." In *The Routledge Companion to World Literature*, ed. T. D'haen, D. Damrosch, and D. Kadir. London, New York: Routledge, 180–93.

Woolard, K. (1989). *Double Talk: Bilingualism and the Politics of Ethnicity in Catalonia*. Stanford: Stanford University Press.

12

"In Agatha Christie's Footsteps": *The Cursed Goblet* and Contemporary Bulgarian Crime Fiction

Mihaela P. Harper

A peculiar list circulates in virtual space, its heading—"You are a treasured offspring of socialism, brought up in the 70s, if ..."[1]—is followed by a number of situations that pertain to the last two decades of life under the socialist regime in Bulgaria. Among these ironic, but not devoid of veracity situations, one stands out in its relevance to literature and crime fiction in particular. "You are a treasured offspring of socialism," the entry reads, "if you traded at least once your mother's brand new cookbook or your father's encyclopedia for a tattered Agatha Christie volume" (Administrator 2011). Indeed, the sentiment is genuine, since crime fiction was one of the most popular entertainment options even in the socialist East. And, as the entry indicates, crime fiction was capable of defying the firm correlations between gender and genre that existed during that period because of its ubiquitous appeal. Though Eastern Europe generated its own particular specimens of the crime fiction genre, a few Western representatives were permitted to slip behind the Iron Curtain. These constituted an instant draw for readers—as they still do, judging by the ceaseless reprinting of Christie's novels in Bulgaria and around the world. But the presence of Christie's works in the socialist context raises a number of questions: why were her novels permitted to enter the Eastern block and Bulgaria in particular? That is, why were they translated and offered on the Bulgarian reading market, when the overwhelming majority of Western texts were not? And, what made them gain their fairly instantaneous popularity in that part of the world?

Some of the forewords to Christie's novels, as well as some of the critical commentaries regarding her works, printed in Bulgaria in the interval between 1944 (the beginning of the socialist regime) and 1989 (its official end), suggest several possible responses as to why her books gained admission to the country. In 1979 Dimitri Ivanov asks, "For whom did Christie write? ... For which reader?" his answer—"For the mass reader, of course" (Ivanov 1979: 6). Ivanov elaborates that, although it is "people from the upper middle and high classes of English society that populate the literary world of Agatha Christie's works" (6), she aims to reach the common reader. This endeavor is especially appreciated in socialist Bulgaria, where the common reader is associated with the working class. In this sense, it is her immense popularity abroad, her absence of pretentiousness, as well as her works not being considered art (but rather "instant literature" akin to instant coffee, as Ivanov explains) that make her novels not only eligible for entry into the Eastern Bloc but also quite welcome there. Moreover, Ivanov mentions that Christie has sometimes been grouped with writers who created the idea of the "murky Balkans" and cites the murder on the Orient Express (1934), occurring in a sleeper car between Vienna and Istanbul—"a microcosm on wheels that passes through the oppressive setting of an unfamiliar and hostile world" (7). In other words, Christie's placing Bulgaria "on the map" by popularizing the Balkans—though a somewhat tangential explanation—may have contributed to the interest of East European readers in her novels.

Aiming to introduce Christie to the Bulgarian readership in 1967, Tsvetan Stoyanov describes her *And Then There Were None*[2] as a "novel of 'logic,'" which, in its pure form, "resembles a mathematical problem, a theorem, a chess composition ... And from a more generally philosophical stance, it is a kind of a victory of reason over chaos, confusion, absurdity" (Stoyanov 1967: 5). He proposes that "perhaps this is precisely why lately, vis-à-vis the progressing overall philosophical and psychological crisis in Western literature, the novel of 'logic' is becoming passé" (6). Yet, considering the steadfast interest in crime fiction and Christie's works in particular, it may actually be how her works order the world that appeals to readers who experience reality as disordered, confusing, and absurd. Stoyanov asserts that "Christie continues to bear the old, honorable flag of 'logic,' of reason that in spite of everything overcomes absurdity" (6) against a general tendency of Western literature at the time to present the world as "profoundly confused," its mysteries inaccessible, a jungle without reason, "where you hit and are hit, where chaos and cruelty triumph from beginning to end" (6). Interestingly, this is the world from which the socialist system claims it rescued its citizens. And it is not far-fetched to imagine that Christie's novels of "logic" appealed to authorities who sought to convince the population that the socialist world was ordered, reasonable, and far more conducive to one's wellbeing than the capitalist alternative.

In the 1981 foreword to the translation of *Three Act Tragedy*, Svetoslav Kolev shares the opinion of Dorothy Sayers that "the crime story is a contemporary continuation of the medieval morality plays ... It condemns the crime and is meant to exonerate the innocent, punishes the guilty and is on the side of justice, not of evildoing" (1981: 11). To the socialist authorities, works that presented a clear distinction between good and evil were not only useful but also fit the bona fide purpose of the fictional text. As Vladimir Trendafilov writes in "The Sotscrime," during the years of the socialist regime, "epithets such as 'pure,' 'crystal,' 'transparent,' 'bright,' and 'clear' " dominated the spheres of literary criticism and journalism. There was a "romantic aura" that surrounded such terms and emphasized the ability of the " 'pure' people of the new time," that is, of socialism, to sense evil instinctively and identify it immediately. Thus, a brilliant detective was not necessary, since every *true* member of the socialist society was equipped with the capacity to discern "the evil other" (Trendafilov 2010a: par. 12). "The literary conditionality during that phase of socialism," Trendafilov points out, "is so ideologized that it excludes mystery" (Trendafilov 2010a: par. 15).

Nevertheless, there were certainly disputes regarding the place and function of crime fiction in socialist Bulgaria. Boris Tsvetanov, for instance, reveals that soon after the establishment of the regime in 1944, the "progressive writers," true to socialist realism, "hurried to condemn the crime fiction genre as their brothers [the USSR] had done. There, Maxim Gorky dubbed it 'the favorite reading of the glutted West' " (Tsvetanov 2012: par. 16). Taking up the role of Gorky in Bulgaria, the writer Mladen Issaev, pronounced that "the crime novel is a weed that must be mercilessly uprooted from our literary field" (Tsvetanov 2012: par. 18). Issaev's persecution of crime fiction lasted for twelve years, but it failed to "uproot" the genre, although there were others who shared his sentiment. Kolev offers a general critical note on the genre in an article on Agatha Christie printed in 1972, but keeps open a positive possibility in terms of its value. His points are in line with the claims of the socialist doctrine that distinguished between East and West on moral grounds. He writes:

> The task of the criminal genre is not at all only to entertain, as some think. Its main purpose, first and foremost, is to instruct and protect, when it is not used to pursue commercial aims and the satisfaction of base instincts, as often happens in capitalist societies. The famous masterpieces of this literature reflect the noble struggle of society with crime, a serious ulcer from which the young, most of all, must be protected. If in the West crime is the result of the social system, in the socialist countries, to a great extent, it is the result of the still-persisting,

onerous inheritance of the pre-revolutionary past in the psyche and upbringing of a relatively limited circle of people—mostly loafers, friends of alcohol and the easy, non-labor-oriented way of life. In this sense, an active and leading impetus in the works of authors from our countries, writing in this literary area, is socialist humanism, the struggle to protect and preserve the human identity, the significant moral and ethical values of the new person, national property. (Kolev 1972: 10)

In this sense, while crime has the capacity to measure the "health" of a society, crime fiction can have a pedagogical as well as a normative and regulative function. The latter can contribute to a socialist society's proper health.

Most forewords to Christie's books printed prior to the fall of the socialist regime in 1989 aim to introduce her to the audience, though one foreword does reference the availability of her works in Bulgaria even before 1944. Kolev notes that Christie's *The Murder of Roger Ackroyd* was translated into Bulgarian in 1938 under the same title and again in 1967 as *Alibi* (the title change seems to be an ideological marketing strategy, targeting an audience that was supposed to have acquired a much more delicate sensibility regarding murder and crime during the years of socialism). In 1966, it was the writer Hristo Minchev who was able to convince the head of the National Military Press to print Christie's novel, "primarily because in the USSR a dozen of her works had already appeared. Following the rules of the socialist realism, the shocking original title was given a new one, 'Alibi'" (Tsvetanov 2015: par. 16). It is no secret that Bulgaria—sometimes erroneously dubbed the sixteenth Soviet republic—followed the policies of the USSR. Thus, it is not surprising that the availability of Christie's works in the Soviet Union sanctioned their appearance on the Bulgarian market as well. This linking of the markets would remain in effect for some time even after 1989.

But there is another reason for crime fiction's ambivalent presence in the Bulgarian book market, and it lies in the socialist assertion that the regime had eliminated the root cause of crime. Trendafilov notes that while "socialism diligently conceals the actual crimes and throws a positive disguise over the literary in the course of its entire duration … the media constantly endeavor to assert that the main cause for committing a crime disappeared along with the liquidation of private property." Importantly, he continues, "if a murder were to occur somewhere, its roots necessarily had to be sought elsewhere, in a capitalist foreign land" (Trendafilov 2010a: par. 1). Perhaps here it is possible to find a reason for the agreement to translate and disseminate Christie's novels prior to the regime change in 1989—they presented a "degenerate" classed society (primarily upper middle and upper classes) that served as the fecund milieu for crime and a kind of perverse justice, as in Christie's *And Then There Were None*. Thus, solve as they might every crime that they encountered, Poirot and Miss Marple could never eliminate the source of crime itself. In this sense, one of the morals of crime fiction that the socialist regime may have sought to promote was that capitalist, classed societies were doomed to a crime-ridden future, antithetical to "the bright future" that communism itself promised. Emil Lozev implies a similar idea when he writes that, "Without her books being socially critical, through their verisimilitude to everyday life, involuntarily they depict the destructive impact of bourgeois reality on human individuality" (Lozev 1976: 8). On the other hand, it seems that even the socialist party was not convinced by this idea, since, as Tsvetanov recalls, writer and crime fiction editor Hristo Minchev—the same one who eventually persuaded Military Press to publish Christie's novel *Alibi*—was cautioned, after an actual murder took place on a Sofia streetcar in 1957, not to print so many crime novels (even though he had only published six in one year) (Tsvetanov 2015: par. 15). The implication was again that the cause of the crime was elsewhere—in this case, emanating from the pages of the crime novels—and that crime fiction had served as the conductor of this very real influence and effect.

Despite the contradictory interpretations, there was a surge in the publication of crime-related readings in the 1960s, "as a result of the easing of the doctrinarian control over literature [that] managed to assimilate into the national tradition—to 'nationalize' in a sense—the espionage novel of the Soviet kind, a staple of the 50s" (Trendafilov 2010a: par. 61). The term "nationalize" here evokes the process of appropriation of private property by the state, though the notion refers more broadly also to the rewriting of history and to the revision of the citizens' beliefs and their very lives. Though Trendafilov's main focus is the Bulgarian crime novel, he does not include among its influences Agatha Christie's work, which may not have "flooded" the Bulgarian market at that time, but was certainly a notable and welcome presence, as indicated by the "You are a treasured offspring of socialism" list referenced in the beginning.[3] Since 1989, however, her work has indeed flooded the market. In fact, Bulgaria confirms that, as UNESCO found in 2010, Agatha Christie is the most translated author of all time. Along with many other countries around the world, Bulgarian publishing houses—ERA in particular—in 2010 celebrated the 120th anniversary of Christie's birth, the 90th of Poirot's first case, and the 80th of Miss Marple's. As part of the "Days of Agatha

Christie," ERA Publishers set up a number of games for readers, a Facebook photo-competition, and a crime fiction contest. The contest's title, "In Agatha Christie's Footsteps," bespeaks a bit of nostalgia, a desire to recover and remember the past, mixed with the tribute to the "Queen of Crime Fiction." However, there is also an attempt to enter the worldliness of the genre and to reshape it, as any footstep-following does. The winner of the contest, Lora Lazar's *The Cursed Goblet*, will shortly become the focus of my discussion. But before turning to Christie's successor in Bulgaria, I would like to dwell on the question of Christie's popularity in a context far removed from the one that her texts generally set up.

As Trendafilov points out, the Bulgarian crime novel "is a socialist invention, an offspring of the period after the second World War ... that emerges under the normative influence of the Soviet military-intelligence novella" (Trendafilov 2010b: par. 6). Thus, the genre was dominated by a rather stagnant formula: the responsibility for the crime is necessarily found elsewhere (Trendafilov 2010a: par. 1), while "any kind of investigation is fully subsumed by the state" (Trendafilov 2010b: par. 6). This is not the case in Christie's crime novels. Instead, they offer something rather different: ownership of the crime and the criminal, an independent detective—foreign in the case of Poirot and relying nearly exclusively on his "little grey cells"—and even a critique of institutions and authorities, such as the legal system and the police. And yet, Christie's settings are meticulously constructed and representative of a very particular kind of upper-class order—a slower pace of action, opulence, and abundant meals (of which Poirot eagerly partakes). It is precisely these settings that many of her Bulgarian readers found irresistibly alluring—they produced in readers the sense of indulging in a travelogue with the bonus of solving a crime in the process. Though he is not speaking directly about Christie's works, Trendafilov suggests that crime fiction

> replaced the unfulfilled journeys to distant corners, embodied an unconscious rebellion against the impossibility, under the conditions of this place, of taking the initiative for your life in your own hands. They gave an alternative to the mediocre life that people led. They offered a virtual risk, an approved version of the forbidden, a reverie of the luxury not only to live however and wherever you would like but also to do so in the name of your country, that is, at its expense. (Trendafilov 2010a: par. 25)

A great part of contemporary Bulgarian crime fiction operates in a rather different tenor, more as a journey behind political and economic facades. Nikolay Aretov points out that, "As a rule, the new Bulgarian crime literature does not concern itself with incidental murderers and robbers (as are the majority of criminals in line with the classical models from Conan Doyle to Agatha Christie, and even in Mary Higgins Clark); it seeks the professionals, the mafia" (Aretov 2005: sec. 2). These works are inextricably entwined with the country's postsocialist reality of organized crime, mass corruption, financial instability, and spiritual paucity, as narratives turn to exposing underground schemes that involve the highest of political structures: blackmail, racketeering, kidnapping, contract rape, and pyramid schemes as well as common crimes, including document falsification and swindling others out of property and cash. There are, of course, exceptions—novels that maintain a distance from their national crime-ridden setting, which Lora Lazar,[4] author of *The Cursed Goblet*, finds critical to preserving "the mystery," the essence of crime fiction. And, as the classic representatives of the genre do, *The Cursed Goblet*, too, turns to murder as the centerpiece crime.

To be precise, the murders are seven—which confirms the suggestion that one-murder crime fictions are passé (at least in the Bulgarian strand of the genre)—and the murderer follows an imaginary ancient Bulgarian runic calendar in committing them. The narrative begins with a treasure hunter, Ignat Kazandjiev, who discovers a rune-inscribed Rosette and believes it to be ancient (the runes are proto-Bulgarian). While every chapter is dedicated to a day of the week, from Sunday to Saturday, and then from Monday to Sunday (skipping Saturday), the text is written in seven alternating segments within each chapter, dedicated to different characters. It commences with the treasure hunter and a nonverbal graveyard caretaker, bai Dushko, before introducing the female figure who finds herself at the center of the events to unfold—restorer and migrant from a small village in rural Bulgaria, Yana Srebreva, called Sparrow by her partner, archeologist Boyan Gradev. *The Cursed Goblet* both maintains and disrupts the way in which female Bulgarian crime fiction characters have traditionally been presented. According to Trendafilov, "As a literary character, the woman serves primarily as a backdrop to events (the faithful wife of the investigator, [etc.] …) or fulfills the function of a passive object in their chain (a crime victim) … Rarely does she have a key part in the development of events, unless she is an antiheroine" (Trendafilov 2010b: par. 25). By the murderer's design, Yana is present at practically every crime scene, which makes her a suspect, but she is certainly not an antiheroine; timid, anxious, often terrified, and insecure, she finds comfort from her anxieties almost exclusively in her profession (which she practices with expertise and flair) and, on occasion, in the arms of her beloved. Her character undergoes the deepest change, as she grows to trust herself and musters the strength to fight the murderer. Her kindness and unique spirit are noted throughout the text by the two "best" characters (in terms of innocence, ethics, likability)—Ignat Kazandjiev, the treasure hunter, and bai Dushko, the graveyard caretaker—despite the suspicions that the police harbor about her involvement in the murders.

The two police officers, Commissioner Mihail Donov, the Target, and his rookie partner Radoslav (Rado) Angelov, are introduced shortly after the beginning of the novel, when Yana happens upon the first body in front of her own apartment door. The rest of the murders follow at regular intervals, connected to Yana and a bottle of the best wine in the area, "Krumovo kale," spiked with a dose of belladonna. As the mystery of the murders slowly unfolds, by the end of the novel all of the characters are working together to solve it—an implication of community-building that is reinforced in the epilogue and constitutes an important reconfiguration of the traditional model of a single crime-solver. Ultimately, the final segment of the murderer's meticulously designed and executed plan backfires, and he, regional governor Savin Sonev, imbibes a lethal dose of the poison that he has been dispensing. Readers find out later that he was brutally abused by his father, the most prominent former communist leader in the town, who—the text suggests—is responsible for the son's aberration, identified by the police psychiatrist as pathological narcissism. The diagnosis itself can be read metaphorically as pertaining to the time both during and after the collapse of the socialist regime—a time also marked by a sense of self-importance and aggrandizement, envy, exploitation, as well as an absence of empathy. In part, the identity of the murderer remains unknown for as long as it does because he occupies the prominent public office of regional governor and because most people have come to know him as a generous and nice person. Among the multiple motives for his murders—including desires for revenge, to outsmart others, and to overshadow his father—is to obtain from Yana "the cursed goblet," a mysterious historical artifact that makes wishes come true, but brings damnation along with their fruition.

While in its numerous murders Lazar's novel echoes *And Then There Were None*, there are certain formulaic elements of Christie's works in general that the text exhibits as well. According to Kostadina Yordanova these include: a closed circle of participants, a second murder, the staging of the murder and provoking the murderer to reveal himself, as well as the murderer's having "no 'external' motives, [since] he is an 'insider,' one of the group's 'own'" (Yordanova 1990: 6). Each of these is present in Lazar's novel, but *The Cursed Goblet* also follows

Christie in the choice of a murder method. As Claire Reynolds indicates, "The intricate set-up of a situation in which the victim will be exposed to a deadly dose of poison seems to have been one of Christie's favourite methods for setting in motion her stories" (Reynolds 2012). Yet, by selecting the blend of belladonna and wine, Lazar does more than follow Christie. The blend points to something upon which Bulgaria prides itself—wine—as well as to the townspeople's appreciation of *good* wine. In fact, Lazar traces the route of the wine pre- and post-production, emphasizing particularly its role as pay-off, as the wine-maker (a suspect) sends countless boxes of his excellent beverage to the police department, the governor's office, and the rest of the local authorities and luminaries. Thus, the current of the precious substance—which also bears the name of one of Bulgaria's most successful and formidable khans, Krum—becomes a singularly apposite vehicle for the "beautiful woman," belladonna. The poison itself has national significance and is a part of folklore, familiar to many Bulgarians as "mad herb," possibly because of its hallucinogenic properties in certain doses. But the combination of wine and belladonna used by the murderer is symbolic of an easily corruptible heritage as well as of its loss and perversion at the hands of the murderer.

Sonev, the villain, shows an intriguing amalgam of qualities. He constitutes an innovation to the genre in its Bulgarian strand, as he dwells among the townspeople indistinguishably, unlike the easily discernible villain in the earlier representatives of the genre that Trendafilov discusses. Lazar's criminal has the appearance of "purity"—he is perfectly likable—but constitutes "a disease" within the town's body that is no longer recognizable. On the one hand, this is because of his high social and political position, and, on the other, because he has convinced everyone that he is friendly, kind, safe, that is, "pure." Even the police commissioner, the Target, who otherwise boasts a keen eye, fails to conceive of the possibility that Sonev is suspect, despite his partner's implying that possibility. The implication seems to be that socialism is still very much alive, operating indistinguishably at the heart of the town and unrecognizable as "other" to the new system and its members. Still, in his attempt to complete his plan, Sonev involuntarily commits suicide—a rather overt hope on the part of the text that the malignant part will eventually eliminate itself.

In his "A Mythology of Crime Fiction," Aretov proposes a distinction between the crime fiction of socialist realism and its Western counterpart. While the former "presupposes an uncritical, if not an enthusiastic attitude toward the national institutions and especially the authorities in charge of security," the police, the latter doesn't praise the police even when a job is well done. For the latter, "the good cop resembles a private detective—a marginal type, an outsider and a failure, who is rather in conflict with the powers of the day, subjected to their blows" (Aretov 2005: sec. 1). What is more, Aretov claims, the private detective is "a liberal and an individualist," who "expresses a spirit of independence and disobedience" (Aretov 2005: sec. 1). The traditional police officer, on the other hand, is conservative, values the collective, and "protects the interests of the state, a high aim that permits violating the rights of the individual" (Aretov 2005: sec. 1). In *The Cursed Goblet*, though the "good guys" form a crime-solving community toward the end, the prime crime solvers are three—Ignat Kazana, the treasure hunter, and the two representatives of the police. The latter two come much closer to the figure of the private detective that Aretov describes than to the traditional police detective. When authorities from the "big city" take over the case and refuse to cooperate, the two policemen in the novel follow their own leads without sharing them and even conceal evidence, thus rejecting the bureaucracy and the system that they are supposed to support. In this sense, all three comprise "the spirit of independence and disobedience" (Aretov 2005: sec. 1). Yet, the crime is no longer solved solely by "little grey cells" (à la Poirot), but rather on the basis of pseudo-historical information found on the internet by the treasure hunter, who is himself more of an outlaw than anything else.

He deciphers the runic "map" of the murders in spite of the disregard with which his ideas are met by the professional historian Gradev and by the police. In this sense, what Lazar's text offers is a reconfiguration of the forces at work in the crime novel. This reconfiguration doesn't subscribe to Aretov's notion of a "good crime novel"—one that "opposes the social status quo and institutions (police, courts) and should attack them rather than rely on assistance from the PD, for instance" (Aretov 2001)—but it does offer a novel way of looking at the representatives of the law. The police are not applauded as they were in socialist crime narratives, and they still fail in multiple ways to solve the crime at hand, as they do in Christie's works. But they are far more cooperative and willing to stand on the side of the outlaw, even to break the law themselves—a gesture indicative simultaneously of a mistrust of the system, of a confidence in their own abilities, and of ownership of the crime setting, literally and figuratively. In fact, the text distinctly sympathizes with the two representatives of the police force. Misho the Target "resembled a boulder, upon which the sandpaper of the sculptor had not completed the final smoothing strokes" (Lazar, 49), a massive figure that "exuded warmth" (Lazar, 60), while Rado has dimples when he smiles, "does not say much, does not pretend to be a know-it-all, and does not postpone tasks until the next day" (Lazar, 23). Their characterization throughout the text exposes an incorruptible work ethic and genuine eagerness to protect their town and community, both qualities that directly contradict the image of the police representative over the last two decades, an image marked by corruption, indolence, and indifference.

Solving the crime does not merely return the world to a preexisting order or subject a context run amok to the laws of logic and justice (as it does in Christie's text). It improves the microcosm, the world in *The Cursed Goblet*; the attitudes, community, and lives of all characters are ameliorated, as the epilogue makes evident. The removal of the criminal presence disencumbers the lives and personalities of the characters: archeologist Boyan Gradev is finally able to propose to Yana, who is herself no longer afraid of life; bai Dushko is reunited with his long-lost love, Siya, after the Target and Rado help him to locate her; Rado finds love, despite his complaint that no young people remain in town; and the Target, in a much improved mood, arrives to celebrate Boyan and Yana's engagement with his wife, Maria. Thus, it is not merely a matter of eliminating the internal problem—simultaneously psychological (the internalization of the abusive father) and political (the socialist past that is not only still alive but rules in a deceptively reformed and actually degenerated present)—but rather that its elimination positively reconfigures the very existence of the community of characters involved.

Order is itself a recurring motif in the text—both Yana and Sonev seek it with compulsive obsessiveness. But while the former imposes physical order on her domestic and professional space, the latter fashions order out of historical and astronomical symbols. Yana's ordering ultimately proves to be the life-sustaining kind, whereas the interpretation/exploitation of celestial bodies—the murder victims are designated as Mars, Jupiter, Moon, and so on—and manipulation of history, undertaken by Sonev, are exposed as self-destructive. The ordering of facts that solves the crimes, on the other hand, emerges on the basis of intimate, lived histories that yield a truthfulness to which popular histories or History in general do not have access. When examining the vandalized tomb of Sonev's father (vandalized by Sonev himself), bai Dushko lets the two police officers know that the deceased was not a "decent man," which the Target contradicts by noting that "You cannot find a single person who would say something bad about [comrade Boevski]" (Lazar, 62). Bai Dushko's intuitive way of accessing truths is corroborated by Ignat Kazana, the treasure hunter, who, late in the novel, reveals his first-hand knowledge of the brutal beatings and abuse that Sonev endured at the hands of Boevski. It is this piece of history—a private story contradicting the general opinion that has entered mainstream history—that helps solve the crime, though the Target wants "facts, clues, evidence, and not empty cogitations" (Lazar, 303). Thus, the ordering of the narrative, and the correction of mainstream history, occurs in the often domestic, intimate realm of private history and communal interlocution, where there is room for intuition and cogitation.

Each of the changes that the text introduces to its predecessors, and particularly to Christie's novels, including grounding the setting in a very particular Bulgarian history and sociopolitical problematic, localizes the globality of the genre. In this sense, Agatha Christie's writing becomes world literature in Bulgaria, but, paradoxically, so does Lora Lazar's. Locating the novel in Christie's "footsteps" doesn't merely give a little-known author access to a broader audience that is familiar with Christie's works; it also reveals Lazar's innovations to the national genre as well as to global crime fiction. The "footstep" itself becomes the space of world literature, "a degree of distance"[5]—it worlds the literature that enters it. In a country that is still developing mechanisms for disseminating texts beyond the national boundaries, entering the space of the "footstep" remains one of few means of becoming world literature, in the sense of literature in a context other than the national.[6] *The Cursed Goblet* thus performs an intriguing maneuver for entering the world: it simultaneously associates itself with world literature—by following in Christie's footsteps—and dissociates itself from it—by localizing the genre in personal and national histories.

Notes

1 Unless otherwise noted, all translations from the Bulgarian are my own.
2 The novel was printed in Bulgaria under the title *Ten Little Niggers* (Narodna Mladej 1967).
3 Bulgarian online forums on Agatha Christie are an intriguing read vis-à-vis the question of the author's popularity during the socialist regime and now. Participants often discuss feelings of nostalgia and pleasure associated with reading Christie, at times linking these with the opportunity to experience British culture and society that her books afford. "But I enjoy this farfetchedness, pretentiousness, and the

humdrum banter between Poirot and Hastings. It is a part of the atmosphere, so to speak. Tedious traditionalism that evokes stability and safety. Like Good old England," one forum participant, Jave, points out. See "Agatha Christie—the queen of crime fiction" on *bg-mamma*, one of the most popular Bulgarian online forums at http://www.bg-mamma.com/index.php?topic=466014.15;topicrefid=20.

4 Lora Lazar is an alias that follows—in the non-Bulgarian sounding name—a tradition that the early Bulgarian crime writers started. According to Tsvetanov, the numerous crime writers that emerged a little more than half a century ago wrote under similarly foreign sounding names: Bisou Polino, M. Dorian, E. Ulas, Dr. Yans, Don Lucio, Jack Ovorbag, George Delaguer, and E. Brin (Tsvetanov 2012: par. 2).

5 In *What is World Literature?* David Damrosch proposes that "a degree of distance from the home tradition can help us to appreciate the ways in which a literary work reaches out and away from its point of origin. If we then observe ourselves seeing the work's abstractions from its origins, we gain a new vantage point on our own moment" (Damrosch, 300).

6 In a brief announcement for the National Library from 2009, Aretov asserts that the Bulgarian crime novel is on the rise and highlights the foci of discussions in the course of the "Bulgarian Crime Fiction" academic conference that took place in 2008. The conference was organized around three roundtables, the queries of which were: "Why don't/do I read Bulgarian crime fiction?" "Why don't/do I trust Bulgarian critics?" "Why don't/do I write Bulgarian crime fiction?" (Aretov 2009: 41). Aretov writes that many of the authors and critics focused on what the Bulgarian crime novel needs to be in order to attract the attention of an international audience. The question raised the issue of dissemination, and particularly of the need for literary agents who would facilitate access to Bulgarian books within and outside of the country.

Works Cited

Administrator (2011). "Вие сте свидна рожба на социализма, ако…" [You are a treasured offspring of socialism, if …]. *LibRev Pregled* (July 23). http://www.librev.com/index.php/mixed-things-stuff-publisher/1303-2011-07-23-08-30-42 (Accessed January 10, 2015).

Aretov, Nikolay (2001). "Рапсодия в черно. Размисли за криминалните жанрове" [Rhapsody in black. reflections on the crime genres"]. *Literaturen Vestnik* 33 (october 10–16). http://www.slovo.bg/old/litvestnik/133/lv0133017.htm (Accessed January 25, 2015).

Aretov, Nikolay (2005). "Митология на литературата за престъпления" [A mythology of crime fiction]. *LiterNet* (February 12). http://liternet.bg/publish8/naretov/mitologia.htm#2 (Accessed February 5, 2015).

Aretov, Nikolay (2009). "Българският криминален роман" [The Bulgarian crime novel]. *Biblioteka* 1, 41–42. http://www.nationallibrary.bg/fce/001/0106/files/bibl-09-1aretov.pdf (Accessed September 15, 2015).

Christie, Agatha (1967). Алиби [*Alibi*]. Sofia: Darjavno Voenno Izdatelstvo.

Damrosch, David (2003). *What is World Literature?* Princeton: Princeton University Press.

Ivanov, Dimitri (1979). "Уловките на старата дама" [The ruses of the old lady]. Foreword to Agatha Christie, *Свидетел на обвинението* [*Witness to the crime*], trans. Theodora Davidova. Sofia: Narodna Kultura, 5–10.

Jave (2010, January 28). Agatha Christie—the queen of crime fiction [Msg 15]. Message posted to http://www.bg-mamma.com/index.php?topic=466014.0;topicrefid=20.

Kolev, Svetoslav (1972). "Агата Кристи" [Agatha Christie]. *Anteni* 2 (January 14), 10–11.

Kolev, Svetoslav (1981). "Агата Кристи и Еркюл Поаро" [Agatha Christie and Hercule Poirot]. Foreword to Agatha Christie, *Трагедия в три действия* [*Tragedy in three acts*], trans. Boris Mindov. Biblioteka Galaktika. Varna: Georgi Bakalov, 5–11.

Lazar, Lora (2011). Чашата на проклятието [*The Cursed Goblet*]. Sofia: ERA.

Lozev, Emil (1976). "Кралицата на детектива" [The queen of crime fiction]. *Narodna Kultura* 18 (May 1), 8.

Reynolds, Claire (2012). "Agatha Christie's Methods of Murder." *Agatha Christie* (November 30). http://www.agathachristie.com/news/2012/agatha-christies-methods-of-murder (Accessed January 16, 2015).

Stoyanov, Tsvetan (1967). "Агата Кристи и 'малките негърчета" [Agatha Christie and "the little niggers"]. Foreword to Agatha Christie, *Десет малки негърчета* [*Ten little niggers*], trans. Nikola Milev. Sofia: Narodna Mladej, 5–8.

Trendafilov, Vladimir (2010a). "Соцкримът" [The Sotscrime]. *PublicRepublic* (August 8). http://www.public-republic.com/magazine/2010/08/44459.php (Accessed January 15, 2015).

Trendafilov, Vladimir (2010b). "Жената в българския криминален роман" [The woman in Bulgarian crime fiction]. *LiterNet* 10:131 (October 17). http://liternet.bg/publish8/vtrendafilov/zhenata.htm (Accessed January 20, 2015).

Tsvetanov, Boris (2012). "Усмъртяването на българския криминален роман" [The killing of the Bulgarian crime novel]. *Desant* 142 (February 8). http://www.desant.net/show-news/23840/ (Accessed March 3, 2015).

Tsvetanov, Boris (2015). "'Ориент експрес'—българската връзка на Агата Кристи" ["Orient Express"—the Bulgarian connection of Agatha Christie].

Bolgari (January 14). http://bolgari.net/sad_quot_orient_ekspres_quot_%E2%80%93_bylgarskata_vryzka_na_agata_kristi-h-867.html (Accessed March 8, 2015).

Yordanova, Kostadina (1990). "Рецептура на мистерията" [A recipe for mystery]. *ABV* 24 (June 12), 6–7.

13

A Missing Literature: Dror Mishani and the Case of Israeli Crime Fiction

Maayan Eitan

Dror Mishani's novel *The Missing File* begins with a question: "Do you know why there are no detective novels in Hebrew?" Police inspector Avraham Avraham poses this question to a mother who has just reported the disappearance of her teenage son. And he immediately answers:

> Because we don't have crimes like that. We don't have serial killers; we don't have kidnappings; and there aren't many rapists out there attacking women on the streets. Here, when a crime is committed, it's usually the neighbor, the uncle, the grandfather, and there's no need for a complex investigation to find the criminal and clear up the mystery. *There's simply no mystery here.* (Mishani 2013b: 4; my emphasis)

The author himself, though, a literary editor of Hebrew fiction, a translator, and a scholar, offered a slightly different answer in a 2013 interview in the leading Israeli newspaper *Haaretz*: "Because Hebrew literature was founded as part of the national project," he said, and as, traditionally, the detective "does not deeply occupy himself with questions of national identity … Hebrew literature has always rejected this genre" (Mishani 2013a). Unlike the soldier or the Mossad agent, who have been depicted as national heroes, Israeli cultural representations of police detectives have been, for various sociopolitical reasons, mostly derogatory. Contrary to the brave endeavors of Zionist heroes, Hebrew popular culture has rarely seen a policeman whose day-to-day work seemed worthy of literary depiction; and thus Hebrew literature has had no serious tradition of crime fiction.

Mishani's own crime novel, *Tik ne'edar* (literally "a missing file or backpack," but also "the [murder] case of the missing [person]"), however, proves to be a completely different and intriguing case, as is also suggested by its speedy translation and circulation. Mishani's protagonist, detective Avraham Avraham, is a Mizrahi, a Jew of Middle Eastern or North African origin, historically excluded from Israeli hegemony and positions of power. He lives and works in Holon, a lower-middle-class suburb of Tel Aviv, watches "Law & Order," and reads Sherlock Holmes tales, but his uneventful life is disrupted when he has to solve a universally horrifying mystery: the sudden, unexplained disappearance of a teenage boy. In the course of the novel Avraham will not, indeed, "occupy himself with questions of national identity," yet Mishani's novel serves as a fascinating example for a genre reinventing itself. Even more fascinating is the relationship between the local (and, at least to some degree, the non-Western) and the (Western) global, or the process of transformation of the local into the global, illustrated by the book's success in non-Israeli markets, a matter to be touched upon later.

Mishani's academic work dealt with the history of crime fiction in Hebrew, but he later neglected this project in favor of writing his own crime novels. He was born in 1975 in Holon, the same suburb in which his protagonist lives and works. *Tik ne'edar*, the first of his Avraham series, was published in Hebrew in Tel Aviv in 2011 and then almost immediately was translated into more than fifteen languages, among them English, French, German, Spanish, Catalan, Polish, Italian, Swedish, and Norwegian. The book was published to very positive, even rave, reviews, and won several prizes both in Israel and abroad. No other Israeli crime novel has ever won such worldwide acclaim.

This essay attempts to answer the following question: Why, in a literary market that produces more and more crime novels, did Mishani's Avraham series move so smoothly from a truly tiny local market into the global one? I suggest that there is a telling connection between the novel's worldwide success (albeit, admittedly, mostly in the West) and the fact that it has been described, framed even, in global markets as a rare depiction of suburban Israeli life. Thus, the back cover of the American paperback edition describes Avraham as dealing with "a crime committed in his quiet suburb of Tel Aviv," and the central blurb below this description tells us that "the sense of place here is fascinating (Tel Aviv's suburbs seem both familiar and exotic)," while the final blurb announces that "Readers of edgy mysteries set in unusual places will eagerly await his planned sequel."

A word about the history of Israeli crime fiction is in order. Crime novels in Hebrew were published in Mandatory Palestine during the 1930s and 1940s, in a time of great political and cultural turmoil—the years before the foundation of the state of Israel, during which the Jewish Settlement (*yishuv*) tried to define itself as a nation (an effort that, of course, never precludes an attempt at cultural world-making). These novels were written mostly by schoolteachers, immigrants themselves whose first language was not Hebrew, hoping that such a popular genre would encourage their students to read and thus learn the new language. The result was an expansion not only of literary horizons but also of the linguistic boundaries of Hebrew, another project attempting to reinvent itself at the time.

After the establishment of the state of Israel in 1948 and during the first half of the 1950s a shift occurred: While less and less original crime fiction was written in Hebrew, more classic world mystery and crime novels were translated into Hebrew (among them, for example, were the works of Conan Doyle and Agatha Christie). And yet crime fiction remained on the margins of Hebrew literature, never entering its canon, perceived as an inferior genre. In the early 1960s, original crime fiction in Hebrew began to emerge once again, now as a popular genre, and Israeli authors, writing in Hebrew, began to publish their own crime and mystery novels. Their work typically dealt with the figure of the Zionist "Sabra" (a Jew born in Palestine/Israel), and their villains, as one can (naturally and unfortunately) imagine, were Arabs, while the detective adventures always had something to do with national goals—from salvaging long-lost Jewish archaeological treasures to preventing terror attacks.

And so by the 1980s Israeli crime fiction was everywhere. Still not considered part of the Hebrew literary canon or perceived as "serious" literature, it was widely read nonetheless. It generally followed similar patterns and plot lines: The Hebrew *sipur balashi*, literally, a detective story, now revolved around a police detective, either a man or a woman, who is called to help the victims of domestic but not national crimes; solving, mostly, almost impossibly mysterious murder cases. It is worth mentioning that these novels were written by both men and women, and that their protagonists, especially during the 1990s—yet another time of political turmoil for the country—came from all strata of Israeli society. Interestingly, very few translations of foreign crime novels appeared in Hebrew during these years. Some of the local authors were translated into other languages, especially English and occasionally French or German, and, not unlike Mishani's Avraham novels, were marketed to foreign audiences as a portrait of the "authentic" Israel, Israelis, or Israeli life.

Despite occasionally portraying working-class Israel, Mizrahi Jews, and non-hegemonic Israel and Israelis, those 1980s and 1990s novels never explicitly dealt with such volatile topics, but rather used them as plot background. Yair Lapid, for example, had written three such novels between 1989 and 2010, while working as a journalist and television news and talk show host, before leaving his literary and journalistic career in 2012 to enter politics, founding a centrist party, and becoming Benjamin Netanyahu's finance minister in 2013-14. Lapid's protagonist, private eye Josh (Yehushua) Shirman, was fashioned after Raymond Chandler's Marlowe. He is a heavy whiskey drinker and witty womanizer who usually fights the generic "bad guys": organized crime, a serial killer, or the occasional gang. Despite earning themselves a relatively wide Israeli readership, none of these novels managed—or maybe even aspired—to deal deeply with social or political problems, or to offer a serious outlook on the crimes they portrayed or their connections to Israeli society and politics. Most were not translated into other languages, and none managed to gain an international readership and acclaim such as Mishani's Avraham series had. Why not?

The first reason would probably be that crime fiction, written in Hebrew or (scarcely) translated, was considered literature for adolescents until the 1980s, when two women writers, Batya Gur and Shulamit Lapid, began publishing their detective fiction. Both their protagonists, one a man, police inspector Michael Ohayon, the other a young woman, journalist Lizi Badihi, were Mizrahi Jews. They were, then, different from both the traditional protagonist of canonical Hebrew Israeli literature, and the protagonist of Israeli crime fiction. Their Mizrahi identity was marked by their Sepharadi family names, Ohaion and Badihi, and they lived and worked in the Israeli periphery. Their biography, then, marks their difference from the protagonist of what had been considered "serious" Israeli literature, whose (male) protagonists were all Ashkenazi, that is, Jews of European origins, who were either Holocaust survivors themselves or were the descendants of survivors, usually growing up under the sun of upward social mobility: born to elite Israeli families, either middle or higher class or in a kibbutz, serving important national positions in the army, and so on.

Before the novels of Batya Gur and Shulamit Lapid, the protagonist of popular Israeli crime fiction in the 1960s and 1970s was a policeman who belonged somewhere else completely, mostly because policemen in Israel have historically been Mizrahi Jews. In the Israeli popular imagination, the best-known depiction is Policeman Azulai, the eponymous protagonist of a popular movie (the film, renamed "The Policeman" was nominated for the 1972 Academy Award for Best Foreign Language Film, and won the Golden Globe for the same category). Officer Avraham Azulai's story, albeit heart-wrenching, is pathetic—and so is he, as soft-headed as he is soft-hearted. He infuriates his wife by falling in love with a prostitute, and is dismissed for incompetence by his superiors, despite the efforts of a group of friendly criminals to stage a heist that he can thwart.

In contrast to such depictions, Mishani wrote in 2013 that the mission of a contemporary realistic crime fiction writer was to reinvent the Mizrahi policeman and create him as the serious protagonist of a serious crime novel; one who is sharp, bright, and capable of solving the most intriguing and complex mysteries. Now, perhaps, the question with which I began can be somewhat clarified. Mishani's *The Missing File* opens with a question, or rather a statement, about the Hebrew literary canon's *lack* of a tradition of serious crime fiction, a question that will continue to haunt the novel till its end: "Do you know why there are no detective novels in Hebrew?" Avraham (Avi) asks the mother reporting the disappearance of her son at the Holon police precinct. In the face of this seeming non sequitur, the confused, overwhelmed mother simply replies, "What?" (Mishani 2013b: 4).

In a frustrated tirade, Avi repeats his original question, "Why aren't there any detective novels?" and immediately adds: "Why doesn't Israel produce books like those of Agatha Christie, or *The Girl with the Dragon Tattoo*?" The mother replies, "I don't read much," whereupon he answers his own question: "Then I'll tell you. Because we don't have crimes like that. We don't have serial killers; we don't have kidnappings ... There's simply no mystery here." He continues: "The explanation is always the simplest. What I am trying to say is that I think there is very little chance that something has happened to your son. And I am not just saying so to ease your mind. The statistics say so" (4). He assures the mother—mistakenly, as it soon turns out—that her son is sure to turn up before long, after having played hooky to be with a girlfriend or to smoke some marijuana, or go and get a tattoo in Tel Aviv. He advises against opening a formal investigation, "when there is a chance we will find him in a situation in which you wouldn't like us to find him" (4). The scene ends, with the mother hesitant but unconvinced: "He fixed his gaze on her, trying to assess the impression his little speech had made. She appeared lost. She wasn't used to making decisions—or insisting. 'I don't know if something happened to him,' she said. 'It's not like him to disappear like this'" (5).

Let me suggest that this scene has less to do with literary depictions than with the social and especially political reality of crime in Israel. Issues of national security are the responsibility not of the police but of the Israeli army and the secret services. Literature, says Avraham, emulates reality; and since there's nothing to emulate in police work, he seems to argue, there's also no literature.

But what I hope this short review of the history of Israeli crime fiction offers is a somewhat more complex depiction of the sociopolitical background against which Hebrew crime fiction has not been written, or, when it was—and it indeed was—these social conditions have shaped what kind of literature was produced. This is also the background against which Mishani wrote his Avraham series, which may offer a different mimetic relationship: Literature first, Mishani seems to challenge us, then, perhaps, a change in social reality. As he said in an interview in 2013 for the German crime fiction site Krimi-couch,

> I think society is extremely important to the good crime novel. This is one of the lessons that the best Scandinavian crime (Sjöwall and Wahlöö, Mankell) taught us: Crime fiction is a good literary tool to write about society, and crimes cannot be fully understood without social context. I hope this is also the case for my novels: I'm not trying to "map" Israeli society (as Batya Gur did, and very well, I think), or refer to every social class or group; but I am trying to root my stories in the social context that they take place in. And I can tell you that writing about Holon, this grey suburb of Tel Aviv that I was born and raised in, was one of the most important aspects of writing *The Missing File*. (Mishani 2013c)

Mishani's position here is ambiguous. Even as he emphasizes the importance of society as a setting, and of Holon in particular, he distinguishes himself from Batya Gur's more programmatic mapping, and his depiction of Israeli society may not be so very different from the depictions in the Nordic Noir novels that inspired him.

In light of these considerations, the fact that the Avraham series has been presented to foreign audiences around the world as a depiction of authentic Israeli life is somewhat bogus. Mishani's novel offers a compelling blend of suspense, humor, and human interest, as well as the distinctive metafictional element signaled by Avi's opening question about the lack of detective stories in Israel. Avi proves to be an avid reader of foreign detective stories, but he is often convinced that the great detective has actually ended up with the wrong solution to the mystery, and throughout *The Missing File* we're invited to question him in the same way. So the novel offers much to its readers; what it doesn't offer is some uniquely local reality. Rather, the novel is a depiction of something closer to a utopian, almost futuristic, vision of Israeli life.

Furthermore, and this is my own explanation for its speedy and impressive circulation, what happens in Holon doesn't stay in Holon, and in principle could have happened anywhere. Both the book's literary aspirations and its international orientation are well expressed by the epigraph that appears, in French, on the title page:

> Comment s'étaient-ils rencontrés? Par hasard, comme tout le monde.
> —DENIS DIDEROT, *Jacques le fataliste et son maître*

A quotation from another crime novel of worldwide fame can help to illustrate this point:

> The skies above the police station and the Ystad Hospital were almost pitch-black when Wallander left the building. It was past seven. He turned right at Kristianstads-vägen and right again onto Fridhems-gatan, getting swallowed up among the walkers ... He tried not to get caught up in their walking pace. Slower, slowly. It was a pleasant early-September evening. There wouldn't be many like this in the coming months.

Some of my readers might have recognized Henning Mankell's protagonist, Kurt Wallander, living and working in Ystad, Sweden. But this is a fake quote; I tweaked it a little. The original quote is actually taken from Mishani's book, whose protagonist was fashioned to a great degree after Mankell's Wallander. Here is the original quote, from the very first pages of Mishani's novel:

> The skies above the police station and the Holon Institute of Technology were almost pitch-black when Avraham left the building. It was past seven. He turned right at Fichman and left onto Golda Meir, getting swallowed up among the walkers ... He tried not to get caught up in their walking pace. Slower, slowly. It was a pleasant early-May evening. There wouldn't be many like this in the coming months. (Mishani 2013b: 10)

As with the setting, so with material culture:

> Another fifteen minutes or so went by with them sitting there like that, in his small room, face-to-face. He hadn't had a cigarette break since 5:00 p.m. His pack of Blend was on the table in front of him, a small black Bic lighter on top of it ... She seemed to him to be the kind of person who did in fact clean every day. Small, with small hands, sitting there on the edge of the chair, leaning forward, a faded black leather handbag on her lap. She had one hand on the bag and the other was clutching a small cell phone, an old Nokia model, in blue. (Mishani 2013b: 5–6)

The only changes needed to "Nordicize" this passage from Mishani were to rename the cigarettes from "Time" to "Blend" and to substitute a Nokia cell phone for the Samsung in the original; the handbag and even the Bic lighter could stay unchanged.

I could have chosen other passages from the book(s) and continued playing with this forever, really (and in earlier drafts of this essay had indeed done so, to my great pleasure). Appropriately, the cover of the American paperback edition bears a blurb prominently displayed on the front cover, from "HENNING MANKELL, INTERNATIONAL BESTSELLING AUTHOR OF THE KURT WALLANDER MYSTERY SERIES," who tells us that the novel is "Impressive! … Mishani writes with profound originality … A truly interesting story." As an expert practitioner in the genre, Mankell may not be referring at all to Mishani's use of his Israeli setting, but to the book's distinctive structure, with chapters alternating between Avi's perspective and that of the—probable—criminal, and to the dramatic series of reversals at the story's end that reveal just how mistaken we readers, as well as Avi himself, have—probably—been all along.

But if being serious in writing (or reading) crime fiction is the topic of this collection, let me conclude with the following remarks, and some questions. When actual, "authentic" local signifiers are so easily and (at least I hope) credibly transformed into other "foreign," globally recognized ones (in this case, Scandinavian), some crime novels may become especially compelling for global markets, even while they are marketed as "authentic." The stakes, however, are not necessarily about authenticity, a problematic concept to begin with, but about the shape and especially the role of literature. When language becomes transparent, and a novel originally written in one national (even minor!) language is so readily made global, what happens to the concrete social and political realities it had tried so seriously to challenge? What remains, if anything, of this aspiration?

Works Cited

Mishani, Dror (2011). *Tik ne'edar*. Jerusalem: Keter Books.

Mishani, Dror (2013a). "The Big Mystery: Dror Mishani on Why Israelis Don't Write Crime Novels." Interview with Ayelett Shani, *Haaretz*, May 16. http://www.haaretz.com/israel-news/the-big-mystery-dror-mishani-on-why-israelis-don-t-write-crime-novels.premium-1.524320 (Accessed March 26, 2016).

Mishani, Dror (2013b). *The Missing File*. Trans. Steven Cohen. New York: HarperCollins. Paperback edition by Bourbon Street Books, 2014.

Mishani, Dror (2013c). "Never Trust a Detective!" Interview by Lars Schafft, Krimi-couch, August. http://www.krimi-couch.de/krimis/interview-with-dror-mishani.html (Accessed March 26, 2016).

14

World Detective Form and Thai Crime Fiction

Suradech Chotiudompant

Crime fiction has been regarded in Thailand as a minor literary genre and its development has been nothing but sporadic, but its local history may tell us how Thailand has interacted with the literary universe in terms of literary production and appropriation. From its beginning right before the twentieth century up to the present time, crime fiction in Thailand has evolved and gone through different phases, determined by both local context and international influence. This essay is not, however, aimed to construct a detailed development of how the genre has taken root in Thailand, but rather to offer useful glimpses at certain landmarks in its history, in which the interaction between world detective form and local renditions are significant. In this light, Thai crime fiction may be understood not as existing ex nihilo, but as a product of interaction and negotiation in the process whereby a world literary form has entered a national literary sphere.

The dawn of Thai crime fiction

The history of Thai crime fiction dates back to the 1890s, during the reign of King Chulalongkorn (Rama V), renowned for Siam's openness to the influx of Western cultural flows. Members of the Thai elite read detective stories from the West and endeavored to translate and adapt them, with various effects. The Sherlock Holmes stories can be regarded as a vital source of inspiration for this group of writers, most of whom came from the aristocracy and the rising middle class.

One of the first stories to be translated into Thai appeared in the journal *Wachirayanwiset* in the early 1890s. "Rudaidoi la-iat" [Having Known in Detail] is a rough translation of Arthur Conan Doyle's "The Boscombe Valley Mystery," stripped off its setting. The Thai edition, not attributed to any author in particular, retains the original chain of major events in which the victim is struck dead by his old friend, who is deeply agitated that the victim will reveal his shady dealings in the past. Vital clues such as footprints and the stone used to knock down the victim are maintained, while various details are significantly watered down—the specific description of the setting in the original is reduced to simply an "area" in the translation—and certain information is domesticized for the Thai audience, including the prize money for helping to capture the murderer, now specified as "400 Thai baht." In her study of the translation of this tale, Panida Boonthavevej claims that it is "translation as adaptation, which means the translation that alters certain significant elements and writing style in the original" (Boonthavevej 2014: 21). This translation reads more like a police case summary, or a fable, given its vague sense of locality. To a certain degree, this example exemplifies how Thai literati first came to terms with world detective fiction, attempting to adapt it for an audience that had yet to be introduced to the genre.

In the early 1910s Liam Winthuphramanakul (formally known as LuangWilatprariwat) tried his hand at *A Study in Scarlet*, *The Sign of Four*, and "A Scandal in Bohemia." Nuan Pachinphayak, whose official title was Luang Saranupraphan, translated *The Hound of the Baskervilles* and more of Doyle's fiction in the popular Thai journal *Senasuksa lae phaewittayasat* over a period stretching to the late 1920s. His translation of *The Hound of the Baskervilles* went through several editions. In 1913 Pleng Disayabut (Luang Naiyavijarn) translated the Holmes story "The Adventure of the Second Stain" and published it in three instalments in the Thai journal *Phadungwithaya*. Although some passages are cut, his translation is more loyal to the original than the translations published earlier in *Wachirayanwiset*. Names are transliterated into Thai, the setting is detailed, and conversations and testimonies are retained. Within twenty years, then, we can see that the Thai language has become more accommodating to Western influences. The 1910s can be regarded as the golden period in which especially Sherlock Holmes stories were translated and adapted.

King Vajiravudh (Rama VI) was a prolific writer, with works in various literary genres. He was also an active translator, and his translations range from Shakespeare to popular literature. Educated at Oxford, he was influenced by the British literary world of the Victorian era, and he probably got to know and read the Sherlock Holmes stories during his years in England (Leuangwongngam,

2010: 179). Still, his first translation, in 1905, was "The Mystery of the Five Hundred Diamonds" from *The Triumphs of Eugène Valmont* by Robert Barr. He translated only one Sherlock Holmes story, "His Last Bow: The War Service of Sherlock Holmes," in 1919, under the pseudonym "Phanlaem," in a journal called *Samutsarn* (Sujjapan, 2012: 19–20). He then went on to translate detective fiction by other authors, such as Sax Rohmer's *The Golden Scorpion*, William Le Queux's *Mysteries of a Great City*, and a collection of Hercule Poirot stories by Agatha Christie in the early 1920s.

King Vajiravudh not only translated works of fiction, but also worked on adaptations. "The Second Ghost of Phra Kanông," written in English when he was at Oxford, finds its inspiration in the local legend of Mae Nak Phra Khanong [Mother Nak in Phra Khanong Village]. The ghost of Nak, rumor had it, could not let go of her excessive love for her husband. In the king's rendition, the village's "second ghost" is that of a dead wife named Nim who doesn't want her husband to remarry. What is interesting is not only the actual mystery but the frame story—a conversation that takes place in England among police officers who were once sent to work in Siam. As told by one of these, Mr. Sidney Kingswell, the mystery of the second ghost can be construed as the rational gaze of the West trying to make sense of mysterious Siam, ironically framed through the eyes of a Siamese king through his character "Kingswell."

"The Second Ghost of PhraKanông" was included in the collection *Nithan Thong In* [The Tales of Thong In] in 1905. This collection constitutes another hybridized beginning of Thai crime fiction. A number of stories, published by the king under another pseudonym, Nai Kaew Nai Khwan, showcase the protagonist Thong In, who is clearly modeled after Sherlock Holmes in his personality, attitude, and habits. His sidekick lawyer Wat recalls Conan Doyle's Dr. Watson. One of these stories, "Khwam lap phaen din" [The Kingdom's Secret], dealing with the mystery of a missing document, is clearly inspired by Doyle's "A Scandal in Bohemia." "Phurai kha khon thi Bang Khunphrom" [The Murder in Bang Khun Phrom] on the other hand recalls Edgar Allan Poe's "The Murders in the Rue Morgue," with the murderer being an orang-utan and the victim locked up in a closed room.

Rachel Harrison (2009) and Thosaeng Chaochuti (2009; 2014) agree that King Vajiravudh's take on detective fiction is by no means neutral, but instead signals Siam's deep anxiety about the imperial West. While Thong In represents the Thai mimicry of the West's reason and logic, the orang-utan can be interpreted as the barbaric Other from which Siam might have wished to distance itself. Taking her cue from Harrison, Thosaeng Chaochuti argues that the orang-utan "represents, within the story, a backward and uncivilized Other. Such interpretation is further reinforced by the fact that the narrator also calls the animal a *khon pa*, a variation of the term *chao pa*, which was ... used by the Siamese elite to describe the primitive and uncivilized peoples that they encountered along the borders of the country" (Chaochuti 2014: 67). In other words, King Vajiravudh's mastery in mixing local tales with the structure of classical detective fiction can also be read as a political move to mitigate the sense of insecurity of Siam in its encounter with the West.

The beginning of detective fiction in Thailand, therefore, was not simply a matter of introducing a new genre to the Thai audience. As the genre, especially in its classical format, prides itself on its strict reasoning or what Poe terms ratiocination, which in this light can be interpreted as part and parcel of the Enlightenment project of the West, its introduction into the Thai literary landscape entailed the dichotomization of reason and mind, materialism and spirituality, as well as civilization and barbarity, with a modernizing Siam being linked simultaneously to both poles of these dichotomies. In translating and appropriating crime fiction, Thai writers needed to come to terms with this complicated state of affairs.

Phrae dam: Crimes and the urbanization of Bangkok

After having done some translations of Sherlock Holmes stories, Nuan Prachinphayak started writing his own crime fiction in the 1920s. *Phrae dam* [Black Silk], published in instalments in *Senasuksa lae phaewittayasat*, was a great success. Readers were hooked by cliff-hangers at the end of each episode, a sign that the Thai audience was becoming familiar with the genre. The plot revolves around a mysterious figure clad in black silk, whose identity the reader is encouraged to guess. Violence and fighting become commonplace, following the pattern set by the hardboiled detective stories in the American pulp fiction magazine *Black Mask*. The setting is contemporary 1920s Bangkok, in the twilight years of King Rama VI's reign, when the city began to spread out under the influence of Westernization. Cars like Buicks and Fords are mentioned, and people entertain themselves with films imported from the West.

The tension in the narrative is localized, however, revolving around the inequality and corruption that plagued Siam at the time. Prasert Setthawong, a well-respected retired civil servant, agrees to adopt a young woman named Prayoon, whose father, a close friend of his, has mysteriously disappeared. Prayoon falls in love with a police officer but one day a newspaper announces that he has died on duty. She is shocked and finds herself approached by Prasert's son, whom she dislikes. The plot thickens when a mysterious figure tries to kill her. It transpires that the would-be murderer is Daeng Phaya, a rural thug who mistakes Prayoon for her sister Prayong, with whom he has fallen madly in love. The plot of *Phrae dam* centers on issues of mistaken identity, disguise, and deception. Prasert, who seems to be a kind gentleman when he adopts Prayoon, turns out to be a criminal who makes counterfeit money, while Prayoon's elusive and seemingly irresponsible father is in reality a good man who has chosen not to become involved in Prasert's illegal business. Prayoon's boyfriend, Chamnong, turns out to still be alive after all, and almost at the end of the narrative appears in black silk fighting Daeng Phaya. The announcement of his death was simply meant to help him work under cover.

Phrae dam is interesting not only for how it adopts the classic detective fiction tradition of the search for the identification of the criminal—each episode ends with the big question: *Who is Phrae dam?*—but also for how it adapts itself to the local context. Bangkok was expanding at an alarmingly quick rate and people were becoming increasingly materialistic due to the influence of capitalism: they needed to get rich in order to gain recognition in society. Behind the façade of a busy city, where everyone tended to his or her own business, people might be respectable by day but engage in wrongdoing by night. Daeng Phaya also serves to critique Thai society: a rural baron, who lives on money that he and his gang rob from corrupt people, the rationale being that this money didn't belong to them in the first place. Though it can be argued that *Phrae dam* is resonant with Western influences, especially from the Fantômas series by the French writers Marcel Allain and Pierre Souvestre, the narrative is still original in at least three respects. The characters are localized with names and titles that allow the reader to learn more about their personalities and about class conflict in Thai society. The events are set in Bangkok neighborhoods such as Petchburi Road and Yommarat, which can still be identified to this day. In addition, the narrative offers a poignant critique of urbanizing Thai society at the time when capitalism marched in and the First World War bred an atmosphere of insecurity and distrust.

Adventures in Thailand's rural backcountry

Detective fiction in Thailand continued to evolve between the late 1920s and the 1950s, even though some of it borders on what we might call adventure narratives rather than crime fiction. The texts produced in this period don't focus on identifying the criminal, as in the whodunit format popularized in the earlier era. Instead, readers are encouraged to understand the main character's development. Even though detection may not take central stage in these fictions, the figure of the narrator can still be compared to the hard-boiled hero. In the West, the emergence of hard-boiled fiction means that the detective can no longer take comfort in an armchair solving a mystery but needs to get out and learn the hard way, fighting with gangsters and corrupt authorities. Thai fiction went through a similar development. The new generation of authors, such as P. Intarapalit, Manat Chanyong, and Liao Srisawake rely on distinctive styles to sketch the plight of protagonists who face tough crimes and fight their way in rural areas of Thailand. Famous narratives by P. Intarapalit include *Suabai suadam* [Bai and Dam the Rural Bandits] series, published around the late 1940s and based on a true story of black-clad rural bandits who robbed only rich people in central Thailand. Clearly reminiscent of Daeng Phaya in *Phrae dam*, Bai and Dam were known for committing crimes with a good intention of helping out the poor. Rumor had it that Bai, in particular, stole weapons from Japanese military transports in Thailand's Central Plain during the Second World War.

First published in 1942, Manat Chanyong's famous short story "Chap tai" [Shoot to Kill] focuses on rural Southern Thailand, where the jungle was dense and prisoners were sent to cut down trees to make way for new roads. The narrator is a man in charge of such a group of prisoners. He has a pleasant and understanding relationship with one of the prisoners, Phorn. Phorn and another official fall in love with the same woman and this leads to tension and a fight, ending in Phorn escaping into the deep jungle. The narrator is ordered to catch him, dead or alive, causing a conflict between duty and friendship. While trying to follow Phorn's trail, the narrator is always concerned with Phorn's health, especially in the tropical jungle where malaria is rife. One day he meets a red-eyed monster and tries to kill it, only to find out later that Phorn's body is found not far from where he has seen the monster. The narrative intentionally focuses on the narrator's point of view to stress his psychological pain:

I felt stunned. His body was decaying all right. He must have been dead for several days—of malaria and hunger. My eyes filled with tears thinking on how he had told the girl to ask me for medicine.

I could not be callous to him. I had really liked him. I told my men to dig a grave at once and we buried him. We stuck up a sign on the grave and stood still for a minute. (Chanyong 1942: 34–5)

The narrative thus points not only to the physical violence that Thai crimes inflict on prisoners and the authorities alike, but also to the spiritual crisis stemming from the age-old conflict between friendship and duty. "Chap tai" is thus complex and adds another subtle layer to crime fiction, this time with existential angst and psychological intrigue in addition to local conflicts in rural Thailand.

In the early 1950s, Liao Srisawake published one of his most celebrated novels, *Phrai kwang* [Wide Jungle], in which the protagonist Phon Phrai-ngam, a charismatic young man, works his way up in a village in the Central Plain of Thailand. At once a womanizer and a relentless fighter, Phon travels to a village in the hope of finding a job. His independent nature and his unwillingness to bow down to corrupt practices in the village don't endear him to the village head, who initially hates his headstrong attitude but eventually learns to accept him. The novel makes use of a recurrent motif in adventure novels: an ambitious young man wishes to transform the community in which he lives, through the guidance of moral conscience, encouraging the villagers to be more independent and to break away from collectivist norms, which are deep-rooted in Thai society. *Phrai kwang* shows how despotism was rampant in Thai villages at the time. Phon's decision to "set the villagers free" leads to an outright conflict with the village head at the beginning, but when they find they have common enemies—Mr. Smith and a Chinese, who come into the village to operate a timber business—Phon manages to show his skills in driving the foreigners out, as well as sponsoring the village head to continue his term, in spite of all the animosity between them.

As suggested by the three examples discussed, the narratives in this period are distinctive in their focus on rural Thailand, where crimes and criminals are not painted in simple colors, as some thieves are portrayed as benevolent while the police and the authorities may be corrupt. This can be historically contextualized, as during the first half of the twentieth century, Thailand underwent an intensive process of modernization countrywide. Popular works written in this period, therefore, tend to elicit the sense of uncertainty and anxiety resulting from clashes between locally influential people, those from the center who seem to be more "civilized," and those oppressed by the existing social structures and trying to carve out their own path. Rural Thailand is portrayed as a dynamic platform on which these clashes are staged. On the one hand, it may be read as a breeding ground for evil and corruption, generating the oppressive system that its inhabitants are too fearful to fight. On the other hand, however, it may be interpreted as a space of potentiality, in which a real hero may prove his mettle. Such a hard-boiled heroic figure is depicted as a highly individualized man, alienated from his environment yet desirous of making a substantial change in his society. What is also noteworthy is that the hero need not be on the side of the authorities, but can be a thief who fights against social injustice and rampant corruption.

Voices of authority: Policing and crime fiction

The sense of individualism in the hero figure was carried over in the next decade, as evidenced from the emergence of the police thriller in the 1960s. Pracha Poonwiwat set up an interesting literary trend, modeling his police officer protagonist after Ian Fleming's James Bond. Portrayed as a womanizer, his protagonist is an outcast from the police organization but works his way up. Representative of his oeuvre, Pracha's second novel, *Thon ik nid thurna* [Be a Little More Patient], showcases Police Major Khatha Khunawat, a charismatic yet idiosyncratic police officer who is forced to resign from the police department due to his hot temper. With his close aide, he sets out on a journey to the north of Thailand, hoping to earn his fortune by working with the Karen tribe in Myanmar. Noza, the tribe leader, is a very beautiful woman. She falls for Khatha and trusts him enough to let him help in the tribe's fight against its enemies—both the Myanmese and Chinese soldiers. In their fight, Khatha manages to save Noza's life with his skills as a police officer. However, the romance between Noza and Khatha is unrequited as he needs to return to work in the police department. His resignation in the beginning was just a ruse to cover up the police's plan to investigate the conflict between the Karen and the Myanmese in the north. Laced with humor, Pracha's novel manages to localize the genre of the spy thriller by using the regional background as the setting and the racial and national conflicts as part of the motive that drives the characters to undertake their adventures.

This creation of cunning police officers was subsequently offset by a model set by Vasit Dejkunjorn in his famous work *Sarawat Yai* [Chief Inspector

Yai], whose protagonist is a paragon of virtue and self-discipline. Assigned to work in Kampaeng Petch, a small province in central Thailand, Yai tries to set a good example for his junior colleagues to follow. A devout Buddhist, Yai refuses to take bribes and his exemplary way of life poses a threat not only to local politicians but also to his fellow police officers who are implicated in a complex corruption ring. *Sarawat Yai* not only sings the praises of the good policeman's determination and devotion but also chastises the general corruption that destroys Thailand's police organization on all levels. In comparison to Pracha's works, Vasit's renditions of the police thriller are of a more serious nature. Unlike Khatha, who doesn't have any qualms about making passes at women, Yai is strictly monogamous and doesn't condone even minor acts of corruption: for instance, he doesn't accept a free meal from a hotel owner as this can be construed as an act of bribery. The novel is also full of details that help make the presentation and investigation of crime scenes look realistic, as the author supplies a wealth of information from his own experience as a police officer.

All in all, police detective fiction in this period moved further away from the earlier hard-boiled fiction in which protagonists tended to be commoners or rural bandits. However, what connects the two groups are original injections of local color and regional context, especially of rural Thailand, in which crimes and corruption were rife and conflicts among local lords were commonplace. In addition, they are also similar in their stress on the role of moral guidance as an indispensable tool that holds Thai society together. With such strong adherence to moral codes, most crime fiction just discussed portrays the heroes' good conscience helping them guide the whole society in the right direction and turn Thai society into a just one. Police investigators in this subgenre of crime fiction represent the voice of the nation to a certain extent. The Thai government at the time was in deep conflict with the communists, fearing that they would re-educate the Thai population and encourage them to follow in the footsteps of countries such as China and Russia. These works thus play out against the backdrop of the Cold War era.

Contemporary imaginings: New debates, old format?

Crime fiction has enjoyed a series of revivals by contemporary writers, often through experiments with the classical British-style format. One case that should be mentioned is the series of Phumrak Phansing stories by Win Lyovarin, a prolific writer who has tried his hand at different genres, from political novels to inspirational tales. In these stories, first published in *Matichon Weekly* in 2003, Phumrak is an idiosyncratic investigator who manages to solve conundrums in Thai society by using his intellect and good observation. A veteran author of historical novels, Vinita Diteeyont also has published a series of novellas called *Khun pa Mathur* [Aunt Mathur], modeled after Agatha Christie's Miss Marple. Like Win's stories, Vinita's detective fiction can be considered an experiment before she turned to other forms, in her case historical novels and fantastic narratives for which she is now best known.

Ruangdej Chantarakiri, an influential figure in the contemporary Thai literary landscape, established a publishing house called Rahatkadi [Mystery Tales] around the turn of the millennium, and launched a magazine of the same name, showcasing both translations and critical pieces on detective fiction. Even though the magazine didn't last long, it created a positive spark in Thai literary circles. Nanmeebooks, a publishing house famous for its literary translations of Nobel laureates, set up the Nanmeebooks Awards for literary achievements in various fields, one of which is crime and mystery. One of the first to receive this award was Phornsak Uratchatchairat, whose work *Kan morana* [Time of Death] received an honorable mention in the 2007 competition. In this narrative, two plainclothes police detectives—Samai and La-Or—set out to investigate a series of crimes in the old city of Bangkok. With the events taking place about a hundred years ago, *Kan morana* turns the old part of Bangkok into a quaint, mysterious place. The first mystery concerns the drowning of a Chinese woman in a local canal. In her hand is found the pocket watch of Chakra, a powerful civil servant's son. The watch is stopped at a quarter past nine, presumably the time when the woman was drowned. Around the same time Chakra's friend Chokchai is found hanging in a store he and Chakra own. It seems logical that Chakra killed both people, but he has an alibi: at the time when the two victims died, he was having a fight with a barber. What complicates the situation is that the drowned woman is a prostitute romantically connected with a Chinese gangster. The latter threatens to kill Chakra without waiting for the Thai judicial system to mete out its sentence.

Chakra's father, Luang Mongkol Silphaisan, plays a significant role in these crimes. Chakra did have a fight with Chokchai earlier on but the latter did not die. It is Luang Mongkol who, after his son has left, orders Chokchai to be murdered by hanging. When Luang Mongkol realizes that the prostitute has witnessed how Chakra escaped from the store, he decides to murder her too, without realizing that she has found Chakra's pocket watch on the ground and thought of returning it to him. The scene at the barber is after all just a setup, to provide Chakra with a false alibi.

Kan morana may be regarded as a contemporary thriller, with some classical detective fiction elements such as clues and inexplicable conundrums. The narrative makes passing references to a number of classical detective works, especially Jacques Futrelle's "The Problem of the Perfect Alibi" from his story collection *The Thinking Machine* (1907). Underneath such borrowed techniques and elements, the narrative rectifies social prejudices as well as creates new ones in the context of contemporary Thai society. First, while the Chinese were depicted as corrupt in such earlier narratives as Liao Srisawake's *Phrai kwang*, *Kan morana* shows how the Chinese gangster abides by his own rules and moral codes. He is fair enough to listen to Samai's explanation in the end and lets Chakra off. He also lets the police officials deal with Chakra's father no matter how desperately he wants to take revenge himself. In addition, the narrative details why the gangster has become who he is in the first place, and especially how he has been discriminated against in Thai society. Second, while the Chinese seem to be relatively absolved, the criminals are Thai, especially those high up on the social scale. Chakra is a young, spoiled Thai, sent abroad by his rich parents, whose love has turned to overprotection and corruption. Chakra isn't a responsible person: the business that he has invested in with Chokchai is not successful as he smuggles some imports from their store to sell for his own gains. Chokchai then threatens to sue him and that is the reason why he is silenced.

Different from works in a former era, in which the Chinese or the Myanmese were portrayed as corrupt, *Kan morana* can be related to the emergence of the multicultural ideology widely promulgated at present. Rather than pointing the finger to people of other ethnicities, Phornsak's narrative confirms that the Other is indeed within. It is in fact the corruption and wrongdoings of Thai people themselves that account for the violence and mysteries. This twist is related to xenophobic anxiety throughout the narrative: the failing business of Chakra and Chokchai deals with the importation of objects from the West, while one of the victims is Chinese. Such anxiety about ethnic alterity needs to be transcended so that Thailand will make good progress in an increasingly globalized world. It is all the more ironic that such a recognition of otherness should be registered in the genre that was once an importation from the West.

In the early 2000s, the launch of Dan Brown's mystery novels in the international market, including the Thai one, changed the Thai landscape of crime fiction once again. In this new literary trend, the hard-boiled hero is retained, but the distinctive elements include decipherment and deep analysis of characters' psychology, leading to yet another interesting cross between the hard-boiled genre and the classic detective format. Chairat Pipitpattanaprap's *Kaholmahorathuek* [In an Uproar], written under his pseudonym of Prapt, was clearly inspired by this line of detective fiction, especially in its focus on the decoding of complex codes and with a wealth of cultural background. Comparable to Brown's *Angels and Demons* set in Rome and the Vatican City, Chairat's fiction makes an interesting use of Bangkok's complex cityscape. Finding codes engraved onto victims' body parts, the police officers need to use their cultural knowledge and deciphering skills to catch up with the murderer's plan and try to get one step ahead. Like Phornsak before him, Chairat renders Bangkok as an uncanny space in which mysteries lurk in small alleys in the old city—the so-called Rattanakosin Island.

What is interesting in this work, long-listed for the prestigious SEA Write Award for the Best Novel in 2015, is not only the deciphering element that depends on the reader's knowledge of complex Thai poetry and Bangkok's geography, but also the detailed explanation of the crime motive, which involves such issues as political slander in Thailand. Set in 1943, the novel portrays how the murderer, a woman named Phanonit, chooses to stage serial killings in order to get the attention of Fueng, who chose monkhood to relieve his guilt in intentionally and wrongly alleging that Phanonit's father was involved in the restorationist Baworndej rebellion of 1933, leading to the latter's unjust imprisonment. The motive is further complicated by the criminal's experience of domestic violence—sexual molestation by her stepfather, who is a reputable doctor.

While sexual molestation looms large in Chairat's first published detective work, concern for the environment is the main focus in his second novel, *Niratmahannop* [Chronicle of the Sea]. The narrative centers on mysterious murders in Chonburi and Bangkok. The victims are linked to Thaichoti, a powerful oil company, whose pipelines aren't properly maintained, leaking oil that pollutes the water and harms fish and other sea creatures. It turns out that the murderers are a special type of hybrid creatures—the half-man, half-fish "Mern." These Mern look exactly like humans but they can stay underwater for a long time and emit sounds that can damage humans' innards. They have long infiltrated human society and their murders have a dual objective: to stop the oil company from contaminating the seawater and to find a precious "ocean stone," which can purify seawater. The only evidence for this stone can be found in a work by Sunthorn Phu, a famous poet in the reign of Rama III.

The environmental crime against humanity is set against complicated interpersonal relationships that are increasingly problematic. Families are portrayed as dysfunctional, with children having closer ties with their maids than with their parents, while personal relationships, be they straight or homosexual, are lacking in communication and thus become distant. Chulakate, the main female protagonist, is unhappily married to a son of the Thaichoti dynasty. Her mother finds herself falling in love with another woman and lives in a state of agony and confusion. If *Kaholmahoratuek* portrays emotional complexity due to domestic violence in which a stepfather abuses his daughter, the psychological drama in *Niratmahannop* results mainly from the deplorable state of interpersonal relationships in contemporary Thai society, where people are deeply influenced by materialism and self-centeredness. For Chairat, this increasing sense of isolate individualism goes hand in hand with human myopia, especially in the exploitation of natural resources for individual gain.

The search for the "ocean stone" links all the murders together, especially in the crime scenes in which one finds the Khao Mo or a small, replica mountain, built in a number of Thai temples to remind people of Mount Meru, which in Hindu and Buddhist cosmology is believed to be the center of our universe. As in *Kaholmahoratuek*, Chairat combines arcane symbolism and Thai poetry with modern psychological drama, resulting in a detective fiction that is at once local and international at the same time.

Niratmahannop signals that Thai crime fiction has come a long way. Earlier translations and adaptations have now been replaced by works that focus on local problems and concerns through acts of decoding that require a wealth of Thai cultural knowledge. Contemporary Thai crime narratives don't simply entertain but offer social criticism on issues ranging from domestic violence to environmental destruction. In a nutshell, since its inception over a century ago, Thai detective fiction has largely borrowed elements and techniques from world detective fiction, especially in its Anglophone variants, while changes in the ideological backdrop have led to substantial variations and developments in Thai crime fiction. Even though a detailed history of Thai crime fiction remains to be written, these glimpses into Thai crime narratives produced in various periods testify to the fact that these texts are highly dynamic, presenting the careful integration of local matter within the nuanced appropriation of the world detective format.

Works Cited

In ThaiChairat Pipitpattanaprap (2014). *Kaholmahoratuek* [In an Uproar]. Bangkok: Phraew.

Chairat Pipitpattanaprap (2015). *Niratmahannop* [Chronicle of the Sea]. Bangkok: Phraew.

Liao Srisawake (1969). *Phraikwang* [Wide Jungle]. Bangkok: KhlangWitthaya.

Manat Chanyong (2011). *Chap tai: ruam rueng ek* [Shoot to Kill and the Collection of Masterpieces]. 4th ed. Bangkok: Sangsan Books.

Panida Boonthavevej (2014). "'Suebsappakan' kub prawat achayaniyai nai prathet Thai" [Tracing Sherlock Holmes and a History of Crime Fiction in Thailand]. In *Reaping the Harvest in the Unknown Fields: History of Contemporary Thai Literature*, ed. Soranat Tailanga and Natthanai Prasannam. Bangkok: Department of Literature, Kasetsart University, in collaboration with Office of Contemporary Art and Culture, 10–31.

Parichat Poopan (2011). "Achayaniyai Thai, B.E. 2541–2550" [Thai Detective and Mystery Novels, 1998–2007]. MA thesis, Srinakharinwirot University, 2011.

Phornsak Uratchatchairat (2007). *Kan morana* [Time of Death]. Bangkok: Nanmee Books Crime and Mystery.

Pracha Poonwiwat (1968). *Thon ik nid thurna* [Be a Little More Patient]. 2 vols. Bangkok: Kasembannakit.

Rattanachai Leuangwongngam (2010). *Sherlock Holmes version kao* [Sherlock Holmes: Old Editions]. Bangkok: Samosorn Nungsue Rahatkadi.

Ruenruthai Sujjapan (2012). "Khwam son phraratharuethai khong phrabat somdet phra mongkutklaochaoyuhua nai 'kadirahat' " [King Vajiravudh's Interest in "Mystery Fiction"]. In Vajiravudh, 13–65.

Vajiravudh, King (2012). *Kadirahat phrabat somdet phra mongkutklaochaoyuhua* [Mystery Fiction of King Vajiravudh]. Bangkok: Sayam Parithat.

Vasit Dejkunjorn (1994). *Sarawat Yai* [Chief Inspector Yai]. 2 vols. Bangkok: Matichon.

In EnglishCawelti, John G. (1976). *Adventure, Mystery, and Romance: Formula Stories as Art and Popular Culture*. Chicago: University of Chicago Press.

De Fels, Jacqueline (1975). "Popular Literature in Thailand." *Journal of the Siam Society* 63:2, 219–38.

Harrison, Rachel V. (2009). "'Elementary, My Dear Wat'—Influence and Imitation in the Early Crime Fiction of 'Late-Victorian' Siam." In *Chewing Over the West*, ed. Doris Jedamski. Amsterdam: Rodopi, 303–44.

Knight, Stephen (2004). *Crime Fiction 1800–2000: Detection, Death, Diversity.* Basingstoke: Palgrave Macmillan.

Priestman, Martin (1990). *Detective Fiction and Literature: The Figure on the Carpet.* Basingstoke: Macmillan Press.

Rzepka, Charles J. (2010). "What Is Crime Fiction?" In *A Companion to Crime Fiction*, ed. Charles J. Rzepka and Lee Horsley. Oxford: Blackwell, 1–9.

Scaggs, John (2005). *Crime Fiction.* London: Routledge.

Thosaeng Chaochuti (2009). "'The Murderer of Bangkhunphrom': The Semi-Colonial Siam and Its Early Literary Adaptation." *Manusya* Special Issue 18, 30–41.

Thosaeng Chaochuti (2014). "Through the Literary Lens: Vajiravudh's Writings and Siam's Negotiations with the Imperial West." In *Disturbing Conventions: Decentering Thai Literary Studies*, ed. Rachel V. Harrison. London: Rowan & Littlefield, 63–78.

Todorov, Tzvetan (1977). "The Typology of Detective Fiction." In *The Poetics of Prose.* Ithaca: Cornell University Press, 42–52.

Worthington, Heather (2011). *Key Concepts in Crime Fiction.* New York: Palgrave Macmillan.

Part Four

Holmes Away from Home

15

Holmes Away from Home: The Great Detective in the Transnational Literary Network

Michael B. Harris-Peyton

The Wikipedia entry for "World Literature" is flagged, as it has been since November 2014, by Wikipedia's volunteer editors. The entry carries two ominous, but not unusual, flags. The first flag is for style violation—the article is "written like a personal reflection or opinion essay that states the Wikipedia editor's particular feelings about a topic, rather than the opinions of experts." The second is a bit more interesting—the entry is flagged for non-neutrality. While these flags don't indicate which parts of the article are the problem, they implicitly refer to the out-of-place final section of the entry, under the section header "Classics of World Literature." This section reads, in total:

> Wide international distribution alone is not a sufficient condition for attributing works to world literature. The decisive factor is an exemplary artistic value and the influence of the respective work on the development of humankind and science [citation needed] in general, and on the development of literature(s) of the world in particular. An agreement on universally accepted criteria to decide what works have literary world ranking is not easy, especially since individual works have to be considered in their respective temporal and regional contexts. (Wikipedia, "Classics of World Literature")

This section contains that famously laconic paratextual notation "citation needed," the marker Wikipedia uses to indicate claims that are undersubstantiated. This final section seems to take issue with all of the prior sections, asserting that circulation—a key factor in a text being considered world literature both in Wikipedia's intellectual free-for-all and in world literature's most prominent scholarly texts—is not a sufficient indicator of a text's value. Originality and artistic merit must also, for some unspecified reason ("citation needed"), be included in any explanation of why a text is worthy of the attention of world literature scholars and enthusiasts.

The argument of the entry's final section is an "old school" argument, though still a common enough one to cause contention among the editorship. Important texts, this old and familiar argument goes, are special because they are firsts, are originals, and possess some ineffable artistic merit. This is what makes them worth reading, printing, circulating, translating, and studying. Scholars across several disciplines have already riddled this argument with holes—Linda Hutcheon, for example, offers a particularly incisive deconstruction of the "artistic merit" argument in *A Theory of Adaptation* (beginning in her preface to the first edition, xiv–xv, where she notes that the almost automatic dismissal of "second" works as "secondary" is more political than numerical). The argument for artistic merit and originality is endlessly subjective and unsustainable, but, I assert, it is worth more than a critical dismissal *precisely because* it is both absurd and long-lived: something is going on there. I assert that both the particular label "originality" and more general labels like "artistic value" are actually after-the-fact justifications—unsubstantiated but easy explanations for the actually complicated phenomenon of wide circulation and popularity. Claiming a text as an (or the) original example of a genre or as its artistic pinnacle allocates it particular referential power over that genre and its history, regardless of its actual position in the timeline and its intertextual dependencies on other works.

The survival of this originality-as-value system, and its complicity in supremacy arguments of various kinds, is evident even in the preparation of one of world literature's more popular teaching texts. *The Norton Anthology of World Masterpieces* changed its title to the arguably less-evaluative *World Literature* only in 1995, in the context of post-Cold War globalization and the abandonment of *World Masterpieces*' implicit mission to promote the monolithic centrality of "The West" in terms of political, philosophical, and literary-generic development. The rhetorical deployment of terms like "original" and "masterpiece" occur frequently and often belie a nationalist or colonial agenda. "We" and the things we like are "original"; "they" and the things they like are "copies" at worst and "their versions," deeply indebted to "us" at best. Assertions of originality mask a project of appropriating a text's success as evidence of the superiority of some in-group—of the author figure, the nation, the language, The West. "The new and unique" remains the primary indicator of the value of a text, even when (thanks to the well-studied concept of genre), it's actually referring to its opposite: the familiar, the conventional, and the referentially connected.

There is a pervasive (but troubled) cultural myth, within and without scholarly disciplines, that what is valuable is what is unique, even though what sells, and what people read or watch or listen to the most—the stuff that marks the day-to-day experience of a culture—tends to be those genre texts (like the crime fiction that occasions this collection) that are less involved in the discourse of artistic or origin-marking value than in a transcultural network of reference, reuse, and circulation. When we study these texts, we feel a pressing need to justify our interest through the language of merit-via-originality (particularly, it seems, when studying "genre fiction"), even though what attracts us to them, in the context of world literature at the least, are their wide circulation beyond their original contexts (see Damrosch 4), their inability to stay in their places of origin, their repeated iteration and promiscuous chains of reference, their ability to have a rich local context in several localities.

A case-in-point: In my research on Sherlock Holmes and Holmes-like texts, I found myself transitioning from the BBC series *Sherlock* to CBS's *Elementary*. My first unguarded thought about this transition was "do we really need another Holmes adaptation? How unoriginal." The ever-present language of originality-as-merit was immediate—I caught myself dismissing a perfectly useful primary text both because it wasn't "the first" Holmes television show and because it was an American take on a character traditionally associated with British national identity. These are particularly counterproductive lines of reasoning when my entire raison d'être for studying Holmesian texts was to investigate their tendency to circulate and be adapted—I was drawn to the Holmes corpus *precisely* because it has proliferated transculturally and was created in a transcultural context, and because a fairly large number of people have wanted to consume texts themed around Holmesian mystery again and again. Despite the titular detective's tendency to stay in London, his texts and narrative patterns most decidedly did not. Originality had nothing to do with my interest—it only served as a blanket term for perpetuating a hierarchy of texts, in this case, based on the uncritical association of "British" and "first" with "valuable." As if, in effect, cultural history began and ended in Britain.

My motives and my justification did not match, and this dissonance was illuminating. The Holmes figure, and the Holmes genre, turned out to be an excellent tracer-text for watching the ways the fetish of originality and the desire for a linear source-to-text relationship were actively challenged by the realities and legacy of circulation in a transnational textual marketplace. When originality is discussed as a value in that marketplace, I assert that two operations occur simultaneously:

1. Theoretically, a critically useful and complex understanding of a text's circulation potential, its translatability, its interconnection, and its adaptability, is obscured by discussions of arbitrary value or merit.
2. Historically, a colonial notion of where (and with whom) culturally important texts are supposed to originate, and which ones are allowed access to scholarly attention and networks of consumption, is perpetuated.

The concept of originality thus conceals the actual motives for scholarly or readerly interest and quietly articulates a cultural assumption that places cultural power in a very specific geographic, economic, and historical arrangement.

Circulation, translation, adaptation

The history of Holmes is illustrative of this two-step process, both because of its status as "common knowledge" and because that artificial history[1] sometimes competes with the actual content of the text, revealing cracks in the process of building a linear historical narrative. The Holmes texts are widely positioned as the first, or among the first, of the "great detective" model of investigative fiction, and are popularly considered "British" in some fundamental way. This history, of course, conceals a long chain of generic predecessors and textual references from non-British and often "peripheral" places—but this Holmes-as-Original history (much like its textual subject) possesses a cultural utility that makes it popular. This history works as a cultural myth grown around a popular, widely circulated text, co-opting its popularity in service of a colonial mission. If originality stands as a byword for what is valuable, the Holmes texts *must be mythologized* into being fundamentally original, fundamentally artistically better, even if their real power comes from their culturally ambiguous origins, their circulation and adaptability, and perhaps a certain degree of luck. If the text is to have cultural power, and if it is to serve a colonial role concentrating the start of a genre in historically British hands, it can have *no history itself*. A textual empire, to borrow obliquely from Hardt and Negri, has to be outside history. It must be original and inevitable, or else we must admit that its power comes from outside, is hybrid or mixed, and is contingent. The Holmes stories themselves ardently refuse to disguise their own history, however—they variously illustrate just how poorly originality, especially with its connotation of independent cultural purity, explains their value.

This, in and of itself, is not news: Caroline Reitz and other scholars have traced the movement of Holmes, and of detective fiction, from a very un-British notion of superman-detective to a text (and a genre) retroactively embraced during the British empire-to-nation self-definition project of the late nineteenth and early twentieth centuries. Sherlock Holmes stories became a paradigm of British identity because they hit on a late-nineteenth-century need for narratives exploring the distinction between aggression and policing that helped justify imperial ambition, not because anything in them was fundamentally British—as Carlone Reitz points out, they were made British due to their cultural utility in that imperial context (Reitz xiii–xviii). Pablo Mukherjee points out throughout *Crime and Empire* that even prior to the popularity of Doyle's detective stories, the language of crime—ranging from the integration of terms like "thug" and "bandit" to the growth of the popular literary genre—was developed via a complex interchange of cultural materials between the empire and its colonial possessions, and this interchange was not unidirectional. In short, Holmes is seen as the "original" and most British great detective even though there really is no pure original, and he's not really very British. The narrative of Sherlock Holmes as British crime-fiction urtext (and urcharacter) disavows a complex process of creation. This disavowal is meant to reinforce the idea that culture comes from the metropole, even as the texts advertise (or sometimes fail to suppress) a messy involvement in the periphery of the British Empire and the continuing formation of Britishness as a concept.

Before I analyze two texts operating in the genre surrounding Sherlock Holmes (one a Holmes story, another one that occasionally advertises its relation to Holmes) in order to highlight the cracks in the ideology of originality-as-value and the textual histories that ideology enables, it would be useful to more precisely define some key terms, many of which I'm using idiosyncratically. The scholarship of world literature over the last two decades has reached the uneasy consensus that *circulation* is a key factor in defining that field's boundaries. David Damrosch's 2003 definition of circulation is, perhaps, the most usefully concise—circulation means that a text "reaches beyond its home base," through translation, physical transportation (4) or, indeed, reference. The ability to "leave home," or the historical circumstance of having left home successfully, is what draws the label world literature to a text. In addition, I occasionally use the term *translation*, whose usage here echoes its origin in the Latin for "to convey across" some boundary more than exclusively to change languages: a text may be altered to fit local codes and conditions, through everything from trans-lingual translation to aggressive censorship to a simple change of title. The term *translation* is overburdened here in order to clear out space for, and call attention to, the use of the word *adaptation* as a replacement for postcolonialism and world literature's notion of *appropriation*—a term, I'd suggest, that is in dire need of replacement. To appropriate, presently, often carries with it the unpleasant note of colonial or politically charged cultural theft, and therefore, of ownership, where adaptation (as work in adaptation studies routinely asserts) carries with it a sense of collective use and reuse that is subversive of archaic, unsustainable notions of cultural property, cultural purity, and freedom from influence. Adaptation, simply put, is how the circulation of texts turns into whole networks and genres of texts—it is a process of creation *and* a politics of membership.[2] All of this might happily fit into an expanded notion of *translation*, but I want to call particular attention to this particular process in the analysis that follows. The anxiety of adapting and being marked subordinate versus the real need to connect with a larger genre marks these texts in ways that disrupt originality-as-value, and the Holmes-as-Original history that ideology sponsors.

The reprint of a (fictional) memoir: *A Study in Scarlet*

While thus far I've referred to the ideology of originality-as-value placing Holmes at the beginning or origin of the detective genre, it's important to note that histories of the detective or crime fiction genre often *don't* explicitly point to Arthur Conan Doyle as a founding author without serious qualification. A typical (though somewhat dated) example of the pattern of genre history might be gleaned by the first pages of A. E. Murch's 1958 monograph, *The Development of the Detective Novel*. The verso of the monograph's title page is a glossy insert with six portraits: Charles Dickens, Wilkie Collins, Sheridan Le Fanu, Lord Bulwer-Lytton, Alexandre Dumas, and Edgar Allan Poe (in that order, left-to-right, in three rows of two). There are two more inserts at the ends of critical chapters of the text featuring authors from later periods, but this insert precedes even the title page of the text itself, a privileged position that is not explained textually. The aim of Murch's text, notably, is a genealogy of detective fiction, recovering genre features from their alleged origins in works of various other genres and national origins. Importantly, all of these origins are Western European and not explicitly colonial, with the possible exception of Poe's ambiguous transatlantic Americanness—a position the text glosses over.

The layout of Murch's history is indicative of the structure of a typical history of the genre: the table of contents implies, and the text substantiates, a history in which Sherlock Holmes can be the origin without necessarily being the first. In this pattern, Holmes is simply the paragon of the genre, the center of the history, the teleology of all the works that surround it, even those that had not yet been written. In this narrative, Doyle's stories are *without* history; they are less a product of evolution than the focal point of a genealogy, an inexorable goal toward which earlier works progressed and from which subsequent works digressed. Arthur Conan Doyle's portrait on a six-person glossy insert is neither the first insert nor the last—it is in the exact center of Murch's text. Doyle's part in the text garners its own chapter, the tenth of thirteen, with (tellingly) the shortest and least creative chapter title. While other authors and texts are provided descriptive titles like "III: The Rise of the *Roman-Feuilleton*. Detective Themes in the Novels of Honore de Balzac, Eugene Sue and Alexandre Dumas," the centrality of Holmes to this history is revealed in its apparent lack of a need for explanation: "X: Sherlock Holmes." It requires no elaboration, its chapter title a triumphant statement of the genre's arrival at an important single point, the culmination of the genre's work, the central peak of the trajectory. Murch's history in that chapter, notably, avoids saying that Doyle played upon a history of detective tropes to build his now-famous characters and texts, positioning it explicitly as an arrival in England of a French genre that could only have been perfected by an Englishman (Murch 177).[3] Like most historical narratives, the desire for origins and consequences organizes events in this genre history as if they were the inevitable result of the past, in the process erasing more complicated connections.

The first Holmes story itself is haunted by the ideology of originality-as-value and those more complicated connections. The text's involvement in not-British (or, more precisely, not-English) textual networks, and the demands that genre play upon old and new necessitates a careful negotiation. *A Study in Scarlet* is, from the beginning, engaging in a complicated avowal-through-disavowal—of genre, of the genre's international dependencies, of involvement in the colonies and the periphery.

Sherlock Holmes, in *A Study in Scarlet*, disavows a relationship with Poe's Inspector Dupin and Gaboriau's Monsieur Lecoq—and there's nothing quite as indicative of a relationship as an explicit disavowal, particularly when being "not original" is a bad thing in the eyes of critics, but integral to participating in a genre[4] and getting readers. Holmes, as a character, at least, is anxious to name and dump these predecessors, and does so in the second chapter—Lecoq is a hapless bungler, and Dupin far too slow and improbably lucky (Doyle 2006: 42–3). Watson's attachment to Dupin leads to a little tension, but ultimately does not undermine his enthusiasm for his roommate's feats. Holmes must perform for Watson a careful act of "yes, that's what I do, but no, not like them." The same enough to be mistaken, different enough for the mistake to matter. They are not so much predecessors or models as learning experiences.

Of course, well before disavowing a relationship with an American paranormal romanticist who resided on the Continent and published transatlantically, and another relationship with a French author, Doyle's first Holmes mystery is fairly riddled with things translated to or translated from other places. In the first paragraph of *A Study in Scarlet*, we have Afghanistan, London, Calcutta, Peshawar, Kandahar province, Afghan Ghazis, Islam, various fevers, contagions and colonial ailments (Doyle 2006: 7–14)—and within a few pages, a dead man with American business cards and mention of the trial of a German murderer. And all before this, just to emphasize the truly recycled, temporally subsequent nature of the text, the first half of *A Study in Scarlet* is subtitled as a "reprint" from the "memoirs" of John Watson, and the second half derived (ostensibly) from the testimony of the criminal. Everything, it seems, is either from the colonies or is a secondary copy of something British deeply in contact with the colonies—and a counterfeit, for these are not really memoirs at all. And this isn't even to spoil the mystery itself, which hops across Europe and the Atlantic and deals with all sorts of foreign objects (German socialist secret societies, an American Mormon love quadrangle involving ambiguous parentage and incomplete religious conversion, the American wilderness, an American living among Indians and adapting their skills before becoming an itinerant London cabbie) and myriad secondary, or faked, clues.

The text, in other words, plays with its own confused origins and position, just as a British national and imperial project tries to assert a unique identity out of a frankly chaotic (and not atypical) history of cross-cultural circulation, borrowing, and membership.[5] Doyle's longer works, like *A Study in Scarlet*, contained these complicated avowal-disavowals of both generic interconnection and the purity of Britishness, and were among the first and most common of the Holmes texts to spread to colonial libraries (Joshi, 64–5).[6] Doyle's texts, with all their complex wrangling with origins and identity, got sent to Indian libraries and bookstores in the 1890s as part of the imperial project of training colonial subordinates to be almost-but-not-quite British, the mimic men of Bhabha's famous scholarship.

To tell whether the boy is Indian or not: "Feluda in London"

Holmesian mystery stories—either structured like, using characters like, or explicitly paying homage to Doyle's detective—spread through the English and local-language literary marketplaces of British colonial possessions rapidly because the discourse of crime and criminality that detective fiction like Doyle's plays upon was articulated in the context of justifying colonial intervention and management (see, for example, Reitz's *Detecting the Nation*, and Mukherjee's *Crime and Empire*, among others). In other words, crime fiction was always already about colonialism. These new marketplaces for Holmes were prepared because they had been partially responsible for the genre in the first place—and, being contextually relevant and useful for a British colonial education regimen, the marketplace was supplied well.

It doesn't take more than a few years' postindependence for India, in particular, to add new Holmes figures to the many pre-independence and trans-independence detective figures in a Holmesian type that India had already produced. In the 1960s, Satyajit Ray, more famous in the West as a filmmaker, launched a series of short stories sending a Bengali sleuth nicknamed Feluda and his Watsonesque young nephew Topshe on a series of train-bound adventures to the edges of India (rather than the British suburbs) to solve mysteries. These stories are usually contextualized as Holmesian homage or as local Holmesian substitution. Critical and press commentary about Feluda, particularly in English, are quick to mark him as India's Sherlock Holmes, or India's "echo" of Holmes (Das), or a "pseudo-Holmes" (Mathur, 89)—an avowedly national alternative brand to another brand who apparently isn't India's (despite Britain and colonial India's high level of integration at the time of Holmes's inception). Feluda is marked as a subordinate version: Holmes is everywhere, Feluda is India's local variant, a regionalized or nationalized echo.

Ray himself acknowledges a debt to Holmes in his notes, though he is careful not to articulate the same sort of direct connection that an "Indian Holmes" might. Ray comments in an author's note (in a statement without strong connection to the sentences on either side) that he "read all the Sherlock Holmes stories while still at school" (Ray, viii). The statement acknowledges the presence of Holmes as generic raw materials existing in a common cultural, educational, and literal public domain unique in its power, but not so unique or originally British that it cannot be altered, extended, transported, and adapted in post-British India. Predictably, when describing and marketing an English translation of Ray's stories, translator Gopa Majumdar draws a more direct relationship to Holmes as an impetus for the creation of Feluda (Majumdar's "Introduction" in Ray xi), perhaps hoping to capitalize on the popularity of Holmes to reach non-Bengali readers, not unlike the move to identify Feluda, in other places, as "India's Holmes."

While operating in a Holmesian mode—sanitized, domestic criminality, missing historical objects, trains, and a comparatively slow but actually sharp sidekick—the Feluda stories might be better described as a sort of adaptation or translation (or, as Suchitra Mathur puts it in the title of her 2006 essay, "Holmes' Indian Reincarnation") rather than a local substitute or postcolonial homage. Feluda inhabits the role of Holmes, rather than his features. He is the ideal investigative citizen, normal enough to be respectable but odd enough to be a good sleuth, with a narrative-composing sidekick. Unlike Holmes, Feluda imbibes rather than rejects superfluous information, mirroring a different relationship to space and knowledge: Holmes's mind "attic" can be filled (Doyle, 33–34), and is based primarily in London and its immediate suburbs, as complex and heterogeneous as they are. Feluda, on the other hand, has a "mind-weapon"[7] continually sharpened by wide reading, a much more useful metaphorical tool for investigative intellect if most of your investigations take place days away by train from the home space of Calcutta. An attic, after all, is far less mobile than a weapon, and might be enhanced, rather than cluttered up, by additional extraneous knowledge—and the notion of extraneous knowledge enhancing, rather than crowding, an investigative tool represents a different (arguably less imperial) notion of what is important or useful. In short, the powers of the detective are adapted to the spatial and cultural demands of the new setting and scope.

While most of the Feluda stories avoid any explicit relationship to Sherlock Holmes as an original, one of the later stories—"Feluda in London," published in the Bengali-language magazine *Desh* in its 1989 Durga Puja issue[8]—tackles the connection head-on. Feluda and the now adult Topshe (who has gradually moved from naive boy-sidekick to Watsonian assistant and ostensible author of the stories) are sent to London to solve a mystery of identity. While there, Feluda and Topshe attempt to locate 221B Baker Street, noting that "seeing the sights of London would have remained incomplete if we hadn't seen Baker Street" (Ray 554). Of course, as Feluda discovers, the actual location does not exist, and so they must make do with 220 Baker Street, where Topshe informs the reader that Feluda had previously made clear how much he admires Holmes, and (acknowledging the fictionality of the character) his "creator," Arthur Conan Doyle. While Topshe's narration makes clear that Holmes remains just as fictional in Feluda's universe as in our own, Feluda insists upon paying his respects to "the guru" of his methodology—Holmes, *not* Doyle. His use of "guru" (in both the original and Gopa Majumdar's English translation, 554) identifies Holmes not as a source, but as a teacher, a reference document rather than an origin, a vector of transmission rather than an originator. Feluda's relationship to the fictional Holmes emphasizes those stories' relation to the genre that Holmes acts as an avatar for—raw prior material, *not* aspirational model. Interestingly, for Feluda, the function of London as a home to the fictional avatar of rational detection is that city's single determining value; everything else is assessed in relation to Calcutta.

A complex relationship to Doyle's fiction, and to London as an icon of cultural heritage, is articulated further by the mystery that sends Feluda to London in the first place. Ranjan Majumdar, a client whose features seem "European" (Ray 535), arrives in Feluda's office attempting to locate a friend he had in London as a teenager, and whose identity he does not recall. Majumdar is unable to recall this close friendship because of a head injury he suffered shortly before returning to India—an injury so severe that he had to restart his education. Further complicating the search is the unknown friend's appearance—it is "impossible to tell whether the boy is Indian or not" (536), pointing to a collapse of the stereotyped and colonially essential racial differences between Europeans and Indians that furnishes much of the mystery. The boy, as it turns out, is British and a member of a family both heavily involved in colonial economics (542, 555) and deeply, pervasively racist (555).

Feluda's investigation, once he is sent to London, reveals that the boy is Peter Dexter, and that he died while Ranjan Majumdar and he were schoolmates in Cambridge, during a boating incident that involved both boys. The boy's brother, the now terminally ill Reginald Dexter, is living in India running a tea plantation. After interrogating several expatriate Indians and some British schoolmasters—in the process advertising the surviving postcolonial connection and circulation between Britain and India—Feluda's breakthrough comes from Mr. Hookins, the aging groundskeeper at Cambridge, who reveals that Peter and Ranjan constantly fought about Peter's vehement anti-Indian racism. Peter Dexter's racist diatribes had led to a confrontation during which the teenaged Ranjan struck him with a boat oar and allowed him to drown in the Cam. Peter's brother Reginald is unable to pin the blame on Ranjan Majumdar because he is, perhaps ironically, too openly racist for British authorities to take seriously as a witness (Ray 558). The only other witness, Mr. Hookins, covers up the murder to protect Ranjan (561–2). Hookins's sympathy with Ranjan Majumdar, rather than with the Dexters, works to illustrate that the colonial relationship is effectively a two-way street. Most British subjects in the story are happy to acknowledge (via action or direct assertion) that the relationship with India was complex and not unidirectional, that metropole and periphery were not so different. Likewise, Ranjan Majumdar's father's involvement with the anti-British independence "terrorists" is understood as a badge of principle, rather than a fault, even among the British and Indian expatriate community (551), and the easy, unremarked hybridity of Feluda's British contact, Dr. Sen, and his wife Barbara challenges colonial and racial boundaries, indicating a lived interconnection produced by the historical reality of colonialism and migration (550) more complex than political and national histories indicate.

The Dexters's racism combined with their ambiguous appearance and involvement in the tea industry, it is implied, are a result of an attempt to compensate for a racial ambiguity or for cultural "contamination" resulting from too much time in colonial India, rather like the sinister colonial doctor of Doyle's "The Speckled Band." However, unlike several of Doyle's antagonists, the problem for the Dexters originates not in how closely they are involved with India, but on their near-pathological denial that such involvement actually connected and merged Britishness with Indianness. The groundskeeper's willingness to talk to Feluda originates in his dislike for the Dexters, whose racism he finds distasteful because of the family's involvement in colonial enterprise (561). In the end, however, most of this (post)colonial circulation and narrative building is a moot point, for moments after Feluda solves the mystery, Ranjan Majumdar urgently recalls Feluda and company to Calcutta. Upon their return, they find Majumdar shot and killed and the Calcutta police baffled. Feluda notes, only to Topshe, that the gunshot suicide of one Reginald Dexter, in a local hotel, has been reported in the morning paper (562–3), implying that the cycle of racism, revenge, and death started by Peter Dexter and Ranjan Majumdar has reached its conclusion. Feluda's unwillingness to notify the police or the press of his findings in the final moments of the story, like Hookins's original cover-up, marks his refusal to dig up narrow-minded colonial grudges and reintroduce them into the public discourse of Calcutta or London.

The juxtaposition of Feluda's pilgrimage to 220 Baker Street with Feluda's central investigation necessitates an exploration of the lived connections between former colony and colonizer that actively subverts those easy, binary roles—both in the larger ethnic-national case, and in the smaller case of Ray's stories' relationship to a generic predecessor. The mystery itself is produced by the mismatch between the discourse of national and ethnic origins and the realities of colonial circulation of people, texts, and wealth. The Dexters's denial and racism, Feluda's realization that the origins of his methodology reside not in actual London but in a fictional version written by a British citizen of colonial origin, and Feluda's deliberate reference to the fictional English detective as a "guru," not a predecessor, mark "Feluda in London"'s obsession with the complexity of British-Indian circulation. Likewise, the parallels between Feluda's homage and *A Study in Scarlet*'s avowal-disavowal of predecessors troubles Feluda's localness. Feluda's status as "Indian Holmes" is subverted because Holmes is a part of a fictional London equally available (or unavailable, as the search for 221B illustrates) to the Indian Feluda as to any British investigator: Sherlock Holmes, in other words, is *also* the Indian Sherlock Holmes, having been produced in a Britain deeply and bilaterally connected to its colonial possessions. Colonial circulation reveals the fragility of cultural ownership, of the origins of a cultural artifact and the boundaries of culture, since for a text or genre to circulate and be adapted into a new iteration locally means, in a real sense, that it has *become local* while being globally available—that the local area has become involved in the text's history of cultural migration and influence. An apparent reference to an origin text is transformed into continuity rather than repetition, the text produced via adaptation rather than mimicry.

Conclusions

Erasing the complex connections (avowed or disavowed) to other texts in other places happening in these stories for the sake of a coherent or facile narrative of genre history has seriously affected how texts are labeled for circulation and which texts are selected for study, reprinting, archiving, and sale. Entire archives of texts, particularly popular fiction produced in formerly colonized nations, are cut out of the transnational network (despite being integral to it) because they're "not unique enough," not original. They are identified as local knockoffs or regional stand-ins and not worthy of attention as remarkable texts outside those spaces, even though, from a theoretical perspective, they're doing some of the key things world literature as a discipline finds most interesting—evincing an exchange, a circulation, a translation or sharing of cultural mechanisms, adapting and sometimes breaking genre conventions.

Thinking of a genre—like crime fiction in general, or a particular Holmes-inflected brand of storytelling—as a world literature leaves us in an excellent position to brush away the myth of originality as value because it allows us to shift value from an archaic notion of originality to the notion of circulation, adaptation, and growth. A focus on connection and circulation—on a text's role in a transnational cultural marketplace—allows us to be less arbitrary about what we think is "worth reading and worth studying," highlights the cultural mechanisms that have particular power in a particular time or place, and has the power to break down the notion that culture flows from centers outward, and from the artist-author to the audience, in a unidirectional fashion.

Examining the contradictions inherent in Holmes-as-Original gets us away from the assumption that peripheral adaptations, as the supposed products of "weak literary cultures," are limited to writing back to a hegemonic, metropolitan original. There is no real center or periphery here—just raw materials and adapted productions. This analysis places us where world literature (as a site of scholarly inquiry) wants to be—talking about circulation, cultural use, and global connection, about texts leaving home and coming into contact, rather than texts as an eternal product only of their own homes, which travel sometimes without bringing anything back. This is the fundamental contradiction of originality as a marker of value and power: in order to gain that power, the text must leave home and connect with alternative traditions while pretending that those traditions didn't influence the text at any point. It must adapt while pretending it emerged ex nihilo.

The problem occurs, of course, when we forget or deliberately set aside the fact that Holmes was doing the same thing, and so we ignore Ray's "local Holmes" because it is a "local Holmes"—a derivation, violating the originality rule—even though Holmes, as a supposedly "local British" product at the core, was necessarily a "local Dupin or Lecoq" as well as a transnational product. The power of Doyle's detective across cultural boundaries, however, mandates we find some special ability or quality to attribute to it—and so, originality. First because best; best because most widely read; most widely read because first.

Historically, both texts are participating in a genre older than themselves that they modify, using older texts whose conventions they adapt. One, however, is presented as a special original of the genre in order to control who gets to be in the genre, and whose authors (on a national or social scale) are supposed to be worth looking at. All others, in a move far more dangerous than being marked "bad" or "second," are simply not marked for attention at all—they are made specific and local while also being generally the same as another, contradictorily both obscure and unoriginal. Thus, they are doubly obscure.

Notes

1 All histories are, of course, artificial. In this context I mean that the actual printed or taught histories are altered, often in the face of empirical evidence, to support a certain narrative.
2 Here, again, I'm indebted to Linda Hutcheon, who begins *A Theory of Adaptation* by asserting that adaptation pushes the notion that texts are "created and received *by people*," and thus the cultural status of a text (as normal or "secondary" or "inferior") is political rather than a result of some altered or inferior process of creation (Hutcheon, xiv).
3 This ignores Doyle's Britishness versus his Englishness, or perhaps moves to claim Doyle as an example of the troubled relationship between these two categories. In fairness, however, Murch attributes the popularity of Holmes to the central paradox of genre—the combination of old with new—before positioning the Sherlock Holmes stories, and their author, as a master of this whole genre-making process (Murch, 177–8).
4 Though the proliferation of Holmes-mode stories in British periodicals, and their fans among scholars, indicates that the reading public at the time (to say nothing of the present) doesn't seem to worry much about originality, but instead crave genre participation and continuity—otherwise, why would Doyle have had to take Holmes to the Reichenbach Falls, only to be forced to bring him back from the dead?
5 Several recent histories of the genre, like Maurizio Ascari's *A Counter-History of Crime Fiction*, note the genre's shared development with the Gothic—a genre concerned with the horror of and tension about the discovery of buried histories and origins.

6 At least eleven colonial libraries in India carried Doyle's novels by the mid-1890s, according to Joshi's statistics. The most common texts she locates are found in fourteen libraries, putting Doyle rather near the top of the availability rankings.
7 This is "mogojostro" or "magajastra," sometimes translated as "brainpower" or "brain weapon" depending on editions and translators.
8 Rather like the first Holmes narrative appearing in a periodical's Christmas issue, most of the Feluda stories were published in Durga Puja special issues. The holiday occurs in autumn, and coincides with a work and school holiday that helped to explain why Topshe—a young teenager in the first story, and roughly a year older in each subsequent one—is able to travel with Feluda on his investigations.

Works Cited

Ascari, Maurizio (2007). *A Counter-History of Crime Fiction: Supernatural, Gothic, Sensational*. New York: Palgrave Macmillan.

Bhabha, Homi K. (1994). *The Location of Culture*. New York: Routledge.

Damrosch, David (2003). *What is World Literature?* Princeton: Princeton University Press.

Das, Antara (2009). "The Cult of Feluda." *Indian Express [New Delhi]*. January 4. http://archive.indianexpress.com/news/the-cult-of-feluda/405830/ (Accessed May 6, 2012).

Doyle, Arthur Conan (2006). *The New Annotated Sherlock Holmes: The Novels*, ed. Leslie Klinger. New York: W. W. Norton.

Elementary (2012). CBS. September 2012–Present. TV Series.

Hardt, Michael, and Antonio Negri (2000). *Empire*. Cambridge MA: Harvard University Press.

Hutcheon, Linda with Siobhan O'Flynn ([2006] 2012). *A Theory of Adaptation*. 2nd ed. New York: Routledge.

Joshi, Priya (2002). *In Another Country: Colonialism, Culture, and the English Novel in India*. New York: Columbia University Press.

Majumdar, Gopa (2004). *Introduction* to Satyajit Ray, *The Complete Adventures of Feluda*, trans. Gopa Majumdar. New Delhi: Penguin Books India.

Mathur, Suchitra (2006). "Holmes's Indian Reincarnation: A Study in Postcolonial Transposition." In *Postcolonial Postmortems: Crime Fiction from a Transcultural Perspective*, ed. Christine Matzke and Susanne Mühelen. New York: Rodopi, 87–108.

Mukherjee, Upamanyu Pablo (2003). *Crime and Empire: The Colony in Nineteenth-Century Fictions of Crime*. Oxford: Oxford University Press.

Murch, A. E. (1958). *The Development of the Detective Novel*. New York: Philosophical Library.

Ray, Satyajit (2004). *The Complete Adventures of Feluda*, trans. Gopa Majumdar. New Delhi: Penguin Books India.

Reitz, Caroline (2010). *Detecting the Nation: Fictions of Detection and the Imperial Venture*. Columbus: Ohio State University Press.

Sherlock (2010). BBC TV Series, July 2010–Present.

"World Literature." *Wikipedia: The Free Encyclopedia.* November 12, 2015 (Accessed December 11, 2015).

16

Sherlock's Queen Bee

Theo D'haen

> *It is of the highest importance in the art of detection to be able to recognize, out of a number of facts, which are incidental and which vital.*
> —Sherlock Holmes in "The Reigate Puzzle"

If there is one crime fiction character who indubitably belongs to world literature it is Sherlock Holmes. At least in English and probably also in many other languages, the novels and stories detailing the adventures of Arthur Conan Doyle's hero serve as the inevitable point of reference for most later fictional detectives and their creators as well as their readers. As such, Sherlock Holmes has entered the collective consciousness first of the West, and ultimately of the world. Proof of Sherlock's enduring appeal is that, like the mythical heroes of Homer, the legendary champions of the *Chanson de Roland*, the Knights of King Arthur's Round Table, and such more recent creations as Robinson Crusoe or Don Juan, he has become the subject of various forms of recycling. An article by Gary Susman mentions that by 2014 already more than seventy actors in over two hundred productions had impersonated Conan Doyle's hero, including Basil Rathbone, Peter Cushing, Christopher Plummer, Jeremy Brett, and more recently Robert Downey Jr., Benedict Cumberbatch in the BBC series *Sherlock*, and Johnny Lee Miller in its American CBS counterpart *Elementary*. The latter two series, at variance with most earlier adaptations of Conan Doyle's stories, are set in the present rather than in the time the stories were written. *Elementary*, while keeping Sherlock an English character, has as its setting New York, where Sherlock has gone to cure himself of his drug addiction.

Just as Virgil's recycling of Homer, Dante's of Virgil, and Joyce's of Homer, Virgil and Dante served particular purposes for their particular time and place, so too contemporary recyclings of Sherlock Holmes serve specific purposes.

A number of today's reworkings of Conan Doyle share a feature that can also be seen in J. M. Coetzee's reworking of *Robinson Crusoe* in *Foe* (1984), or Michel Tournier's doing the same in *Vendredi ou les limbes du Pacifique* (1967): a gendered recycling that fastens upon what from our contemporary, or perhaps presentist, perspective is perceived as a biased lack in the original. Coetzee adopts a feminine and partially also a "colored" perspective, giving a voice to a category of characters—women—barred from Defoe's *Robinson Crusoe*, and intimating the future acquisition of a voice by the colored character Friday, present but barred from speaking in the eighteenth-century original. Tournier adopts a gay perspective, together with what perhaps in retrospect we can already call an ecological one, both again conspicuously absent (to a contemporary eye) from Defoe's text. We can see exactly the same thing going on in *Elementary*, with Sherlock's all-white male roommate and companion in detection Dr. John Watson being replaced (at least in the initial season of the series) by an Asian American named Joan Watson (played by Lucy Liu) as the female housemate and psychological counselor to the latter-day incarnation of Conan Doyle's protagonist. Moreover, Irene Adler, the only woman Sherlock ever loved, according to the Conan Doyle canon, turns out to be Sherlock's ultimate opponent, Moriarty, in *Elementary*.

The BBC series *Sherlock* concentrates on expanding the humor, only glancingly present in the original, for contemporary viewers. *Sherlock* also gives more prominent roles to women, in the characters of Molly Hooper (played by Louise Brealey) as a pathologist and Mary Morstan (played by Amanda Abbingdon), first as Watson's girlfriend and later as his wife. And the special episode "The Abominable Bride" aired on January 1, 2016, which has Sherlock, by means of a drug-induced trance, return to late Victorian times and thus to Conan Doyle's original setting, is a strong defence of women's rights. If in *Elementary* Joan Watson takes on two of the functions of the original Dr. Watson, she doesn't assume his role of narrator of Sherlock's adventures. This does happen, though not without a twist, in yet another recycling of Sherlock Holmes in a detective series authored by the American Laurie R. King, the so-called Mary Russell series.

The first novel in the series, *The Beekeeper's Apprentice* (2000 [1996]), is a marvelous cross between Conan Doyle, *A Manuscript Found in Zaragoza*, Agatha Christie's Poirot and Miss Marple stories, John Buchan's spy thrillers, and Maurice Maeterlinck's *La vie des abeilles*. The latter book, a 1901 philosophical treatise on beekeeping by the 1911 Belgian Nobel Prize Winner, provides the epigraphs to the various parts of what is in fact a collection of tales loosely inspired by Conan Doyle rather than a fully integrated novel. In fact, it is Maeterlinck's reflections on the various stories that create a web holding them together. The same purpose is served by the two prefaces to the volume, one by Mary Russell, ostensibly the author of what follows, and the other by Laurie R. King casting herself as "the editor" of Mary Russell's hitherto unpublished writings. The action of *The Beekeeper's Apprentice* is set in Sussex, in the South of England, from 1915 to 1919.

Mary Russell is fifteen when she first meets Holmes, now sixty-one, and since 1903 a retired beekeeper living in the countryside as first announced in Conan Doyle's "The Adventure of the Second Stain" (1904), and reiterated in "His Last Bow" (1917) and "The Adventure of the Lion's Mane" (1926). Throughout the various stories, retrospectively told by Mary Russell, she will become Holmes's apprentice in beekeeping, but more importantly in sleuthing. Unlike Conan Doyle's somewhat naïve and clumsy Dr. Watson—who is portrayed in *The Beekeeper's Apprentice* as even more of a dunce—Mary Russell proves to be Holmes's match in everything. In fact, the subtitle to the volume: *Or, On the Segregation of the Queen*, indicates that she may actually surpass her teacher. The same thing is intimated at the end of the volume when Holmes and Mary start on a game of chess, Holmes's favorite pastime when not working on a case. Holmes is willing to "spot" Mary a piece, to which she replies: "But not a queen?" Holmes, who has lost to Mary before by doing exactly that, retorts with "Oh no, never again. You're far too good a player for that." So, she says, "We'll start equal then." "I shall beat you if we do," Holmes muses, whereupon Mary replies: "I don't think so, Holmes. I really don't think you will" (King 2000: 347). That she becomes the "Queen" is also underlined by her signing her author's preface "M. R. H.," the "H" standing for ... Holmes! In fact, in subsequent volumes of the series, Mary Russell will become Holmes's wife, regardless of the decades separating them in age. Her change of station in life is in fact already hinted at by the note to her "Dear Reader" with which she starts off her preface, echoing the "Reader, I married him" that introduces the final chapter of Charlotte Brontë's *Jane Eyre*.

However, there is more—in a beehive it is the queen that rules, not any finally pretty superfluous male, whose only useful function is to get the "action" going. This is exactly what happens in *The Beekeeper's Apprentice*, with Mary Russell quickly taking over from Holmes as the true leading character, as she continues to be in the subsequent volumes of the series, named after her and not Holmes.

In fact, she looks back upon her initial days with Holmes from the vantage point of the late 1980s, and she concludes her preface with:

> Holmes and I were a match from the beginning. He towered over me in experience, but never did his abilities at observation and analysis awe me as they did Watson. My own eyes and mind functioned in precisely the same way. It was familiar territory. So, yes, I freely admit that my Holmes is not the Holmes of Watson. To continue with the analogy, my perspective, my brush technique, my use of colour and shade, are all entirely different from his. The subject is essentially the same; it is the eyes and the hands of the artist that change. (King 2000: xvi–xvii)

The difference, of course, lies in the gender and the time of writing of the artist, purportedly Mary Russell herself, but by extension also her "editor," Laurie King. In her "Editor's Preface," King claims that the package containing Mary Russell's "On the Segregation of the Queen," along with several other manuscripts, was delivered to her one day by UPS, and that all she had to do with its publication was correcting spelling, sorting out handwritten notations, finding a publisher through her own agent, and giving the thing a more appealing title. In fact, she asks any reader "out there" who "knows who Mary Russell was, could you let me know? My curiosity is killing me!" (King 2000: xii). Obviously, King is here posing as a faux-naif, and in fact she subverts the real import of Mary Russell's text by re-titling it: King's title *The Beekeeper's Apprentice* casts Mary Russell as Holmes's understudy, while Mary's own *On the Segregation of the Queen* emphasizes her rise to equality and ultimately preeminence and power. The aptly named King, it seems, has upstaged the Queen. In fact, the intricate game of *imitatio* and *aemulatio* being played even gains in complexity if we learn at the very beginning of *The Beekeeper's Apprentice* that the subtitle to the *Practical Handbook of Bee Culture* which is first mentioned as having been authored by Sherlock Holmes in Conan Doyle's "His Last Bow" reads: *With Some Observations on the Segregation of the Queen*.

But Mary Russell's intended title at the same time subverts accepted hierarchies as they played out in the period in which her text is set. The alternative titles discussed in the "Editor's Preface," and the ostensible casting of the subsequent text as a Sherlock Holmes adventure, turn *The Beekeeper's Apprentice* into a case of embedded structures, one gainsaying the other. As an image for this pattern, I would like to invoke the practice of the parenthesis, with the proviso that whereas it is ordinarily the parenthesis that is the shorter text inserted in the larger one, in this case I would see the larger text, that is to say the ostensible "body" of the novel, as the long parenthesis to the two prefaces, interrupting the unity of meaning overlaid on the various stories by the structural device of the bee-metaphor in the Maeterlinck epigraphs and in the final paragraph of the volume. Or, inversely, the prefaces and the epigraphs can be looked upon as serving as parentheses. In fact, for the epigraphs this is actually the case, as they intervene in the body of the text. The two prefaces can then be seen as parentheses between the title of the novel and its narrative "body." In any case, what I would want to argue, following John Lennard's suggestion in his *But I Digress: The Exploitation of Parentheses in English Printed Verse*, is that a parenthesis registers an "ontological disjuncture" between the private and the public (1991: 242). In *The Beekeeper's Apprentice*, the disjuncture is between the "public" imagination relative to a Holmes story and the "private" truth of Mary Russell, and by extension of Laurie King.

The Mary Russell series is not the only crime series for which Laurie R. King is known. She also runs another series featuring San Francisco police inspector Kate Martinelli, set in the present. Interestingly, however, King brings the Mary Russell series and the Martinelli series together in her 2006 novel *The Art of Detection*. And again she uses an embedded or parenthetical structure. Martinelli is called to investigate the death of a middle-aged man found murdered in a disused gun emplacement on a difficult-to-reach promontory below the Golden Gate Bridge. When accessing the murdered man's San Francisco house, Martinelli and her associates find the lower floors to be done up in Victorian style, complete with gas fittings and other paraphernalia, looking, in fact, much like Baker Street 221B. The murdered man turns out to have been a great Sherlock Holmes fan, actually making a living as a collector and trader of Holmes memorabilia.

A central role in the plot is played by a purportedly unpublished Sherlock Holmes story that Arthur Conan Doyle would have written during a stay in San Francisco in the early 1920s. This story has just recently come to light, and it was in the possession of the murdered man. As Martinelli realizes when she reads a copy of the story, marked as such by the use of a different font, imitative of typescript, the present-day murder is copycatted, at least as to where the murdered man was found, from the unpublished Holmes story. In fact, that this should indeed be a Sherlock Holmes story is only indicated, or even merely suggested, by its being labelled as such in the third-person Martinelli parts of the novel. Unlike with the great majority of the historically documented Sherlock Holmes stories (I can only recall "The Case of the Blanched Soldier" and "The Adventure of the Lion's Mane" from *The Casebook of Sherlock Holmes* as exceptions to this rule), this particular story is told in the first person singular, presumably by Holmes himself. Presumably, because the narrator never lets out his real name. Instead, in the opening paragraphs of the story, when making the acquaintance in a cheap dive of a young man very much like the street urchins Conan Doyle's Sherlock Holmes deployed as his Baker Street Irregulars, he apparently introduces himself as "Mr Sigerson." This, at least, is the name that the young man in question, who gives as his name Martin Ledbetter, uses when he asks the narrator what his business in San Francisco is. The narrator replies with "My wife's family lives here." Immediately though he adds "which statement has as much truth in it as the names we had given each other" (King 2007: 198).

There are various ironies here. To begin with, as we know from the Conan Doyle story "The Adventure of the Empty House," Sigerson is the name the historical Holmes used during the so-called Great Hiatus, the period from 1891 to 1894 when Holmes remains absent from London after his supposedly fatal fall into the Reichenbach Falls in "The Final Problem." Then, for the attentive reader of the Mary Russell mysteries, the reference to "his wife's family" is as good as an admission that the narrator indeed is also King's Sherlock Holmes. In *The Beekeeper's Apprentice*, Sherlock, when first meeting Mary, applies his famous gifts for detection to determine her background. He locates her by her accent as having come "recently from her father's home in the Western United States, most likely northern California" (King 2000: 17). By the time in which the Sherlock Holmes story featured in *The Art of Detection* is set, Mary would have been married to Sherlock. Again, though, Mary is never named as such, the narrator at the very beginning of his story only mentioning that he found himself "in San Francisco one spring evening, my travelling companion temporarily about other business and my mind at a loss for a load to carry" (King 2007: 192). It is perhaps not too wild a guess that the "other business" the narrator's partner is engaged upon is the settling of her family affairs in San Francisco, the city of her parents who died in an accident some ten years earlier. This, in any case, is what the King Mary Russell novel immediately preceding *The Art of Detection* is about, and which is set in 1924. It strikes the reader as a further irony then when one of the characters in the Sherlock Holmes story that features so prominently in *The Art of Detection*, upon being subjected to a minor instance of detection by "Mr Sigerson," remarks; "what are you, some kind of Sherlock Holmes?" To which the narrator replies: "It was a question I had encountered before" (King

2007: 225). Even if only on the basis of "circumstantial evidence," then, a reader acquainted with either/or, and a fortiori both, both Conan Doyle's historical Sherlock Holmes and King's appropriation of him in her Mary Russell series would certainly understand this narrator to be nothing but "the real thing."

The plot of the purported Sherlock Holmes story hinges upon gender, in this case gay relationships. In fact, it resonates with an issue much debated during the early 2000s: the DADT ("Don't ask, don't tell") policy on gays, lesbians, and bi-sexuals in the US military in effect from 1994 to 2011. The narrator helps "Miss Billie Birdsong," a male transvestite singer in a dance hall for homosexuals, find out what happened to Jack Raynor, the man s/he is in love with and who she thought was also in love with her, and who has inexplicably disappeared. Jack is a soldier in the US army. It turns out that he has been killed by Gregory Halston, the only person in his company he considered a friend, interested in "books and music and life" (King 2007: 326). Raynor and Billie, while taking a stroll in public, one day cross Greg and his girlfriend, Merry, on the street. Only, Merry is not a girl but, like Billie, a transvestite.

She is, moreover, a female impersonator singer who feels upstaged by Billie. Jealous, she tells Greg that Billie is a transvestite. Jack fears that Billie will tell Jack the same thing about Merry. Later, Jack tells Greg that he plans to leave the army and get married—married moreover to Billie. As the narrator tells Billie in the final pages of the purported Sherlock Holmes narrative: "With Raynor still in uniform, Halston was safe. But from the outside, anything Raynor said could put Halston behind bars, or worse" (King 2007: 326). Consequently, Gregory Halston kills Jack Raynor. "Telling" amounted to a death sentence for Jack. What makes the whole thing even more bitter is that Jack Raynor actually might have found a way to indeed marry Billie, even though gay marriages were of course forbidden in 1920s America. In any case, the lawyer whom Jack had consulted on the matter had apparently been willing to draft legal papers allowing for the marriage; the condition for success however would have depended on Billie continuing to convincingly pose as a woman. And as the narrator further confirms to Billie, who can hardly believe that Jack would indeed have been willing to risk all this for her, a letter by Jack's sister "makes very clear that he was determined to proceed without the benefit of law, were you willing to undertake the performance of a lifetime" (King 2007: 330).

If the gay plot of the Sherlock Holmes story transgresses not only the accepted *mores* of the time in which it is set, it also goes against the period racial attitudes. Billie is described as being "small and exotically handsome, her theatrical make-up emphasising the large eyes and full lips Nature had given" (King 2007: 211). She has a "warm coppery skin" and "blazing green eyes" (212). The narrator calls her "a fine womanly figure of a man, five feet four inches or smooth racially mixed skin over a dancer's muscles and pleasingly languid bones" (214). And in a yet more explicit description: "Birdsong... was by feature and accent from the American south-west, Arizona or New Mexico. The thick, straight black hair and exotically tinted skin revealed a percentage of blood older to these lands than that of the European settlers, although the light green eyes were imports—in northern India one found this mixture of brown skin and green eyes, but not in America, and not with those cheekbones" (226). Billie's lover, on the other hand, is described as "a fit young man in his early thirties, pale of hair and eye" and with eyes "blue as lapis lazuli" (234). The "hair-cut and the straight back" that "say soldier" (229) make Jack Raynor come out even more of an "all-American boy"—except for the fact that he is gay. But even if Jack and Billie had not been gay, 1920s America would scarcely have tolerated such a racially uneven union.

The Sherlock Holmes story functions as a (large again!) parenthesis in the story of Martinelli herself, which is about solving the murder, but which is also about Martinelli's life outside of the police force, in this case as one partner in a lesbian relationship. Martinelli's partner Lee, like Watson in Conan Doyle's Holmes stories, is crippled from a professional wound, and serves as sounding board to Martinelli discussing her cases with her, but she also regularly reminds Martinelli that there is life beyond her professional life. Lee has a little daughter, Nora, who serves the same purpose. Significantly for the contemporary meaning, and highlighting the "ontological disjunction" between the social realities depicted in the parenthetical Holmes story and the embracing Martinelli story, is that the latter ends with the marriage of Martinelli and Lee on the first day gay and lesbian marriage was legalized in California. The contrast between then and now is emphasized when Martinelli, waiting with Lee and hundreds of other gay and lesbian couples for the marriage ceremonies to begin, "caught a glimpse of someone she knew, or thought she knew. Down where the hallway turned, a tall young man with close-cropped blond hair and eyes the color of lapis lazuli stood gazing down at his brown-skinned, green-eyed beloved" (King 2007: 490). This is the modern counterpart to the doomed gay couple from the embedded Holmes story.

Now, where does all this lead us to? Just as a parenthesis in a text reveals an "ontological disjunction" between "the real" and "the ideal," the very act of reading fulfils the same role in the life of the reader. A text, perhaps particularly a novel or short story, offers "as if" models, or "scripts" for life; in many respects this is also Martha Nussbaum's argument in *Cultivating Humanity* (1997) and other essays. Traditionally, however, this has been exclusively argued with regard to "serious" or High Literature. On the contrary, formula fiction, to use the term John Cawelti has familiarized for all popular genre fiction, is usually deemed to serve only the aims of evasion. In other words, reading a serious work of literature constitutes a "parenthesis" in the life of a reader, and through the "ontological disjunction" thus invoked, leads to a form of individual catharsis and to the reader's intellectual and emotional growth. With formula fiction, the argument goes, such is not the case. Instead, the ontological disjunction here is usually thought to lead to daydreaming and wishful thinking.

In *The Theory of the Novel* (1915), Georg Lukács argued that the novel is the form that epic takes when the bourgeoisie rises to power, evocative of a middle-class world as true epic was of that of the warrior nobility. Franco Moretti takes up and at the same time problematizes the same argument in his *Modern Epic* (Italian 1994, English 1996) and again in *The Bourgeois: between History and Literature* (2013). The novel that Lukács and Moretti have in mind is the realist, or the historical realist one, which Lukács sees entering upon its decline with the turbulences of 1848, leading on the one hand to monopoly capitalism, and on the other to organized lower-class or proletarian resistance in the form of trade unions and political parties. It is no coincidence that we see the rise of the detective novel in this same period. As social reality started slipping from the control of the bourgeoisie, the novelistic form expressive of that control was replaced, for the sake of the middle class, by formula fictions projecting the status quo of bourgeois order by combating the will to power of both the capitalist monopolist and the proletarian common crook, both of whom are depicted as destabilizing forces of chaos. In Europe, this generic development takes the form of the Sherlock Holmes stories, and later, in the interwar period, of the Golden Age fiction of Agatha Christie, Dorothy Sayers, and Ngaio Marsh. Somewhat later in the United States, as Sean McCann has argued in *Gumshoe America* (2000), it will take the form of the hard-boiled crime novel à la Hammett and Chandler, holding out the promise of the restoration, at least temporarily, of an order supportive of an American blue-collar male readership disoriented and economically and politically dispossessed by the First World War and the concomitant entry into the workforce of large contingents of women and African Americans.

In my view, King takes up these ideas of order in the embedded or parenthetical stories of *The Beekeeper's Apprentice* and *The Art of Detection*, but precisely shows them to have been projections in the service of, in Britain, a male middle class, and in the case of the United States, a white male blue- and lower white-collar class, clinging to power in the face of impending defeat. She also shows these projections to already contain the seeds of their own subversion *in absentia*, so to speak, in the Holmes stories' lack of women and minority characters. Although King doesn't take up the colonial aspect of the Holmes stories (as seen in *The Sign of Four* and in such stories as "The Speckled Band"), this too, of course, offers opportunities for recycling, as in Jamyang Norbu's *The Mandala of Sherlock Holmes* (1999). In fact, using the "parenthesis" terminology I am proposing, we might say that all those social elements "parenthesized" in normative or typical formula fiction return in recyclings in the work of subtly subversive writers such as King or Norbu. Or to take another recent example, Anthony Horowitz in *House of Silk* (2011) revives Holmes, Watson, and Lestrade in a case that involves a pastor and his wife running an orphanage for boys. These they rent to wealthy customers looking for sexual thrills. Just as King's *The Art of Detection* picks up on the actual issue of DADT, and Norbu's *The Mandala of Sherlock Holmes* on the plight of the Nepalese and the followers of the Dalai Lama, so too Horowitz's novel resounds with scandals recently come to light, such as issues of sexual abuse in the church but also in Britain's higher circles, including members of the aristocracy and of parliament. Just as the recyclings of serious literary works, then, reflect upon the genre and its implications for later times, so do the recyclings of formula fictions, and with similar import.

Taking a still broader view, we might borrow Reinhart Koselleck's idea, expressed in *Futures Past*, that history writing at any given moment is not only about the present, but also looks at the past with an eye to what the present thinks the future will be, or, put differently, in terms of what it expects the future to be. From this perspective, it might be a good thing to give more attention than is usually the case to popular genres in literary historiography. From the perspective of world literature, we may recall Homi Bhabha's claim in *The Location of Culture* that "the currency of critical comparativism, or aesthetic judgment, is no longer the sovereignty of the national culture" but is now the province of transnational categories favoring new "modes of cultural identification and political affect that form around issues of sexuality, race, feminism, the lifeworld of refugees or migrants, or the deathly social destiny of AIDS" (Bhabha 1994: 6). In light of this observation, we can see Laurie King's Sherlock Holmes recyclings as fitting at least one or several of these new modes, showing us how formula fiction can be recast as the epic of the historically dispossessed, now poised to take over the world.

Works Cited

Bhabha, Homi K. (1994). *The Location of Culture*. London and New York: Routledge.

Cawelti, John G. (1976). *Adventure, Mystery, and Romance: Formula Stories as Art and Popular Culture*. Chicago and London: University of Chicago Press.

Doyle, Sir Arthur Conan (1981). *The Penguin Complete Sherlock Holmes*. London: Penguin.

Horowitz, Anthony (2011). *House of Silk*. London: Orion.

King, Laurie ([1996] 2000). *The Beekeeper's Apprentice: Or, On the Segregation of the Queen*. London: HarperCollins.

King, Laurie ([2006] 2007). *The Art of Detection*. New York: Bantam.

Koselleck, Reinhart (2004). *Futures Past: On the Semantics of Historical Time*, trans. and intro. by Keith Tribe. New York: Columbia University Press.

Lennard, John (1991). *But I Digress: The Exploitation of Parentheses in English Printed Verse*. Oxford: Clarendon Press.

Lukács, Georg ([1915] 1974). *The Theory of the Novel*. Cambridge MA: MIT Press.

McCann, Sean (2000). *Gumshoe America: Hard-Boiled Crime Fiction and the Rise and Fall of New Deal Liberalism*. Durham and London: Duke University Press.

Moretti, Franco (1996). *Modern Epic: The World System from Goethe to García Márquez*. London: Verso.

Moretti, Franco (2013). *The Bourgeois: Between History and Literature*. London: Verso.

Norbu, Jamyang (1999). *The Mandala of Sherlock Holmes*. New Delhi: HarperCollins India.

Nussbaum, Martha (1997). *Cultivating Humanity*. Cambridge MA: Harvard University Press.

Susman, Gary (2014). "Holmes, Sweet Holmes: 10 Great Movie and TV Sherlocks." http://entertainment.time.com/2014/01/21/holmes-sweet-holmes-10-great-movie-and-tv-sherlocks (Accessed April 4, 2016).

17

Sherlock Holmes Came to China: Detective Fiction, Cultural Meditations, and Chinese Modernity

Wei Yan

One important criterion for deciding whether a text belongs to world literature is its ability to circulate among different regions in various languages. If we apply this standard to early Chinese detective fiction, which appeared in the beginning of the twentieth century and flourished during the Republican China period until 1949, it is probably the case that none of these works can be regarded as world literature, due to the fact that few of them have been translated into other languages; still less have had influence on the production of crime fiction globally.[1] Chinese detective fiction was mainly consumed in China at that time. However, if we examine classics of detective fiction in world literature, Sherlock Holmes stories have a far-reaching influence on the overall Chinese detective fiction. Since 1896 when the first Sherlock Homes story was introduced through translation, Conan Doyle's tales immediately became popular with the public. Chinese readers abandoned their traditional court-case literature of incorruptible judges to embrace this new, modern Western detective, and Chinese publishers competed with each other by claiming to have the newest or the most complete collections of the stories. Native writers either wrote sequels of Holmes's trip in China, or created their own local detectives with Holmes as their archetype. Stories of Arsène Lupin by the French writer Maurice Leblanc (1864–1941) accidentally became popular in China simply because Lupin had once outwitted Holmes. Local writers invented their own "Oriental Lupin" to compete with those "Oriental Holmes." How were the Sherlock Holmes stories introduced into China and how did they influence Chinese detective fiction? Why did Chinese translators stress the moral superiority of Sherlock Holmes, and what cultural meditations did the native writers make when they created their own detective heroes? What kind of Chinese modernity did these writers try to convey in their own detective fiction? These are some preliminary questions addressed in this essay.

In September 1896, *The Chinese Progress*, an influential newspaper in late Qing Shanghai, published a short story entitled "British Detectives Solved a Case of Stolen Confidential Letters," a translation of the Sherlock Holmes story "The Navel Treaty." According to extant records, this was the earliest translation of Western detective fiction published in China. Because of its popularity, three more Holmes stories were translated in short succession. These translations were later collected and published together as *Dr. Watson and Sherlock Holmes Stories*. At that time, these stories were used in part to educate Chinese readers about Western law. Late Qing reformists believed that Western scientific, legal, and law enforcement techniques and systems, as presented in detective fiction, provided viable models for educational, legal, and institutional reform. Their pedagogical purpose notwithstanding, these stories were well received by the Chinese audience, who believed that the Western methods of investigation and detection they espoused were diametrically opposed to the workings of the traditional Chinese judicial system, which largely relied upon physical torture to extract confessions.

The contrast furthermore led some of the Chinese literati to challenge the traditional belief in the incorruptible judge as the embodiment of law and justice, for instance, in *The Travels of Lao Ts'an* 1907), one of the most popular and influential novels of late Qing China. In this novel, the author Liu E (1857–1909) arranged a murder case: The suspect, Mrs. Jia Wei, is accused of poisoning thirteen of her husband's family members; worse, as was customary at the time, her father tries to bribe the judge in the hope of lessening her sentence. It just so happens that the judge presiding over this case is one known for his "incorruptible" virtue. Doubly suspicious of Jia Wei's guilt, he orders torture of the cruelest kind to obtain her confession. Unable to bear the cruelty of this judge, Lao Can decides to solve the case. After examining evidence and conducting an extensive investigation, he sets a trap to catch the criminal's accomplices and eventually arrests the murderer. For solving the murder mystery, Lao Can is lauded by Prefect Bai as a Chinese "Sherlock Holmes" (Liu 1990: 206).

Before Lao Can, the Sherlock Holmes of traditional Chinese crime literature was a character named Judge Bao. Traceable to the Song Dynasty, Judge Bao is a semi-mythical folk hero: an official hailed for his impartiality, incorruptibility, wisdom, and power of divination in numerous pieces of late imperial drama and fiction. The appeal of Judge Bao began to diminish in Liu E's time, when everything associated with what was seen as the fundamentally corrupt institutions of government came under suspicion. For the late Qing writers, independent and scientifically oriented detectives like Sherlock Holmes became the model protagonists for a new genre of detective fiction. Lao Can is not a judge appointed by the government and assumes no legal authority. Instead, he is merely an itinerant doctor compelled to intervene by compassion and a sense of moral responsibility. The emergence of Lao Can as a self-styled detective in modern Chinese fiction is emblematic of a sea change in the discourse of Chinese legality and investigative agency.

Detective fiction was the most popular Western literary genre translated into China The critic A Ying estimated that of the approximately one thousand translations of Western fiction between 1840 and 1911, at least five hundred were translations of detective stories (A Ying 186). Almost all the important translators at that time, such as Lin Shu, Zhou Shoujuan, and Zhou Zuoren, translated detective stories. In addition to the bestselling Sherlock Holmes, Chinese readers also knew well the British detectives Martin Hewitt, created by Arthur Morrison (1863–1945), and Dick Donovan created by James Edward Preston Muddock (1848–1934); the American detectives Nick Carter, created by "Chikering Carter," the pseudonym of Frederic van Rensselaer Dey (1861–1922); and the French gentleman-burglar Arsène Lupin. Chinese translations of Western detective stories came from two sources. Whereas most British and American novels were translated directly from English, European stories (other than British stories) were based on the Japanese translations by translators such as Kuroiwa Ruiko (1862–1920) and Tokutomi Roka (1868–1927). These translated detective fictions greatly influenced the late Qing Chinese novels. Some of the narrative methods used by Chinese writers during the late Qing period, for example, the suspenseful beginning of *The Strange Feud of Nine Murders* (1903), and the perspective of a first-person narrator in *Eyewitness Reports on Strange Things from the Past Twenty Years* (1910) by Wu Jianren (1866–1912) owe much to the influence of the narrative techniques and unique format of Western detective fiction. The popularity of Western detective novels also encouraged the writing of native Chinese detective fiction, leading to collections like *Chinese Detective Cases* (1902) by Wu Jianren and *Chinese Women Detectives* (1907) by Lü Xia (1884–1957).

The golden age of Chinese detective fiction came between 1911 and 1949, when the Republic of China was established. During this period, several magazines specifically devoted to detective fiction were launched in Shanghai, and much Western detective fiction was translated into the modern vernacular. Complete collections of the Sherlock Holmes stories, as well as those of other famous Western literary detectives, including Philo Vance and Charlie Chan, were published. Most importantly, a group of native Chinese detective writers emerged. Imitating or borrowing literary prototypes from Western detective writers, these writers also created several Chinese literary detectives who were well received among Chinese readers at that time.

Sherlock Holmes stories remained most popular throughout the Republican China era. As soon as Conan Doyle's stories began to appear in Western literary journals, they were immediately translated into Chinese. From the 1910s to the 1940s, over thirteen Sherlock Holmes collections were published by twelve different publishers in China. Most Western scholars agree that the appeal of Sherlock Holmes stories comes largely from the Victorian culture they embodied. For example, anointing Holmes "the last Victorian hero," Rosemary Jann believes the true appeal of this character "lies in his ability to satisfy a middle-class ideal of preeminence earned by talent rather than by birth while still retaining the trapping of older, leisured aristocratic ideals" (Jann, 39). Republican Chinese readers, however, seemed to have a slightly different understanding of the value of the Holmes stories, appreciating them in particular for the ethical values inherent within them. For example, in the colophon to a 1916 collection of Holmes cases, the famous writer Liu Bannong wrote:

> If someone asks how Holmes could make himself such a moral model for society, I think that it is because he possesses high morality. If he were immoral, then Baker Street would have turned into a den of bandits and thieves; if he loved money and fame, he would have been confined by the trap he made. In that case, how could he find time to serve society and how could he win the trust of society? With moral characteristics, if he serves as a detective, he will be a famous one; if he serves as an officer, he will be a good one; and if he serves as a high official, he will be a righteous one. (Bannong, 2)

It is true that Holmes is indeed a respected Victorian gentleman, but if we more closely examine Holmes's character, we will find that he is a man who follows his own code of conduct rather than submitting to conventional moral or legal limits. As his intellectual curiosity for new knowledge and sensations is sometimes quite apart from moral considerations, this serves him well. For example, he is willing to administer poison to a person simply to observe the result, or to beat a cadaver to see how long after death bruises could form. Between cases, Holmes often injects cocaine and falls into long spells of total listlessness and depression, and he displays contempt for any kind of knowledge unnecessary to his detective work. The reason why Chinese intellectuals disregard the disagreeable aspects of Holmes's character in their description of him as a scientific man of high morality is because of the close relationship between science and morality in China.

During the New Culture Movement of 1917 to 1923, which culminated in the May Fourth Movement of 1919, science was rapidly elevated to ideological status. Scientism was so popular and widespread that science sometimes appeared the focus of nationwide worship. New intellectuals called it "Mr. Science" and used it to attack traditional Confucian philosophy and to call for national rejuvenation. Traditional intellectuals also tried to embrace this fashion, and set out to prove that science existed in traditional Chinese classics. Despite their differences, both revolutionists and conservatives extended the concept of science into the realm of life philosophy.

Most Chinese detective fiction native writers belonged to the Mandarin Duck and Butterfly School, a school that was often associated with traditional Confucian ideas and old modes of writing, such as classical poems and martial art fiction. When they started to write detective fiction, these writers needed to build connections between Western science and Confucian teachings. In fact, such moral scientism can be traced back to the late Qing period. As Charlotte Furth has observed, the first Chinese intellectuals exposed to Western science attempted to associate science with the intellectual predispositions inherent in traditional Chinese philosophy. Specifically, "When thinking of nature, they imagined an organic, harmoniously functioning cosmos, where the social and moral order was integrally linked with natural processes ... Because they assumed the fundamental unity of natural and moral truth, Chinese were quick to conclude that Western scientific theories were applicable to the whole world and had ethical relevance" (Furth, 12). As an example of such belief, Furth described how Tan Sitong (1865–1898), an important reformist thinker of the late Qing period, believed that goodness (*ren*) was a function of ether (13).

Republican revolutionists, despite the fact that they attacked traditional Confucian values, also asserted that science has a moral educational function. They believed that by replacing traditional Chinese philosophy, science could be a new means of gaining understanding of the self. For example, Hu Shi (1891–1962), one of the most important May Fourth intellectuals, believed that science should be used to "reconstruct the order of the universe, the world, society and the individual, as well as their interrelation, and to afford life a source of value and meaning" (Hui, 38).

Overall, it can be concluded that since the late Qing period, although different schools had different views of science and traditional Confucian teachings, they all agreed that science had been endowed with a moral aura that equated scientific knowledge with moral superiority. Consequently, a hero like Sherlock Holmes, who has an almost encyclopedic grasp of knowledge, is conversant in logical deduction, and appreciates the essence of science, must be a man of high morality.

The most famous Chinese detective fiction writer was Cheng Xiaoqing. He was lauded as "the Master of Chinese Detective Fiction" and was the creator of the well-known Chinese literary detective Huo Sang, the so-called Oriental Sherlock Holmes. Cheng was born into an ordinary Suzhou family and taught himself English. It is said that he began reading Sherlock Holmes stories at the age of twelve and immediately became enamored with the character. Cheng familiarized himself with detective techniques by undertaking massive detective fiction translation projects, and he took courses in criminology and criminal psychology from an American correspondence school in order to gain expertise in forensic science. Cheng wrote his first Huo Sang story for an essay competition held by the newspaper *Fun Grove* in 1914. Huo Sang's initials reveal his connection with his literary model, Sherlock Holmes—H. S., after all, is an inversion of S. H. From 1942 to 1945, Cheng published a thirty-volume collection that included all seventy-three Huo Sang stories. Besides writing Huo Sang stories, Cheng Xiaoqing was part of the team that translated the complete Sherlock Holmes stories into classical Chinese in 1916 and into the modern vernacular in 1927. Cheng Xiaoqing also translated detective works by Western authors such as Wilkie Collins (1824–1889), Anna Katharine Green (1846–1935), Austin Freeman (1862–1943), Dorothy L. Sayers (1893–1957), S. S. van Dine (1888–1939), Earl Derr Biggers (1884–1933), Leslie Charteris (1907–1993), Agatha Christie (1890–1976), and Ellery Queen. Cheng was familiar with the history of Western crime fiction. In his short essay "On Detective Fiction" (1946), Cheng introduced the history of Western detective fiction, focusing one Poe's creation of the detective genre and Conan Doyle's contribution to the popularization of the genre. In addition to his debt to Conan Doyle, Cheng also expressed his appreciation for S. S. van Dine's contributions to behavioral psychology as well as Leslie Charteris's development of the beyond-the-law character Simon Templar, alias "The Saint."

For Cheng Xiaoqing, Huo Sang is an idealized modern Chinese hero, who on one hand shares many similarities with his literary model, Sherlock Holmes, while on the other hand he upholds a few traditional values. Huo Sang is 5 feet 9 inches in height and weighs over 150 pounds (by comparison, Holmes was over 6 feet and excessively lean). Like Holmes, Huo Sang plays the violin very well and has a varied and curious range of knowledge. His paring with his assistant, Bao Lang, is also an imitation of the partnership of Holmes and Watson. Bao Lang is a writer who had been a classmate of Huo Sang's for six years at the fictitious Dagong University and Zhonghua University. They lived together before Bao Lang got married, and sometimes they disguise themselves as a couple to solve cases. Like Dr. Watson, Bao Lang primarily plays the active narrator and records most Huo Sang cases, or sometimes provides irrelevant details to confuse the reader. And, as a spectator of Huo Sang's adventures, Bao Lang's role is also to persuade readers of his friend's intellectual acumen.

Huo Sang differs from Holmes in his breadth of knowledge. He abandoned traditional Chinese textual analysis, was conversant in both the natural and social sciences, was very knowledgeable in aesthetics and psychology, and most importantly, he was a man of high morality, and he appreciated traditional ethnical values. As has been discussed before, Cheng Xiaoqing was a Butterfly School writer. By depicting Huo Sang as conversant in both Western science and traditional ethnics, Cheng Xiaoqing was able to position and market himself in the name of science by identifying the point of interaction between Confucian values upheld by the Butterfly School and values of science promoted by Republican revolutionists.

The second difference between Holmes and Huo Sang is that, while both of them are on the side of law and order, they serve the interests of different socioeconomic classes. While Holmes upholds the values of the middle and upper class, Huo Sang belittles the wealthy class and stands for the poor. Bao Lang explains that this is because Huo Sang is a keen believer in Mozi's idea of *jian'ai* (universal love), a belief long immersed in a heroic tradition of *youxia* (wandering errants). The school of Mohism originates in the teaching of Mo Di, or Mozi. Its core idea, *jian'ai*, as King-fai Tam notes, means to "advocate a primitive form of equality that threatens to eliminate differentiation of human society by social roles" (King-fai, 148). Holding the spirit of *jian'ai*, Huo Sang is deeply concerned with the deterioration of social morality, unequal distribution of resources, poverty, and injustice, caused by a myriad of social evils and crimes, including the exploitation and control of resources by Western occupiers. He can be seen as a *youxia*, a type of man naturally inclined toward individualism, revolt, and extravagance, cherishing honor and belittling wealth. The Mohists were similar to the *youxia* in their sense of altruism and justice. Like the *youxia*, Huo Sang is more likely to be motivated by a sense of poetic justice and obeys a higher code of morality. In some cases, he would allow the criminal to escape, either because the victim represented a greater threat to society than the criminal, or because the crime was a pardonable act of revenge for acts that the law was helpless to redress.

Huo Sang's admiration for the *youxia* spirit sometimes leads him to respect some beyond-the-law characters. In a story entitled "The Aftermath of the Romance," a ventriloquist kills a wealthy man, but when he realizes that some innocent people were caught as suspects, he turns himself in to the police. Huo Sang hires a lawyer for him, but it doesn't work out. After one month, the ventriloquist breaks out of prison. Both Huo Sang and Bao Lang feel satisfied with this ending and think that the ventriloquist's action was quite romantic: "The Oriental national has a great romantic tradition. I had thought that because of the modern material culture's influence, now everything became rational and boring, and such romantic passion had gradually disappeared. But I am wrong. Such noble and passionate chivalric spirit still exists in the blood of our Chinese nation."[2]

Unlike Holmes, who is an intellectual superman with an air of superiority, Cheng Xiaoqing deliberately portrayed Huo Sang as an unobtrusive and modest man. Bao Lang attributed this choice to the cultural differences between the writers. In a story, he notes: "I remembered the Western detective Sherlock Holmes—although he is a genius, he is arrogant and often looks down on others. If we compare Holmes with Huo Sang, we can see the different manners between the Oriental and Western people" (Cheng, 1986b: 56). As a firm supporter of the British Empire, Doyle is confident in bourgeois institutions of law and order, in the stability of individual identity, and in the scientific ideal of objective truth. Part of Holmes's attraction, as Julian Symons suggests, was that "far more than any of his later rivals, he was so evidently a Nietzschean superior man" (Symons, 65). Huo Sang, on the other hand, looks more "human" than Holmes. In some cases, he makes the wrong judgment, and he can even be outwitted by Bao Lang. However, whenever he makes mistakes, Huo Sang is not afraid to admit and correct them on time. This is probably what Cheng Xiaoqing aimed to prove: Huo Sang is both a man of virtue and an approachable, as well as imitable, model for the modern Chinese citizen.

Cheng Xiaoqing's portrayal of Huo Sang as an ordinary man who often made mistakes and sometimes relies on poetic justice as a final solution is probably also due to the governmental and economic turbulence in China at that time. Many Chinese detective writers were also keen on portraying a detective whose work was marked by failures. Several writers wrote stories about the failures that Sherlock Holmes made when he tried to solve cases in China. Other writers created different Chinese literary detectives who often could not solve the cases in the end. Why did most of them stress the fact that any talented detective would fail in China at that time? After its ancient dynastic system ended in 1912, China was occupied by different warlords and its economy and social order were being heavily damaged by continuous wars. Most crimes in Chinese detective stories took place in Shanghai. After the Opium War, Shanghai was divided into three districts—the International Settlement, the French Concession, and the Chinese-controlled area—each of which had its own law enforcement authority. The coexistence of these three different juridical and administrative systems, as well as the increase in population due to the influx of refugees from other regions, complicated the structure of law enforcement in Republican Shanghai. Criminals could flee to foreign concessions to seek for extraterritorial protection, and foreign imperialists preferred maintenance of a poorly policed Chinese municipality of Shanghai so that they could justify maintaining their extraterritoriality and other special privileges.

The universal collaboration of the police with underground gang members made a bad situation even worse. For example, Huang Jinrong (1867–1953), the chief of the French police's Chinese detective squad, was a gangster who joined the Green Gang in 1927. Chinese detectives were notorious for extorting money from the innocent, raping young girls, falsely accusing people of belonging to gangs, and conspiring with the gangs themselves. As a result, detective squads were generally held in low esteem is China, and have been called "a group of swindlers, rascals, and villains ... absolutely lacking in scientific training ... using a thief to catch a thief" (Wakeman, 24). Therefore, even Sherlock Holmes would feel helpless facing such a dark and chaotic reality. Huo Sang is rather an idealized image of a Chinese detective and his stories are part of Cheng Xiaoqing's fantasy of social control.

Chinese literature has a long tradition of viewing literature as an important way to provide readers with moral education. Western detective fiction and films were sometimes criticized for their sensational and vivid description of crimes. To avoid such critique, Cheng Xiaoqing adopted a didactic way of telling stories.

He viewed his detective fiction as "disguised textbooks for science." This slogan was also often adopted by other Chinese detective writers when they tried to advertise their stories in literary journals and newspapers. Although his didactic stance might discourage a modern appreciation of the literary value of his stories, from 1920 to 1950, when the worship of science was fashionable in Chinese society, the didactic potential of his stories must have had a magnetic effect on his readers. It succeeded in positioning Chinese detective fiction, considered a genre of popular literature, at the nexus of serious literature. Holding out great hope for self-improvement and national rejuvenation to a new generation through the values of science, detective fiction reading and writing appeared to be noble endeavors indeed.

Western detective fiction was introduced into China during the late Qing era, a time when China was facing unprecedented national crises. The writing of Chinese detective fiction ceased in mainland China after 1949, when the new Communist regime believed that detective fiction belonged to the bourgeois ideology of capitalism: there should be no crime in Socialist China. Detective fiction was replaced by anti-spy literature. Where once figures like Huo Sang outsmarted corrupt government officials, now plots, influenced by Soviet literature, centered on how the Communist Party police exposed counterrevolutionary conspiracies. But from the late Qing through the Republican period, detective fiction flourished in China. During the New Culture Movement, science was far more than a tool for logic thinking, but became a highly moralized philosophy of life. Chinese popular writers employed detective fiction as a powerful vehicle to disseminate science and promote traditional ethical values. As a result, they transformed Sherlock Holmes to fit into their Chinese modernity: detectives are not only thinking machines, but also men of virtue.

Notes

1 Only two detective stories, "The Sunglasses Society" (1924) by Sun Liaohong and "The Ghost in the Villa" (1947) by Cheng Xiaoqing, have been translated into English in 2003. See Wong (2003).
2 Cheng Xiaoqing, 259 (1986a). Cheng Xiaoqing's sympathy for chivalric outlaws can also be found in his translation in the 1930s of the Saint series created by Leslie Charteris in 1928. The "Saint" Simon Templar is called "Robin Hood of Modern Crime." Cheng Xiaoqing commented that the Saint was a humorous and

righteous outlaw who was full of energy and had a keen sense of justice (Cheng Xiaoqing, 3[1946]). In his Huo Sang stories, Cheng Xiaoqing also created a chivalric underworld character whose nickname is "Swallow of the South" and called him "the only rival in Huo Sang's heart."

Works Cited

A Ying (1980). *Wanqing xiaoshuo shi*. Beijing: Renmin Wenxue Chubanshe.

Cheng Xiaoqing ([1944] 1986a). "Langman yuyun." *Qingchun zhi huo* [Fire of Youth], Shanghai: Shijie Shuju, repr. *Huo Sang tan'anji*, vol. 2. Beijing: Qunzhong Chubanshe.

Cheng Xiaoqing ([1944] 1986b). "Wuzui zhi xiongshou." *Xin hun jie* [Marriage Disaster], Shanghai: Shijie Shuju, repr. *Huo Sang tan'anji*, vol.3. Beijing: Qunzhong Chubanshe.

Cheng Xiaoqing (1946). "Lun zhentan xiaoshuo", *New Detective* (January 1946), 3–11.

Furth, Charlotte Furth (1970). *Ting Wen-chiang, Science and China's New Culture*. Cambridge MA: Harvard University Press.

Jann, Rosemary (1995). *The Adventures of Sherlock Holmes: Detecting the Social Order*. New York: Twayne.

Liu Bannong (1916), *Fuermosi zhentanan quanji [The Complete Collection of Sherlock Holmes Detective Stories]*, Shanghai: Zhonghua shuju.

Liu E ([1907] 1990), *The Travels of Lao Ts'an* (1907), trans. Harold Shadick. New York: Columbia University Press.

Symons, Julian (1985). *Bloody Murder: From the Detective Story to the Crime Novel: A History*. New York: Viking.

Tam, King-fai (2001). "The Traditional Hero as Modern Detective: Huo Sang in Early Twentieth-Century Shanghai." In *The Post-Colonial Detective*, ed. Ed Christian. New York: Palgrave, 140–58.

Wakeman, Frederic (1995). *Policing Shanghai: 1927–1937*. Berkeley: University of California Press.

Wang Hui (1995). "The Fate of 'Mr. Science' in China: The Concept of Science and Its Application in Modern Chinese Thought." *Positions* 3:1, 1–68.

Wong, Timothy C. (2003). *Stories for Saturday: Twentieth-Century Chinese Popular Fiction*. Honolulu: University of Hawaii Press.

18

A Sinister Chuckle: Sherlock in Tibet

David Damrosch

In 1903, a decade after a Sherlock-weary Arthur Conan Doyle killed off his famous detective in "The Final Problem," he bowed to public demand and brought Sherlock back to life. In "The Adventure of the Empty House," Holmes astonishes Watson by reappearing in London. He explains that he hadn't in fact fallen into the Reichenbach Falls along with his nemesis Professor Moriarty, but had fled Europe incognito in order to escape the revenge of Moriarty's henchmen: "I travelled for two years in Tibet, therefore, and amused myself by visiting Lhassa, and spending some days with the head lama. You may have read of the remarkable explorations of a Norwegian named Sigerson, but I am sure that it never occurred to you that you were receiving news of your friend" (Doyle 2:488). Nine decades later, the Tibetan activist and writer Jamyang Norbu decided to tell the story of that sojourn. In *The Mandala of Sherlock Holmes* (1999), Sherlock solves a murder mystery in Bombay before journeying to Tibet, where he saves the life of the young Dalai Lama of his era. In the process, he becomes both a global detective and a strikingly otherworldly figure, even as Norbu uses crime fiction for very worldly political ends.

Jamyang Norbu was six years old when the Chinese invaded Tibet in 1950. He'd already been sent to study at a British school in Darjeeling, where his family joined him after fleeing Lhasa. The mostly impoverished Tibetan refugees received a lukewarm welcome in northern India, where they were fairly isolated from the Hindi-speaking society around them. For Norbu, the English language and its literature were passports to a wider world, as he tells us in a preface to the novel:

> My life at St. Joseph's college was, at first, a lonely one, but on learning the English language I soon made many friends, and best of all, discovered books. Like generations of other schoolboys I read the works of G. A. Henty, John

Buchan, Rider-Haggard and W. E. Johns, and thoroughly enjoyed them. Yet nothing could quite equal the tremendous thrill of reading Kipling or Conan Doyle—especially the latter's Sherlock Holmes adventures. (Norbu 1999: x)

The militantly anti-imperialist Norbu leaves implicit the irony that it was hearty champions of empire such as Kipling and Rider Haggard who opened up the world to him through literature. Yet unlike Indians of his generation, Norbu never experienced the British as colonizers or English as the language of colonial oppression. The imperial power that had overrun Tibet was China, and he became devoted to the struggle for independence. He joined the abortive armed uprising against the Chinese, before settling in the Tibetan exiles' capital of Dharamsala. There he helped set up the administration's finances and began to write eloquent essays on cultural and political issues. Yet his essays reached few readers beyond the Tibetan community in India, and reactions were mixed even there. In a preface to *Shadow Tibet*, a collection of his essays written between 1989 and 2004, Norbu says that

> I have to be straight with the reader. I was not prolific; neither did my essays reach a wide Tibetan audience as they were written in English. To make matters worse, I could not resist throwing in the odd Latin tag I had retained from school. But however inadequate or limited in readership, these essays did somehow make an impression on the main players. The Tibetan government became hugely annoyed, and His Holiness once gave me a severe dressing down, and I daresay, I just might possibly have deserved it. (Norbu 2006: 5)

Norbu's essays may have had little local effect, but "it was the Chinese who convinced me that I was making a real impact as a writer" (2006: 5). Chinese officials in Lhasa let it be known that even though his essays "were as futile as the wings of a fly beating against a rock," they were harming Chinese-Tibetan relations. They recommended that "as an educated Tibetan I should return to Tibet to join in the socialist reconstruction of Tibet" (6). Declining this generous invitation, Norbu continued his essayistic activism, first in print and subsequently in a website (jamyangnorbu.com) featuring a monthly blog, also entitled "Shadow Tibet," with provocative entries on topics such as "The Real Threat to the Dalai Lama" (February 2016) and "The Subliminal Clarity of Blurry Cellphone Videos" (March 2016).

These blog posts offer a vital platform for international discussion, but their impact remains largely limited to the English-speaking Tibetan exile community; the posts typically receive a couple of hundred responses at most. It has been through the global medium of detective fiction that Norbu has reached a far larger audience. In *The Mandala of Sherlock Holmes,* Norbu created a sparkling pastiche praised by reviewers around the globe, as blurbs on the back cover of the American edition inform the prospective reader: "a master-stroke" (*The Times of India*); "a ripping tale of deadly intrigue and dastardly crimes" (*South China Morning Post*); "a page-turning thriller" (*Boston Globe*). No less an authority than *Alfred Hitchcock's Mystery Magazine* declared that "Good sense and irrepressible good humor … permeate this dashing and colorful tale of an exotic land steeped in mystical power. All Holmes fans should curl up with this book tonight and learn the truth behind the great man."

None of these blurbs hints at the book's strongly political dimension, and the description on the flyleaf similarly characterizes the novel as "an exciting, often richly humorous detective story" that moves from "the hot, dusty plains of India … to the medieval splendor that is Lhasa"—an Orientalizing description quite at variance with the book's actual portrayal of Lhasa as "a surprisingly cosmopolitan town" where the market sells merchandise from England, Russia, China, and India, and where the Dalai Lama's chief secretary serves Holmes "tea and Huntley & Palmer's chocolate-cream biscuits" (Norbu 2006: 149–50). The flyleaf indicates that the story moves "to the remote, icy Himalayas, where good and evil battle for ascendancy," but says nothing specific about the nature of this battle. Only gradually as we read the novel do we find Sherlock confronting the evil agents of the Chinese Empire, which is already intent in the 1890s on gaining control over Tibet. Reversing Winston Churchill, we could say that Norbu has wrapped the enigma of Tibetan politics inside a Sherlockian mystery. As Kristin Guest has argued, "Norbu's use of pastiche is self-consciously political, drawing together literary and historical contexts to connect past imperial cultures to comment on the contemporary situation in Tibet" (Guest, 79).

Neither published in Tibet nor written in Tibetan, *The Mandala of Sherlock Holmes* is very much a work of Tibetan literature, drawing deeply on Tibetan history and religion; Tibetan concepts of reincarnation play a central role in the story's dénouement. Yet it is equally a work of world literature, framed in the genre of global detective fiction. It was first published in 1999 in India, where it won a literary prize, then in the United States in 2001 under the title *Sherlock Holmes: The Missing Years*. (The American publisher evidently didn't think that American readers would be interested in mandalas, or perhaps even know what they are.) The English edition, meanwhile, decided to have it both ways, titling the book *The Mandala of Sherlock Holmes: The Missing Years*; even in English, the book takes on new forms for different national markets.

Norbu's creative use of Sherlock Holmes was key to the novel's success, but in framing his anti-imperial detective story, Norbu did more than play with Conan Doyle's tales; he drew heavily on Kipling to create his evocation of Victorian British India. He mined Kipling's 1888 collections *Plain Tales from the Hills* and *The Phantom Rickshaw* for a host of Anglo-Indian phrases and period details—his characters enjoy "tiffining at Peliti's," a popular restaurant in Simla (Norbu 1999: 86)—and he drew especially on *Kim* (1901), Kipling's great tale of imperial rivalry and adventure. Always faithful to the Conan Doyle canon, Norbu needed a Watson-style narrator, but he couldn't use Watson himself, since Sherlock's confidant and chronicler only learns of Sherlock's adventures upon his return to London. Instead, Norbu filled Watson's shoes with Kim's florid, excitable friend and companion Hurree Chunder Mookerjee, elevating him from the status of minor character to make him the first-person narrator of the entire novel.

The book is a stylistic tour de force. Norbu certainly isn't enamored with Kipling's imperialist politics, but nonetheless he has great fun with Hurree's Babu English, creating vertiginous slippages between colloquial English and Hindi—"a bounteous baksheesh of a rupee" (Norbu 1999: 5), "the blighter of a ghariwallah" (48). He also bestows on his narrator his own weakness for Latin tags; admiring one of Sherlock's disguises, Hurree exclaims: "By Jove, you were, if I may say so, a Bhotia to the boot heels; a Bhotia *ad vivum*, if you will pardon the expression" (101). Norbu's creative hybridization of English is nowhere better seen than in a ten-page glossary that concludes the novel. There, he sets Tibetan, Hindi, Sanskrit, and Anglo-English terms on an even plane, even using French to elevate the term "baksheesh," which he glosses as "alms, a *pour boire*" (269). The glossary teaches us that dekchis are cooking pots (Hindi), a chilingpa is a foreigner (Tibetan), a khafila is a caravan (Arabic), a lingam is a phallic symbol (Sanskrit), and a "poodle-faker" is a "womanizer, especially in hill stations, hence 'poodle-faking' (Anglo-Indian)" (276). The very selection of entries has a political resonance: it is surely no coincidence that Norbu's glossary starts with "Amban: the imperial Manchu commissioner in Lhasa (Manchu)" and ends with "zoolum: oppression (Hindustani)" (269, 279).

As Steven Venturino has said, in the most extended discussion of the novel to date, "The vertigo of intertextuality in this novel therefore leads us to reject totalizing assumptions regarding a single 'proper place,' or even dimension, for a person, nation, story, or memory. Kipling, Doyle, Jamyang Norbu, British India and Tibet are each shown to result in and may be the result of superimposed texts" (Venturino, 312). The vertigo induced by the novel's linguistic and textual overlays involves time as much as the narrow pathway above the Reichenbach Falls. As we can see in the case of other peripheral writers such as Russia's Boris Akunin, the Sherlock Holmes tales are doubly useful for Norbu, both as globally popular detective stories and also, by now, as *historical* fiction, set in a time equidistant from contemporary readers in peripheral and metropolitan locations alike. In his preface, Norbu speaks of the puzzling period language that he encountered when first reading Conan Doyle: "For a boy from Tibet there were details in those stories that did at first cause some bewilderment. I went around for some time thinking that a 'gasogene' was a kind of primus stove and that a 'Penang lawyer' was, well, a lawyer from Penang—but these were trifling obstacles and never really got in the way of my fundamental appreciation of the stories" (x). These phrases, however, aren't likely to bewilder only Tibetan boys; few readers anywhere today will know the meanings of "gasogene" (a seltzer-maker) and "Penang lawyer" (a cane). The historical detective novel thus levels the cultural and linguistic playing field for Norbu: he can master Conan Doyle's fictional world, and its language, as fully as can any contemporary English or American writer.

In particular, Norbu makes sure that we know how fully he has mastered the Holmesian canon as a "perfetto conoscitore del canone holmesiano," as Mario Faraone has put it (Faraone, 57). Norbu tells us in his acknowledgments that the initial idea for the novel was suggested to him by the American mystery writer John Ball, "a Master Copper-Beech-Smith of the sons of the Copper Beeches, of Philadelphia, who on a cold winter night at Dharamsala in 1970 examined me carefully on my knowledge of the 'Sacred Writings,' at the conclusion of which he formally welcomed me to the ranks of the Baker Street Irregulars" (Norbu 1999: 267). In his preface, Norbu presents himself as the editor of Hurree's manuscript, found in a tin box in a crumbling wall by Hurree's great-grandson Siddharth Mukherjee ("or 'Sid,' as he insisted I call him," xii), and throughout the novel he inserts periodic footnotes referencing relevant Holmes tales. At one point, he even corrects a linguistic mistake, which he ascribes to Watson rather than to Doyle:

> One of Dr Watson's less celebrated gaffes as a reporter is cleared up here. In *The Empty House* Watson records Holmes as crediting his defeat of Moriarty to his knowledge of "... *baritsu* or the Japanese system of wrestling ..." In point of fact,

the word baritsu does not exist in the Japanese language. The actual term used by Holmes and correctly reported by Hurree is *bujitsu*, the generic Japanese word for the martial arts. (Norbu 1999, 33n)

He then cites "the Japanese statesman-scholar, Count Makino," who corrected this error in a paper read at the founding meeting of "the Baritsu chapter of the Baker Street Irregulars in Tokyo, on 12 October 1948." The deadpan precision of this scholarly reference overrides the fact that Holmes couldn't possibly have used the correct Japanese term, nor could Watson have misreported it, as neither character ever actually existed. The mistake, of course, was Conan Doyle's, but Norbu inscribes himself within the inner sanctum of the Holmesian universe by adopting the Baker Street Irregulars' pseudo-solemn commitment to the historical factuality of Holmes and his world, a tendency for which the hyperrealism of much detective fiction provides ample warrant.

In this context, Hurree Chunder Mookerjee is a particularly apt companion for Holmes, since he is a fictional character whom Kipling had based on a real-life scholar-diplomat, Sarat Chandra Das (1849–1917). An expert in Tibetan language and culture, author of a Tibetan grammar and of an ethnographic travelogue, *Journey to Lhasa and Central Tibet* (1894), Das also worked as a spy for the British in Tibet. As Guest remarks,

> Norbu himself appears in the story as a metadetective, whose search for evidence of Holmes's travels in the east culminates in the discovery of a manuscript penned by Mookerjee: a fictional character who is himself a tribute to Sarat Chander Das, the real historical person referenced by Norbu in the acknowledgements. Taken together, these references ask the reader to reflect on the relationship between different texts and histories as they inform the present. (Guest, 82)

In Norbu's novel as in *Kim*, Hurree works as a spy for the secret service overseen by Kim's mentor Colonel Creighton. An Indian Sherlock, Hurree often travels in disguise in order to uncover conspiracies, solve mysteries, and thwart rival foreign agents. He meets his match, however, when he is sent to sound out the motives of a mysterious Norwegian who has just arrived in Bombay—none other than Sherlock Holmes in disguise. Hurree tries to ingratiate himself in a disguise of his own; he poses as a shipping company's guide, "Satyanarayan Satai, Failed Entrance, Allahabad University." Yet Holmes instantly discerns a contradictory fact of Hurree's past: "You have been in Afghanistan, I perceive." (A brilliant use, here, of Holmes's famous remark to Doctor Watson when they first meet in *A Study in Scarlet*.) Discomfited, Hurree bursts out in a kind of hyper-Babu-speak:

> Wha ...! Oh no, no sahib. I am most humble Hindu from Oudh, presently in remunerative and gainful employment in demi-official position of agent, *pro tem*, to respectable shipping firm. Afghanistan? Ha! Ha! Why, sahib, land is wretched cold, devoid of essential facilities and essential amenities, and natives all murdering savages—Musselmanns of worst sort—beyond redemption and majesty of British law. Why for I go to Afghanistan? (Norbu 1999, 6)

Holmes isn't fooled. "'Why indeed,' said he, with a low chuckle that sounded rather sinister" (6).

Norbu isn't just making fun of Mookerjee, however; instead, he builds on Kipling's original portrayal of Hurree as a shrewd undercover operator. Yet more than this, Kipling's Babu is a keen observer of native customs for their own sake, and his undercover work for the British is actually a cover for his true passion: ethnography. As he carries out covert missions for Colonel Creighton, Hurree takes the opportunity to make detailed anthropological observations. He pursues this avocation with scientific zeal, and his highest ambition is to publish ethnographic articles in England and one day to be elected a Fellow of the Royal Society. Given his position as a native Babu working for the British, this dream is unrealizable, even absurd. Yet instead of mocking Hurree for his pretensions, Kipling makes this unlikely dream a bond with Colonel Creighton:

> No money and no preferment would have drawn Creighton from his work on the Indian Survey, but deep in his heart also lay the ambition to write "FRS" after his name ... nothing save work—papers representing a life of it—took a man into the Society which he had bombarded for years with monographs on strange Asiatic cults and unknown customs ... So Creighton smiled, and thought the better of Hurree Babu, moved by like desire. (Kipling, 147–8)

Conan Doyle and Kipling were both drawn to quasi-mystical secret societies equipped with private rituals and codes known only to the elect. Both had periods of involvement as Freemasons, and during the Boer War in 1901—the year of *Kim*'s publication, two years before Holmes's resurrection—they were active together in the formation of a new lodge in Bloemfontein. (See Beresiner for a full account of Conan Doyle's connections with Freemasonry.) In *Kim*, Hurree uses his knowledge of quasi-Masonic Indian societies to develop a kind of secret code for use with his fellow spies. As he instructs Kim,

> "Suppose we get into a dam'-tight place. I am a fearful man—most fearful—but I tell you I have been in dam'-tight places more than hairs on my head. You say: 'I am Son of the Charm.' Verree good."
> "I do not understand quite. We must not be heard talking English here."
> "That is all raight. I am only Babu showing off my English to you. All we Babus talk English to show off," said Hurree, flinging his shoulder-cloth jauntily. "As I was about to say, 'Son of the Charm' means that you may be member of the *Sat Bhai*—the Seven Brothers, which is Hindi and Tantric. It is popularly supposed to be extinct Society, but I have written notes to show it is still extant. You see, it is all my invention. Verree good." (Kipling, 153–4)

Hurree has his most signal success when he wins the confidence of a pair of disguised Russian and French spies by playing the role of an angry, drunken opponent of British colonial rule. Having gotten them to let down their guard, he makes off with their secret stash of maps and papers, in much the same way that Sherlock uses disguises to retrieve the compromising photograph from Irene Adler in "A Scandal in Bohemia."

Norbu heightens Hurree's skills both as a spy and as an ethnographer; on the novel's title page, we learn that he has in fact become a Fellow of the Royal Society—and a recipient of the Founder's Medal of the Royal Geographical Society, no less—as well as a member of learned societies both in Calcutta and in St. Petersburg. As in *Kim*, Hurree applies his ethnographic knowledge in his dealings with Europeans as well as Indians. As he tells us in describing his attempted ruse on meeting Holmes, "It is always an advantage for a babu to try and live up to a sahib's preconception of the semi-educated native" (Norbu 1999: 6). His problem in this scene is that his usual strategy fails to work on Holmes, who is free of the racial prejudices that blind most visiting Europeans; immune to stereotyping, Sherlock can actually see what's before his eyes. As the novel progresses, both Hurree and Holmes learn a great deal from each other, as they come to confront Tibet's Chinese enemies, and they part as the best of friends.

To be sure, as a good Indian, Mookerjee has a low opinion of Kipling, whom he knows only as a sometime journalist whose rhetoric of "the Great Game" he rejects with scorn at the outset: "This excretious appellation was the creation of one Mr Rudyard Kipling, late of the Allahabad *Pioneer*, who with deplorable journalistic flippancy, managed, in one fell stroke, to debase the very important activities of our Department to the level of one of those cricket matches so eloquently described in the poems of Sir Henry Newbolt" (xix). Norbu further undercuts Orientalist preconceptions by making Hurree a thoroughgoing rationalist, in keeping with the scientific and ethnographic ambitions he already displays in *Kim*, and conversely Holmes becomes a mystical seeker who uses his formidable powers of observation to pierce the veil of earthly illusion.

As early as the second chapter, when Holmes is confronted with a horrific murder (a hotel employee is the victim of a poisonous leech intended for Holmes himself), Hurree is struck by Holmes's meditative aspect as he examines the blood-soaked corpse: "Mr Holmes seemed more stimulated than shocked by the situation. There was no trace of the horror which I had felt at this distressing sight, but rather the quiet and interested composure of a holy sadhu, seated cross-legged on his buckskin mat, meditating on the mysteries of life and death" (Norbu 1999: 19). As the novel progresses, we learn that Holmes's famous cocaine habit represents an attempt to blunt the emotional impact of his implicitly Buddhist awareness of the essence of life as suffering:

> He was not a happy man. It seemed that the great powers he possessed were sometimes more of a curse than a blessing to him. His cruel clarity of vision seemed often to deny him the comfort of those illusions that permit most of humankind to go through their short lives absorbed in their small problems and humble pleasures, oblivious to the misery surrounding them and their own inevitably wretched ends. When his powers thus overwhelmed him, Sherlock Holmes would, unfortunately, take certain injurious drugs such as morphine and cocaine in daily injections for many weeks. (Norbu 1999: 96)

Once he and Hurree reach Tibet, however, Holmes gets in touch with his inner bodhisattva. Refreshed by the Himalayan air and by the landscape's deep spirituality, he gives up drugs and pays his respects to the gods, declaring that "from here on, science, logic and Mr Herbert Spencer simply cease to exist. *Lha Gyalo!* [Victory to the gods!]" (Norbu 1999: 138). Unlike the discomfited Hurree, Holmes accepts the seemingly impossible events that take place there: the evil Chinese Amban can make objects fly through the air by sheer mental force, and a gigantic mandala inside a Himalayan ice cave magically opens to reveal vast buried chambers where a stone of infinite power is hidden. There Holmes and Hurree are attacked by no less a villain than Professor Moriarty, who is revealed as a reincarnated lama who had managed to transmute himself back into his Asian body as his British incarnation was about to perish at the bottom of the Reichenbach Falls. Holmes in turn proves to be the reincarnation of "the renowned Gangsar *trulku*, former abbot of the White Garuda Monastery, one of the greatest adepts of the occult sciences" (242). In a dramatic confrontation, Moriarty and Holmes battle to the death using their spiritual powers. Moriarty is definitively defeated, and his Chinese patrons' quest to control Tibet is stymied, at least for the remainder of the pre-Communist era.

The rationalist Hurree is completely baffled by these events. He rejects the explanations Holmes gives, based on ideas drawn from particle physics and biochemistry, concepts that Norbu presents not as anachronistic prophecies but as ancient Tibetan wisdom:

> He then embarked upon an extraordinary lecture which was chock-a-block full of very fanciful ideas and wild theories, that he, in a very superior way, considered to be more scientific than the scientific laws formulated by such great thinkers as Mr Dalton or even Mr Newton. Of course it was all bakwas, as we say in Hindustani... I mean he even said that light waves were electric and magnetic vibrations, when everyone knows that light is just colours... Even more crazy was his idea that human thoughts were mere electrical discharges in the brain cells. I mean, how can a scientific man like me even begin to tolerate such ravings. (Norbu 1999: 238)

Norbu is no Buddhist believer; two extended essays in *Shadow Tibet* bemoan the superstitions current in the Tibetan community, and as Lapamudra Basu has observed, there is a touch of parody in the climactic spiritual battle for the sacred stone of power, in which Hurree saves the day by tripping Moriarty up with his umbrella (Basu, 316). In the novel itself, Holmes remarks that "anyhow, there is a surfeit of religion in this country already. Why should the missionaries want to bring in another?" (Norbu 1999: 139). Yet Norbu presents Tibet as the world's great storehouse of ancient wisdom. Following his defeat of the reincarnated Moriarty, Holmes instructs Hurree in the meaning of the story:

> The Buddha once said that there were as many worlds and universes in the sphere of existence as there were grains of sand on the shore of the Ganges... You know the prophecy of the Lamas, that when man succumbs absolutely to greed and ignorance, causing ruin and desolation everywhere on the land... then the Lords of Shambala will send their mighty fleets across the universe,

and in a great battle, defeat evil and bring about a new age of wisdom and peace. (Norbu 1999: 255–6)

The rationalist Hurree skeptically replies, "Do you believe in the story, Sir?" Holmes responds: "It is not necessary to subscribe to such a belief to see where man's blind worship of money and power must eventually lead him ... No, I do not think it would be simple-hearted to give serious consideration to this ancient prophecy, and also to take some solace from its hopeful conclusion" (Norbu 1999: 256).

In bringing Sherlock Holmes into the realm of what can be called Tibetan world literature, Jamyang Norbu has done more than reinvent the great detective for his present political purposes; he has also revealed a spiritual dimension—seen in a notably humanist light—already encoded in the original tales but rarely seen by Western readers. At several points Norbu cites chapter and verse from the "Sacred Writings" (as Holmesian devotees call them) as evidence for Sherlock's crypto-Buddhist spirituality, as can be seen in passages such as the final lines of "The Adventure of the Cardboard Box": "'What is the meaning of it, Watson?' said Holmes solemnly as he laid down the paper. 'What object is served by this circle of misery and violence and fear? It must tend to some end, or else our universe is ruled by chance, which is unthinkable. But what end? There is the great, perennial problem to which human reason is as far from an answer as ever'" (Doyle 2: 901).

Norbu takes his bold blending of religion and science directly from Holmes, who tells Hurree that "There is nothing in which deduction is so necessary as in religion. It can be built up as an exact science by the reasoner" (Norbu 1999: 45). These lines are lifted verbatim from "The Naval Treaty." In a footnote, Norbu mentions that this is the story that directly precedes "The Final Problem," adding that "it is interesting that the metaphysical strain in him should surface so conspicuously" shortly before his climactic life-and-death confrontation with Moriarty (45n). In a later footnote, Norbu says that "it is remarkable that neither Watson nor the generations of Holmesian scholars should have noticed the clear spiritual bent in Holmes's character" (146n).

Grounded in Norbu's creative rereading of Conan Doyle, *The Mandala of Sherlock Holmes* blends genre fiction and political advocacy in a mode of metafictional play, in which Tibetan Buddhism is shown to be a moral resource for the whole world, transcending greed and the quest for domination, in an ideal blend of religion and science, ancient and modern, East and West together. Norbu doesn't expect that his book will in itself change the tide of history; at the book's end, we discover that Holmes, reincarnated once more, is living quietly as a monk in exile. As Venturino says, "Holmes himself is not to be the final answer to the novel's conflicts; instead the novel's own multilayered materiality, its circulation among readers, and its effects on future narratives serve as responses to the novel's own challenge" (328).

The book has indeed achieved a global circulation, and it has been translated into many languages, including French, German, Hungarian, Spanish, and Vietnamese. In a further twist of the book's adaptation to a foreign market, it was reissued in 2003 in the United States under its original title, *The Mandala of Sherlock Holmes*, and yet this restored title didn't involve some reorientation toward Tibetan authenticity (see Figure 18.1). Rather than showing a Tibetan map or temple scene, the American reissue uses a cover illustration geared for a postmodern audience: this is a 1990 painting by an American artist, Mark Tansey, entitled "Derrida Queries de Man," which shows the great deconstructionists in the guise of Holmes and Moriarty wrestling on the narrow path above the Reichenbach Falls. The towering cliffs around them are formed not of stone but of text. So the novel has had very different lives, half-lives, and shadow lives just in English.

As Mario Faraone has said, "Through the lens of a Sherlock Holmes 'case,' popular literature and the detective genre become a vehicle adapted to advance the argument for the liberty of the Tibetan people ... which can be transformed from a simple and somewhat utopian hope into a lasting reality" (Faraone, 87). In its various reincarnations, *The Mandala of Sherlock Holmes* testifies to the power of crime fiction to reach a worldwide audience, at once entertaining and educating its far-flung readers. In this, the novel embodies Norbu's hope, expressed in *Shadow Tibet*, that literature can succeed where more direct political action fails:

> Somehow, Lu Xun's writings have outlived the propaganda and ideology of his old nemesis, the Kuomontang, and will no doubt continue to be read and admired long after the disappearance of the Chinese Communist Party and its hacks and apologists. Good literature not only seems to be able to outlast tyranny, but further seems to have a regenerative effect on devastated political and psychological wastelands left behind by the likes of Hitler, Stalin or Mao.
>
> So, Nietzsche was wrong and the apostle John right. "In the beginning was the word." (Norbu 2006: 7)

Figure 18.1 *Cover for Jamyang Norbu,* The Mandala of Sherlock Holmes: The Adventures of the Great Detective in India and Tibet (New York: Bloomsbury, paperback edition, 2003).

Works Cited

Basu, Lapamudra (2009). "Tales of Tibet: Representing Religion and Resistance in Contemporary Film and Fiction." *South Asian Review* 30:1, 302–18.

Beresiner, Yasha (n.d.). "Arthur Conan Doyle: Spiritualist and Freemason." http://www.freemasons-freemasonry.com/beresiner10.html (Accessed March 11, 2016).

Doyle, Arthur Conan (1930). *The Complete Sherlock Holmes*. 2 vols. Garden City, NY: Doubleday.

Faraone, Mario (2006). "'You Saw, but You Did Not Observe!' Sherlock Holmes, il buddismo e l'indipendenza del Tibet." *Merope* 18:48, 55–88.

Guest, Kristin (2010). "Norbu's *The Mandala of Sherlock Holmes*: Neo-Victorian Occupations of the Past." *Neo-Victorian Studies* 3:2, 73–95.

Kipling, Rudyard ([1901] 2002). *Kim: Authoritative Text, Backgrounds, Criticism*, ed. Zohreh T. Sullivan. New York: W. W. Norton.

Norbu, Jamyang (1999). *The Mandala of Sherlock Holmes: The Adventures of the Great Detective in India and Tibet*. New Delhi: HarperCollins Publishers India, New York: Bloomsbury, 2003. Previously published by Bloomsbury as *Sherlock Holmes: The Missing Years*, 2001.

Norbu, Jamyang (2006). *Shadow Tibet: Selected Writings 1989–2004*. New Delhi: Bluejay Books.

Norbu, Jamyang (n.d.). http://www.jamyangnorbu.com/blog/2016/02/05/the-real-threat-to-the-dalai-lama/ (Accessed March 9, 2016).

Venturino, Steven J. (2008). "Placing Tibetan Fiction in a World of Literary Studies: Jamyang Norbu's *The Mandala of Sherlock Holmes*." In *Modern Tibetan Literature and Social Change*, ed. Lauran R. Hartley and Patricia Schiaffini-Vedani. Durham: Duke University Press, 301–26.

19

Detecting Conspiracy: Boris Akunin's Dandiacal Detective, or a Century in Queer Profiles from London to Moscow

Elizabeth Richmond-Garza

It is uncomfortable for a sober person to be in the same house with drunks.
—Entry on Boris Akunin's blog, August 30, 2014

On August 30, 2014, Boris Akunin posted to his blog, *Liubov' k istorii*, his unwilling decision to leave Vladimir Putin's Russia for an unspecified elsewhere. In this daring post, he explains his decision as being about a divergence of perception and ethics. Akunin is not willing to remain in an environment where his "sober" view of current affairs is overwhelmed by one who is without restraint, "drunk" with the delusions of the moment. Outspoken on issues of Russian policy both domestic and international for some time, Akunin declares himself queer in the sense that he is out of sync with Russia's current official policies, especially with the aggression in Ukraine, curtailment of individual liberty for Russian citizens, and increasing censoring of the arts. His departure is unwilling ("Many things 'keep' me in Russia"), and he expresses a desire to return one day, but for now he can only promise that "I will periodically visit to see whether the binge is over." What advice does he give to Russia's leadership in the meantime? If they have read his books, then they will understand his point of view. Akunin isn't a political scientist; he writes popular fiction, especially detective stories. These delightful volumes, however, continue the Russian tradition of writers like Aleksandr Pushkin who use the fictional, and even the fantastical, to address the actual.

Of the many literary and verbal *tours de force* that characterize Akunin's career, the creation of Erast Petrovich Fandorin is perhaps the most beloved and the most provocative. A kind of "pulp fiction for the intelligentsia" (*New York Times*, March 17, 2003), this series of period detective stories delights their readers with a reprise of Sir Arthur Conan Doyle's great Sherlock Holmes, while at the same time embedding thoughtful and witty commentary on Putin's Russia, via the choronotope of late imperial Russia. From the start, Akunin's entertainment comes with a subversive bite. These police procedurals (*kriminaly*) are set in the "elsewhen," but not in the elsewhere. With Moscow and St. Petersburg as their primary locales, and places like London, Istanbul, and Baku as additional settings, Akunin offers a critique of contemporary Russian culture and politics in the guise of historically remote diversions. Any reader who reads even the title of the initial Fandorin volume detects a polyglossic voicing. It seems, once again in the 2000s, that Mikhail Bakhtin's dialogism is a necessary foil to official attempts at controlling the heteroglossic actuality of how Russian citizens think and behave (Bakhtin, xxxiii).

Boris Akunin's first detective story in the series that features Fandorin bears the subtitle *Konspirologicheskii Detektiv*, promising its readers not only a detective story but also a conspiracy. Under the main title *Azazel'*, retitled *The Winter Queen* in Andrew Bromfield's graceful and attentive English translation, Akunin (the *nom de plume* of Shalvovich Chkhartishvili, a Russophone Japanologist of Georgian origin and prolific fiction writer, essayist and blogger when he isn't indulging in the genre of the detective story) connects the subversive and the conservative in a single phrase. The rational and empiricist project of sleuthing depends upon the existence of a threat to investigate and the subtitle contains one of Akunin's characteristic multilingual puns. While the word *detektiv* usually designates the detective story as genre (*syshchik* is the person who detects), Akunin capitalizes on the homophony of the English "detective" and the Russian *detektiv*. He suggests that the *detektiv* is both the investigator and the thing investigated. Russia's new *detektiv –konsul'tant* (consulting detective) will make his debut in and *as* a *Konspirologicheskii Detektiv*. As a detective, he detects conspiracies. As a civil servant himself, he is part of one. There are in fact two conspiracies in the novel, an international criminal network and a cabal within the government, and Fandorin will have to defeat both. With the witty play on consulting/conspiring in the word *konspirologicheskii*, Akunin introduces the Russian detective story par excellence whose *fin-de-siècle* sleuthing adventures have delighted Russia's reading public since 1998, even as they subsequently earned their author the risk of having his passport revoked. On August 19, 2014, a list was published of individuals considered to be "enemies of the people." Akunin's name is number 35 on this list, along with the names of Russian performers, musicians, and other writers, and even of non-Russians like Arnold Schwarzenegger (#6) and Milla Jovovich (#25).

In the summer of 2014, Akunin's witticism returned to haunt its coiner, as the Russian authorities elide Comrade Akunin with his fiction. With his name on the "black list," Akunin finds himself translated (*Glavnoe*, August 19, 2014). The consultant has become the conspirator, and the national protector has become the enemy, while both his persona and tactics remain the same: closely observing how other men of interest behave.

The ambitious narrative of nationalism requires a nation and a protector, and that protector needs to be one of us, a compatriot who participates in the culture he preserves. Moreover, not all but many nations are literally feminized. While *Vaterländer* (fatherlands) do exist certainly, many nations such as Russia are first and foremost *Rodina-mat'*, the motherland. Like W. B. Yeats's remembered martyrs from Cathleen ni Hoolihan, the nation's feminization ensures the self-sacrificing loyalty of her sons, who are willing together to give themselves for "her" (Yeats, 31). These protectors of the nation share loyalty and selflessness, but there is a particular protector whose queer way of being troubles the nation as much as it protects "her." Sir Arthur Conan Doyle's Britannia, as much as Boris Akunin's Russia, however, both depend upon him and are destabilized by him. There is a fine line between profiling and cruising, one that perhaps both Conan Doyle and Akunin transgress. Moreover, such transgression is not suppressed in the narratives inhabited by Holmes and Fandorin. It is on the surface. Both characters are fashioned as dandies *and* detectives, a combination that dates back at least as far as C. Auguste Dupin in Edgar Allan Poe's *Murders in the Rue Morgue* (1841), and maybe even to Shakespeare's Hamlet himself, in his elegant black suit observing his uncle's every move and imagining Claudius's inadequacy in bed with Gertrude.

Of course, Russian literature has its own practitioners of detective and crime fiction, often writing under pseudonyms like Akunin. An easy case could be made for it featuring at the heart of Russian Silver Age literature Fyodor Dostoevsky's *Crime and Punishment* (1866) giving us the first indigenous *syshchik* (detective) in the character of Porfiry Petrovich, the St. Petersburg magistrate in charge of investigating murders. It is his fascination with psychological profiling that is crucial to the capture of the double murderer, Rodion Raskolnikov. Moreover, Akunin regularly cites Dostoevksy and has written two volumes, which pun on Dostoevsky's initials, *F. M.*, and the use of the same letters for FM radio. *F. M.*

(2006) is told from the perspective of Porfiry and traces the exploits of Fandorin's grandchild, Nicholas, as he looks for the lost variant of Dostoevsky's novel in the twenty-first century. Akunin's oeuvre participates in a genre that has shown great energy especially since the Second World War. To name only one among many popular crime writers in Russia today, Yulian Semyonov, writing under the name Yulian Lyandres, wrote detective and spy novels both before and during Perestroika and even cofounded a theater, "Detektiv," in Moscow in the late 1980s, which specialized in staging suspenseful and detection-themed works. Often credited with pioneering Soviet investigative journalism as a foreign correspondent, he is best known for novels like *Seventeen Moments of Spring* (1968), which follows the exploits of undercover Soviet agent Colonel Isaev in 1945 as he infiltrates the SD, the Nazi political Intelligence Agency.

Akunin capitalizes on the popularity of local Russian detective stories and on the Russian taste for adaptations of their British forerunners, but his revival retains a complexity often elided by other Russian writers in the genre: dandyism. From Beau Brummel's famous *levées* and tie-tying ceremonies in the 1790s, to Sherlock Holmes's understated black suits in the 1890s, to Fandorin's lifesaving corset in a nostalgic revisiting of the *fin de siècle*, dandified attire and attitude have been connected unexpectedly to an intellectual and even nation-preserving masculinity. Even 007's nonchalance seems to continue the tradition of the old-Etonian dandy as national protector. Thomas Carlyle, who defined the "dandiacal" in *Sartor Resartus*, sees in the appreciation of the dandy his actualization. More than merely living to dress, the dandy fashions himself as critic; the dandy lives to be observed and to observe. As Oscar Wilde quipped, "One must either be a work or Art, or wear a work of Art" (Wilde, 3).

Behind this focus on the aesthetic construction of the self, however, lie not only a vision of ideal masculinity, but also an assumption that such masculinity is both visible and readable. Considering Akunin's protagonist in juxtaposition with his English predecessor, this dandified detective poses questions about heteronormativity and patriotism. How is it that dandyism's masculinized but controversial and marked aesthetic comes to be connected to the pinnacle of masculine rationalism in the face of threat, to criminal investigation and the policing (which is meant literally here) of deviance in both its social and ideological variants? Conan Doyle's preoccupation with Holmes's intimate domestic relationship with Dr. John Watson is only the most obvious reprise of the dandy's publication of his private self-construction. Such artifice arises in the context of Sir Francis Galton's arrogant proto-eugenic composite portraits, which claimed to read internal ethics and criminal predispositions based upon physiognomy.

Such phenomenological overconfidence must be calibrated against the need for real intimacy which Holmes's own method emphasizes, and then can be used as a point of departure for considering the implications of a dandiacal performative identity both in the *fin de siècle* and in our current moment. Does the dandy, and do the dandiacals who are trained to read his fabrications, offer an alternative epistemology, which both subverts and lampoons the dominant desire to profile and define? And might there be something worth considering, in the context of a Georgian Japanologist writing nostalgic detective stories in Russian under Putin's gaze, about the deployment once again of the archetype? Becoming dandiacal is an interstitial position, one that allows hypermasculinty to become its other.

Akunin has chosen his lineage carefully, tracing across the space of a century of historical and cultural affinities that permit his invention to captivate his audience. The experience of Sherlock Holmes relies upon an awareness of British imperial conflicts as the backdrop for the stories. One might say that a reader of Conan Doyle's stories in *The Strand Magazine* was expected also to be a reader of *The Evening Standard*. Pleasing even without their historical contexts, the English presence in Hong Kong underlies the opium-den intrigue of "The Man with the Twisted Lip," for example, and "A Scandal in Bohemia" is grounded in the dynastic uncertainties and instabilities of the Habsburgs who would ultimately precipitate the First World War. Indeed, one story in particular, "The Resident Patient," is perhaps the inspiration for the "Azazel'" conspiracy in Akunin's first volume. Holmes is challenged in this story to account for the death of a very nervous Russian patient who is under the care of a live-in doctor. Perhaps above all else, Dr. John Watson's status as a field surgeon and veteran of the Afghan wars serves as a constant reminder that these cases and characters, while invented, are plausible inhabitants of Victorian and Edwardian London. Just as Martin Freeman's recent portrayals of Watson in the BBC series *Sherlock* poignantly capitalize on twenty-first-century global conflict in Afghanistan, Akunin invokes and reworks his English model for his readers.

Russian readers and viewers have a long tradition of devotion to the police procedural, and especially to those two most admired practitioners Conan Doyle and Agatha Christie. The immense popularity of Sherlock Holmes, Miss Marple, Hercule Poirot, and others includes not only translations but also adaptations for film and television throughout the Soviet period and beyond. Ruben

Dishdishyan's 2013 television series, *Sherlok Kholms*, is only the most recent in a long line of successful remediations of the stories, beginning with Vasily Livanov's highly successful series of television films, *Prikliucheniia Sherloka Kholmsa i doktora Vatsona*, directed between 1979 and 1986 by Igor Maslennikov, which remain the most faithful filmic adaptations of the original stories. The appeal of the stories lies not in their suspensefulness per se, as the solutions are often foreshadowed or even revealed, but in the ways in which the solutions are found and in the characterization of those who do the solving.

Just what about Holmes, and now Fandorin, is so attractive and so unnerving? Despite his reassuring "solutions" to cases, our ambivalence about Holmes himself remains, whether imagined in Sidney Paget's original illustrations for the stories or in Ilya Noskov's 2002 portrayal of Fandorin in Aleksandr Abadashyan's *Azazel'*, in which one of Putin's few remaining staunch supporters from the artistic community, Sergei Bezrukov, perhaps appropriately plays the corrupt state official, Ivan Frantsevich Brilling, who is working with an international syndicate. Indeed, it needs to be mentioned that one of the few things that is lost in the English versions of the novels is their multimediality. Bromfield sensitively preserves the period wit and eloquence of Akunin's Russian, and the intrusion of things like dispatches, advertisements, and letters also makes its way into the English versions. What is lost in translation is the pleasure of the elaborate interplay of text and image that the various illustrators (Aleksey Kuzmichev, Igor Sakurov, and others) contribute to the original volumes. Although Paget's remediational sensibility contributes to the Russian versions, sadly it doesn't make its way back home again.

The success of the Holmes stories hinges upon creating a shared cultural space between the characters and the audience, each of whom hopes that empirical deduction with its combination of logic and observation can render a threatening world intelligible. For Conan Doyle, the emergent technologies of investigation were as exciting as ours. Dactyloscopy and photography profiling promised not only to account for what had happened but, in the latter case, even to predict future violations. Sir Francis Galton's composite photographs superimposed multiple images of individuals, who shared a particular profile, to create a generic profile, holding out the hope that criminal tendencies could be mapped physiologically, especially in the geometry of the face. Galton argued that predispositions to criminality, even to the particular offense likely to be committed, could be detected in the careful measurements he made of nasal length or forehead height. Holmes's close observation of physical characteristics stops short of fully predicting behavior, but he is confident in using his capacity to "read" physiology, behavior, and attire as an index of past action and current accountability.

The allure of legible bodies in an increasingly diverse and cosmopolitan London, and the impulse to name and taxonomize them extends beyond Galton and Conan Doyle. There has been a persistence of interest in Holmes's sexuality. Sometimes the prompting of this interest has taken the concrete form of, for example, the actor Jeremy Brett, who had played Basil Hallward in John Gorrie's ground-breaking 1976 television version of Oscar Wilde's *The Picture of Dorian Gray*, taking on the role of Holmes for Granada Television's decade-long series beginning in 1984. Brett retains from John Osborne's adaptation of Wilde the complex relationship to masculinity and same-sex attraction that Hallward confesses for Dorian Gray, just as the other principal actors in the adaptation, John Gielgud as Henry Wotton and Peter Firth as Dorian Gray himself, risked controversy in playing the other two points in Wilde's love triangle. More often, Holmes's queerness has been remarked by critics interested in the representation and repression of homosocial masculinity in Victorian culture. In 1895, while Oscar Wilde was serving his first year in prison for gross indecency, John Addington Symonds wrestled with this very matter of naming identities, in his case the one "that dare not speak its name." On the opening page of *A Problem of Modern Ethics*, Symonds suggests that certain identities cannot be named, despite their very real existence: "There is a passion, or a perversion of appetite, which, like all human passions, has played a considerable part in the world's history for good or evil; but which has hardly yet received the philosophical attention and the scientific investigation it deserves" (Symonds, 1). Symonds goes on to suggest that homosexuality ("inversion") is global and transhistorical (1–2).

Despite its actuality, and even its legibility to the initiated, however, it doesn't register in contemporary discourse as a profile. Unlike other identity markers, which often have to do with race, ethnicity, and gender, homosexuality is a practice that cannot be read with confidence. While a Russian and an Englishman may appear similar, or a woman may seem to have the mental tenacity of a man, Victorian London seems replete with profiles that defy categorization. For homosexuality the challenge is even greater since, apart from the anti-sodomy laws like the Labouchere amendment of 1885, it doesn't exist as a category that would render it intelligible. It is not who you are so much as what you do. How then do the protectors of the national identity detect various potentially subversive profiles circulate in cosmopolitan cultures? With individuals able to pass for ideal citizens, for being patriotic, for being English, or even for being heterosexual, how does the detective detect them? Moreover, what risks to normativity does the nation run in relying upon individuals who are able to read such profiles and even to adopt them themselves?

Holmes and Fandorin are both snappy dressers, and they adopt a similar style. Fandorin's style, however, entails at least the same level of risk as Holmes's pose, thanks to Putin's recent passage of anti-homosexuality legislation. On June 29, 2013, Putin signed a federal act banning "information promoting non-traditional sexual relations," thereby amending the Administrative Code and the federal law "On Protecting Children from Information Harmful to their Health and Development" (Federal'nyi zakon). Indeed, one might argue that were Fandorin living in 2014, he would be at a greater risk himself and a greater risk than Holmes . The Duma's controversial federal act, unlike the Labouchere Amendment that criminalized "gross indecency" in Victorian England, criminalizes not a concrete act but an impression specifically the forming of an "attraction" to something non-traditional (Article 3, chapter 6). Rather than addressing the legality of sodomy, the new legislation focuses on how a person's behavior appears and might influence others' attitudes, especially those of the young.

Both Conan Doyle and Akunin repeatedly invite us into the intimate private world of the detective as he puts on his pose, often with another man watching. This "nontraditional" scene of the detective "dressing up" while his friend watches run throughout both texts. Of course, Holmes and Watson share rooms, until Watson marries and moves out, and the stories are filled with their "intimate" scenes of bachelor life, as Watson repeatedly describes them. Most of the stories begin with the two men reading the paper after breakfast, and Holmes taking on his detective identity, which involves props (his pipe), gestures (his closed eyes and pressed-together finger tips), and clarity of mind:

> "You have erred, perhaps," he observed, taking up a glowing cinder with the tongs, and lighting it with the long cherrywood pipe which was wont to replace his clay when he was in a disputation mood ... He looked her over in his searching fashion and then composed himself with his lids drooping and his fingertips together to listen to her story. ("The Adventure of the Copper Beeches," Doyle 166–7)

Akunin's protagonist, a twenty-year-old orphan assigned to the Criminal Investigations Department of the Moscow Police, doesn't have a roommate, and the stories aren't narrated in the first person. Nevertheless, a level of intimacy is created from Fandorin's first appearance as observed by his new boss, Xavier Feofilaktovich Grushin, as they read the newspaper together in the office, pausing especially over an advertisement for the latest American corset "Lord Byron" (Akunin 2003: 9).

In slightly different ways each is a "dandy," and early on their inventors make this ambivalent identity clear. Beau Brummell invented the dandiacal pose, using his style as an entré into the most elite aristocratic circles of the Prince Regent, the future King George IV, beginning in 1795. Brummell's natural wit and understated dress captivated the prince, earning him a position of exceptional influence, until the two fell out over a disastrously ill-conceived joke at the prince's expense in 1813 (Kelly, 190–1). Brummell's devotion to fastidious grooming, his introduction of the well-cut plain black jacket, and his obsession with the well-tied cravat survived his personal disgrace and introduced the nineteenth century's focus on expressing and reading the self through understated attire. Thomas Carlyle, however, in his satirical masterpiece, *Sartor Resartus*, already foregrounds the possible risks of this focus on the hermeneutics of attire. For Carlyle, the dandy is troublingly obsessive, and the "drudge" functions as the dandy's even more alarming inverse. Carlyle's piece purports to be a treatise by a fictitious German philosopher called Diogenes Teufelsdrökh. Teufelsdrökh's topic is how people dress and what these sartorial decisions entail and imply. He writes about the dandy in the section entitled "The Dandiacal Body": "A Dandy is a clothes-wearing Man, a Man whose trade, office, and existence consist in the wearing of Clothes. Every faculty of his soul, spirit, purse and person is heroically consecrated to this one object, the wearing of clothes wisely and well: so that as others dress to live, he lives to dress" (Carlyle, 207). For Carlyle, the dandy is the ultimate surface text and surface reader, someone whose clothes are coextensive with being alive. Long before Judith Butler's insights about the constructedness of gender and identity, Carlyle's dandy relies upon the fictionality of the attired self as the basis for who he is in the world.

I am using the word dandy here very intentionally, since there is another Russian word, *frant*, for the self-fashioned and fashion-conscious man. With a lineage that can be traced back to the great national poet Aleksandr Pushkin, who aspired to being a second Lord Byron, *frant* is a more than ambiguous term. Although often considered to be one himself, in a famous passage from *Eugene Ongein*, Pushkin reduces Onegin as a person to his clothes alone: "as regards his clothing he was a pedant, what we call a dandy" (Pushkin, 707). *Frant* bears with it some of the negative associations of "fop," suggesting an inverse proportionality of attention to dress and intelligence. Russian complements the somewhat dubious Czech loan-word *frant* with the equally foreign *dendi*, and a number of other far more negative imported words like *shschiogol'*, whose common ground is that they are not properly Russian words.

Akunin's own choice of the unusual Erast, as Fandorin's given name, entails the same ambivalence about fancy gentlemen, invoking for any Russian reader the callous aristocratic seducer and destroyer of a poor Moscow flower girl in Nikolai Karamzin's "Poor Liza" (1792). Somehow the Russian language needs to retain linguistically the otherness of the dandy. Indeed, among Pushkin's works that portray the dandy-infested superficial and ruthless St. Petersburg society, there is also a work that relies upon suspense and detection, and which Akunin explicitly invokes. In Pushkin's 1833 supernatural story "The Queen of Spades," a Russified German finds himself caught in a magical world of gambling where his success or failure depends upon acquiring a secret numeric code that will tell him which cards will come up and thereby secure his victory and future (Pushkin, 1048–59). Its successful acquisition requires deduction, profiling, and spying. By chapter 8 of *Azazel'*, Akunin makes Pushkin's relevance explicit, subtitling the section "in which the jack of spades turns up most inopportunely" (93). Indeed, the whole chapter reprises the Pushkin story, from snippets of French to the intricacy with which Akunin describes the high-stakes card game being played. Like the tragic Hermann, however, Fandorin is not a *frant*, since his very life depends upon his dandyism, especially in an early scene in *Azazel'*, where his fashion consciousness saves his life.

On the one hand the visibility of the male might be viewed as a testimonial to masculine subjectivity. The dandy's *soigné* appearance is the source of his influence and the basis of his claim to admission to the halls of power. How he looks controls how he is seen and what he is permitted. This carefully constructed self is created for other men, to be the object of their viewing and approbation. Only a few chapters earlier, Fandorin makes the fortunate decision to enhance his already attractive physique through the donning of that slimming male corset he and Grushin had seen in the newspaper. This particular garment, regularly featured in Victorian advertising, flirts with cross-dressing and troubling intimacy. Indeed, every detail of the relationship between the dandy and his clothes is potentially troubled. Brummell and the Prince Regent watched each other dress, and this intimate physical relationship is regularly preserved in the dandy's relationship to his tailor. When writing about tailors, Carlyle's Teufelsdrökh notes:

> Still more touching was it when turning a corner of a lane, in the Scottish Town of Edinburgh, I came upon a Signpost, whereas was written that such and one was "Breeches-Maker to his Majesty;" and stood painted the Effigies of a Pair of Leather Breeches, and between the knees these memorable words, SIC ITUR AD ASTRA. (Carlyle, 220)

Carlyle's shop sign reveals the anxiety of the tailor's job, the intimate knowledge of the body that he is to clothe and the awareness that "this is the way to the stars."

Akunin's Fandorin is more decorous in his fixation on a slender waist rather than well-clad thighs, but the flirtation remains. In fact, the text addresses this anxiety directly. Fandorin's superior jokes about his protégé's interest in the corset, and we are told that Fandorin "became inexplicably embarrassed; his cheeks flushed bright red, and his long girlish eyelashes fluttered guiltily" (Akunin 2003: 9). Although actual historical advertisements (Farrer, 64) confirm the acceptability of these garments, Grushin is less certain. However, that corset stands in as a knife-proof vest and saves Fandorin's life when he is ambushed by assassins after dinner with the dandiacal student and duelist Arkhtyrtsev. Grushin may be too traditional to approve of the corset, but when an energetic new boss, Ivan Franzevich Brilling, comically refers to as "the man of the future" (Akunin 2003: 69), comes to visit recuperating Fandorin in his bedroom along with Grushin, the corset is praised. In a room that includes only a divan on which the patient is lying, his clothes, and a collection of foreign books (about English philosophy, French police stories and Indian breathing exercises), Brilling reassures the again blushing Fandorin and even begins to imagine the benefits of this garment for his whole department: "Yes, it was a splendid idea. It wouldn't save you from a bullet, of course, but against cold steel it serves pretty well. I'll give instructions for a batch of such corsets to be bought for agents assigned to dangerous missions" (74). Brilling will emerge as the most powerful member of the international conspiracy. Gently and playfully, as the three police officers discuss underwear in a bedroom, Akunin introduces the trope of cross-dressing, inviting his readers to see a parallel between women's underwear and a police uniform. The protectors of the nation will wear corsets from now on.

If sporting a corset to defeat an English-backed international conspiracy represents a doubly delightful reversal of modern expectations about the national origins of organized crime and the best ways to defeat it, Akunin's game of echoing contemporary issues in Russia is far more pervasive. Small flourishes—such as naming a game in which young orphaned men tempt fate by spinning the barrel of a gun loaded with a single bullet and shooting themselves "American roulette"—are accompanied by more complex critiques. Like many who have contemplated the character of Holmes, Akunin decides to provide a backstory for his eccentricity and his confirmed bachelorhood, one that confirms him as a heterosexual romantic. For Akunin, Fandorin's reticence around women is innate, but it is the death of his fiancée on their wedding day that assures his detachment from conventional society, both masculine and feminine. Terrorists take revenge on Fandorin for his defeat of the *Azazel'* conspiracy, and the first volume of his adventures finishes with his wedding day and the murder of his new bride. Elizaveta von Evert-Kolokoltseva and Fandorin are presented as genuinely in love. When Fandorin breaks his promise to the head of *Azazel'*, Amalia Bezhetskaya, to spare the young men in her organization from prosecution, she takes revenge by sending a bomb to destroy his happiness. As he pursues the assassin who has delivered the bomb to his hotel suite, Elizaveta is blown to pieces. The gruesome details of the scene are suggestive, as a single right hand with her wedding ring is all that remains of the unlucky bride: "Then he recognized it: a gold ring glittering on the third finger of a slim girl's arm severed at the elbow" (Akunin 2003: 242). Akunin capitalizes on modern anxieties about terrorism in Moscow, and at the same time ironically demonstrates the incapacity of faith to protect in the face of people who are determined to harm.

Characteristically, Akunin's image is ambivalent. The bomber is not a government agent, but a criminal mafia has infiltrated the government under the guise of a charity for orphans. The tracking and defeat of that threat requires that a "nontraditional" individual use "nontraditional" methods. As long as corsets are used for security they don't constitute queer propaganda. When the terrorists win, however, the queer emerges and is not attractive. As Fandorin staggers along Tverskoi Boulevard, Akunin attempts to let us see him through the eyes of the Muscovites he encounters. For the first time Akunin calls him "foppishly dressed" and says that he has "the deathly pallor of a dandy." Bromfield accurately translates *shchëgol'* as dandy, but he loses the distinction Akunin is making by using the less flattering *shchëgol'* rather than *dendi* or even *frant*. In his moment of personal tragedy, Fandorin becomes a curious and eccentric superfluous figure, more risible than pitiable. His queerness that had saved lives and defeated enemies is placed on display, at the mercy of the amateurish and heteronormative profiling of the Moscow public.

After this tragic incident, placed in 1876, Fandorin will remain unable to have intimate relationships with anyone, male or female, until he is posted to Japan. His loss is inscribed on his body, since the instant that the bomb detonates, his hair turns white. Fandorin's white hair seems to affirm detection's epistemological sufficiency, even as it signifies his loss. At the same time, it is despite this apparent stability of signification, he becomes a master of disguise. If the tragic start to his career is not very Holmesian, Fandorin's professional carer is also a curious riff on Holmes. Fandorin is an amalgam of Sherlock with Mycroft Holmes, a character whom Conan Doyle claimed he based upon his friend Oscar Wilde. Indeed, since Fandorin combines detection with a series of official governmental appointments, he may even represent a fusion of Sherlock with Agent 007. Akunin's novels, novellas, and short stories featuring Fandorin capitalize on his many jobs for government agencies, leading up to the most recent novel, *Chërnyi gorod* (Black City) (2012), which takes place in Baku during the First World War, in which he faces off against one of the leaders of the Russian Revolution, who is charged with financing "the Party." Fandorin's precise and elegant appearance, whether in its Orientalist or its Westernizing bureaucratic variant, seems to echo James Bond's dandyism. Akunin spends as much time telling us about the details of Fandorin's appearance and manners as he does in creating portraits of his opponents. Fandorin is very much subjected to our observation and profiling. By contrast, however, with the always recognizable and recognized Bond, Fandorin retains from Holmes the capacity to be the dandy, and at the same time the dandy's inverted double. Unlike the overt dandiacal spy "on her majesty's secret service," Holmes and Fandorin embody the danger of the drudge, who can pass for anyone:

> In strange contrast with this Dandiacal Body stands another British Sect, originally, as I understand of Ireland ... They are Generally called the *Drudge* Sect ... Their raiment consists of Innumerable skirts lappets, and irregular wings, of all cloths and of all colours; through the labyrinthine intricacies of which their bodies are introduced by some unknown process. (Carlyle, 212–13)

The attire of the drudge defies interpretation, presenting instead a multilayered excess of possible meanings. The drudge's appearance creates its own supplements, thereby undermining the possibility of any of them being a sincere expression of who the drudge is or even of who the drudge aspires to be.

The dandy's attire, albeit artificial, is aspirational, in Carlyle's words "heroic." The drudge's attire resonates with the "irregular" and the "unknown." Carlyle is explicit that something of the unknownness of the drudge and his "sect" is literally foreign. Drudges are and are not British. Although now considered British, they are "originally ... of Ireland." The drudge represents the inner edge of an empire, the Irishman in London, the Georgian or the Japanese in Moscow, the stranger among us. The drudge is a multicultural cipher, able to become and unbecome at will through the rearrangement of multiple and diverse layers of identity. If Holmes's plain black suit and silk top hat mark him as a dandy, an elegant and recognizable Victorian, this Dr. Jekyll personality has his Mr. Hyde.

Echoing stories like "A Scandal in Bohemia" and "The Man with the Twisted Lip," *The Turkish Gambit* (2005b) involves Fandorin going under cover. Holmes is consistently a master of disguise, be it as a frail priest or an opium addict whom even Watson cannot recognize in the two stories just mentioned. Although essential to solving the cases, since it allows Holmes to access information that he would be denied in his own person, these disguises are troubling. They are both too readable, as they encourage superficial surmises, and fundamentally unreadable as they are mostly false. The cases of Holmes pretending to be someone else are numerous, but the opium-den impersonation is particularly complex. Holmes, who is in fact a cocaine addict, poses as an opium addict. The falsity of that pose is arguably far less than his usual pose of being a "consulting detective" with national and individual security as his priority. Each drudging moment destabilizes the everyday pose, suggesting that it too is a matter of wearing the right hat and jacket. Holmes seems to have become his other when he goes under cover only because we have decided that his Baker Street self isn't a pose in the same sense. In *Azazel'*, Fandorin is initially able to disappear in Moscow society and to pass unnoticed until the bombing, and he learns to pass unnoticed anywhere when he goes abroad.

The opening scene of *The Turkish Gambit* involves the need for two Russians to pass for Central Asian men. Neither is Central Asian, and only one of them is a man. Fandorin, who is completely undetectable after his release from Turkish imprisonment, rescues a young Nihilist woman by winning her in a bet at an inn in a Bulgarian village. Despite her modern views on gender equity, Varvara Suvarova is following her fiancé, who has volunteered to liberate the Slavic people who are at risk from Turkish rule. Fandorin, in despair after Elizaveta's death, has followed the example of the suicidal Count Vronksy in Part 8 of Leo Tolstoy's *Anna Karenina* and has volunteered to help the Serbs as well, and is working for the Russian government in the area. He must recue Varvara from two orientalist fantasies—the sexual predation of the men in the inn and from a group of

Bashi-Bazouks, whose saddles are decorated with the severed heads of their enemies and who have with them a final living Russian prisoner (2005b: 21–22).

Although Varvara fails to pass for local or male, Fandorin here passes for both. Akunin chooses from the start of this text, one which is punctuated with apparently authentic bulletins from the front and newspaper articles, to allow us to see the story, including Fandorin himself, through Varya's eyes: "He had become totally Turkish in captivity, Varya thought angrily. He could at least have seated the lady on the horse. Typical male narcissism! A preening peacock! A vain drake, interested in nothing but flaunting himself before the dull gray duck" (19). Akunin coins the wonderful word "*oturechilsia*" (turkified) to capture Varya's impression of someone who had translated himself internally and externally into an enemy on the inner edge of the Russian empire. Having observed that he looks like all the other Bulgarian men, other than being a bit cleaner and blue-eyed, Varya condemns him as a narcissist, and as both "peacock" and "drake," concerned only that others perceive him as attractive. Varya, who has failed to detect Fandorin's subterfuge, profiles Fandorin as the dandy's inverse, the drudge who passes for the dandy's other while mirroring his vanity. Both the Fandorin created by his "turkified" attire, and the Fandorin who speaks French and sees though her impersonation by noticing a stray lock of her long hair, are potentially as undermining as the Bashi-Bazouks, unless his skills are harnessed in the service of the state. Fortunately, they are, and Fandorin will save Russia from a terrible plot by detecting an Occidentalizing dandy, Anwar Effendi, who has been passing military secrets in the guise of being a French journalist. Like Brilling, the villain is characterized by exceptional charm and the capacity to ingratiate himself, in ways that mimic Fandorin's own talents.

Turetskii gambit seems to promise a companion for Fandorin, or at least a sidekick in Varya. Despite their feelings, however, the two part. Akunin chooses not to create a character like Watson who becomes the narrative voice of the stories while at the same modeling an ideal reader of Holmes and his adventures. Fandorin is more isolated, both as a character and as a function of the conventional third-person narrative choice that is closely aligned with his point of view. Watson is our entré into Holmes's world, an intelligent and psychologically complex figure who mirrors and flatters the reader as he records the dazzling deductions of his friend, providing a narrative buffer between the quirky and dangerous Holmes and us. Fandorin is less egregious and more understated. We are soon placed far closer to his thoughts and impressions, thanks, however, to the assistance of a confidant rather than a chronicler. After two novels set outside of Russia, *Turetskii gambit* (1998) and *Leviafan* (1998), and *Almaznaia kolesnitsa* (*The Diamond Chariot*, 2003) about his service in Japan, Fandorin returns to Moscow in 1882 to investigate the premature death of war hero Mikhail Sobolev in *Smert' Akhillesa* (*The Death of Achilles*, 1998). In a move that allows Akunin to introduce his expertise about Japan into the texture of the novels, he is now accompanied by his Japanese manservant, the fallen *yakuza*, Masa. Akunin combines a witty allusion to Inspector Clouseau's manservant Cato Fong from the Pink Panther films with resistance to the racist stereotyping that characterized those filmic farces (Edwards, 1964). Fandorin's relationship with Masa merges two Russian anxieties, intimacy with the West and with the East, as Masa's quiet deference embodies both the *ancien-régime* classism of the European aristocracy and the stratified fastidiousness of shogunate Japan. In the course of largely nonverbal interactions, the two men work as a team, with Masa's presence assuring both the social prestige and the humanity of white-haired and emotionally remote Fandorin. Although alienated, ultimately Fandorin isn't alone.

When Fandorin returns to Moscow at the start of *Smert' Akhillesa*, to find the city so changed he isn't able to recognize it, Masa, who is mistaken for Chinese, is with him. Masa provides him with a confidant, a secret language (Japanese) to which even the reader is denied access, and an avatar who can voice disapproval of Western behavior with impunity. Masa expresses blunt opinions about Russia as the decadent West, about Moscow's women, architecture, and manners especially, which mirror Russia's uneasiness about the decadent European West. Like the orphans in *Azazel'*, Masa loves duels and insists upon Fandorin meeting important officials wearing a sword, even though the narrative persists in describing the response of those who meet Fandorin as being very much a dandy. Masa's fantastical presence is that of an actual drudge, semiotically as unreadable to the Russians he meets as his Japanese is unintelligible to them. His total unfamiliarity with Moscow, and Fandorin's long absence from it, allow the text to present the city as though it were unknown, highlighting the gaps in its symbolic power as capital. The simple mistaking by Fandorin of the new statue on Tverskoi Bul'var for being of Lord Byron, rather than Pushkin, embodies the fluidity of national identities. Pushkin emulated Byron, but to mistake him for Byron is to sign over Russia's greatest poet to the English.

Fandorin and Masa form a dialogic pair, each correcting the other's errors, and at the same time voicing those errors so that they become part of the text. Each draws logical conclusions based upon observation, which Fandorin will reject based upon what is acceptable. The Sobolev case centers on the cover-up of the circumstances of the assassination of a military hero, who is killed in the company of his mistress and seems to have acquired political ambitions. The novel insists upon diversity of perspective in a manner that again recollects Conan Doyle. Like "A Study in Scarlet," for example, the story is told twice, from Fandorin's point of view and from that of his antagonist, Achimas Welde, killer-for-hire, until the two characters and narratives meet in the last chapters. Welde, a Moravian kidnapped and brought up in the Caucasus, is the narrative point of view for the central third of the novel, as Akunin again insists upon the hybridity and multiplicity with which identities are performed in Tsar Alexander III's Russia.

Fandorin's queerness echoes that of Russia itself, central and peripheral to modernity, a dialogic and polylingual terrain on "the extreme edge of the semiosphere," as Yuri Lotman has suggested (Lotman, 142). Akunin foregrounds the extent to which Russia is not only on the boundary, but is a place of "creolized semiotic systems" (Lotman, 142). Fandorin's queerness is borderless, taking place in an East that is somewhere else's West, in a masculinity that is someone else's femininity. Close observation and logical deduction have caused both Fandorin and his creator to see Russia as a place where "everything in it is alien to me" (Akunin Blog). Such alienation, however, is perhaps what is always required of the detective. Anyone who sees the world so precisely can always underwrite or undermine a conspiracy, whether it threatens or forwards the interests of the establishment. As Holmes notes in "The Adventure of the Blue Carbuncle," "It is my business to know what other people do not know" (Doyle, 104).

Works Cited

Akunin, Boris (2003). *The Winter Queen*, trans. Andrew Bromfield. New York: Random House Trade Paperbacks.
Akunin, Boris (2005a). *Murder on the Leviathan*, trans. Andrew Bromfield. New York: Random House Trade Paperbacks.
Akunin, Boris (2005b). *The Turkish Gambit*, trans. Andrew Bromfield. New York: Random House Trade Paperbacks.
Akunin, Boris (2006). *The Death of Achilles*, trans. Andrew Bromfield. New York: Random House Trade Paperbacks, 2006.
Akunin, Boris (2012). *Chërnyi gorod*. Moskva: Zakharov.
Akunin, Boris (2014). *Liubov' k istorii*. Blog. August 30. http://borisakunin.livejournal.com/135653.html.

A Shot in the Dark (1964). Blake Edwards, dir. United Artists.
Azazel' (2002). Aleksandr Adabash'ian, dir. Moskva: Pervyi kanal [Channel One].
Bakhtin, Mikhail (1981). *The Dialogic Imagination: Four Essays*, ed. Michael Holquist, trans. Caryl Emerson and Michael Holquist. Austin and London: University of Texas Press.
Belinsky, Vissarion (1962). "Thoughts and Notes on Russian Literature." In *Belinsky, Chernyshevsky, and Dobrolyubov: Selected Criticism*, ed. Ralph E. Matlaw. Bloomington: Indiana University Press, 3–32.
Carlyle, Thomas ([1838] 1987). *Sartor Resartus*, ed. Kerry McSweeney and Peter Sabor. Oxford: Oxford University Press.
Dostoevsky, Fyodor (1993). *Crime and Punishment*, trans. Richard Pevear and Larissa Volkhonsky. New York: Vintage.
Doyle, Arthur Conan (1976). *The Original Illustrated Sherlock Holmes*. Secaucus, NJ: Castle.
Farrer, Peter (1994). *Borrowed Plumes: Letters from Edwardian Newspapers on Male Cross Dressing*. London: Karn.
Federal'nyi zakon ot 29.06.2013 № 135-F3: http://pravo.gov.ru:8080/page.aspx?50556. Trans. http://www.sras.org/russia_gay_propaganda_law.
"Fisht Olympic Stadium set to provide iconic centrepiece for Sochi 2014" (2013). Official Website of the Olympic Movement, May 28 (Accessed June 26, 2016). http://www.olympic.org/news/fisht-olympic-stadium-set-to-provide-iconic-centrepiece-for-sochi-2014/199682
Karamzin, Nikolai (1998). "Poor Liza"/"*Bednaia Liza*." London: Bristol Classical Press.
Kelly, Ian (2007). *Beau Brummell: The Ultimate Man of Style*. New York: Atria.
Kivinov, Andrei (1994). *Koshmar na ulitse Stachek*. Moskva.
Lotman, Yuri M. (2000). *Universe of the Mind: A Semiotic Theory of Culture*, trans. Ann Shukman. Bloomington: Indiana University Press.
Mesto vstrechi izmenit' nel'zia (1979). Stanislav Govorukhin, dir. Odesskaia kinostudiia khudozhestvennykh fil'mov.
Myers, Steven Lee (2003). "A Russian Intellectual Turns to Crime." *New York Times*, March 17.
Poe, Edgar Allan (1984). "Murders in the rue Morgue." *Complete Stories and Poems of Edgar Allan Poe*. New York: Doubleday, 2–26.
Prikliucheniia Sherloka Kholmsa i doktora Vatsona (1979–1986). Igor' Maslennikov, dir. Moskva: Lenfil'm, 1979–86.
Pushkin, Aleksandr (2008). *Polnoe sobranie sohinenii v odnom tome*. Moskva: Al'fa-Kniga.
"Putinskie SMI opublikovali spisok vragov Rossii" (2014). Obshchestvo. *Glavnoe*. August 19. http://glavnoe.ua/news/n188000.
Semnadtsat' mgnovenii vesny (1970). [*Seventeen Moments of Spring*]. Tat'iana Lioznova, dir. Moskva: Kinostudiia im. M. Gor'kogo.

Shakespeare, William (1986). *The Tragedy of Hamlet*, ed. Harold Jenkins. London and New York: Methuen.

Sherlock (2010–2014). Steven Moffat and Mark Gatiss, producers. BBC One.

Sherlock Holmes (2009). Guy Ritchie, dir. Warner Brothers.

Sherlok Kholms (2013). Ruben Dishdishian, dir. Moskva: Tsentral.

Symonds, John Addington (1896). *A Problem in Modern Ethics: Being and Inquiry into the Phenomenon of Sexual Inversion Addressed Especially to Medical Psychologists and Jurists*. London.

The Adventures of Sherlock Holmes (1984–1994). Michael Cox, producer. ITV Granada.

The Picture of Dorian Gray (1976). John Gorrie, dir. BBC.

Tolstoy, Leo (2002). *Anna Karenina*, trans. Richard Pevear and Larissa Volkhonsky. New York: Penguin.

Ulitsy razbitykh fonarei (1998) [*Streets of Broken Lights*]. Aleksandr Rogozhkin, dir. Sankt-Peterburg: Studiia "2 V" Peterburg.

Vainer, Arkadii and Georgii (1975). *Era Miloserdiia* [*The Age of Mercy*]. Moskva.

Wilde, Oscar (1894). "Phrases and Philosophies for the Use of the Young." *The Chameleon* 1:1, 1–3.

Yeats, William Butler (1964). *Cathleen Ni Hoolihan*. In *Eleven Plays of Willliam Butler Yeats*, ed. Norman Jeffares. New York: Macmillan, 221–31.

Notes on Contributors

Susan Bassnett is Professor of Comparative Literature at the universities of Warwick and Glasgow. She has published extensively on aspects of literature and translation, her most recent book being *Translation* (Routledge, 2014). She is a Fellow of the Royal Society of Literature, a Fellow of the Institute of Linguists, and a member of the Academia Europea. In addition to her academic work, Bassnett is a poet and journalist.

Karl Berglund is a PhD student in Comparative Literature at Uppsala University, Sweden. His dissertation "A Market of Murders" will be completed in 2017. It investigates the commercial success of Swedish crime fiction in the 2000s and how book trade structures interconnect with the fictions it distributes. He has published several articles and two monographs on the subject: *Deckarboomen under lupp* ("Crime Boom Investigated," 2012) and *Mordförpackningar* ("Packaging Murder," 2016).

Michaela Bronstein is an Assistant Professor of English at Stanford University. Her essays have appeared in *MLQ*, *Journal of Modern Literature*, *Essays in Criticism*, and elsewhere; her first book, *Out of Context: The Uses of Modernist Fiction* (forthcoming from Oxford), examines the transhistorical dimensions of modernist novels in light of the political uses later authors have made of them. "Four Generations, One Crime" is drawn from a second book project focusing on the parallels between literary futurity and utopian violence in novels about revolutionaries.

Suradech Chotiudompant is Assistant Professor in the Department of Comparative Literature, Faculty of Arts, Chulalongkorn University, Thailand. He has written widely on contemporary international and Thai literature, and he is also interested in the relationship between literary studies and contemporary social theory and such related topics as identity politics, consumer culture and urban studies. His recent publications in Thai include *Magical Realism in the Literary Works of Gabriel García Márquez* and *20th-Century Literary Theory in the West*.

David Damrosch is Ernest Bernbaum Professor of Comparative Literature at Harvard. His books include *What Is World Literature?* (2003), *The Buried*

Book: *The Loss and Rediscovery of the Great Epic of Gilgamesh* (2007), and *How to Read World Literature* (rev. ed., 2017). He is the general editor of the six-volume *Longman Anthology of World Literature*, editor of *World Literature in Theory* (2014), and co-editor (with Theo D'haen and Djelal Kadir) of *The Routledge Companion to World Literature* (2012).

Dirk de Geest teaches literary theory and Dutch modern literature at K.U. Leuven, Belgium. His research covers a broad field of issues in 20th-century literature. His theoretical work **focuses** mainly on systems theory, the historiography of literature, and discourse analysis. Currently, De Geest is preparing a book on the Dutch avant-garde magazine *De Tafelronde*.

Theo D'haen is Professor of English and Comparative Literature at the University of Leuven in Belgium. His books include *Contemporary American Crime Fiction* (Palgrave Macmillan 2001, with Hans Bertens), *American Literature: A History* (Routledge 2014, with Hans Bertens), *The Routledge Concise History of World Literature* (2012), and, as co-editor, *The Routledge Companion to World Literature* (2012, with David Damrosch and Djelal Kadir) and (with César Domínguez and Mads Rosendahl Thomsen) *World Literature: A Reader* (Routledge 2013).

Maayan Eitan is a PhD candidate in the Department of Comparative Literature at the University of Michigan, Ann Arbor, where she is writing her dissertation about love in modern Hebrew and Jewish poetry and thought. Her short stories have appeared in *Mita'am: a Review of Literature and Radical Thought*, and she is currently working on her first novel (in Hebrew).

Mihaela P. Harper is an assistant professor in the Cultures, Civilizations and Ideas Program at Bilkent University in Ankara, Turkey. Her research interests span Eastern Europe, translation and transnationalism, interdisciplinary and comparative perspectives, cultural critique, political theory, as well as continental philosophy. She has published in *symplokē*, the *Slavonic and East European Review*, the *Journal of Modern Literature*, and *Modern Language Studies*. Her current project examines post-apocalyptic narratives, both literary and visual, against the backdrop of theories of exception, lawlessness, language, and community.

Michael P. Harris-Peyton is a doctoral candidate in the English Department at the University of Delaware. His research focuses on transcultural adaptation in world literature, global popular culture, and the politics of genre. He is currently working on his dissertation, "Holmes in the Empire: Colonial Textual Agency, Circulatory Power and the Adaptation of Detective Fiction."

Andreas Hedberg is acting lecturer in the Department of Literature, Uppsala University. His research interests include sociology of literature, world literature, processes of canonization and literature as critique of modernization. Since 2011, he has been part of the research group Swedish Literature in the World (SIV) at The Section for Sociology of Literature, Uppsala University, where he is especially interested in the mediation of Swedish literature to France. Since 2016, he has also been in the research program Cosmopolitan and Vernacular Dynamics in World Literature at Stockholm University.

Stewart King teaches in Spanish and Latin American Studies and coordinates the International Literatures program at Monash University, Australia. He has published extensively on contemporary Spanish and Catalan narrative and on crime fiction as a form of world literature. He is the author of *Escribir la catalanidad. Lenguas e identidades en la narrativa contemporánea de Cataluña* (2005) and has edited or co-edited *The Space of Culture: Critical Readings in Hispanic Studies* (2004, with Jeff Browitt), *La cultura catalana de expression castellana* (2005), and "The Global Crime Scene" (*Clues* 32:2, 2014, with Stephen Knight).

Anneleen Masschelein is a lecturer in cultural studies and literary studies at K.U. Leuven, Belgium. She has published widely on contemporary theory, arts and literature. Her book, *The Unconcept*, was published by SUNY Press in 2011. She is currently working on a book project on literary advice within the framework of a consortium on Literature and Media Innovation, sponsored by the Belgian government program Belspo.

Louise Nilsson is a researcher at English Department, Stockholm University where she's currently working on the project, "Mediating the North in a Transnational Context: Vernacular and Cosmopolitan Places in Nordic Noir," within the research program *Cosmopolitan and Vernacular Dynamics in World Literatures*. She's a member of the Australian-based research network *Detective Fiction on the Move* (Newcastle University) and one of the contributors to the network's collection *Criminal Moves* (forthcoming). Further information: http://worldlit.se

Elizabeth Richmond-Garza is UT Regents' and Distinguished Teaching Associate Professor of English at the University of Texas at Austin. She is the Director of the Program in Comparative Literature and served as chief administrative officer of the American Comparative Literature Association from 2002-2011, and has held both Mellon and Fulbright Fellowships. She teaches theater, aesthetics, and the fine arts, and writes on Orientalism, Cleopatra, European drama, the Gothic, and literary theory. She is currently finishing a study of Oscar Wilde.

Bruce Robbins is Old Dominion Foundation Professor of the Humanities at Columbia University. His books include *The Beneficiary* (forthcoming in 2017), *Perpetual War: Cosmopolitanism from the Viewpoint of Violence* (2012), *Upward Mobility and the Common Good* (2007), *Feeling Global: Internationalism in Distress* (1999), *Secular Vocations: Intellectuals, Professionalism, Culture* (1993), and *The Servant's Hand: English Fiction from Below* (1986). He is also the director of a documentary entitled "Some of My Best Friends Are Zionists."

Tilottama Tharoor teaches at New York University's Global Liberal Studies Program. Her areas of teaching are Literature, Art History, Cultural Studies and Women's Rights. Research and writing cover Postcolonial and Feminist Theories, British and World Literatures and South Asian Cultures. She edited *Nari*, an essay collection about Women in Calcutta's History, and is currently working on a book, *The Empire Within: Women and Empire in the Late 19th and Early 20th-Century British Domestic Novel*.

Delia Ungureanu is Assistant Professor of Literary Theory in the Department of Literary Studies at the University of Bucharest and Assistant Director of Harvard's Institute for World Literature. Her research fields include politics and ideology, sociology of literature, poetics and rhetoric. She is the author of *Poetica Apocalipsei: Razboiul cultural in revistele literare romanesti (1944–1947)* [*The Poetics of the Apocalypse: The Cultural War in the Romanian Literary Magazines (1944-1947)*, 2012] and of *From Paris to Tlön: Surrealism and World Literature* (forthcoming).

Michael Wood was born in Lincoln, England, and studied Modern Languages at Cambridge. He taught at the universities of Cambridge, Columbia, Exeter and Princeton, where he is now Professor Emeritus of English and Comparative Literature. He writes frequently for the *London Review of Books* and the *New York Review of Books*, and his most recent longer publications are *Literature and the Taste of Knowledge* and *Yeats and Violence*. His brief life of Alfred Hitchcock appeared in 2015.

Wei Yan is an assistant professor in the Department of Chinese at Lingnan University, Hong Kong. Her research interests include modern Chinese popular literature and Sinophone Studies. Her PhD dissertation is "The Rise and Development of Chinese Detective Fiction: 1900-1949" (Harvard, 2009). Her research is published in *Journal of Modern Literature in Chinese*, *Sino-Humanitas* and *A New History of Modern Chinese Literature* (Harvard, 2017).

Index

Abadashyan, Aleksandr 276
Adler, Irene 234, 264
Akunin, Boris 8, 261, 271–87
Allain, Marcel 201
Andaç, Münevver 132
Andersen, Hans Christian 124–5
Anderson, Jean 85
Aragon, Louis 7, 134–6, 138–9
Aretov, Nikolay 176, 179–80, 183
Aritzeta, Margarida 164
Arjouni, Jakob 146
Ascari, Maurizio 229
Auden, W. H. 91, 97, 98, 146–8, 151, 154
Auster, Paul 91

Bakhtin, Mikhail 272
Ball, John 261
Bannong, Liu 248
Barr, Robert 199
Bassnett, Susan 7, 143
Baudelaire, Charles 157
Beinhart, Larry 101
Benjamin, Walter 21, 98, 119
Berglund, Karl 6, 77
Bertens, Hans 3
Berwick, Ray 120
Bhabha, Homi 242
Biggers, Earl Derr 250
Bloch, Robert 120
Bloom, Harold 20–1
Bolaño, Roberto 54
Boonthavevej, Panida 198
Borges, Jorge Luis 30, 36, 125, 158
Bourdieu, Pierre 111, 118
Bradford, Richard 3
Brand, Dana 119, 128
Brande, Dorothea 93
Breton, André 135–6
Brett, Jeremy 233, 277
Bromfield, Andrew 272
Bronstein, Michaela 6, 59

Brontë, Charlotte 235
Brooks, Peter 35
Brown, Dan 208
Brummell, Beau 274, 279
Buchan, John 234
Burgess, Gelett 96
Burroway, Janet 93
Butler, Robert Olen 93
Byron, Lord 279

Cain, James M. 162
Camilleri, Andrea 145, 146, 152–3, 154
Camus, Keith 59
Capmany, Maria-Aurèlia 163
Carlyle, Thomas 274, 279–81, 283–5
Casanova, Pascale 2
Casares, Adolfo Bioy 158
Cawelti, John 241
Cela, Camilo José 118
Chandler, Raymond 4, 25, 31, 99, 147, 162, 165, 190, 241
Chantarakiri, Ruangdej 206
Chanyong, Manat 202
Chaochuti, Thosaeng 199, 200
Charteris, Leslie 250
Cheng Xiaoqing 250–4
Chernyshevsky, Niolay 60
Chotiudompant, Suradech 7, 197
Christie, Agatha 1, 7, 19, 71, 144, 146, 148, 149, 151, 152, 154, 158, 163, 171–82, 189, 191, 199, 234, 241, 250, 275
Clark, Mary Higgins 177
Clover, Carol 125
Coetzee, J. M. 234
Collins, Wilkie 143, 162, 250
Conan Doyle, Sir Arthur 8, 143–4, 146, 149, 151, 158, 162, 177, 189, 198, 199, 219, 220–5, 226, 228, 229, 233–40, 245, 248, 250, 257, 260–3, 272, 275, 278, 283, 287
Connelly, Michael 4, 121

Conrad, Jospeh 6, 59–60, 62–4, 66, 67, 68, 71, 72
Crameri, Kathryn 160
Crofts, Freeman Wills 147
Cronin, Michael 158
Cumberbatch, Benedict 233
Cushing, Peter 233

Daeninckx, Didier 162
Dahl, Arne 112, 113, 114, 118, 120, 121
Damrosch, David 8, 20–1, 29, 36, 78, 86, 159, 183, 219, 257
Das, Sarat Chandra 262
Davidson, Peter 124
de Geest, Dirk 7, 91
Defoe, Danial 234
Dejkunjorn, Vasit 204
Dey, Frederic van Rensselaer 247
D'haen, Theo 3, 8, 233
Di Renjie 2
Dibdin, Michael 152
Diderot, Denis 193
Disayabut, Pleng 198
Dishdishyan, Ruben 276
Diteeyont, Vinita 206
Dostoevsky, Fyodor 4, 6, 59–60, 62, 63, 67, 68, 71, 72, 273
Doucet, Jacques 135–6
Downey, Robert, Jr. 233
Dreiser, Theodore 60

Eco, Umberto 21, 91
Edelman, Lee 61
Eitan, Maayan 7, 187
Eliot, T. S. 4, 98
Ellis, Sherry 101
Eluard, Paul 132–3
Emre, Merve 54
Engels, Friedrich 1, 2
Ephron, Hallie 101
Erdmann, Eva 26, 31, 84
Esenwein, Joseph Berg 94
Espriu, Salvador 166
Evanovich, Janet 91
Even-Zohar, Itamar 150, 159–60

Fanon, Frantz 71
Faraone, Mario 261, 268

Faulkner, William 131
Ferraté, Gabriel 166
Fincher, David 4
Fleming, Ian 151, 163
Folch i Camarasa, Ramon 163
Forshaw, Barry 85
Franco, Francisco 164
Frazer, June 35
Freeling, Nicholas 146
Freely, Maureen 131
Freeman, Austin 250
Freeman, Martin 275
Frey, James 101
Furth, Charlotte 249
Fuster, Jaume 163, 164
Futrelle, Jacques 207

Gaboriau, Émile 143, 157–8
Galton, Sir Francis 276
Gardner, John 93
Gatiss, Mark 144
Genette, Gérard 111
Gikandi, Simon 70
Goethe, Johann Wolfang von 20
Goldberg, Nathalie 93
Gorky, Maxim 173
Gorrie, John 277
Graham, Caroline 151
Gramscis, Antonio 13
Green, Anna Katherine 157, 250
Grimm, Jacob and Wilhelm 120
Guansé, Domènec 161
Guest, Kristin 259, 262
Gunning, Tom 119, 128
Gur, Batya 190

Halldén, Kåre 14, 20
Hammett, Dashiell 4, 99, 158, 162, 165, 241
Harper, Mihaela P. 7, 171
Harris, Thomas 4
Harrison, Rachel 199
Harris-Peyton, Michael B. 8, 215
Haycraft, Howard 98–100, 105
Hayden, G. Miki 101
Hedberg, Andreas 5, 13
Hedlund, Magdalena 80, 82
Heilbron, Johan 82
Heine, Maurice 133–4

Index 299

Higashino, Keigo 152
Highsmith, Patricia 93, 148
Hitchcock, Alfred 1, 120–1, 125
Hoeg, Peter 149
Hoffmann, E. T. A. 157
Holt, Anne 149
Hopkins, Nevil Monroe 96
Horowitz, Anthony 151, 242
Hu Shi 249
Hughes, Langston 44
Hugnet, Georges 139
Hume, Fergus 158
Hutcheon, Linda 216, 229

Indridason, Arnaldur 149
Intarapalit, P. 202
Issaev, Mladen 173–4
Ivanov, Dimitri 172

Jakobson, Roman 165
James, P. D. 144, 146
Jann, Rosemary 248
Japrisot, Sébastien 162
Jatawaluck 7
Jefferies, L. B. 121
Joensuu, Matti 149
Jordana, Cèsar August 162

Kallentoft, Måns 114
Karamzin, Nikolai 280
Kåre Halldén 18–9
Kepler, Lars 119
King, Laurie R. 234–8, 242
King, Stephen 93
King, Stewart 7, 78, 157
Kipling, Rudyard 8, 20, 236, 260–1, 262, 263–4
Knox, Ronald A. 95, 98
Kolev, Svetoslav 173–4
Koselleck, Reinhart 242
Krajenbrink, Marieke 3

Lacan, Jacques 133
Laclau, Ernesto 112
Lagercrantz, David 77, 81, 85
Lamott, Anne 93
Lamson, Laurie 101
Lane, John 144

Lapid, Shulamit 190
Lapid, Yair 190
Larsson, Åsa 114
Larsson, Stieg 18, 48, 77, 79, 80, 81, 84, 104, 110, 119, 125, 127, 149
Lawson, Mark 145, 148, 152
Lazar, Lora 7, 176–82, 183
Le Carré, John 162
Leblanc, Maurice 245
Lefevere, Andre 147–8
Lennard, John 237
Leon, Donna 152
Levy, Andrew 93, 105
Lin Shu 247
Liu E 246
Livanov, Vasily 276
Lotman, Yuri 287
Lovitt, Carl 35
Lozev, Emil 175
Lü Xia 247
Lu Xun 268
Lucarelli, Carlo 6, 33
Lukács, Georg 241
Lyovarin, Win 206

Macdonald, Ross 162
Maeterlinck, Maurice 234–5
Majumdar, Gopa 224, 225
Mankell, Henning 4, 48, 52, 79, 104, 110, 145, 149, 153, 192, 193
Mann, Thomas 131
Marklund, Liza 121
Márquez, Gabriel García 24
Marsh, Ngaio 241
Martín, Andreu 164
Martinelli, Kate 237
Marx, Karl 1, 2
Maslennikov, Igor 276
Masschelein, Anneleen 7, 91
Mathur, Suchitra 224
McCann, Sean 241
Mendoza, Elmer 6, 23–30
Merkel, Angela 152
Messent, Peter 3, 38
Meyer, Stephanie 149
Miller, Frank 91
Miller, Johnny Lee 233
Miller, Vivien 3

Minchev, Hristo 174, 175
Miranda, Carolina 3, 85
Mishani, Dror 7, 187–94
Moffat, Steven 144
Molino, Edicions 163
Monsiváis, Carlos 30–1
Moretti, Franco 2, 3, 21, 35, 37, 42, 44, 78, 241
Morrison, Arthur 247
Mosley, Walter 158
Mouffe, Chantal 112
Muddock, James Edward Preston 247
Mukherjee, Pablo 219, 223
Mūkoma wa Ngũgĩ 6, 34, 59, 60, 62, 64, 67–71, 72
Muñoz, José 61, 72
Murch, A. E. 220–1
Murray, Simone 82

Nesbo, Jo 145, 148, 149
Nesser, Håkan 121, 124
Nestingen, Andrew 48
Neville, Barbara 101
Ngũgĩ wa Thiong'o 6, 59, 60, 62, 63, 65, 66, 70, 71, 72
Nickerson, Catherine 38
Nilsson, Louise 7, 109
Norbu, Jamyang 8, 110, 242, 257–69
Noskov, Ilya 276
Nussbaum, Martha 241

Oakley, Helen 3
Ohlsson, Kristina 124
Oliver, Joan 163
Oliver, Maria-Antònia 164, 165
Osborne, John 277

Pachinphayak, Nuan 198
Paget, Sidney 276
Palau i Camps, Josep-Maria 164
Pamuk, Orhan 4, 7, 36, 131–2, 134–8
Pastor, Marc 165
Pedrolo, Manuel de 162, 163, 164
Pepper, Andrew 3
Péret, Benjamin 132–3
Peters, Ellis 144
Pezzotti, Barbara 3, 85

Phu, Sunthorn 209
Piglia, Ricardo 24–5, 29, 30, 31
Pipitpattanaprap, Chairat 208
Plummer, Christopher 233
Poe, Edgar Allan 21, 26, 94, 96, 119, 120, 121, 127, 137, 143, 157, 199, 200, 221, 250, 273
Poonwiwat, Pracha 204
Porter, Dennis 13, 35
Prachinphayak, Nuan 200
Prapt 7, 208
Pushkin, Aleksandr 271, 279–80, 286

Qiu Xiaolong 152
Queen, Ellery 250
Queux, William Le 199
Quinn, Kate M. 3

Rankin, Ian 25–6, 30, 145
Rathbone, Basil 233
Ray, Robert J. 101
Ray, Satyajit 222–3, 228
Reitz, Caroline 219, 223
Remick, Jack 101
Rendell, Ruth 144
Reynolds, Claire 179
Richmond-Garza, Elizabeth 8, 271
Rimbaud, Arthur 137
Robbins, Bruce 6, 47
Rodell, Marie F. 98, 100–1, 104–5
Rohmer, Sax 199
Roka, Tokutomi 247
Rowe, Rosemary 101
Rowling, J. K. 150
Rubinstein, Helena 136
Ruiko, Kuroiwa 247
Ruiz, Edouard 135, 136, 139
Russell, Mary 235, 236, 237

Sade, Marquis de 133
Santorelli, Stephen 153
Sarenbrant, Sofie 14–18, 20
Sayers, Dorothy 4, 97, 99, 144, 151, 173, 241, 250
Scharnhorst, Garry 60
Sciascia, Leonardo 25, 30
Seguí, Josep Lluís 164

Index

Semyonov, Yulian 274
Serra, Antoni 164
Serrahima, Maurici 163
Shakespeare, William 273
Sigurdarsdottir, Yrsa 56, 149
Simenon, Georges 144–5, 157, 158, 159, 162
Sjöwall, Maj 114, 145, 153, 154, 192
Smith, Alexander McCall 91
Söderberg, Alexander 80–1
Solana, Teresa 165
Sophocles 3, 119
Souvestre, Pierre 201
Srisawake, Liao 202, 203, 207
Steiner, Ann 78, 84, 149
Stewart, David 38
Stoppard, Tom 72
Stoyanov, Tsvetan 172
Susman, Gary 233
Swirski, Peter 3
Symonds, John Addington 277
Symons, Julian 252

Taibo, Paco Ignacio, II 30–1
Tam, King-fai 251
Tan Sitong 249
Tansey, Mark 268
Tarantino, Quentin 125
Tasis, Rafael 161, 163, 164
Tharoor, Tilottama 6, 33
Thomas, Ross 25
Thompson, John B. 81
Thompson, Stephen 144
Thomsen, Mads Rosendahl 20
Thomsen, Rosendahl 20–1
Thong In 199
Titus, Edward 135–7
Todorov, Tzvetan 35, 42, 64
Tolstoy, Leo 284
Torrent, Ferran 164
Tournier, Michel 234

Trendafilov, Vladimir 173, 175, 176, 177, 179
Tsvetanov, Boris 173, 183

Ueland, Brenda 93
Ungureanu, Delia 7, 131
Uratchatchairat, Phornsak 206–7

Vajiravudh, King 199, 200
Valls, Àlvar 159
Vallverdú, Josep 163, 164
Van Dine, S. S. 95–6, 250
Van Gulik, Robert 2
Venturino, Steven 260
Venuti, Lawrence 159
Vidocq, François-Eugène 157

Waade, Anne Marit 86
Wahlöö, Per 114, 145, 153–4, 192
Walcott, Derek 44
Walker, Ronald 35
Wallentin, Jan 80, 81
Walsh, Rodolfo 30
Webster, Henry Kitchell 96
Wei Yan 8, 245
Wells, Carolyn 94, 96, 99, 105
Wheat, Carolyn 101
Whited, Lana A. 71
Wilde, Oscar 274, 277, 283
Wimsey, Lord Peter 151
Winthuphramanakul, Liam 198
Wood, Michael 6, 23
Wright, Richard 60
Wu Jianren 247

Yeats, W. B. 273
Yordanova, Kostadina 178

Zhou Shoujuan 247
Zhou Zuoren 247
Žižek, Slavoj 48

www.ingramcontent.com/pod-product-compliance
Lightning Source LLC
Chambersburg PA
CBHW052151300426
44115CB00011B/1625